19.95

901
ARO

Aron, Raymond, 1905–

Politics and history

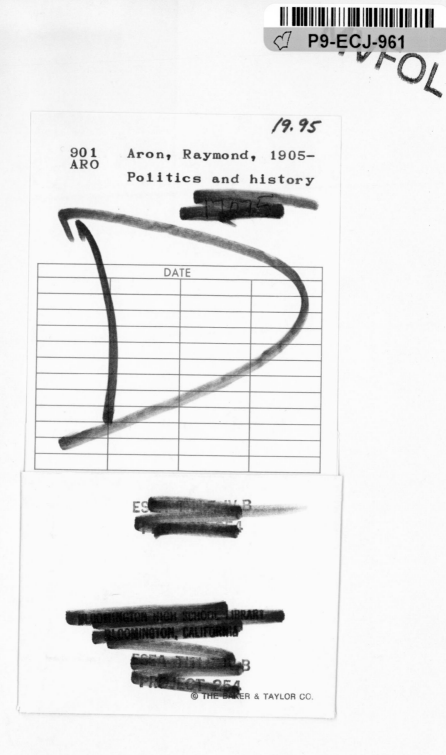

DATE

POLITICS
AND
HISTORY

POLITICS
AND
HISTORY

SELECTED ESSAYS BY
RAYMOND ARON

COLLECTED, TRANSLATED, AND EDITED BY

MIRIAM BERNHEIM CONANT

Fp

THE FREE PRESS
A Division of Macmillan Publishing Co., Inc.
NEW YORK

Collier Macmillan Publishers
LONDON

Copyright © 1978 by The Free Press
A Division of Macmillan Publishing Co., Inc.

All rights reserved. No part of this book may be reproduced or transmitted in any form or by any means, electronic or mechanical, including photocopying, recording, or by any information storage and retrieval system, without permission in writing from the Publisher.

The Free Press
A Division of Macmillan Publishing Co., Inc.
866 Third Avenue, New York, N. Y. 10022

Collier Macmillan Canada, Ltd.

Library of Congress Catalog Card Number: 78–54122

Printed in the United States of America

printing number

1 2 3 4 5 6 7 8 9 10

Library of Congress Cataloging in Publication Data
Aron, Raymond
  Politics and history.

  Bibliography: p.
  Includes index.
1. History—Philosophy—Addresses, essays, lectures.
2. Political science—Addresses, essays, lectures.
3. Social sciences—Addresses, essays, lectures.
I. Conant, Miriam Bernheim. II. Title.
D16.8.A725   901   78–54122
ISBN 0–02–901000–4

Contents

Part III *Conclusion*

Acknowledgments

I wish to thank Sarah Lawrence College for a sabbatical leave that enabled me to do this work.

I also wish to express my deep gratitude to John Shepley for his invaluable help with the translations and editing. His talents and thoroughness have greatly enhanced this book.

Many thanks go to Audre Proctor, a typist whose skills and good humor provided constant encouragement; to Isabelle de Lajarte, Raymond Aron's secretary, for her cooperation and thoughtfulness; and to Phyllis L. Marchand for the index.

Finally, at the Free Press, I want to thank Charles E. Smith and Kitty Moore, for their understanding and patience with the inevitable delays and difficulties that beset a volume of this sort, and George E. Magee, for overseeing the production of the book.

Preface

What kind of understanding is possible of one's own times? Raymond Aron, in the essays that appear in this volume, brings to contemporary history the insights of both philosophy and social science. This is the first collection in English offering the reader material that focuses on Aron's lifelong attempt to bridge the gap between knowledge and action, to understand the dialectical relationship between history and politics.

Aron addresses himself to fundamental questions. What constitutes a good life for individuals and for the societies they live in? How may we define justice and freedom and reconcile the conflicts between these two values in modern times? What are the chances of peace in a nuclear age? In his approach to these problems he relates traditions, present consciousness, and the will to action and change. Aron shows us how the past *as conceived in the present* helps make comprehensible the folly or the wisdom of human decisions. Perceptions of the past are a political statement about the present and future. Aron avoids the extremes of determinism and relativism and instead creates a framework in which the future is open but choices are limited by social, economic, and political realities and the necessity of including these realities in policymaking.

Raymond Claude Ferdinand Aron was born in Paris on March 14, 1905. His academic career spans the years between 1928, when he came out of the Ecole normale supérieure at the top of his class, and 1970, when he became a professor at the celebrated Collège de France. His scholarly works cover a host of fields and command worldwide recognition.[1]

Aron is also a journalist, for decades a regular columnist for the conservative French newspaper *Le Figaro* until his resignation in June 1977. He now writes for the more progressive *L'Express*. His interest in journalism dates from the fall of France in World War II and his exile in Lon-

[1] See pp. 260–261 for a selected list of Aron's major works and a chronology of his academic career.

don, where he was chief editor for the monthly *La France libre*. Aron's ongoing involvement with current affairs also has taken the form of debates with French intellectuals—most notably, Jean-Paul Sartre and Maurice Merleau-Ponty.[2] Aron is very much aware of the ambiguous nature of power, of the crushing responsibilities and hard choices facing statesmen, who, unlike theorists, have to cope with short-range, middle-range, and long-range issues all at once.

As have many other acute observers of power before him, Aron has been tempted to take part in politics. That he has not chosen to do so, or that circumstances have not favored such a possibility, is seen by him as a mixed blessing.[3] In his work, intellectual honesty has been a form of action in itself, forcing a confrontation between abstract theorizing and public policymaking. If citizens and their leaders, intellectuals and their followers can be made to face choices within known limits, the preconditions for a more tolerant and humane world would emerge.

In an age of specialists the scope of Raymond Aron's work is refreshing. The clearly interdisciplinary nature of classical political philosophies has been challenged today by the increased complexity of modern life and the exponential growth of knowledge. A synthesis of the kind offered by Plato, Saint Augustine, Saint Thomas Aquinas, Hobbes, Hegel, or Marx is possibly an unrealistic goal for modern thinkers. Aron does not attempt to provide us with any closed, final system—indeed, his views are flexible and open-ended. He does, however, try to shed some light on the twentieth century *as a whole*. He brings the approaches of philosophy, history, political science, economics, and sociology to bear at once on his subject matter. Although he has the highest respect for contemporary social science, its empirical and statistical methods and its attempts at objectivity, he believes that no social science can ever neglect with impunity historical and philosophical dimensions. In the essays collected here, there are many examples of the fallacious results obtained when social scientists isolate themselves from reality. On the very eve of World War II professional sociologists continued to ignore the impact of fascist ideology; professional economists stuck to narrow technical interpretations of the need for "temporary" unemployment while remaining oblivious to the crisis dimensions of the Great Depression. In our own day, we build sophisticated "scenarios" and computer assisted simulations of war involving peoples in the non-Western world whose history and value systems are a crucial and yet an ignored dimension in our attempt to predict the outcomes of international political struggles. We construct in-

---

[2] See *L'Opium des intellectuels* (Paris: Calmann-Lévy, 1955), among others. Aron's debates with the Left are well known. His polemic against the Right should not be neglected, however. See *Espoir et peur du siècle* (Paris: Calmann-Lévy, 1957) and *Polémiques* (Paris: Gallimard, 1955).

[3] See the concluding paragraph of "Machiavelli and Marx," p. 101, and "On the Historical Condition of the Sociologist," p. 68.

tricate models of our own society and fail to discern basic differences between political and economic power or between the impact of past values and that of present ideological forces.[4]

No social scientist can escape confrontation with the values that determine the nature, scope, and direction of much of what he or she is attempting to understand. Even linguists and economists, who perhaps have come closest to discovering models with predicitive scientific validity, must come to terms with the values they have inherited and unforseeable human events.

In his work Aron fuses the Anglo-Saxon, pragmatic, behavioral approach to society with the classic philosophical tradition of continental Europe, particularly that of the German historical school. His deep study of Marx and ongoing debate with Marx's ideas are alternately a source of profundity and rigidity in Aron's own positions. At the same time, his affinity for Montesquieu and Tocqueville makes Aron an heir to that tradition, with its focus on history and its emphasis on liberalism and realism. In "The Liberal Definition of Freedom" Aron contrasts the views of Tocqueville and Marx on freedom and the future of the industrial order: in the process we can see how he brings together historical perceptions and present political realities and dilemmas.[5]

Aron's comparative sociological studies of the industrial order East and West are thus both empirically oriented and philosophically and historically rooted. Although his work on class structure and bureaucratic imperatives has inspired the so-called convergence theory between "capitalist" and "communist" regimes, or between "planned" and "market" economies, Aron himself subscribes only partially to such an approach.[6] For him the *political* system is crucial. Does it admit or exclude genuine opposition? Does it protect individual rights? Whereas hierarchical structures of production and modern technology similarly affect social life, highlighting the common features of industrial society whatever the political regime, the past values of a society, and its formal political rules for implementing them, remain critical to understanding the vast *differences* between two forms of industrial society that seem well on their way to dividing the entire world. Both systems loudly proclaim an egalitarian ethic and both have to face a nonegalitarian reality, as the most cursory study of income distribution, prestige differentiation, and power concentration amply demonstrates. However, as Aron points out in the two concluding essays of this collection, leaders in capitalist as well as communist societies are aware of the problem and address it in a variety

[4] See "On the Historical Condition of the Sociologist," p. 63 and p. 65; "Macht, Power, Puissance," pp. 102–103; "The Evolution of Modern Strategic Thought," p. 195.

[5] "The Liberal Definition of Freedom," pp. 139–165.

[6] See *Dix-huit Leçons sur la société industrielle* (Paris: Gallimard, 1963), *Démocratic et totalitarisme* (Paris: Gallimard, 1965), and *Les Désillusions du progrès* (Parib: Calmann-Lévy, 1969), among others.

of ways that differ significantly. Again, traditions influence the choice of options; values are in conflict; and success and failure are necessarily differently perceived despite similarities in the basic problems tackled.[7]

Although Aron's preference for the West is explicitly stated, he does attempt to treat each system on its own terms and present the advantages and disadvantages of each. His success in this respect is open to question. This is not surprising since according to Aron's own analysis objectivity is a highly desirable goal for the social scientist and yet commitment to specific values is an inescapable human necessity. Many of the essays in this volume grapple with this dilemma from a variety of points of view and levels of perception.

In the English-speaking world Aron is perhaps best known for his work on international politics and his studies of peace and war in the twentieth century. One of his recent works is an exhaustive study of Karl von Clausewitz, whose theories about war have had a great influence on our time.[8] Aron notes with irony that for a century wracked by wars they seem to play a singularly small part in scholarly interpretations. War has gone out of fashion as a subject of inquiry and economics has taken over in the explanatory schemes of historians. In the essay "Thucydides and the Recital of History" Aron draws analogies between the Peloponnesian wars and the wars of this century; in the process, he draws our attention to the roles filled by great historical figures, a matter often underplayed in modern historical thought.[9]

The essays presented in this volume give an idea of the range of Aron's contributions to a variety of disciplines, but this is not the main rationale for their selection. They were chosen to offer an introduction to Aron's own philosophy of history, a theme that is central to all of his concerns. In a recent interview Aron declared:

> I found my way at about twenty-six when I chose the theme of my philosophic thought: the relations between action and history, and it is out of this query, the relations between action and history, that all my books have emerged.[10]

Surely it is time for more attention to be paid to a theme that Aron himself endows with such importance. In the concluding essays to this volume he shows how our perceptions of the past and our will to act in the future are closely related. Historical experience and political programs—*what has been and what ought to be*—must be understood as a continuing dynamic whose progressive or regressive features for human dignity and the good of the whole community often depend on the very

---

[7] See "History and Politics," p. 247, and "The Social Responsibility of the Philosopher," pp. 254–259.

[8] *Penser la guerre, Clausewitz*, 2 vols. (Paris: Gallimard, 1976).

[9] See "Thucydides and the Recital of History," p. 45.

[10] *Journal de lire*, no. 18 (February 1977): 34; editor's translation.

terms under which the dynamic is perceived, that is, the very lengths people and their leaders are willing to go to realize their beliefs about the future.

All politics is rooted in history and all political doctrines have a position toward the past. The reactionary wishes to preserve or return to the past at all cost and denies change. The revolutionary attempts to abolish the past and transcend it. Neither end is achievable yet both partisans will go to inhuman extremes in the name of an impossible goal: absolute definitions of justice. The key to resolving this impasse is an enlightened attitude toward change, neither denying nor accelerating the conflict beyond reason, *and* fewer illusions about the perfect nature of the future societies change is expected to bring about.[11]

In "Three Forms of Historical Intelligibility" Aron argues that a probabilistic approach is best because it sheds light on the past *and* the future, accounts for the contingent *and* the necessary, and allows us to think in terms of trends and underlying forces without becoming enslaved to fallacious determinisms. We should look back to see in past events a logical development yet we must also be aware of how everything *could* have been different. Napoleon *could* have decided not to attack Russia. So could Hitler. Likewise, although we can confidently expect the industrial order to develop in a certain direction with a focus on efficiency and production there is no *certainty* that it will. According to Aron, in looking back and in looking ahead a probabilistic outlook is both intellectually sound and politically progressive.[12]

This brings us to perhaps the heart of Aron's perception of the dialectic between politics and history. He suggests that the work of the true statesman, weighing probabilities and their future consequences, resembles the work of the historian in retrospectively weighing the probability of the motivations of past actors:

> Just as the statesman, depending on the possibilities that he can foresee, designs the contours of the world in which he acts, so the historian, by a retrospective analysis of possibilities, reveals the articulations of the historical process.[13]

The statesman and the historian must understand and work within given general frameworks, recognizing the underlying political and economic forces that affect society. But they also must be able to recognize the unique, events that will never be seen twice. Distinguishing between the systemic and the unique means steering a difficult course between these two sorts of knowledge and actions based upon them. Whereas

---

[11] See "History and Politics," pp. 247–248, and "The Social Responsibility of the Philosopher," pp. 254–258.

[12] "Three Forms of Historical Intelligibility," pp. 50, 54, 60–61.

[13] *Introduction à la philosophie de l'histoire* (Paris: Gallimard, 1938), p. 204; editor's translation.

some decisions seem to confirm the course of history, others seem to change it. Neither the historian nor the statesman can afford to minimize "necessary" *or* "contingent" explanations or understandings. When they bring them together to explain or influence human affairs they are making a political statement or taking a political decision. The decision toward the end of World War II to land in Normandy rather than attack Germany through the Balkans profoundly influenced the future of Europe and the world in the second half of the twentieth century—this decision has to be understood in terms of broad, underlying factors *and* in terms of individual views and psychology of those who happened to be in command at the time.

The essays included here illustrate both a method and a position concerning the relationship between knowledge and action, history and politics. The interaction of historical experience and political will is the theme behind most of these short studies. It provides in concentrated form the theme behind many of Aron's larger works as well.

Aron's philosophy of history is progressive and, if closely read, leaves room for a degree of hope about the future. With an open future, possible progress awaits those who would intelligently wed idealism and realism. In history and politics there can be no final determinism:

> Unlike phylogenesis, history cannot be arrested. We cannot observe humanity's adult stage. Thus each one imagines it as he would wish it or as he predicts it. Such images are always uncertain if they claim to be an anticipation of reality, but they are perhaps inevitable and legitimate if human truth is not something received but rather something in the process of creation.[14]

There is of course also much pessimism in Aron's writing. A classical realist such as he cannot fail to point out the tragic dimension of human existence, past, present, and future. With a focus on the twentieth century this tendency is reinforced. As a young, Jewish, postdoctoral scholar in Hitler's Germany in the early thirties, Aron adopted a pessimism that was the only lucid and responsible response to events around him. He lost faith, as he put it in his inaugural lecture to the Collège de France, and could retain a degree of hope only with effort.[15] Both of these attitudes have remained with him and intermingle in many of his works. Pessimism, with a degree of hope, seems half a century later still to be a reasoned attitude toward the world and its future.

The essays in this volume help us to start asking the right questions about our times, whatever our opinions and orientations. For instance, it is possible to remain within Aron's framework and agree with his basic assumptions and be either more reformist or more traditionally oriented

---

[14] *Introduction à la philosophie de l'histoire*, p. 176; editor's translation.

[15] See "On the Historical Condition of the Sociologist," p. 65.

than he himself is. I lean to the former and feel comfortable advocating a policy of active reform on the basis of an Aronian analysis—at least for the developed areas of the Western world. For the Third World serious problems arise, as Aron himself has pointed out.[16] The dimensions of the problems to be solved and the historical background of the societies involved all but preclude the compromises and timing of liberal politics.

Aron's comparative, empirical approach to society leads to a pragmatic reformism. How to reconcile this with his abstract neo-Kantianism and his belief in certain crucial values and the impact, however undetermined, of human reason on history requires a longer analysis of his work than anything attempted here. Aron's problem is the very problem of liberalism itself, that eclectic and at times ambiguous commitment to both commonsense compromises and absolute principles. As an observer and a scholar of the twentieth century he has done more than most to give heart to liberals and pause to its critics.

Aron's essays help us to anchor our own times in times past, conciliate political activism with social reality, and temper a quest for justice with an awareness of past values and traditions. They warn us against dogmatism and illusory thinking, which are often associated forms of thought. In the life of individuals and the life of communities, hope without illusion or fanaticism is a rare and precious commodity. It is called wisdom. It is the only path to whatever secular truth is humanly accessible. The work of Raymond Aron puts us on this path.

M.B.C.

---

[16] See *Colloque de Rheinfelden*, Raymond Aron, George Kennan, Robert Oppenheimer, and others (Paris: Calmann-Lévy, 1960).

Introduction

Fifteen or so years ago I gave two series of Gifford Lectures entitled "Historical Consciousness in Thought and Action." The first series dealt with some questions that had constituted the central theme of a book written forty years ago, *Introduction à la philosophie de l'histoire*,[1] namely what are the specific characteristics of the reconstructed human past, of historical knowledge? The second series pursued the task announced in a footnote on the last page of the *Introduction*: to become conscious of man's historical condition.

Even if I stand up against my society, it is that very society, inscribed in myself through the values it instills in everyone, that provides me with the justification for my revolt against the official authorities. Many dissidents in the Soviet Union justify their opposition by a "betrayed" Marxism, or by fundamental principles of equality or freedom that have been violated or misunderstood, or even beyond this by the Christianity of eternal Russia.

The title chosen by Miriam Bernheim Conant for this collection of essays expresses what has been the inspiration for my labors, the inquiry that runs throughout my books, from the first three, prior to the war, until the most recent, the two volumes I devoted to Carl von Clausewitz (1976) and *Plaidoyer pour l'Europe décadente*, the former far removed from, the latter very close to, present-day politics. Though an author should leave to his readers the task of interpreting his texts, which he knows better, by definition, in terms of what he meant to say than what he actually has said, a few remarks will perhaps help the reader better understand the whole configuration to which these essays belong, written as they were under different circumstances and at widely separated dates.

---

[1] *Introduction to the Philosophy of History: An Essay on the Limits of Historical Objectivity*, trans. George J. Irwin (Boston: Beacon, 1961).

It was in 1931, at the age of twenty-six, that I formulated my own intellectual goals. I decided then, at a time when I was finding life hard to cope with and severely judging the narrowness of the philosophic training I had received, to subject my own political opinions to a critique. My temperament and natural ambition inclined me toward metaphysical speculation. But Léon Brunschvicg—a neo-Kantian engaged in the history of mathematics and physics—discouraged me in advance. What metaphysics is possible in an age when the natural sciences are demonstrating in action their correspondence with reality and are overturning our civilization? In any case, a philosophy radically detached from science (in the narrow sense of the term) seemed pointless to me. Not having received a real initiation in mathematics, I despaired of ever filling this gap; I had spent a year studying various books of biology, in particular the genetics of Mendel and Morgan, at a time when the chair in general biology at the Sorbonne was occupied by Etienne Rabaud, who rejected in one stroke the whole of genetics. The thesis subject suggested to me by Léon Brunschvicg was based, if I remember correctly, on the notion of the individual or of individuality in the realm of living matter. At the end of a year, I had enough sense to realize that I had better either become a biologist or else leave to the biologists the task of criticizing their science. At best, I would only have been able to approach the level at which the best biologists, conscious of their profession, establish themselves with ease.

Brunschvicg's neo-Kantianism, which had turned me away from metaphysics, still left me dissatisfied. Ethics, drawn from the history of science or epistemology, seemed to me both partial and every bit as arbitrary as any other philosophy. The attitude of the scientist in his quest for truth, the detachment from self by which one sees a situation and oneself through the eyes of another—I admire the grandeur and accept the necessity of all this. But the total, flesh-and-blood man that I am—that we all are—does not live each moment like a scientist over his test tubes or microscope; he loves, hates, acts, believes; he is a citizen, soldier, teacher, militant, bourgeois, rich or poor, French or German, in the midst of others and of events. Because science and science alone brings true knowledge since its findings can be verified, philosophy no longer possesses a field of its own in which it can attain verifiable knowledge; however, this does not mean that philosophical thought, for lack of system, relinquishes all ambition and leaves it up to the novelists to ponder the human condition. A society cannot do without a certain overall vision of itself and the world. A philosopher still has the choice between the two paths: the analysis of the natural sciences or reflections of a moral and historical nature. It may well be that these two paths meet somewhere.

In subjecting my political opinions to a critique, I hoped to overcome a duality that was perhaps inevitable but one that made me suffer. On the one hand, I read Kant's *Critique of Pure Reason*; on the other, I observed Weimar Germany, where I had been living since 1931. Kantian philosophy fascinated the student and scholar in me but not the social and historical man who was painfully witnessing the rise of German National Socialism and the conditions that spawned a second European and world war. In asking myself several questions—why did I join the Socialist party? why did I leave it after a few months, tired of the revolutionary prating of bourgeois young people in the fifth *arrondissement* of Paris?—I discovered, almost in spite of myself, another critique: to question my political opinions was also to question the limits of sociohistorical knowledge. On the way I discovered Marxism, which already, in the Germany of 1931, obstructed the future. Thus, I traveled from a critique of biology to a critique of the human or social sciences, and in so doing I reestablished a unity between myself and my life—a unity, both dangerous and exhilarating, of thought and action, of teaching and journalism, of history and politics.

Of course, when in 1931 I took up the study of Marx or even when I wrote the *Introduction* in 1936–1937, I had no idea that from 1947 to 1977 I would regularly write one or two articles every week for *Le Figaro*. There was no way of knowing that I would have the talent, albeit minor, necessary to convey a few ideas in four or five pages and in a style intelligible to the general public. My participation in the daily press was the result of circumstances: the war, my role in the monthly review *La France libre* in London, the delay in my return to the university. Without journalism, my books would probably have had a somewhat different character—better or worse, I cannot say, but certainly more in conformity with the rules of academic works. This point being conceded, I am still convinced that the four categories of my postwar works constitute a logical, if not necessary, continuation of the basic question raised in the *Introduction à la philosophie de l'histoire*.

I can sort my books into the following categories: those that discuss current ideologies, in Paris or throughout the world, of which the best known is *L'Opium des intellectuels*;[2] those that elaborate the concept or the implications of *industrial society*, of which the best known are *Dix-huit Leçons sur la société industrielle*[3] and *La Lutte de classes*; those that deal with international relations, among which I might mention *Paix et guerre entre les nations*[4] and *Le Grand Débat*;[5] and finally those that

[2] *The Opium of the Intellectuals*, trans. Terence Kilmartin (London: Secker & Warburg, 1957; Garden City, N.Y.: Doubleday, 1957).

[3] *Eighteen Lectures on Industrial Society*, trans. M. K. Bottomore (London: Weidenfeld & Nicolson, 1967).

[4] *Peace and War; A Theory of International Relations*, trans. Richard Howard and Annette Baker Fox (Garden City, N.Y.: Doubleday, 1966). There is also an abridged edition, prepared by Remy Inglis Hall and translated by Howard and Fox (Garden City, N.Y.: Doubleday, Anchor, 1973).

[5] *The Great Debate: Theories of Nuclear Strategy*, trans. Ernst Pawel (Garden City, N.Y.: Doubleday, 1965).

analyze the regimes of our times, *Démocratie et totalitarisme*[6] and *Essai sur les libertés*.[7] I leave aside interpretations of economic, social, or political theories or doctrines *(Les Etapes de la pensée sociologique,*[8] *Penser la guerre, Clausewitz)* and studies of history in the making *(Le Grand Schisme, La Révolution introuvable,*[9] and *Plaidoyer pour l'Europe décadente).*

All of these works, it seems to me, express a commitment and display an effort toward understanding, along with, if not objectivity, then at least honesty toward those whom I oppose. Personal commitment is more evident in *La Révolution introuvable* than in the *Dix-huit Leçons*; it appears, certainly, in all my works, as does, I hope, the effort at understanding. And if this is so, these books illustrate and carry out my initial and permanent plan conceived forty-five years ago and of which the *Introduction à la philosophie de l'histoire* revealed only a part: I wanted simultaneously to be a spectator of history in the making and an actor, through words written and spoken, in politics.

By taking my political opinions, and at the same time Marxism, as a subject for consideration or philosophical criticism, I encountered not only the huge Marxist, Marxological, and anti-Marxist literature but also the philosophical literature, almost exclusively German at that time, on the specific nature of historical knowledge or the sciences of the mind. Because of the neo-Kantianism I had absorbed at the university, I was fascinated both by the notion, equivocal by the way, of the *critique of historical reason* (Wilhelm Dilthey) and by the *critique of the economy*, a permanent theme of Karl Marx's. When, in 1938, I published the *Introduction*, inspired by the critiques of Dilthey and Weber, I conceived the idea of writing a critique of political economy, or rather an introduction to the social sciences, along the lines of Marx's critique of the economy. After the war I largely lost interest in writing introductions to the social sciences or to political economy; concrete problems won out over formal or epistemological problems. Nevertheless, I continue to study, as best I can, the literature on historical knowledge, in particular, the works of Anglo-American analysts.

Of the three books published before the war, the first, *La Sociologie allemande contemporaine*,[10] was, so to speak, commissioned by my "sponsor" of the time, Célestin Bouglé—a rather ad hoc work, diversely re-

---

[6] *Democracy and Totalitarianism*, trans. Valence Ionescu (New York: Praeger, 1969).

[7] *An Essay on Freedom*, trans. Helen Weaver (New York: World, 1970).

[8] *Main Currents in Sociological Thought*, trans. Richard Howard and Helen Weaver, 2 vols. (New York: Basic Books, 1965, 1967; London: Weidenfeld and Nicolson, 1965; reprint ed., Doubleday, Garden City, N.Y.: Anchor, 1968, 1970).

[9] *The Elusive Revolution. Anatomy of a Student Revolt*, trans. Gordon Clough (New York: Praeger, 1969).

[10] *German Sociology*, trans. Mary Bottomore and Thomas Bottomore (London: Heinemann, 1957; New York: Free Press, 1957).

ceived by the senior members of the university. Likewise, the study of Dilthey, Rickert, Simmel, and Weber met with severe criticism from my thesis adviser, Léon Brunschvicg. This severity was probably excessive and today I understand its motivation; in any case, it served me well. Since he, who had my interests at heart, predicted inevitable failure if I offered this historical essay (on German philosophers hardly known at the time to the French) as my principal thesis, I had to express *my* own ideas directly and not present them through thinkers of secondary rank. Historical events pushed me to complete the *Introduction* more quickly than I might have wished. War was coming: I reasoned that even if I survived, I would not have the heart, at the close of hostilities, to resume an unfinished work.

The *Introduction* surprised the members of the jury, but the three leading judges at the university—Henri Bergson, Léon Brunschvicg, and Lucien Lévy-Bruhl—expressed, both publicly and privately, flattering or indulgent opinions. As a thesis, but also in the intellectual world at large, the book was a success. Yet, twenty years later, when the work appeared in Great Britian and the United States in an imperfect translation, it was, on the whole, rejected.

Two ideas oriented and guided my thinking in the *Introduction*. The object of the knowledge we call historical differs from that of physical or chemical knowledge. This object is constituted by men, by lived experiences, by human actions; it is possible that the essence and method of science do not and should not depend on the object itself. But this statement is open to discussion. None of the social sciences, not even economics, which today passes for the most advanced, enjoys a status comparable to that of the exact natural sciences. In the United States a number of universities have split their economics departments: one section teaches neoclassical economics; the other, progressive economics.

The second point of departure was not the *human* but the *past* nature of the object of historical knowledge. Or again, one would hold narration to be the form par excellence of historical knowledge. However, the reconstruction through documents or monuments of what no longer exists and the alignment in time of successive events do not resemble the activities of the physicist or chemist. It is enough to evoke the reconstruction of the evolution of the planet earth or of the solar system to select another typology: no longer the alternative between natural sciences or the sciences of the mind but the opposition between the sciences of laws and those of facts, or again, to use Wilhelm Windelband's terms, between nomothetic and idiographic sciences.

I did not attempt to settle the debate: do all sciences, whatever their object, belong to a single and unique category? Or should one differentiate between them according to their object (nature or humanity)? Or again, do the sciences of laws and the sciences of change typically oppose each other? I attempted to describe the steps that take one from lived experience to the knowledge of self and of others, a knowledge that does not attain the ungraspable moment of experience: I do not myself relive the experiences I have had in the past but I *understand* my behavior and the behavior of others by reconstructing the motivations of the actor or I *explain* through precedents and the social environment the human or social event, an event that constitutes an objectification of the ungraspable experience.

The duality of understanding and explanation has not disappeared from the philosophical literature. Von Wright demonstrates this.[11] The inexhaustible Dray-Hempel controversy never refers to German works of the end of the last century and the beginning of this one, though it comes up with the same problems: the historico-human fact cannot be separated from the intentions of the actor. When we try to take account of a historico-human fact, situated and dated, can we explain it by subsuming it under a universal proposition or are we reduced to seeking the motivations of the actor, or again, in the words of Karl Popper, the *logic of the situation*, which, the character of the author being given, produced the event or decision?

Because of peremptory formulas (for example, the *dissolution of the object*) and the lack of adequate distinctions among the various kinds of uncertainty or interpretation, the book gave the impression of a historical relativism bordering on skepticism. By now I thought quite differently. I pointed out the dogmatic scientism of vulgar Marxism and insisted on the plurality of historical interpretations not to open the way to the arbitrariness of grandiose visions but to take into account the plurality of modes of intelligibility.

Historical relativism—in its limited sense, meaning that each society gives itself a past in terms of its own present—is rightly thought of as a cliché. The curiosity of historians turns in this or that direction. That a reconstruction or a narrative contains material that may differ in part according to the researcher or narrator does not affect the intrinsic truth of the judgments stated. I assumed that the historian sets the truth as his goal and also that he reaches it, as far as his data allow. But I also recalled the distance between what is experienced and what is known (*le vécu et le connu*). The macroscopic event—the Battle of Waterloo—was diversely experienced by tens of thousands of different actors. The reconstructed battle substitutes for the chaos of innumerable individual acts and impressions a limited plurality of collective movements that converge in a logical, if not necessary, outcome. Retrospectively, the entity "battle" becomes intelligible because we know how it ended. When we discuss matters at a higher level—for example, U.S. foreign policy between 1945

[11] Georg Henrik von Wright, *Explanation or Understanding* (Ithaca, N.Y.: Cornell University Press, 1971).

and 1973—we do not know the outcome. A fortiori, we do not know the outcome of universal history, of which we live only a tiny fragment. Ignorance of the outcome does not nullify judgments of what went before but does modify the meaning, the role, and the importance of any given event. Who would have recognized the significance of the split between Mensheviks and Bolsheviks before the seizure of power in 1917?

Of course, if we possessed a general theory of societies or of each social formation, a properly historical narrative, with no loss thereby in meaning, would derive its intelligibility from just such a theory. Out of the contradictions of capitalism would logically flow the successive stages of the regime. But the theory does not exist. Though political economy and sociology provide history with concepts, regularities, and, in the absence of laws, patterns of interpretation, the future of the entity "Western capitalism" remains a history in the usual sense of the word, that is to say, a series of events, comparable to the scenario of a drama, with anonymous forces, individual decisions, and unpredictable connections. In other words, I did not want to suggest that each historian tells the story in his own way but that no historian can boast that he has presented the definitive version of the drama; not only is the last word not yet spoken but the intelligible reconstruction of experienced chaos never exhausts the facts or connections capable of appearing in knowledge.

The plurality of interpretations when it is a question of the spiritual universe—the world of the mind—takes on another and a deeper meaning. Contemporary history offers both a privilege and a weakness. Thucydides tells the story of a war he had participated in; the organization of armies or cities, the values and concepts of the actors, he knew them all at first hand, without embarking on the discovery of the *other*. Because of this very fact, the *History of the Peloponnesian War* is a story in its pure and basic form: a series of decisions, at some moments crucial, with the unfolding of the motivations of the actors, and the tragic outcome, the work of actors who did not will it and yet at the same time are responsible for it, a destiny stronger than the men who produced it. On the other hand, to *comprehend* the polis or Plato's philosophy requires from us an effort of detachment in relation to ourselves and one of sympathy toward another.

Detachment and sympathy define, so to speak, the ethics of the historian. If I called some great works of the past—the *paideia* of the Greeks or the plays of Shakespeare—"ambiguous and inexhaustible," I was not so much thinking of dissipating or exposing the illusion of truth as of reiterating an idea more trite than paradoxical: the masterpiece harbors not one secret but many; that is, it possesses multiple aspects, multiple meanings, that reveal themselves little by little to the men who come after it. Historical knowledge consists in a dialogue; the object passively submits to the questions of the historian but nevertheless continues to live.

What the artist has painted, or what the philosopher has thought, or what the writer has written remains forever immutable, but its meanings were never posed in such a way that it could be proclaimed that one interpretation, and one only, was valid. Not that the interpretation thereby becomes arbitrary: to question a work is not to apply our concepts and values to it but, quite the contrary, to elaborate and discover the mode of thought, the evidence, and the problems of the *other*. Great works usually contain contradictions, or at least divergent tendencies, from which the interpreter can legitimately extend one interpretation at the expense of others. On the other hand, to substitute our concepts for those of the *other* is to abuse the historian's rules of conduct.

The second panel of the projected diptych involved an introduction to the social sciences and above all to political economy. These sciences, for the same reasons as history, aspire to a reality that results from the objectification of lived experiences consisting of human actions, sometimes intelligible without reference to conscious intentions but in the final analysis performed by actors endowed with consciousness. Indeed, historians are more interested in lived experiences than are sociologists or economists. But they, too, discern amid the words of men, the goals they have pursued, and their actual behavior, the results they have provoked. The aggregates of macroeconomics cannot be explained by the psychology of individuals; they are nonetheless influenced, if not determined, by the behavior of social groups. Phillips's law—the inverse correlation between rates of unemployment and rates of inflation—is verified or invalidated according to the way social groups (trade unions and employers) react to unemployment.

The critique of the social sciences in no way leads to the radical relativism professed by Karl Mannheim in the first phase of his career. What remains valid in my eyes, however, is the absence of an all-encompassing, totalizing social science. Each of the disciplines— economics, sociology, politics, social psychology—uses a vocabulary and a system of concepts of its own. Each aspires to a partial social reality or, if you like, approaches the whole of a society from a particular angle. At best, a system such as that of Talcott Parsons embraces, at least in its conception, the different elements of the social totality—family, power, classes, the economy—but even this system remains doubly incomplete: it leaves undetermined, or poorly determined, the relationships among the various subsystems and the conceptual vocabulary carries with it a certain representation of the social unit, a representation very remote, for example, from the one suggested by Marx. All these theories contain true and verifiable propositions; each remains marked by what could be called, for want of a better term, an ideology, an image of society, charged with positive or negative values. Theorists in the Parsonian tradition see American society tolerably close to the good society; Marxist theorists see it unacceptably remote; yet both camps would agree on quite a number of facts.

I outlined in my courses for the Collège de France a "Critique of Sociological Thought," too imperfect to be published. And the Aberdeen Lectures still require more years of work than fate may have in store for me.

☆ ☆ ☆

The ambition I have nurtured since 1931—to live as both historian and social actor—required a conscious commitment that guides, assuming it does not distort, my perception of society. The element of relativism, inevitable in our knowledge of the past, a fortiori in our knowledge of the present, urges on us both detachment and reflection.

In our time—by the fact of fascism and national socialism before 1945 and that of communism especially after 1945—we have encountered the *other* at our side. It was not necessary to sail to a distant and unknown country to ask oneself: how can one be a Persian? It is enough to meet one's colleague, at one's side, to ask: how can he be a Hitlerian? or a Stalinist? In the United States, as I have already mentioned, certain universities simultaneously offer neoclassical economics and progressive (or revolutionary or neo-Marxist) economics. Of course, all professors, on one side and the other, accept certain facts, certain regular sequences, certain outlines, and certain concepts. Though, in this sense, they belong to the same club, they offer a very different view of reality and suggest very different courses of action.

This political relativism, the equivalent of historical relativism, can be refuted or surmounted by the analyst by either excluding one of the schools from science or discerning partial truths in both. Personally, I draw two lessons: one must *understand incompatible visions* in academic disciplines and in the ideologies of political parties; and one must *justify the taking of a stand* by the study of the regimes our period offers.

Before World War II, I insisted on the inevitable risk of decision. To accept our regime, political or economic, sometimes entails as many risks as to reject it. Between 1933 and 1939, while, powerless and desperate, I watched the decline of France in the face of a mortal threat, I understood the legitimacy of a revolt against a power so paralyzed as to be incapable of saving the nation. After 1945, at the close of hostilities, it seemed obvious to me that the totalitarian threat came once again from the East, but from much farther East, and from the far Left not from the far Right. By the same token, to lead the life of an active witness, it behooved me to justify my rejection of the revolutionary option.

The books of the second category, *Dix-huit Leçons sur la société industrielle* and *La Lutte de classes*, were a response to this duty even more than *L'Opium des intellectuels*. This last book was judged polemical—which I willingly grant—but the first two are not or were not intended to be. They attempt to describe and analyze two types of social organization in two concrete historical societies, the Soviet Union and the United States.

Seemingly I was slipping from one philosophy or existential attitude to another. Before the war, in keeping my distance from a certain academic moralism, I stressed the historical condition of man, marked by the values of his society and condemned to a hazardous commitment to ever doubtful causes whose ultimate outcome no one could predict with certainty. Since 1945, I have not ceased to plead rationally against communism, for the industrialization of a France retarded in its development by the calamities of the century, for the Atlantic alliance, and for resistance to Soviet expansion in order to save both peace and the regimes of freedom.

The positions taken on postwar problems are not, in my eyes, automatically justified since both camps—communist and liberal—claim to uphold the same values. It was not the same before 1939. Fascism and national socialism explicitly rejected, with violence and scorn, the legacy of the Enlightenment. Communism, on the other hand, claims to be, in Engels's words, the heir of classical German philosophy. It does not consider itself authoritarian or totalitarian but quite the opposite, the agent of human liberation, of the realization of a freedom higher than that of bourgeois democracy. Thenceforth, appeals or polemics must compare proclaimed values with the actual condition of men, or if you like the respective ideologies of regimes with reality.

I have never doubted that the standard of living of various classes, the choices open to individuals, and the different forms of inequality could be *objectively* assessed; I believe that in this sense facts, examined in a scientific spirit, determine the outcome of some debates. If commitments remain precarious and can in no case be confused with a judgment of truth it is because all regimes, economic or political, are imperfect and to some extent betray the ideals they proclaim; it is also because modern regimes, unlike most traditional civilizations, are turned toward the future—they are based neither on tradition nor on the present but on their goals. Communism is what it will be; it demands to be understood and appreciated as a transition, as a moment in a march that will lead to a finally human community worthy of the destiny of the human species. Depending on the importance one gives to the respective deficiencies of each type of regime, according to the future promised by each, one will take a stand for one or the other.

Let me add that taking a stand for the world called capitalist or free has one meaning for a Frenchman or a citizen of the United States and another for a Cuban, Russian, or Pole. Neither the Russian nor the Pole, even if he is opposed to his country's regime, thereby necessarily desires a revolution. Many dissidents in Eastern Europe have derived from their experience of this bloodstained century a lesson in wisdom and moderation. Of course, there will still be revolutions, tomorrow as yesterday, but why should we pretend that a revolution aimed at "changing life" and eliminating all the ills of humanity by setting up an absolutely new society would not result once again, after spilling torrents of blood, in another despotism?

The books of the four categories I have singled out and that do not follow directly from the prewar books—*ideological criticism, theory of industrial society, international relations*, and *institutions and political values*—were suggested to me by events. Launched by chance on the path of journalism, I felt the need to include ad hoc judgments in an overall framework. Why Marxism-Leninism? Why were liberal democracies superior, in the light of experience, to the so-called people's democracies under the actual domination of the state, which in turn merged with a party holding a monopoly of power and political activity? How could a state use nuclear arms in diplomacy without ever carrying out the threat being leveled?

The diversity of these works stems from a single question that can be formulated in a number of ways. Marx took no account of the distinctions among today's academic disciplines—economics, sociology, politics, international relations. Though the major part of his scientific work rested on economics, many of his essays and articles relate to other disciplines. As for a theory of society as a whole, which he outlined and which Marxists or Marxist-Leninists have retained and little developed, it exists, in the dogmatic texts, only in the form of vague indications or ambiguous concepts. How do production relations or the infrastructure determine or condition the political regime? Marx never really worked out a general theory of the connections between production relations and political power that would hold for all social formations, or even for capitalism alone. I have attempted to analyze the relations between economic and political regimes in the different types of societies in our time. I have also followed in the footsteps of Marx himself in examining the ideologies of our century in relation to institutions, ruling classes, and the situation of intellectuals.

All of my books, in a way, can be linked to this scrutiny of Marxism, begun in 1931. In another sense they can also be linked to epistemological thought about the way historical or sociological knowledge is rooted in society itself. Whether it is a question of industrial society or international relations, I make every effort to define the limits of our knowledge or our certainties. Some specialists in international relations nourish the ambition of building a science on the same model as the natural sciences. They have poured their anger and scorn on the "traditionalists," the "historians," and the "literary types." I feel no desire to participate in these diatribes: their stake is not mere truth but rather the distribution of academic posts.

There is nothing to keep us from substituting *actors* for states, from utilizing the concept of *system* to designate the totality of the *actors* and their mutual relationships, and from seeking *correlations* between the type of regime and the type of foreign policy. Abstract constructions—observed regularities or patterns of situations—are not unknown to the traditionalists, who have no objection in principle to so-called scientific research. But no so-called scientific research results in a *doctrine*, for example, in matters of nuclear strategy. A strategy cannot ignore the individual man, unique, concrete, of flesh and blood, who performed the role of abstract *actor* in the theory. At the same time, it asks the question: what if another man had made another decision?

What if another had done otherwise?

The duality of understanding and explanation reappears: a crisis becomes intelligible in the light of the behavior of the actors, behavior that itself is understood in the light of the bureaucracy or the opinions of advisers. There is nothing in the research on *decisionmaking* that differs from comprehensive sociology as it was interpreted by Weber. This sociology establishes regularities; when it takes as its object a single decision it may refer back to regularities but it can neither present this decision as necessary in view of precedents and the setting nor dictate to strategists the proper doctrine or the proper choice in any given circumstance. The social sciences or the sciences of action lay hold of sectors, selected and isolated, from the whole that has been experienced. The natural sciences also delineate their objects by their method and concepts, but the techniques, drawn from physical and biological knowledge, are operative and manipulate forces in the service of their needs. Techniques of economic manipulation are also drawn from scientific knowledge and succeed to a certain extent. The limits of their success differ, however, from those of the techniques deduced from the natural sciences; economic theories necessarily exclude exogenous circumstances that influence the result they are seeking; they also necessarily take it for granted that the behavior of the majority of actors conforms to a constructed rationale. But even the majority of actors do not always conform to this rationale.[12] Finally, actors, unlike atoms, are more or less conscious of the science elaborated by sociologists or economists; they sometimes belie the expectations of experts because they are aware of them.

An observer of history in the making but one engaged also in taking a stand, simultaneously preoccupied with objective knowledge and epistemological awareness, I have sought to base my rejections and my

---

[12] The rationale of strategists, assumed in the schemes of scientists, is more ambivalent still.

choices on reason by the comparative analysis of types of regimes and to mark the point at which verifiable knowledge ends and leaves the responsibility to one's conscience. Out of the partial and inevitable subjectivity of the representation of the universe in which each of us lives, I have done my best to elicit the example of an effort, one that must always be renewed, to understand others and myself.

Because of this, friends and colleagues find it difficult to know where to place me or what to call me. Philosopher or sociologist? In politics, should I be put on the Right? But in 1957, long before most men of the Left, I wrote a pamphlet in favor of Algerian independence. Antirevolutionary—that I am for sure. So was Alexis de Tocqueville: must he be ranged on the Right, among the conservatives? Furthermore, I do not feel the kinship with the Ancien Régime that Tocqueville transcended out of historical consciousness. I accept the democratic ideas that opened the gates of freedom to our ancestors, and to the Jewish community, and which allowed me to become a full-fledged French citizen.

I have been isolated and sometimes almost alone, but not today. Tocqueville, at the time of the Second Empire, wrote in a letter that he felt more solitary than in the deserts of the New World. I would write nothing of the sort, though between 1947 and 1953 I was proscribed by the intelligentsia: I denounced Stalinism with more moderation than my opponents of that time do today, when they sometimes strive to outdo Khrushchev in his speech of 1956.

To some extent, I remain on the fringe of the French intelligentsia. Of the two values invoked by our times, equality and freedom, I give first place to the second—not for intellectual comfort but as a result of historical experience. Now neither the Right nor the Left in France cares for economic liberalism. Though both proclaim democratic values, both reinforce state power in many ways. The Right in power restrains, corrects, blocks, paralyzes, and deforms the mechanisms of the market. The Left would push this age-old propensity of the French nation even further. Of course, I am well aware that popular demands lead irresistibly to a certain degree of socialism whether it be social security, guaranteed employment, the redistribution of income, or fiscal growth. Like anyone else, I largely subscribe to these demands. But the conflicting examples of Great Britain and the German Federal Republic seem to me instructive and decisive. There is a certain distributive, and not productive, socialism that leads a nation to ruin or in any case condemns it to decadence. An economy, liberal in its functioning, social in its goals, holds the most promise.

I am not dreaming of a France other than the one the past has created. France, built by the monarchy, is still maintained by its state structure. Accustomed to an administrative and centralizing regime, the French seem hardly gifted in the art of participatory democracy (*autogestion*). In this respect, the case of the universities is enlightening; the system of selection through competitive examinations and the *grandes écoles*—which in itself I do not much care for—is rooted so deeply in the national soil that even a revolution would not succeed in extirpating it. This having been said, I choose, once and for all, not the role of the reactionary but that of the adversary, he who reacts against the tendencies of the social body and his country, against the statist regime, against the unrealizable ideologies that so many Parisian intellectuals delight in, and against the disregard of economic necessities.

During the 1930s France, by absurd mismanagement, nearly died of pernicious anemia; divided by everlasting quarrels within, it refused to see the armies gathering beyond the Rhine. Since 1945, the recovery of France has surpassed the most optimistic hopes. Fourth exporting nation in the world, a great industrial power, France, despite colonial wars, despite errors, and sometimes despite the pretensions of its leaders, again holds an honorable place in the community of nations, considering the size of its population.

As I write, in the summer of 1977, France is once again on the threshold of a new adventure, with two camps, Right and Left, massing against each other as though engaged in an inexpiable conflict. As a historian of history in the making, I wrote a little book on the passage from the Fourth to the Fifth Republic, *Immuable et Changeante;*[13] as early as July 1968 I published *La Révolution introuvable,*[14] which caused a scandal and continues to arouse impassioned and conflicting judgments. Perhaps in 1978 I will write, on the occasion of the birth of a new republic, a pamphlet called *Le Socialisme introuvable.*

R.A.

---

[13] *France, Steadfast and Changing: From the Fourth to the Fifth Republic,* trans. George J. Irwin and Luigi Einaudi (Cambridge Mass.: Harvard University Press, 1960).

[14] See note 9 above.

PART I

HISTORY AND SOCIETY

THE NATURE AND LIMITS OF HISTORICAL AND SOCIOLOGICAL KNOWLEDGE

In Part 1 of this volume Aron discusses the interdependent nature of historical and sociological knowledge. In the opening essay, The Philosophy of History, *Aron poses the problem modern historical science presents to the philosopher of history. Science and technology have made the quest for human meaning and the unity of human experience both more urgent and more difficult to grasp. In* Thucydides and the Historical Narrative *he goes on to remind us that fifth-century* B.C. *and twentieth-century problems have much in common. Although economics and sociology have taken center stage in modern efforts at explaining the human universe, war and politics remain as basic as ever to any understanding of our times. Aron's own approach, as illustrated in* Three Forms of Historical Intelligibility, *focuses on probabilistic determinism and speculates on the effort to synthesize the history of events or actions and the history of works or human creations. In the last essay,* On the Historical Condition of the Sociologist, *Aron demonstrates the necessarily historical base of all sociology.*

1.   The Philosophy of History

ENGLISH, FRENCH, AND GERMAN each use one word for what has happened in the past and for our knowledge of it: *history*, *histoire*, and *Geschichte* mean both man's past and the knowledge men strive to build up about their past. (This ambiguity is less in German, which has two words, *Geschehen* and *Historie*, for these two concepts.)

This ambiguity seems to have a sound basis because reality and knowledge of reality are inseparable in a way that has nothing to do with the unity of object and subject. Physical science is not a part of those natural phenomena that it studies even though it becomes such by changing the course of nature; however, consciousness of the past is a constituent part of the historic process. Man has in fact no past unless he is conscious of having one, for only such consciousness makes dialogue and choice possible. Without it, individuals and societies merely embody a past of which they are ignorant and to which they are passively subject; they merely afford to the outside observer a series of transformations, comparable to those of animal species, that can be set out in a temporal series. If men have no consciousness of what they are and have been, they do not attain the dimensions proper to history.

Man, then, is at the same time both the subject and the object of historical knowledge. It is only by starting with man that we shall understand the real nature of the science and philosophy of history. Such an understanding is the sole aim of so short an article as this, which is not concerned with expounding a philosophy of history any more than with giving an account of philosophies of history from Saint Augustine to Spengler and Toynbee. Such accounts already exist, and the shorter they are the less satisfactory they are. What has to be done here is to explain the origin, function, and characteristics of a philosophy of history; how it differs from the science of history, which also aims at reconstructing and interpreting man's past; and to ask whether the philosophy of history is a

"The Philosophy of History" from Chambers's *Encyclopedia* published in 1950. Reprinted by permission of The Caxton Publishing Company Ltd.

survival from prescientific ages or whether it is indispensable to all civilizations, which can no more do without an overall view of the adventure of man than without a picture of the universe as a whole.

History is the reconstitution by and for those who are living of the lives of those who are dead. It is born therefore of the present interest that thinking, feeling, and acting men find in exploring the past. The endeavor to get to know an ancestor whose prestige and glory have survived to the present; the praise of the virtues that have made the city; the recital of the misfortunes, decreed by the gods or incurred by human error, that have ruined the city—in every case the memory, be it of the individual or the group, starts from fiction, myth, or legend and clears a painful path toward the truth. We must not be deceived by the freshness of impressions: a good memory is not a prerogative of the young.

Historical science, then, begins (speaking of course of a logical and not a temporal succession) by reaction to the imagined happenings of the past. An effort is made to establish and reconstruct the facts in accordance with the most rigorous techniques and to fix the chronology; the myths and legends themselves are used in order to discover the tradition underlying them and thereby to reach the events that produced them; briefly, in Ranke's famous phrase, the highest aim of the historian is to discover and relate *wie es geschehen ist*—how it happened. His ultimate and sole objective is pure reality.

The results achieved by several generations of historians trained in the methods of historical criticism are well known. Thanks to the achievements of historical science, even though there are still vast gaps in our knowledge, our civilization, for the first time in history, has been able to form a picture of the majority of former civilizations. It stands as a living civilization among those that are dead, conscious of its uniqueness and its frailty. It is true, of course, that no modern historian is able to master the whole body of material that has accumulated. The victory of historical science has been a victory for the specialists. The unity of history is lost in the multiplicity of disciplines, each confined to a fragment of the ages or to one aspect of past societies. What does this dispersion of interest mean? Specialization is the inevitable weakness but at the same time the triumph of science, and in this history does not differ from the natural sciences. The age of the encyclopedist has passed and everyone now has to reconcile himself to limitation. What has been achieved is that the past, forever gone yet still surviving in its monuments and documents, has been bit by bit reconstituted in its precise dimensions and infinitely varied perspectives through generations of patient inquiry.

There is no question here of throwing doubt on the merits of the scientific method or, by any cheap skepticism, of impeding the proper development of learned research and disciplined exposition. But it would be a fundamental misconception of the present position of history to forget that the second dialectical stage, that of scientific achievement, is necessarily followed by the third, namely, the stage of critical reflection, which, although it does not reject scientific achievement as science rejects mythological credulity, determines its limits and value. This critical method appears in two forms: that of the *Untimely Meditations* of Nietzsche and that of the application to historical knowledge of Kantian philosophy (Dilthey, Rickert, Simmel, Max Weber).

Nietzsche's *Untimely Meditations* have, it is true, been interpreted and exploited in a great variety of ways. But the essential idea behind them still seems valid. The *Meditations* amount to this simple proposition: the reconstruction of the past is not an end in itself. Just because it is inspired by a present interest, it has a present purpose. What the living seek from a knowledge of the past is not merely the satisfaction of a thirst for knowledge but an enrichment of the spirit or a lesson.

What has survived of Nietzsche's thesis is the conception of history as something "monumental," directly opposed to the pure science of the positivists. Nothing is more obvious than that all men and all events are not equally worth studying and that certain persons and certain achievements have a value and significance that make them particularly deserving of our attention. Science itself works on this assumption in spite of the fact that erudition for erudition's sake would tend to consider any and every phenomenon interesting. Above all, the application of concepts of value to reality itself dispels the illusion of a reproduction pure and simple of that which has been and makes clear the inevitable and legitimate links between the present and the past, the historian and the historical person, the masterpiece and the admirer.

Nietzsche indeed does not deny either the necessity or the merit of erudition, the accumulation of materials, the rigorous criticism of sources, and the ascertainment of the facts. He merely maintains that these preparatory steps are justified by what follows, namely, history proper, "monumental," critical, and archeological. History is the handmaiden of life as long as it provides examples, judges the past, and puts the present in its proper place in the historical process. History is a dialogue between the past and the present in which the present takes and keeps the initiative.

Whatever its faults or merits, Nietzsche's theory ran a grave risk: it was easy for it to slip into contempt for learning and truth. It suggested an opposition between types of historians and of history: those who merely collect materials and those who expound their significance. Such opposition is both unreal and fatal because the essence of history, the science of the concrete, is to search for significance at the level of a unique event or unique society; because an interpretation that is not disentangled from the facts is arbitrary; and because "bare fact" is nonsense, or rather, unthinkable.

Historical analyses of the type inspired by Kant have had the merit of reestablishing this unity and bringing to light a solidarity in practice, a logical necessity; whereas the Nietzschean concept aroused a suspicion of a duality that was not inevitable but only desirable in the interests of living society.

The Kantian type of critique of historical knowledge derives fairly simply from certain controlling ideas. Historical science is no more the mere reproduction of that which has been than natural science is the reproduction of nature. In both cases mind intervenes and, starting with the raw material, constructs an intelligible world. History, like natural science, is a reconstruction, but it is a reconstruction of a very different type. The ultimate aim of natural science is a systematized complex of laws, each of which is capable of being deduced from the others. The ultimate subject of history is a unique series of events that will never be repeated, the procession of human societies and civilizations. Natural science searches for law, history for particulars.

No science is concerned with total reality; each has its own principle of selection, seeking to isolate that which is worth examining or that which serves to explain what is worth examining. The scientist's principle of selection has, it is true, often varied during the centuries from Aristotle to Einstein. The scientist is not interested in the particular stone that fell and killed Archimedes but in the way in which bodies fall, for science is not concerned with space-time data, the precise where and when, but with the abstract and, so to speak, theoretical considerations that are deduced by the reduction of the complex to the simple, such as gravitation in a vacuum or in air. Such a reduction in the historical field is inconceivable. What, then, is the method of that selection without which research would forever fail to reveal the smallest fragment of reality or the least moment of time? The Kantian critique has answered this question by introducing the concept of value. The events that survive in historical consciousness are those having some relation to the values in which either the actors or the spectators believe. There is not space here for any closer analysis of the concept of value. In the simple form given to it by Max Weber, "value" is nearly equivalent to the conception of a "center of interest." We preserve from the past whatever interests us. Historical selection is guided by the questions that the present asks of the past. The succession of pictures that we make of past civilizations is determined by the constant changing of the primary questions we ask.

This succession is all the more significant because selection is not to be understood as an initial step taken once and for all but as a continuing orientation of historical work. Selection is not merely the decision to study or ignore this or that fact; it is a certain way of construing facts, of choosing concepts, arranging complexes, and putting events and periods into perspective. This also explains how it is that the Kantians have succeeded in this case not in establishing the universal validity of knowledge but in suggesting a kind of relativity. Forms of sensibility and mental categories are the guarantee of universality to the same degree in which, as conditions of knowledge, they are valid for all men. But the values and interests that are the concern of history have no universal validity because they vary from age to age. Thus, it is that they justify a dictum that has already become classical: every society has its history and rewrites it as often and as far as the society itself changes. The past is never definitively fixed except when it has no future.

Must we today envisage a fourth stage of historical approach, one that will integrate the two previous stages on a higher level and be yet another dialectical development? It does not seem necessary to go beyond relativism as relativism went beyond the antithesis of legend and science; it will be enough to define the limits of that relativism at which we have arrived.

One of the Kantians, Rickert, has defined these limits by using the concept of values. Historical selection is valid only for those who accept the system of reference employed; therefore, in this sense it is not universally valid. Nevertheless, once such a decisive, if not arbitrary, selection has been made, the subsequent steps of the historian may well be rigorously scientific and claim to be universally valid. More concretely and simply, Max Weber said that each historian asks his own questions and chooses them freely. Once the questions have been asked the answers to them are given solely by the facts. The causal relations between the facts, even if the assemblage of facts has been dictated by some topical interest, are either true or false (however difficult the proof may be and whatever the resultant coefficient of probability). Over and above this hypothetical universality, that is, the universal validity of the deductions following on a free choice of starting point, Rickert believes that even the initial relativity due to selection can be overcome either by studying each period in relation to the values proper to it or by elaborating a universal system of values.

This latter conception would inevitably subordinate scientific truth to the truth of the system of values, that is to say, to a philosophy. On the other hand, the universal system of values is bound to be formal, but the questions the historian asks of reality are usually precise and concrete. Finally, the simple fact of relating one epoch to the values of a later epoch introduces a principle of constant reinterpretation of the past. It is not clear why a historian should be made to rethink a society exclusively in the same way in which it thought of itself (or, what comes to the same thing, to relate each society to its own values and not to later values). It is by no means certain that the historian can achieve complete detachment from the present, nor that he ought to do so: it is only by relating the past to the unfinished present that it can be made to yield up the secrets that have hitherto remained hidden even from the most careful research. In short, the theory of hypothetical objectivity that satisfied Max Weber, and which incontrovertibly applies to causal relations, rests on too simple a conception of selection. If the totality of a historical reconstruction is oriented by the question asked or the values of reference, the total reconstruction will bear the mark of the historian's chosen principles of selection and will be consistent from a single point of view, which at best can be recognized as legitimate and fruitful but not necessarily universally true.

Nevertheless, this relativism, which the very history of historical science evinces, does not seem to be destructive of scientific history as long as it is correctly interpreted. The fact that we acknowledge the existence of such relativism is a sign not of skepticism but of philosophical progress. In the first place, the degree of relativity is limited by the utmost rigor in establishing facts and by that impartiality which the scholar can and must have as long as he is merely unraveling texts and assessing evidence. Next, it is limited by the partial relationships that, starting from certain data, can be discerned in reality itself. A degree of uncertainty (but not of essential relativism) is adduced by the causal relation between an event and its antecedents and by calculating in accordance with probability the part played by each of the antecedents. The relation between an act and the motives behind it, between a ritual and a faith, or between the problems bequeathed by a philosophical system and the solutions given by subsequent systems is capable of being understood because the subjects studied are themselves intelligible. Furthermore, relativism is itself transcended as soon as the historian ceases to claim a detachment that is impossible, identifies his point of view, and consequently puts himself into a position to be able to recognize the points of view of others—not that it is strictly possible to move from one center of perspective to another since there is no numerical constant or calculable equation that makes such a transition possible. Nevertheless, one can comprehend different perspectives even when they seem contradictory and see in their multiplicity a sign not of defeat but of the richness of life.

This is what corrects the vulgar idea of historical relativism. When we cease to interpret our knowledge of the past by the criterion of a transcendental ego that gives form to an inert mass of material, when we put the historian back into reality and take the structure of reality as the point of reference, then the whole sense of the relativist formula is transformed. Past human existence is rich in the same significances and the same fruitful ambiguities as historical knowledge itself. History cannot give a final, universally valid account of societies, epochs, and extinct civilizations for the very reason that they never had a unique and universally valid significance. The never ending discovery and rediscovery of the past is the expression of a dialectic that will last as long as the human race and is the very essence of history: individuals and communities alike find contact with other enriching and self-revealing.

It is more difficult than is usually supposed to distinguish the science and the philosophy of history. If the investigation of the past is inspired and given direction by our present interests and system of values, is there not then a sort of philosophy in all historical interpretation? As a matter of fact, it has proved possible to elucidate the philosophy implicit in the work of all the great historians. Whether it is a question of the relation of the individual to the community, the relative importance ascribed to political units or economic systems, the dependence or independence of ideas in relation to the social substructure, or the reciprocal influence of historical factors, it is always possible to discover in any historical work a theory that has in part been suggested by the research itself and in part has preceded and suggested such research. This leads to the conclusion that there is no difference between the science and the philosophy of history; it would seem that the former cannot achieve its object unless it is permeated by philosophy; the latter cannot achieve concrete truth except through facts.

Such an identification of the science and philosophy of history, however, seems to misconstrue the very considerable differences between them. There are some elements of historical philosophy in every historical work, but they remain implicit and inarticulate, tending to be in practice merely working hypotheses or topics of inquiry. A real philosophy of history would want to systematize these elements by stating them explicitly. The historian makes his philosophy an integral part of an interpretation of some fragment of the past; the philosopher tends to use his philosophy of history for the interpretation of the past as a whole. The historian finds the truth in conclusions obtained by means of directive ideas but which go beyond them. For the philosopher ideas are what are essential as the foundation and guarantee of truth.

Thus, there are two opposite approaches to research and speculation. This opposition in essence seems twofold: on the one hand, it is a matter of dimension, the philosopher aiming always at the whole, the scholar at a part; on the other, even when the historian is writing a universal history and therefore is also concerned with the whole, he tends not to go beyond the facts and to elucidate the main lines of his narrative from the material, not seeking to establish the truth about the evolution of man but simply to discover what really happened.

In order to clarify this abstract exposition, let us follow the successive steps of historical knowledge from the part to the whole. At all stages the same sort of steps are taken. It is commonly said that the philosophy of history is the interpretation of the meaning of the whole of man's past. Now, the two essential and complementary stages, the building of the ensemble and the discovery of the meaning, are inseparable whether one is examining an isolable event, like the Battle of Cannae, or something as difficult to delineate as the evolution of a civilization.

A historian telling the story of the Battle of Cannae will describe how in the first phase the Roman infantry attacked the Carthaginian center. But he does not merely describe a movement, the infantry charge; he enables us to understand the movement by connecting it with two plans of battle: that of Hannibal to envelop the Roman legions and that of the Romans to break the enemy's line. In an example like this, we can establish the significance of an action by discovering the intentions of the actors.

This example is a very simple one. The intention in the actor's mind (at least, in Hannibal's) coincides at almost every point with the course of the battle. This coincidence is the result, first of all, of the strictly rational purpose of the commander, who formulates the exact means necessary for the achievement of his end, that is to say, the tactics necessary for victory. The coincidence of intention and event is the result also of the victory of one will over another, of the Carthaginian over the Roman.

But let us suppose that the event to be expounded is the sacrifice of victims before the battle: what we shall be looking for in this case is the significance of this rite in the system of beliefs that makes it intelligible. At once we are up against a multiplicity of problems of historical importance: the original significance of the rite, its significance at the time of the battle, the genuine belief or disbelief of the persons who performed it, and so on. A large part of the historian's task is to unravel such interlaced and superimposed factors, to elucidate the different states of mind of the actors about the meaning of their actions. The historian has to try to understand the traditions that are an intrinsic part of the life of the societies he studies.

It is not, of course, very often that a human intention is able to realize itself in action complete and unmodified. It is almost always either diverted by some obstacle (there may not be the munitions the tactical plan demands) or traversed by the intentions of others (there are usually two plans of battle, not one); likewise, irrational impulses may cause the actors to abandon both the end and the means of their action (panic may seize the troops). The intention and the event diverge far more often than they coincide. History, whether military or political, has to pursue the interplay of complementary and contrary intentions, which events may either implement or thwart. The historian is able to understand events by studying what men thought, and he discovers what they thought by reconstructing the heritage of the past in which men were faced with a given situation.

It is easy to see unity and significance at the level of a simple event. The Battle of Cannae was not merely a physical event in space and time; what singularity it had was given to it by the significance it had for the actors or the observer. In the case of this sort of battle, it had such clear limits in space and time that it is easy to forget that it was in fact a multiplicity of individual actions. But if one takes the struggle for the frontiers of an empire or the Russian campaign of 1812, it is obvious that the event is an intellectual creation, more or less inherent in the historical process, since the actors live the event as a unity but within limits that are constantly changing and open to revision in accordance with the interest of the observer.

Although it is true that the totality emerges only when its meaning has been elucidated, it is also true that the meaning can be discovered only in relation to the whole event. It is possible to understand the movement of each particular regiment only by seeing it in relation to the battle as a whole. Similarly, only by putting the battle in its place in the history of the Punic wars is it possible to understand its causes and consequences and only by putting the Punic wars in their place in the whole course of ancient history—in the struggle for mastery of the Mediterranean, in the ups and downs of imperial unification and the balance of power—is it possible to understand the Punic wars themselves. At every level, whether one is concerned with a fragmentary event confined within the limits of a battlefield or the course of a single day or with an immense phenomenon such as the Roman empire or the Mediterranean world, it is the historian who makes it a unit and weaves the pattern of meaning—the twofold process characteristic of the reconstruction of the past.

Nothing could be more useful to the study of the logic of both the science and the philosophy of history than a careful analysis of the different types of historical units from the bottom to the top of the scale. There are undoubtedly enormous differences between a historical complex like the Battle of Marathon and one like the Middle Ages. But these differences, which are not susceptible of precise definition, are differences of degree rather than quality.

The concept "the Battle of Marathon" is, we may say, a way of bringing together the events of a single day in a definite locality; the concept "the Middle Ages" is a way of coordinating historical epochs but not a way of relating particular events to the whole; it allows us, by putting the emphasis on such and such an aspect of the period, to study one part of reality and neglect other parts or at least to subordinate what is secondary to what is essential. In other words, one type of complex allows us to group events; the other, to select and orient. But there is no absolute contradiction here. The thoughts of the individual Greek and Persian soldiers on that famous day have no place in the narrative; events are recounted only as they serve a function in the battle: the plans of both sides, the clash of the armies, the victory of the Athenians. That is to say, selection and orientation have their function, even if it be small, in the narration of but a single historical event.

Now, whereas the participants in the battle thought of it as a battle, the Middle Ages is only a retrospective concept. Nevertheless, the Greco-Persian wars were less clearly thought of as such at the time. And even if the Middle Ages could not be thought of as such because they came to be defined by later events, the idea of an epoch subsequent to that of the Roman empire lingered in the minds of men who looked with nostalgia to the idea of the empire long after it had ceased to be a reality. So it is true that the historian sometimes takes the names of the historical complexes, political societies, or periods from that past he is re-creating and sometimes himself gives names to historical complexes. But he never creates a complex that has not been at least adumbrated by the past itself; he is always rethinking the complex that the records themselves reveal.

In the examples we have taken, the essential difference is between a single, static event and one complex in the historical process. The Middle Ages can be understood only in relation to what preceded and followed that period, the ancient and the modern world. A battle or a political organization or an economic system can be understood of itself by being related to its own principles. There is a host of other such distinctions that it would be interesting to explore. For example, the relations among persons or among ideas or those among the material factors that give unity to an economic system are not the same as relationships within a political or cultural unit. A purely ideal phenomenon such as a religion has an entirely different structure and different principles of permanence and transformation from a material phenomenon such as the capitalist system.

For the present purpose, that of discovering the frontier between the science and the philosophy of history, the basic problem is that of the broadest units of history, namely, societies or civilizations. To put it more exactly: what happens when the historian in his effort to grasp the totality of man's past deals with a unit embracing phenomena that differ radically, such as societies and civilizations that have had no actual relations with each other? As long as one keeps within modern Western civilization, one has the feeling of never going outside a definite historic unit. That unit may be vague, the line of division between ancient and medieval and between medieval and modern may be imperceptible, and historians may shift the demarcation backward or forward at their pleasure; that much is granted, such a lack of definiteness being inseparable from reality and from historical knowledge. The best way of dealing with such indefiniteness is to take one's stand at the very heart of the period or civilization to be studied and to proceed thence from point to point until the charactertstics of the period or civilization disappear and give rise to something essentially different.

But when the historian is attempting a universal history or a comparative history (or sociology) of civilizations, two new difficulties arise. What are the limits of those higher units that Spengler and Toynbee christened "cultures"? How are they to be defined? How many of them are there? Also, is it enough merely to set them in juxtaposition? And if an attempt is made to integrate them in an all-embracing history, from where are the principles of integration to be derived?

There seem to be two divergent approaches. An attempt can be made to extract from the reality the evolutionary rhythm or the essential nature of the units to be integrated. Or an attempt may be made to grasp the truth of the past from a universal philosophy of man, the truth of such a philosophy being the guarantee of the truth of the proposed interpretation of the past. Spengler follows the first line; Hegel, the second. Either the complex (even if it be multiple) is real or it derives its unity from the truth, even if the truth reveals itself throughout history.

No doubt it will be objected that philosophical opinions enter as well into the universal history that attempts to report only what happened. What is to be included in such a history? What system of values is implied by the various criteria selected for the evaluation of the cultures dealt with? Some philosophy is implicit in every universal history and such philosophy is always as much projected onto the documents as suggested by them. In any case, a universal history or a comparative history of cultures, like Spengler's, is at the same time more ambitious and more modest than a philosophy of history: more ambitious because it attempts to discover in reality itself the main lines of the historical process; more modest because it makes no explicit attempt to attain the truth about man.

It remains to inquire whether a straightforward philosophy of history is not both more honest and more instructive than these philosophies presented under the guise of empiricism. If the philosophic historian is to get any idea of the past as a whole and interpret it, must he not know the truth about man and his history? It is only by relating the past to the freedom of the self-conscious mind or to the classless society that history can become a unity and that the glorious and bloody succession of states and empires has any meaning.

Marxism is the sole philosophy of history in this sense with which we need to be concerned for it is the only interpretation of man's whole past related to a metaphysical system that today exercises any wide or deep influence on Western civilization. And yet most of those who profess Marxism, forgetful of the Hegelian origins of their faith and transferring dialectical materialism to the plane of science and fact, debase their philosophy into an ideology of justification.

In contrast, essays in universal history or the comparative sociology of civilization (that is, historical philosophies claiming to be empirical, like those of Spengler or Toynbee) seem to be a peculiar achievement of our own age. Though historians scorn them, they nevertheless exercise an influence on the historical conscience of our day.

This contrast is most instructive. The only philosophy that treats the whole of the human past as a unity dates from the nineteenth century. Philosophies of irreducible plurality are modern creations. That statement, if correctly understood, will explain what is characteristic of the present position of the philosophy of history in Western thought.

The decline of the philosophy of history is, in one sense, the counterpart of progress. The scientific nature of the detailed and patient examination of reality makes ideological and schematic constructions unwelcome. Never at any time have men observed such diversity; never have they been faced with such a mass of political, social, and economic experience; never have they had such an abundance of evidence to demonstrate that in every sphere of human activity, individual and collective, different institutions are equally possible, equally workable, and equally transitory. Whether it is a matter of the transition from democracy to tyranny, from private enterprise to government control, from nations to empires, in every case the past at once suggests precedents that, at the summons of the historian and the man of action, become alive and afford us a choice of contradictory lessons.

The enlargement of the known past and the accumulation of historical knowledge have rightly discredited the simplifications of popular philosophy and the naive conceit of those who but yesterday made our civilization the criterion of all civilization. Universal historians and comparative sociologists are merely trying to continue this movement. Since there is an irreducible plurality of social systems, political institutions, and conceptions of the world, the historian must endeavor to understand each of them in its peculiarity, to discover the inspiration and specific genius of each great historical phenomenon. What Meinecke calls "historicism," the attentive awareness of past modes of being and of man's achievements throughout the ages in their inexhaustible richness, is incontestably fundamental for our historical knowledge.

On this ineluctable plurality there is now grafted a philosophy of pluralism that goes far beyond the facts. When Spengler talks of cultures enclosed in their isolation, incapable of communicating with each other, he goes as far beyond experience in the direction of plurality as historical philosophers once went in the direction of unity. All overall surveys of the past, whether they claim to be empirical or metaphysical, are, as has been shown, bound up with the method of approach selected by the expositor. Spengler chose to set cultures in opposition and he pushed that opposition so far that his theory, if literally interpreted, would destroy the very possibility of doing what he set out to do. If civilizations are incapable of mutual comprehension, how is it that Spengler is capable of understanding them all?

Even if we approach the subject less formally, the philosophy of pluralism is at least suggested by the spectacle of the wealth of human achievement and our interest in such irrational things as modes of feeling, religious beliefs, and art forms. Insofar as one is dealing with the unceasing stream of myth and art as much as with the progress of knowledge and power, history inevitably dissolves into an infinite number of human societies, each different in its habits of thought and life, each with a different conception of the universe.

This leads to a philosophy of history whose essence is a conscious denial of the unity of history. It is possible to conceive the process of temporal things as the fragmentation of the being, which, timelessly considered, is itself intelligible. Viewed from such a philosophy, history dissolves into a mere juxtaposition of more or less accidental facts more or less causally connected. There is no coherent historical whole, no possibility of conceiving man or of seeing a single idea in the time process. Such a negation of history, which was, generally speaking, characteristic of the thought of the ancient world, was not a sign of spiritual crisis for man then saw the basis of order not in history but in the cosmos and his immutable destiny in the realization of the essence of his being. But the modern philosophical negation of historical unity in the doctrine of pluralism is very different. It does not resolve the totality of the past into a chaos in which each individual or group makes its own unhindered way and fulfills its own separate vocation: it acknowledges that there are historical complexes each of which is real and each of which controls the destiny of the men who compose it. Each historical phenomenon blossoms according to its kind, like a flower of the field fated to wither as soon as it has bloomed. History, ineluctable and purposeless, without universal unity but unified in each of its parts—such is the dogmatic philosophy of pluralism, which today weighs on our historical thinking, teaching that there is no total unity, no meaning in the whole.

Marxism, in contrast, claims to discern the reality of the whole by giving it a meaning. By triumphing over capitalism, by creating a society in which the individual can communicate immediately with the state—the particular with the universal—by reassuming what he has alienated, man will enter into the rule of freedom and realize himself. The succession of the phases of society, a necessary feature of the historical process, will have meaning for the totality of history; total not in the sense that it records all the facts, which is absurd, but in the sense that it relates all the facts to the truth about man. The class struggle, itself bound up with the factors of production, will make it possible to see every period and every society as they really were. Not, as positivist philosophy requires, because the factors of production determine everything (which is meaningless) but because the development of factors of production and the relations between production and class conflicts make it possible to establish the dialectical steps by which humanity climbs toward freedom.

Marxism, however great its political domain today (often indeed in a vulgarized form), is, it seems, already a phenomenon of the past. By its optimism it belongs to the nineteenth century. At the lowest level it gives no answer to the questions raised by its own development or by the development of the historical phenomena it has begotten.

The original contribution of Western civilization in modern times is the development of positive science, of the industrial techniques based upon it, and of the power that man has thereby gained over nature and over himself. Historical optimism is linked with faith in science, or rather with faith in the civilizing power of science. Knowledge is bound to bear the fruit of wisdom. Man, the lord and master of nature, cannot as such but gain mastery over himself. Victory over matter must bring peace between men.

It is true that Marxist philosophy does not claim that progress is determined and inevitable; it proclaims that struggle is necessary to resolve contradictions. It is not concerned with progress as such. But as interpreted by its disciples it does the same thing in a different way by preaching that the development of science and of the factors of production do lead in fact to the liberation of man on the single condition that at a given moment the capitalist system is overthrown and collective property established. In other words, Marxism maintains that man will become master of himself and of nature at the same moment, provided that a revolution has put power into the hands of the organized working class.

Now, experience of socialism in a single country has shown at least that the disappearance of capitalist exploitation does not necessarily involve that of other kinds of exploitation. It has proved that bureaucratic tyranny is one of the possible forms that may be taken by the regime that succeeds that of the market and private enterprise; it has proved that control of the masses, joined to control of nature, makes it possible for the governing elite to enjoy an absolute power compared with which the power of the kings and dictators of yesterday is as derisory as that of spears beside muskets or three-inch guns beside the atomic bomb.

The current ascendancy of pluralist philosophies of history and the decline of unitary philosophies, which since Saint Augustine have seen the stages of the ascent of man in the succession of empires or social orders, seem to be equally characteristic of the present day. Never before has the human race all over the world been closer to forming a unit. Science, the pride of the West and creator of irresistible power, has leveled the ramparts of the old civilizations of the Far East, and the machine has gone in triumph all around the globe. But the West, inasmuch as it is not sure whether science will bring forth wisdom or whether it will not in its turn be the victim of its own creation, is now asking itself whether it prefers what it has made to what it has destroyed. It mourns that which the noise of the machine has drowned and the smoke of the blast furnace obscured.

Since the power, science, and industry that effectively unify the human race no longer inspire the confidence they did a hundred years ago, universalist philosophies have been rudely shaken. The West no longer believes in itself since it no longer believes in the virtue of its mightiest achievement. Without cosmos and history, man finds himself thrown back on his unique relationship with God. Existentialism, whether negative or positive, atheistic or Christian, is the final result of a crisis that has robbed man of order in nature and of history and left him, naked and alone, face to face with his mysterious destiny.

The absence and the need of a philosophy of history are equally characteristic of our time. Man today is conscious of being engaged in a game in which the stakes are his soul and his existence. He can no longer entrust himself to the vain gods of progress and history. It is not regret for comfortable mythologies dissolved by the research of scholars that inspires our nostalgia, for we willingly tolerate the patience and slowness that their still uncompleted task involves. But we cannot give up the determination to plan and to create our future.

2. Thucydides and the Historical Narrative

THE HISTORY OF WARS has gone out of fashion. Forces of production, social structure—these lay more claim to the attention of posterity. Almost no academic historian any longer sees armies and armaments as the major cause of events. It is only the economic factor that seems capable of supplying the principle of "synthesis" or "integration."

Historians are rarely militarists or warmongers. Though logically one may attribute a dominant role to men or institutions one detests, psychologically one is inclined to neglect what one likes the least. Any reconstruction of the past is a selection; after all, it is perhaps legitimate that we measure the importance of an aspect of the past by the interest it has for us today. The historian who underrates "economics" in favor of "battles" runs the risk of alienating "progressive" and "enlightened" opinion.

At first sight, this attitude does not seem to be in accord with the experience of our century. One is tempted to cry out with the poet: what century has ever spawned more wars! Compare the Europe of a half century ago, its hegemony visibly symbolized by the march on Peking of a tiny European army under the command of a German general, with the Europe of today, divided and powerless, governed here by a Soviet commissar, there by American senators. Can one conceive of such a change except as the result of two deadly wars in which the weaker contestant appealed to non-European powers to help it to victory? The first half of the twentieth century has been the age of great wars, as foreseen by the visionary Nietzsche. Will future historians so regard it?

We all hesitate to reply to such a question. But why? Thucydides described, in detail, the expeditions, the maneuvers, the clash of hoplites

"Thucydides et le recit des évènements." Copyright © 1960 by Wesleyan University. First published in *History and Theory*, Volume 1 (1961) and reprinted by permission of Wesleyan University Press.

on land, of triremes by sea. It was the Peloponnesian war that interested him, nothing else. In a rapid survey of the centuries, he analyzed its remote causes in the formation of the city-states. His detailed exposition was reserved for the deliberations of assemblies, for the speeches of statesmen and generals, for the tactics of commanding officers in the field, and for the valor of soldiers. *Human action* as such—and I mean by that *the struggle of one man or several with one or several others*—that is the center of interest for Thucydides, the focal point of a work that remains, in our eyes, a masterpiece, *the* masterpiece of ancient historiography. Why is it that the German war of 1914–1945 will not have its Thucydides? Why is it that we are sure of this claim even before we give it thought, convinced as we are that a Thucydides of the twentieth century does not and could not exist? It is this inquiry that the following essay attempts to answer. Is it that the history to be told is different or is it the historians themselves who have changed?

☆   ☆   ☆

History,[1] as told by Thucydides, carries in the telling its critical interpretation, its pragmatic or philosophical lesson. Seldom does the historian break the thread of his narrative to speak in his own person. When he does so, it is almost always as commentary by a spectator whose detachment allows him to be just. Thus, at the end of Book VII, appears this epitaph on Nicias: "He was, among all the Greeks of my time, the one who by his application to the good in entire conformity with its rules least deserved to come to this miserable end." Ordinarily the words of his characters permit Thucydides to formulate general propositions without being obliged to intrude himself. The Greeks of the fifth century, as they live again in Thucydides' *History*, are not exposed to the double peril of hypocrisy and cynicism that ideologies give rise to. Addressing the Greeks of Camarina, the envoys from Athens say quite coolly:

> We shall exercise our hegemony over our allies according to the usefulness which each of them has for us, giving autonomy to the people of Chios and Methymna in exchange for their equipping our ships, exacting generally from the others a more rigorous payment of tribute, and finally leaving to certain ones complete liberty in the alliance, though they are islanders and could easily be conquered, for the reason that they occupy essential points around the Peloponnesus (VI, 85, 2).

Neither the Soviet commissars nor the American senators would dare to use such language.

The absence of ideology—camouflage or justification—is surely one of

[1] Readers familiar with the interpreters of Thucydides will perceive at once how much the following pages owe to Madame de Romilly. I could, and should, have mentioned her on every page if I had not been afraid of embarrassing her by the expression I have given to ideas belonging to her.

the reasons why the narrative itself contains the critical analysis and, in part, the philosophical interpretation of the event. It is not the only reason. In order to understand the satisfaction Thucydides' narrative provides, it is necessary to grasp both the nature of the events and the nature of the significance that the historian ascribes to them.

War is certainly not in the opinion of Thucydides a pathetic and ridiculous commotion on the surface of the "wave of history." It is not a cruel and bloody method either of carrying out the decrees of destiny or of bringing about changes that are inevitable whatever the causes. But we shall see that there is in Thucydides a sense of a historic destiny, perhaps a "historical determinism." The historian does not pay any less attention to human actions because they alone are worthy of being brought to the attention of posterity and are also the essence and means of historical development. To write the history of the Peloponnesian War is to recount how the Athenians, having ignored the advice of Pericles and carried away by pride and will to power, ended by succumbing in spite of their heroism and superhuman efforts. Just as in a tragedy whose denouement is known to all the spectators, the outcome of this struggle of giants is known to the readers as early as the speech of Pericles delivered at the moment when hostilities are about to begin. If we are reasonable, we shall be victorious because we are the strongest—this is virtually the orator's theme. Thucydides[2] appears to suggest that actually the Athenians would not have been defeated if they had remained reasonable until the end, but he does not prevent the reader from believing that the reasonableness that would have allowed the Athenians to avoid defeat was *psychologically* impossible.

The historian, with his perspective of years or centuries, may not take an interest in the narration of events since he knows their outcome. He would be like the spectator at the tragedy who did not interest himself in *Oedipus Rex* because he knows, from the beginning of the performance, that Jocasta will kill herself and that Oedipus will put out his eyes. This analogy is not as paradoxical as it appears *for he justifies his narration only in terms of the given circumstances*. There are no valid grounds for writing the lives of men whose memory is not worthy of being handed down to future generations. The narrative history presupposes a certain *quality* of the historical object, that is, of the men who have lived through the events to be retraced. This *quality* is found essentially in the *political* order and, in the eyes of Thucydides, in that supreme act of politics, *war*.

The word "politics" has, in our time, become ambiguous because of the Anglo-Saxon duality of "policy" and "politics," arising from doubt over the primacy of what was generally called "politics." "Policy," that of

---

[2] Was Thucydides familiar with the outcome at the time when he wrote or revised Book I? The interpreters are not in agreement. It seems to me likely that Thucydides, being aware of the final defeat of Athens, modified or preserved the text of this famous speech because it has kept its ring of truth and takes on its tragic significance in the light of the final event.

Michelin or General Motors, of gasoline or beets, is the plan of action defined either by reference to those who have conceived it (Michelin, General Motors) or by reference to the area to which it applies (gasoline, beets). "Politics" in the broad sense designates, in all the fields of social existence, the plans of action conceived by men with a view to organizing or directing other men. "Politics" thus reaches its completion in the search for a regime, that is to say, for the method by which the rules of organization and direction are determined. One may speak of the political regime of large corporations (their regime being authoritarian in the sense that those who direct do not need either to consult those to whom they give orders or to seek their approval). But the regime of the city-state is important above all else, at least in the eyes of the Greeks, because there the leaders presided over not a partial activity (work) but the activity constituting the existence of the free man, that is to say, politics.

We are not going around in a circle. A city is life lived in common by men. Each collective activity allows for a policy pushing it toward submission to an organization. But the art of organizing diverse activities in a single direction is the art of politics par excellence. Each regime represents a certain kind of organization of common existence. The citizen realizes himself in politics because he wishes either to influence other citizens within the framework of a regime or to establish or modify a regime so that the relations between individuals will conform to his ideas of mankind, freedom, or morality.

Defined in this way, politics always carries with it an element of dialogue between the two poles of constraint and persuasion, of violence and discussion between equals. Politics is dialectic when it unfolds between men who mutually acknowledge each other. It is war when it brings into opposition men who, while mutually acknowledging each other's freedom, wish to remain strangers to one another, members of city-states each jealous of its total independence. By the same token, we perceive why war is the completion of politics and at the same time its negation.

The aim of politics is the life of reason. Now this life is possible within the city-state only under the rule of law. If there is one who commands arbitrarily and another who must obey, whatever the command and whatever his feelings, the first will be the slave of his passions and the second deprived of freedom, incapable of being virtuous. Political virtue implies laws and hence the city-state and peace.

Wars bring into opposition not individuals but city-states. Whereas the putting to death of a citizen is a crime unless it is performed legally by the executioner, the putting to death of an enemy in combat is a duty. The violence of war contradicts the political order that is arrived at only within the city-state, but it does not imply the return to primitive savagery. Man at war expresses certain of his animal instincts, but he channels and disciplines them.

This dual character of war, animal and human, appears at all levels. Insofar as they were Greeks and free men, the soldiers in combat mutually acknowledged each other, except that their cities wished to be free and the freedom of collective beings, as distinct from that of citizens, excluded submission to laws. In combat, victory usually goes to the more skillful and better organized side, that is, to the side that obeys reason in spite of the fury of combat.

War is at once cooperation and competition. It puts to the test the capacity of men to unite in order to fight other men, equally united in the will to resist. It unleashes pride of domination and of conquest, but this rivalry does not go entirely beyond reason. Sparta and Athens entered into truces and made pledges to each other (not to attack each other, not to entice the other's satellites, and so on). There is international law, fixed by custom if not formulated, which determines the obligations of the leading city-states, the obligations of those city-states that are not in-volved, and of those that are in one camp or the other. In each camp, the relations between the ruling city-state and its allies or satellites are governed by precise rules. Thucydides explains simply, without camouflage and without cynicism, the unequal positions of the city-states and the various reasons (constraint, conviction, interest, prudence) why they allied themselves with one side or the other. We are far from the modern principle of the equality of states but equally far from an even more gross metaphysic that would disregard these rules, which are neither unknown nor respected. That, in the last analysis, in war interest wins over right and justice, Thucydides is not so naive as to doubt, but war would not be supremely human if force did not have to transgress right in order to carry out its own destiny, its own ruin.

A dialectic of cooperation and competition, of discipline and passion, of courage and intelligence, of right and force, war oscillates between conflicting aims because it is enmity in action, contradiction in motion. Politics in its perfected state is the stilling of these contradictions; it is peace. War is the unleashing of contradictions that have been overcome in stable regimes. If politics is reason, virtue, and peace, war is its nega-tion. If reason, virtue, and peace are achieved only in brief, happy periods, war offers the image of the moving train of human existence, in-capable of the order it conceives and of the end toward which it tends.

Now, in the eyes of Thucydides, the Peloponnesian War is a perfect one, ideal,[3] because it manifests, fully realized, the potentialities of war and because all the conflicting aims appear and flower in it. It was a war to the death that lasted thirty years and was terminated by what we would call "all-out victory": the taking of Athens by Sparta and her allies, the destruction of the thalassocracy. It was a war unparalleled in the duration of its operations, the number and stubborn spirit of the

[3] In the sense in which Max Weber would have used the word.

belligerents, the heroism of the soldiers, the expansion of the theater of operations, and the magnitude of its consequences. But, even more than its spatial and temporal dimensions, the stylization of the war's elements, both concrete and abstract, makes it ideal.

At the moment the war begins, the city-states are at their height, like Greek civilization itself. In this brilliant civilization, Athens and Sparta glow in all their splendor, each so to speak exemplary in its own way. They have fought together against the Persians, but they have become enemies because neither can expand without causing the other to feel threatened. The real cause of the conflict—one remembers the celebrated phrase of Thucydides—is the fear aroused in Sparta and other cities by the rise of Athens. But once this hostility has emerged from the "relation of forces" and been recognized by both sides, each of the leading cities finds in the other's differences from itself additional reasons for enmity, and the historian, in the comparison of enemy brothers, new reasons for admiring the work of fate.

Democracy versus oligarchy, sea versus land, audacity versus prudence, adventurousness of spirit versus conservative wisdom, there is no end to the enumeration of antitheses formulated or suggested by the Greek historian. Even if so many exploits had not been carried out by the actors, the beauty of the events would fascinate the observer and justify their narration. It is well that the modern reader remember that it was democratic Athens and not oligarchical Sparta that appeared, and rightly so, imperialistic in the eyes of the other Greeks. Open to strangers, always in motion, Athens was, if one dares use this modern word, more liberal than its rival. But Athens was no less a threat to the liberties of the other city-states.

The terms we have used to describe the event may be taken both in the current sense and in the sense given them by Max Weber. Thucydides has told the story of the war in such a way that it seems to us stylized and seemingly reasonable in spite of the fact that the narrative adheres to the singularity of successive episodes. The interpreters of today have had considerable difficulty in bringing out this originality of Thucydides because they use concepts that are too vague—particular, general—all obviously ill-suited to Thucydides' practice. He does not formulate any law; he does not turn aside from whatever has happened at a certain place, at a certain moment; yet, the meaning of the narrative is never dissipated in anecdote. An analysis inspired by the methodology of Max Weber dispels, it seems to me, the sense of paradox.

The historian writes of actions. The statesman or the warrior does not act haphazardly, by reaction or instinct: he reflects. When the delegates from Corinth address the assembly of Sparta in order to make known to its members the threat created by the power of Athens, when Pericles urges the Athenians to take up the challenge and aid Corcyra, they plead, they argue, they try to persuade, and they appeal to the desire for security, the self-esteem, and the patriotism of those whom they are addressing. In other words, the conduct of diplomacy and strategy, is, in itself, *intelligible*. The man of today, who has difficulty reconstructing the organization of the Greeks in combat and who does not share with Thucydides' characters the certitudes (intellectual and moral) constituting the structure of their existence, is essentially still capable of understanding directly, without passing them through laws and general propositions, the speeches of ambassadors and the decisions of military commanders.

Why? Because these are actions that Max Weber would have called *zweckrational*: they allow a calculation of means in view of an end. The end, in the search for allies, is simple; the comprehension of means—words or maneuvers—is equally so. But the Weberian formula of *purposive rationality* seems to me inadequate for specifying the characteristics of diplomatic or strategic action. The Weberian definition in fact covers the conduct of the *engineer*, the *politician*, the *military commander*, and the *speculator*. Now, four categories at least must be distinguished according to how the actor manipulates materials, or manipulates men from whom he exacts obedience, or puts himself in opposition to other men in a more or less regulated, more or less violent enterprise, or, finally, tries to derive profit from an enterprise that has become, so to speak, impersonal, wherein the success of one party does not involve an equivalent loss by the other. Let us put aside speculative and technical action. Diplomatic and strategic action belongs to the two intermediate categories, the manipulation of men in order to act against other men. The speeches in Thucydides are symbols of this action, which is peculiarly human in its various forms.

Nicias' speech, before the final escape attempt by the Athenian fleet, is an effort by a commander to act upon men who owe him obedience. The speech of Pericles is of the same kind; he is not trying to instill courage but to impose a certain decision on the assembly. The opposing speeches of the delegates from Corinth and Athens before the assembly of Sparta, or of the Athenians and Syracusans before the assembly of Camarina, seek to incite men who are neither friends nor enemies, who do not owe obedience, and to whom recourse to violence has not yet become inevitable. Of course these speeches were not delivered as we know them and we shall never know to what degree the speeches that were actually delivered resembled the ones presented to us by Thucydides. The important point for us is that these speeches could have been, or must have been, in reality as they appear in the book. Rational in their attempt at persuasion, they reflect the virtual rationality of the conduct of diplomacy or strategy as, or rather above all, regarded in its particular content.

At first analysis, the rationality of the history related by Thucydides does not agree with the generality of laws or of concepts but with the nature of the object, that is to say, human action. We understand why Athens, Sparta, Corinth, Corcyra, Nicias, and Demosthenes acted as they did in any particular circumstance: the contingency being given and the end—independence or victory—being almost evident, the decision results from a calculation. This decision appears rational to us even when it is not given by Thucydides as the only possible one; it appears intelligible to us even when it finally turns out to be wrong.

Whether it is a question of diplomacy or of combat, one passes from rationality to irrationality without departing from immediate intelligibility. Battles, as Thucydides never tires of telling us, sometimes confirm, sometimes contradict, the calculations of military commanders. The historian usually points out the strength of the two sides, the preparations made, the generally accepted qualitative superiority of one side or the other (the superiority of the Spartan hoplites or of the Athenian fleet). Then chance intervenes, under manifold aspects, particularly the one against which the commander can do nothing: the loss of control over the soldiers in the heat of battle (remember the first attack by night of the army of Demosthenes, coming to reinforce Nicias, which began successfully but turned into a disaster in the darkness and confusion). Thucydides endeavors to make the battles intelligible by relating them to the plans of the commanders, to the interplay of minds grappling with each other. But at the same time he renders intelligible the event itself, which has deceived the hopes of one or the other of the commanders, sometimes both. When the battle is not intelligible in its broad outlines, there is nothing to do but note the result.

In the daytime the combatants see more clearly; though even then only what is going on immediately around them, and that imperfectly—nothing of the battle as a whole. But in a night engagement, like this in which two great armies fought—the only one that occurred during the war—who could be certain of anything (VII, 44, 1)?

The intelligibility of conduct, either deliberate or dictated by chance, extends, in the eyes of the observer, to the event that has been neither desired nor foreseen by any actor, whether it is the "accidental" result of a chaos of individual actions (in the case of the night battle), or whether the ruse of one of the combatants has thrown the other into confusion, or whether, finally, natural phenomena—the night, the wind, the eclipse of the moon—have precipitated reactions that are understood as the opposite of the decision adopted. The passage from the individual act to the supraindividual event is made through the narrative, with no break in continuity, without any substitution of general propositions for a reconstruction of facts, by the simple comparison of what the actors wished and what actually happened.

At the same time that Thucydides gradually extends the intelligibility of the action desired by an actor to the event that has not been desired by anyone, he raises the event, whether or not it has been in accord with the intentions of the actor, above historic particularity, clarifying it by the use of abstract, sociological, or psychological terms.

Innumerable examples could be given of this analysis in abstract terms. We will take only one, that of the allies of Athens whom Thucydides passes in review before the final battle of the Sicilian expedition. Why do those who are neither Athenians, Syracusans, nor Spartans fight on one side or the other? Thucydides begins by distinguishing four factors: justice, racial kinship, interest, and constraint. In the case of Athens, the racial opposition is clear: Ionians, they are going to fight against Dorians, and they are accompanied by colonists who possess the same language and institutions as they do. But racial kinship does not explain the composition of the Athenian army since the people of Euboea or of the islands were all, or nearly all, of Athenian origin; though they paid tribute and supplied ships under constraint, they were subjects of the empire. Among the non-Ionians, the Aeolians were obedient to constraint. The Plataeans alone, because they were Boeotians, hated the Boeotians, obeying not necessity but their own passions. The stand taken by the inhabitants of the islands was above all dictated by necessity (Athenian mastery of the seas). Hatred pushed the people of Corcyra against Corinth, whose colony they were. There remain only a few rare cases: the Acarnanians, who came chiefly because of their friendship for Demonsthenes and their devotion to the Athenians; the exiles from Megara (political adversaries of the party in power in their city); and finally the Greeks of Thurii and Metapontum because of revolutionary circumstances.

The narrative does not stop, and yet the analysis, which we would call sociological, crops out on the surface. In the case of general war within a system of political entities jealous of their independence, a small number of motives determines the allegiance of each: necessity does not allow small entities situated in the area of domination by a large entity to remain neutral or even in general to join the other large one, the enemy of the power that dominates them. Sometimes it is kinship of race, of language, or of regime that determines alliances; sometimes, on the contrary, it is hatred between brothers in race or language, hatred against fellow citizens who have seized power, that pushes the Greeks of Corcyra or the exiles from Megara into the Athenian camp. It is hardly necessary to generalize further to make these interpretations of particular cases applicable to other centuries.

Is the insertion, so to speak, of sociological analysis into a narrative the result of art or the reflection of reality? I will gladly speak of both these points *at the same time*. The Peloponnesian War is in itself *stylized* and, as it were, *idealized*. Each of the two great protagonists represents an

almost pure type. Athens, continually in ferment, governed by a passionate and unstable people, based its power on its navy and its wealth.
The decisions of the assembly were to be, in turn, the result of *necessities*
to which any maritime power must ultimately have yielded, of *unthinking enthusiasms* that the people could not avoid, and of that *will to
domination* which the spokesmen for Athens themselves presented as the
most universal and normal impulse. It is sufficient to bear these three
reasons in mind to grasp the difference between possibilities of interpretation and of foresight and to understand also the feeling of so many commentators that Thucydides formulates and suggests laws or at least
general propositions.

A maritime power is forced, in order to preserve its mastery of the
seas, to subjugate the islands, isthmuses, and peninsulas one by one in the
seas it wishes to dominate. This proposition is obviously too vague since
the strategic importance of islands varies according to the technique of
naval warfare, the resources of the settled populations on the bases, and
so forth; it remains intelligible because it conforms to the necessities of a
life-and-death struggle. Naval power seeks to control the islands from
which a rival power may threaten it, along with the isthmuses or peninsulas that command the waterways. Thucydides maintains that Athens
could not escape from this abstract necessity. He does not try, as a
sociologist would, to justify or prove this proposition by enumerating the
circumstances that determine it or limit its application. He holds it to be
implicit in order that the determinism of war not be separated from men
at the very moment that it holds sway over them.

These resemblances, psychological or psychosocial, render intelligible
at one and the same time the humanity and the inhumanity, the tragic
character of historical destiny. The maritime power is pushed into a sort
of forward flight by being enslaved to its own mastery of the seas and by
the obligation to be, or appear to be, always superior in order to maintain
its empire. But to increase its strength, the maritime power must undertake new conquests (Sicily) and exact from its allies more ships and
money. The empire of Athens, by the very fact of the war, became more
and more unwieldy. Athens had to show itself to be ruthless toward rebels
and dissenters because it could no longer count—and Athens knew it—on
the good will of allies and tributaries.

Below, on the level of battle, three factors create the contrast between
intentions and the event: the impact of the intentions, the loss of
discipline (that is, desired order) among the actors, and the intervention
of an unforeseeable phenomenon, particularly a cosmic one. At the level
of politics, the causes of the disparity between intentions and events are
different, more complex, and above all more tragic.

The war itself induces in its participants a sort of irrationality. It was
provoked, at the time of secondary conflicts, by the fear that Athenian

power inspired in the Greek cities, particularly Sparta. How could it end? By the triumph of Athens, which could have extended its empire over all the Greeks, including those of Asia Minor, Sicily, and Italy? Probably, in the eyes of Thucydides, this victorious end was excluded from the beginning: the Athenian power base was too narrow. Athens increasingly borrowed a great part of its resources from allies and tributaries; it was becoming vulnerable to a revolt of its empire, more and more so as the empire was extended. Pericles, probably on this point the interpreter of the lessons that Thucydides himself drew from events, advises the Athenians not to extend their empire and promises them that if they follow this rule of prudence they will be victorious. But if they do not extend their empire, they will have to be satisfied with a defensive and partial victory. They will have demonstrated to Sparta that Athens is incapable of subjugating it. The peace would be, after the war, what it had been before, a precarious equilibrium of many city-states, most of which were grouped around the two largest, Athens and Sparta. Was such a return to the status quo possible? Does Thucydides think, does he himself suggest, that this was possible?

One hesitates to reply. A critic of democracy and of those he holds responsible for the final catastrophe, the Cleons and the Alcibiadeses, Thucydides denounces the excessive pride that, against the wisdom of Pericles, swept the Athenians into huge enterprises. But considering the nature of democracy, as well as human nature, could the Athenians remain content with not being vanquished? Once the war has been unleashed, must not one side be completely vanquished? The overthrow of Athens or the overthrow of Sparta[4]—was there a third possibility? Thucydides does not ask these questions clearly but he implants the question in the minds of his readers. The ultimate motive of the city-states is the dual desire for independence and for domination. Each city-state wishes to keep its independence, and the largest ones, Athens especially, desire to dominate, justifying this domination by the need for security: "We declare that we maintain our empire so that we may not have to obey another, and that we are here as liberators to keep from being ruined" (VI, 87, 2). This rivalry of the city-states for security and power could have lasted without erupting into a war to the death; nevertheless, it is understandable, considering the very nature of rivalry, that this war, to speak like Clausewitz, would go to extremes. Absolute security implies absolute domination. The security of one entity entails the subservience of the other. In putting independence above everything else, the city-states ended by making any peace impossible since this boon, which each wished to attain, was perhaps, as David Hume says, an immaterial one,

[4] The capture of Sparta was perhaps not necessary for the victory of Athens, as the capture of Athens was for the victory of Sparta. Mistress of a maritime empire, Athens could have dominated the whole of Greece without Sparta's being subjected to the supreme humiliation.

the satisfaction of vanity or of glory. Perhaps, in the last analysis, the excesses of the war and the ruin of Athens were less the result of instability among the democracies or passion to rule than of the ultimate goals of the belligerents. If each side wished to have its superiority recognized, only total victory could satisfy the ambition of both. For this stake, elusive and in some way infinite, the combatants fought to the death. Glory or humiliation was the price of success or defeat, not the benefits or losses that followed in the wake of glory or humiliation.

No man wished for *that* war, none thought of it ahead of time, and none appeared after the event as its maker; but even more than the city-states, the regimes, or the necessities of combat, it is man himself, eternal man, driven by unchanging motivations, who reveals himself in that tragic event, the work of actors conscious of their acts and unconscious of their destiny.

☆   ☆   ☆

Is this method of writing history anachronistic? Are we capable, thanks to our methods or our learning, of throwing radically new light on the Peloponnesian War, of reviving the style of the narrative or the mode of interpretation?

First, let us remember that Thucydides himself has two ways of writing history. He employs one in Book I when he broadly outlines the formation of the city-states, the wars against the Persians, and the constitution of two rival alliances—the economic, political, and social history connected with what historians of today seek to know first of all: the development of the city-states and the various regimes, the role of maritime relations, of the fleet, and of money. This sketch is imperfect, inferior to the reconstitution of which today's historians are capable. But it does not differ in fundamentals. The striking fact is that Thucydides enters into the details of the great war and is satisfied to recall the essentials of the centuries preceding it.

Let us leave for the moment the question of whether Thucydides was right or wrong to interest himself in the manner in which events take place. Let us ask ourselves whether, assuming it is worth the trouble of narrating the great war year by year and sometimes day by day, Thucydides' method is erroneous or partial.

We often wonder about the part that "economic interpretation" could have, or should have, played in the narrative of Thucydides. That he was not unaware of the importance of what we today call economic causes is proven by the first book. But once he is launched upon the story of the war itself, the considerations of politics, strategy, and psychology eliminate so-called economic considerations almost entirely. Decisions are doubtless often influenced or determined by the desire to fill the treasury, to obtain tribute, or to assure the replenishment of the grain supply of

Athens or the army. Money and merchandise come under the heading of indispensable means for the life of the city-state and the mobilization of soldiers. But under what other heading could they come once military victory has become the goal?

The so-called economic interpretation of a war may be of three different kinds: first, the belligerents are unwittingly engaged in conflict because of economic needs or difficulties (type: the Leninist theory of imperialism); second, the belligerents use the war to gain economic objectives; third, the formation of alliances, the taking of sides, and the development of the conflict are all determined by economic causes. None of these interpretations is apparent in the case of the Peloponnesian War, or to put it better all three are improbable. One may, strictly speaking, argue that the incessant wars between city-states were *favored* (not determined) by the lack of resources with respect to the number of men. But we have no reason to believe that the citizens desired freedom, each for himself and each city-state for itself, for any other purpose than freedom itself. The desire for domination is as spontaneous and primitive as the desire for riches, and the latter is as normally at the service of the former as inversely. As to friendly or hostile relations, successes or reverses, they are obviously ascribed to multiple considerations that Thucydides has no reason to attribute to a single or special cause.

The contrast between the brevity of the prior history, drawn with sweeping strokes, and the profusion of details in the narration of the war could be lessened in a history written by a modern historian. It would suffice to amplify the prior history and abridge the narrative, and the essence would remain. The sociology of the city-states, their political regimes, and their economic organization, in the manner of Aristotle, and the history of the creation of the city-states, the colonies, and the navies would neither explain nor do away with the narration of events. The only way to comprehend the events in their precise connections is to evoke them in their time and place, as Thucydides does.

It is obvious that the technique of the narrative would be somewhat different. The historian would not assume the right to invent speeches that had not been delivered. As for speeches actually given from the rostrum of an assembly or before a microphone, they do not have the same bearing as the speeches reconstructed by Thucydides because of the concessions that orators of our day make to ideology or to the blindness of crowds. When Winston Churchill cried, "Give us the tools, we will finish the job," he was well aware that the "boys" would be no less necessary than the "tools."

Thucydides, who belongs to the civilization whose supreme test he describes, fails to make clear certain details, unchanged during the thirty years of war, that are indispensable for the reader of later centuries. He does not describe the weapons; he describes only briefly the grouping of the soldiers, the method of combat, and the nonpragmatic rules more or less observed during and after battle. The quantity of technical details introduced by Thucydides in describing the Sicilian expedition may suggest the hypothesis that competition in inventions, trickery, and innovations did not play the same role in other circumstances.

Whatever additions or corrections could be made in Thucydides' narrative, it would not change in character. The sociologist, the historian of cultures, of classes, of prices, of industry, or of ideologies must, if he is interested in the Great War of 1914–1918, make his narrative intelligible by reference to the actors within it and render the final results or the overall picture intelligible by placing them against the contradictory intentions of the actors. *The history of events cannot be reduced to that of societies, classes, and economies.* This was true in the fifth century before our era; it is equally true in the twentieth century after Christ. In what does this irreducibility consist, and what are its causes?

A first observation comes to mind: the irreducibility of the event to circumstances must not be confused with the irreducibility of politics to economics. In economics as well, the event is not reducible to circumstances: the Rockefeller fortune was not implicit in free enterprise or in the rush to the oil fields. Five-year plans are the result neither of eternal Russia nor of the geological, geographical, or economic structure of the country in 1928, but are obviously the result of the will of one man or several. The event—in the sense in which we use this word, namely, *an act performed by one man or several men at a definite place and time*—can never be reduced to circumstances unless we eliminate in thought those who have acted and decree that anyone in their place would have acted the same way. Since the event is an action of an individual (or individuals) one must, if one thinks of it as necessitated, detach it from the actor by substituting a faceless person for him, deindividualizing him (or, if you like, depersonalizing him).

In this first sense of the word "event," it is not only a declaration of war or a Sicilian expedition that is an event but any work at the moment of its birth. That the *Critique of Pure Reason* would not have existed if a unique man, Kant, had not existed is not a theory but an obvious truth. The event, the conjunction of *one* mind with a point in space and time, is not characteristic of politics but of *one aspect* of the human past, whatever may be the category of activity. However, this aspect does not have the same significance in all categories, and the elimination of the event does not signify the same thing with reference to philosophy, science, art, economics, and war.

In specialized histories, which are concerned with a specific work, the historian wishes to preserve the *event*, that is to say, the miracle of a person or of a creation, and to recover the entirety and continuity—the entirety of a style, of a school, of an epoch; the continuity of a discovery, of an elaboration, or of a conquest. The continuity of science is not that of art or philosophy; however, the tension between the singularity comprised by its uniqueness and the singularity that is an element of a whole and the moment of a process is found anew in all cases. One does not wonder whether anything would have been changed if Kant had not existed or had died before the age of fifty: the *Critique of Pure Reason* would not have been written and this lack is in itself something. We can, in theory, ask the question, "Would it all finally come down to the same thing?" But this question hardly interests us because, in the absence of the *Critique of Pure Reason*, can we conceive of the ideas that are today an integral part of our universe?

In the economic order, relative indifference to the event arises from several circumstances. The economy is defined by a problem (how to insure a balance between desires and satisfactions) or a method of reflection and calculation. Work, production, and commerce permit this method of calculation and give a solution to the problem, but no human activity is entirely defined by its economic content. What may be called an "event" in economics is the discovery of knowledge or tools that modify the data of the problem, the sudden modification of a certain solution to the problem, or, finally, the action of one or several men achieving results striking enough in one area to have an influence on the whole problem. Biographies have been written of merchants or capitalists because these great men have been both symbols and expressions of their time and because they have created an *oeuvre*—their fortune—which interests us as such and is inseparable from their individuality. Scientific or technical discoveries are perhaps instantaneous, sometimes accidental, but more often the groundwork has been laid by a series of researchers. These discoveries, called forth by the needs of the milieu, exercise their influence only progressively. As for the modifications brought to the "solution of the problem," whether they are concerned with the mode of production, of exchange, or of distribution, they appear to be political since they are unexpected. The origins of such economic revolutions as the closing of the Mediterranean by virtue of the Arab invasions or the disappearance of private property from the Russian countryside lie in the military victory of Islamic horsemen or the triumph of Stalin in the shadow of the Kremlin.

The different role of the event in the economic sector and the different interest that the historian brings to the economic event are easily explained by each other. The economy as such is a collective phenomenon; it is the life of a collectivity considered in the conscious or unconscious method of solution brought to the disparity between desires, actual or possible, and resources. The economic conduct of individuals lends itself to a rationalistic interpretation, as does that of the diplomat or the military commander. Cooperative at the level of production, this conduct normally admits of an element of sport and rivalry at the level of trade or distribution. But this element is at the level of the individual: the individual decisions of the merchant have only a slight effect on the whole. As we apply the word "political" to an action that tends to unite, maintain, and carry on the social order, political conduct immediately seems to us *an event* since decisions that affect existence, prosperity, or the decline of collectivities are made by individuals and often cannot be thought of as the same if one supposes them made by others. In this sense, the great decisions that overturn economic organization are by definition political since they are made by individuals who, through virtue of their position, are capable of affecting the lives of their fellow citizens.

Historians uninterested in sociology and unacquainted with philosophy have often said, in the manner of Seignobos: "In politics, chance rules." Of course this formula is too simple and ambiguous besides. But naive historians wish to suggest a truth that sociological or philosophical historians fail to recognize. Events *as they have happened* cannot be integrated with or reduced to circumstances—the organization of cities, type of regime, laws governing the functioning of the economic or political regime. It is not illegitimate to place oneself above events as they have happened in order to trace the broad lines of their evolution. The first book of Thucydides is no less legitimate than the seven that follow. But the possibility of summarizing these seven books in the style of the first would not mean that the development of events could not have been other than it was or that this development does not interest us.

The question "What would have happened if . . .?" irresistibly arises for the historian who considers the past in the light of later events. The definition of "event" that we have given immediately conveys the tie between "event" and "accident." Since an event is an action of one man or several, an action we instinctively regard as free or, if you like, *chosen*, we look upon it as not inevitable with regard to the situation. "Not inevitable" means that the actor could, without being essentially different, have made another decision (Nicias could have given the order to retreat to the expeditionary force some weeks earlier) or that another person could have made the same decision earlier or later or a different decision at the same moment. Max Weber saw clearly that there are no accidents in the absolute sense of the word: there is accident in relation to this or that given situation. But an incident, placed against the whole of the given situation, becomes an accident in a quasi-absolute sense. In other words, when the historian tells us how things have happened, he observes chance in the sense of "a series of occasions," bad luck (eclipse of the moon, disorder in the heat of battle), or fatal decisions made by someone or other that could have been otherwise. The burden of proof is on the historian who denies the possibility of chance, and not on the one who naively records it.

Thucydides does not speculate about necessity and accident; he does not work out the line of reasoning that Max Weber formulated on probability. But his very narrative hinges on this polarity, by turns stated and denied. Each deliberation, punctuated by speeches, reminds us that people are speaking and that an assembly composed of people is deliberating. The tournament of words reconstituted by the historian symbolizes, so to speak, the hesitation of destiny and the role of intelligence. The assembly of Athens could have avoided being influenced by the delegates from Corcyra on the eve of the explosion or by the speech of Alcibiades in favor of the Sicilian expedition. Knowing that if war broke out it would be long, bloody, and of uncertain outcome, the assembly could have subordinated everything else to the desire for conciliation with Sparta; it could have listened to Nicias, who pointed out the danger of a second war with Syracuse while the first, with Sparta, was still raging. At each fatal moment, all restraint upon the will of the actors was lacking. But that interweaving of necessity and free choice that constitutes the fabric of history is suggested by Thucydides both in the speeches that he puts into the mouths of the actors and in his comments, implicit or explicit.

Could the outbreak of war have been prevented? Could not Athens and Sparta have avoided following the one Corcyra, the other Corinth? Yes, in the abstract they could have. But the historian also perceives what we call the underlying causes impelling the two great city-states toward the supreme test: Athens was becoming too powerful; Sparta, the Doric cities, and the neutral cities feared for their freedom. Athens, by moderation and generosity, should have rendered its hegemony more tolerable and allayed the fears and envy. But power inevitably inspires fear and envy in others and pride in those who possess it. Thus, each decides freely, but the historian, looking back after the event upon the train of decisions, has a feeling of destiny that he shares with the reader. These literary formulas could have been couched in the more rigorous language of the calculation of probabilities, in the manner of Max Weber. The language of probabilities would be more satisfying to the logician. Present and invisible, it constitutes the texture of the narrative. Men make their history but rare are the men who can change its course. Ordinary individuals submit to a necessity of which historical figures are not always masters.

Politics is, in its essence, *personalized* and *competitive*. Always, at least during the six thousand years of the period called historical, cities had leaders and made war among themselves. At stake in such events were the *choice of regimes* (the method of designating leaders and the mode of exercising authority) and the *choice of the conquerors*. Hence the questions that the historian asks of the past. Was it owing to the regime that the city was victorious? Was it owing to the leaders within the regime that the city was victorious? In the Peloponnesian War, a democracy confronted an oligarchy; an ambitious, unstable city-state, open to ideas and to strangers, vied against a city-state that was traditional, solid, and virtuous. Pericles died before the issue of the conflict was settled. The assembly was going to follow Alcibiades, and not Nicias. What is the lesson? Pericles could perhaps have saved Athens, but would that city have listened throughout to the moderate commander? If the regime makes it conceivable or probable that a Cleon or an Alcibiades would inevitably drag the sovereign people toward mad decisions and ruin, no one will confuse these sociopsychological probabilities with a determinism recognizable in advance. The single event remains more interesting than abstractions.

As for the importance of victory or defeat, the question is not raised by Thucydides. It would be raised only by the observer who would reject the evidence of the actors. To the degree that war is a rivalry of *amour-propre*, a struggle for recognition, victory is the final objective of the combatants, and itself, apart from its consequences, the supreme recompense. To say that after all it mattered little whether Athens or Sparta was victorious, that eventually Macedonia would subdue the Greek city-states all the same and Alexander conquer the Persian empire, is to indulge in a way of reasoning foreign to Thucydides—and not only for the banal reason that he is contemporary with the events he narrates and therefore incapable of wondering what traces were left by the mighty battles and the fruitless heroism. He cannot interest himself in events as they happened if he is not interested in the actors. And he is not able to interest himself in the actors if he is not interested in the goal they gave to life. The history of events makes sense only to those who are not insensitive to the actions of men and to the things at stake in their rivalry. By the same token, we are now in a position to reply to the question we posed at the beginning of this essay: is a history in the style of Thucydides still legitimate or conceivable in the twentieth century?

The unfolding of the history of events has not become *structurally* any different in the twentieth century after Christ. Nothing would be easier than to recognize the typical interweaving of necessities and free choices that we call destiny, in order to convey the divergence between accomplished facts and intentions. The fear that the power of Athens inspired was the fear inspired by the power of Germany in 1914. The disproportion between the occasion for hostilities and the scale of the war is the same; it obliges us to distinguish in the two cases the pretexts or immediate motives from the real cause. There is the same progressive enlargement of the theater of operations, the same increase in the number of belligerents, with neutrals being drawn into the melee either by constraint or in hope of recompense on the day of victory and a share of the spoils. There is the same temptation to inquire into the ultimate motives for the fratricidal fury of Greeks and of Europeans: why was compromise not possible? Why is it that the side that was unable to win succeeded in bringing about the cooperation of powers outside the system of Greek city-states or of European countries? It is legitimate to wonder whether Athens would have succumbed if, satisfied with a defensive victory, it had not used its forces in Sicily, just as one may wonder whether the United States would have intervened in time assuming that the government of the Reich had not resorted to unrestricted submarine warfare. The useless warnings of Nicias before the assembly took the final step correspond to Max Weber's report warning the German chiefs of staff against the fatal consequences of the United States entry into the war. The power that was arousing envy or fear should have, from a certain time on, contented itself with not being vanquished. In the pursuit of total victory, it rushed to its ruin. But, irrational as such action is from the point of view of a calculation of risks and gains, was not this rushing to catastrophe rational with respect to the passion expressed in"conquer or die"? What good is a victory that is not absolute and not consecrated by the submission of the enemy?

Events that can be imputed to the decisions of one man or several produce consequences as far as the eye can reach. Could the two army corps sent to East Prussia and absent from the Marne have perhaps turned the tide of war? With more resolution and confidence, the French and British warships could perhaps have forced the Dardanelles and changed the whole subsequent course of hostilities. The Bolsheviks hesitated to fight the provisional government before the arrival of Lenin. The Russian Revolution, as it actually happened, at the time and in the manner it did, is inconceivable without Lenin. It is easy to show the connection between a war to the death and revolution, or between a war unleashed as a result of conflict among nationalities in southeastern Europe and the breakup of multinational empires, or between the success of the German submarines and American intervention. All these connections are intelligible; all are real in the sense that subsequent events have confirmed them; but none of them is thereby necessitated; none is strictly foreseeable. It is absurd to say that the progression of events could not have been other than it was since no one could have grasped it in advance.

Why is it, then, that the narration of events seems to us not entirely illegitimate or uninteresting—there is no lack of such narratives for the war of 1914–1918 or for that of 1939–1945—but not central to our interpretation of the twentieth century; whereas the narration of the Peloponnesian War seemed to Thucydides worthy of being handed down to posterity and raised as a monument for all eternity? The answer, it seems to me, is the *deindividualization*, the *depersonalization*, of modern events, a phenomenon whose causes are manifold and stem as much from the curiosity we exhibit toward the future as from the very texture of our history.

The decisions of the Peloponnesian War were taken by assemblies that listened to the contrary appeals of orators. Or at least Thucydides presents deliberations and decisions in that style, with no feeling of having distorted what actually happened. The decisions of the twentieth century, those of August 1914, are numerous and complex, none of them having been made by a single man, minister, or head of state. It is true that this very confusion has inspired investigations and caused endless controversy. Interest in the manner in which things take place (*wie es geschehen ist*), and in details, has not vanished; in certain respects, such interest is keener now than in any other epoch. But it has been animated for a long time by the passion of the judge or the inquisitor. When the desire to accuse the enemy of aggression and to exonerate oneself died down, another war erupted, and this time the responsibility was not in doubt. The war of 1914 had taken on the rigidity of fact, of the ir-revocable, of the instrument of fatality. And no one is any longer much interested in knowing how and by whom the suicide of Europe was unconsciously precipitated.

In the Greek city-states, orators and the assemblies carried on a dialogue: the former were the expression of an intelligence that thinks and desires; the latter, of the people, sensitive to arguments but sometimes carried away by emotions. In the Europe of 1914, all the actors ended by becoming small because they were too numerous; because no one clearly said "yes" or "no"; and because it was not known at what moment the scales would tip irrevocably to the side of war. The impersonality of the event is an impression created by the multitude of actors, no one of whom was solely or supremely responsible.

The dramatic character of history emerges from the comparison and contrast between intentions and final results. Yet the contrast must not be too great for otherwise the actors appear ridiculous and the events in-human—as is often the case in the first great war of the twentieth century. No military staff had foreseen it or prepared for industrial mobilization. None had more than a few months' supply of munitions. None had clearly envisaged a long war with victory for the side that held on for the last quarter hour. On the battlefield itself, the contrast between the plans of the generals, settled in the rear, and the daily experience of the or-dinary soldier was at times more like the night battles in which, Thucydides tells us, no one could know exactly what was going on than like engagements between disciplined troops carrying out the orders of their commanders. The overriding aspect became what writers have called a "battle of matériel." Weapons were the chief factor of success. Now weapons are in some manner an expression of intelligence, but a technical intelligence, not a strategical or tactical intelligence, that is defined by the simultaneous organization of cooperation among the combatants and struggle against the enemy.

It seems that the weapons and the grouping of the combatants scarcely changed during the course of the Peloponnesian War. The war of 1914–1918 was a contest of scientists, engineers, and factories, as well as of soldiers. This contest itself contributed to depersonalizing the event, from the fact that the means—scientific, technical, industrial—more and more governed the rationale of its conduct. It would be absurd to deny or depreciate the influence of Ludendorff or Foch, of Lloyd George or Clemenceau. But, in retrospect, the two statesmen are above all, in our eyes, the ones who had the will to go on until the end and who were capable of leading their people. As for the two generals, one was determined to win before the arrival of the American troops and ended by precipitating a total defeat; the other headed a coalition and had the benefit of an overpowering superiority when he was victorious. Finally, this collision of human masses, in combat or in factories, ended in a victory swollen with new carnage. Bolshevism, national socialism, and the war of 1939–1945 have cast their shadows over the Great War. The same is true, of course, for the Peloponnesian War. The hegemony of Sparta was of short duration, that of Thebes even shorter, and all the fraternal enemies were reconciled in their submission first to Philip, then to Rome. It can be said that the heritage of the war is of more importance than the detailed unfolding of the tragedy. Thucydides did not judge the war in this way because he was contemporaneous and shared the passions, the exploits, the sufferings, and the hopes of the combatants and their leaders.

Thucydides' *History* continues to fascinate us for three reasons. As history, that is, as the awareness by the witness, the heir, or the distant observer of what has taken place, Thucydides' book is also, for us, a great achievement: through the narrative, we understand how the Greeks thought, how they governed themselves, and how they fought each other. The war itself, stylized by the historian, has the beauty of an inspired work, the events being illuminated by ideas without losing their uniqueness. Finally, the war has the grandeur of a tragedy whose ending we know but whose vicissitudes we never tire of reliving.

The war of 1914–1918 is lacking in heroes; it is too subject to the laws of numbers, of coal and steel; and its end is not sufficiently spectacular for a description of it to be able to lay claim to a tragic consummation. One is nevertheless tempted, time and again, to remind historians who see history as cut and dried that on various occasions destiny has faltered. But though it is important to resist the retrospective illusion of inevitability, and though it must be remembered that the genius of Churchill and the exploits of the Spitfires were not acquired in advance, the effacement of Europe, the collapse of European empires overseas, and the rise of the Soviet Union and the United States do seem to us contained in embryo in the Great War of 1914–1918. It is the significance of this new world, emerging from a bellicose half century, that raises the ultimate question.

We want to know *what* happened even more than *how* it happened.

☆ ☆ ☆

We who read Thucydides today retain a memory of his implied generalizations, but we tend to forget the tragic narrative. I never tire of reading Thibaudet's essay "Campagne avec Thucydide." Toynbee, according to his own testimony, was struck by the resemblance between the Peloponnesian War and that of 1914. Specialists in international relations in their turn make use of Thucydides in order to find propositions as applicable to the relations between monarchies or national states as to those between city-states.

In general, it can be said that the comparative method has been used for two purposes that I will call, for simplicity, that of *sociology* and that of the *overall interpretation of change* (or philosophy of history, provided we do not include in this concept a determination of values or of ultimate meaning).

The comparison between *Thucydides* and *ourselves* is facile, alluring, and, in the eyes of many historians, risky if not unjustifiable. It is facile because certain more or less abstract similarities are obvious and because the language of Thucydides appeals to us. The conflicts between city-states merge with internal conflicts within the city-states. There is a "Lacedaemonian party," a "peace party" in Athens (but no Athenian party in Sparta). There is in Syracuse a party favorable to negotiating with the Athenian army besieging the city, a party which, by abusing Nicias and preventing him from giving the order to retreat, contributes to the downfall of those it wished to favor. The struggle between the maritime city-state and the continental city-state, the one democratic, the other oligarchic, develops according to a pattern that can be seen in other cases. The equilibrium of forces and, consequently, the prolongation of the struggle arise from the superiority of each side in one of the arenas of combat. A decisive outcome requires either that the Spartan coalition end up dominating the seas or that the Athenian coalition, by mustering allies and satellites, make its forces prevail on land. In the fifth century B.C., the first hypothesis came true; in the twentieth century of our era, the second. What is more tempting than to compare the different positions of the city-states, in one coalition or another, to the subtle relationships between states within the German camp and the camp of the Allies from 1914 to 1918, from 1939 to 1945, and then, even to those of today, since 1945?

Is it only a question of observations that are more provocative than serious or instructive? In one sense, perhaps. It goes without saying that the assembly of the people, the phalanx, the gods of Olympus, and the Platonic dialogues are far removed from modern parliaments, infantry divisions, Christ, or national ideologies. The comparison of certain aspects of the domestic and foreign politics of the city-states, on the one hand, and modern states, on the other, has nonetheless a serious aspect for a reason often not recognized: the finality of politics being in some respects constant and the forms of politics at home and abroad being small in number, the similarities appear and are authentic in spite of differences in technical means of production or killing, in the size of societies, and in religious beliefs. At home, the key concepts point up the diverse forms of relations between rulers and subjects, the greater or lesser sway of the holder of sovereign power. The problem of power is eternal whether one turns over the earth with a pickax or with a bulldozer. The patterns abroad characterize the various forms of the distribution of forces within a system of political units. The relations, in peace and in war, between political units, jealous of their independence, are organized into a sort of diplomatic and military game.

In the fifth century before our era, this game unfolded within a sufficiently restricted space for the whole to become intelligible to the actors and even to distant observers, according to rules sufficiently elaborated for the internal contradiction of international law to appear, and with actors sufficiently numerous and differentiated for most of the possible situations, engagements, and withdrawals to be visible. Concrete events doubtless allowed, beyond these forms or situations (bipolar structure, hierarchy of "units" within each camp), a technical, social, psychological, or religious content. It can be justly stated that the transformations of this content are more important than the similarities of form—a position to which I subscribe with one important reservation. To the degree that any human activity is determined by an eternal problem and a finality, the similarity of forms is neither arbitrary nor unimportant since it rests on an isolable aspect of the past—isolable because the specificity of the action in question indeed sets it apart.

Now, such is the case with strategic or diplomatic action. The problem of political order, that is to say, the authority granted to some or only one over the conduct of all, is eternal. Likewise eternal is the problem of international order, that is to say, the coexistence of political units that wish to be independent, belong to the same sphere of civilization, and hope to escape from the law of the jungle without submitting themselves to that of a tribunal, an arbiter, or a master. The Greek thinkers, observing restricted collectivities, were able to take from them the ideal types of regimes, according to who held the sovereign power and the method of exercising authority. An observer of a great war, Thucydides grasped and stylized the typical antagonisms—of sea and land, of law and force, of the diplomatic conduct proper to a democracy (Athens) and to an oligarchy (Sparta); he understood and made it clear that the will to independence can triumph over the instinct of self-preservation in city-states as in individuals, that community of race and civilization can be torn apart by the rivalry for power just as the national (or civic) community can be destroyed by the opposition of parties. A war to the death, involving an entire system, brings out repeatedly all the antagonisms stifled by peace and restrained during small wars.

External politics are more isolable than internal politics because the problem, finality, and forms are more defined, or less subordinated to changing content. Each city-state is animated by a will to live, which is the desire for nonsubmission. From these desires would result a Hobbesian state of nature, the war of all against all, if a hierarchy were not established between "collective individuals" (alliance, federation, confederation) and if these "collective individuals" did not try continuously to "regularize" their relations. Peace treaties, declarations of war, the reception of ambassadors, the treatment of prisoners, and the obligations of allies, satellites, and neutrals—such is the content of international law, codified or not, rationalized or not. But this regulation has limits: each city-state reserves to itself the right of war and peace, and if it contravenes the regulation, it can be punished only by war. The relation of forces is thus the first *donnée* of the whole international system, the calculation of the relation of forces the rational aspect of diplomatic or strategic action. The situations are similar because the problem—peace or war between states jealous of their sovereignty—is eternal; because the aims of each state—security, independence, power—are in the abstract the same; and because the nature of the deliberation—calculation of power—results from these permanent aims. The irreducibility of international politics to the economic and social situation cannot be imputed to the sole causality of events (partial, individualized facts cannot be deduced from overall data), it depends also on the *specificity of the competition for power between sovereign units*. Let us admit that each of these units always takes on objectives in line with its economic interests (even if vague and indeterminate): in order to attain their objectives, these city-states cannot avoid the obligations and restrictions of power rivalry. This rivalry unfolds in accordance with its own laws and cannot be explained by reference to external *données*. The narrative of the war, diplomatic and strategic, according to these specific characteristics is at once naive and true even if, at this or that moment, other impulses and outside causes (geographic, economic) erupt in the course of the tragedy.

Politics is never *reducible* to economics even though the struggle for the possession of sovereign power may in many ways be linked to the mode of production and the distribution of wealth. The sociology of the Greek city-states, as it is found in Aristotle or in the first book of Thucydides, shows that Greek thinkers were not lacking in perspicacity in this matter. But they would not have had the idea of accepting the equivalence, or confusion, of economic forces with political power. And they would have had much more reason than we for making this mistake: the citizens exercised power directly themselves; whereas the "monopolists" are in the offices of corporations and not in the White House. It is possible, perhaps even probable, that the occupant of the White House might be influenced by the heads of corporations, but that the influence of corporations is decisive and the methods of choosing political administrators or of exercising authority of no significance is a preposterous opinion that can be refuted by the slightest phenomenology of human action or, in more modest terms, by unbiased observation. The political order, modified by all these exterior circumstances but reducible neither to one nor to their totality, retains an autonomy that justifies political history and brings to mind the work of Thucydides.

All this does not mean that the struggle of individuals and groups for sovereign power and for the establishment (or change) of a regime does not take its place within the whole of a type of society, of a period, or of the passage from one period to another. Thucydides himself, in the first book, shows the place and part of tyrannies in the formation of city-states. What kind of regime is rendered likely by underdevelopment? What model of development is favored by a given regime? Such questions are commonplace today. There remains only one more stage to go through in order to place the Peloponnesian War in the evolution of a "society" (in the sense of Spengler or of Toynbee): with the struggle between Sparta and Athens, the society of the ancient world experienced the rupture, the breakdown, that precedes, sometimes by several centuries, disintegration. In this perspective, the war in its entirety becomes an accomplished fact. We may be permitted, in order to restore its dimensions as an event, to wonder whether the war was inevitable, in other words, whether the system of Greek city-states "secreted" a war to the death that was to be common suicide. But neither the question nor the answer any longer has much importance. The fact is that the Greek city-states exhausted themselves in combat and were unable to become reconciled except in common servitude. The war is no longer the tragedy of Pericles, of Nicias, of Brasidas, or even of Sparta and Athens. We are dealing only with personalities whose names are dear to storytellers. The tragedy is that of the city-state, of Greece, and of ancient civilization, for which the Peloponnesian War was a crucial moment and ·an indispensable springboard. Depersonalized, confined to its time and place, that great war becomes the ideal type of death struggle in which all belligerents are consumed together. Is it any wonder that our contemporaries, pondering a humiliated Europe, less than half a century after its apparent hegemony, are inclined to draw instructive and morose comparisons?

We are not inquiring whether the great war of the Peloponnesus or of Europe is the model for the "rupture" that no "society" has been spared. We would be going beyond the limits of this short study and would have to ask ourselves whether these "societies" are real or imaginary, and in what sense real. But we need Toynbee's "societies" in order to place the "great war" within a theory of international relations, the great war that involves all the members of an international system and that, pushed to the end, strikes down the system itself and the principle on which the political units are founded. Never did the Greek city-states, never did national states, seem to be so near to their fulfillment than at the moment they entered into the struggle that was not to spare even the victors. We are not maintaining that all systems must come to this same misfortune, but how can we fail to realize that they are all threatened by it since the internal contradiction in all international systems—the partial rule of the jungle—tends increasingly to deepen as the civilization of brother and enemy states opens out? But the ruin of a system is also the birth of an empire, the enlarging of the historical space pacified by a single ruler, and eventually the formation of another system bound up with another conception of the state.

Thucydides experienced the tragedy; he could not describe its aftermath in the same way that he sketched the process. Limiting his purpose, he was unable to indicate the vast perspectives that become evident with distance. He was not concerned with what we call the history of culture—the understanding of a unique way of living and thinking—nor did he regard the event, of which he desired to be a witness, as an accomplished fact, as a moment in a process of which the actors were unaware, as a prelude to a world alien to the reasons for fighting and dying that inspired its heroes.

The Great War of Europe resulted in the rise of peripheral states, in the division of Europe—seat of a society in the course of universal diffusion—between the two continent-states, in the collapse of European empires overseas, in the rebirth of Asiatic states and the birth of African ones, in a diplomacy global for the first time, and in unprecedented diplomatic relations. After the event, we are inclined to feel that what has happened was inevitable and in conformity with the logic of economics and to forget the evidence: the societies of the twentieth century are economic in that their strength depends upon the means of production and that the development of industry is at once their objective and their calamity. But it is from politics, that is to say, the power rivalry between states or the struggles between parties within states and within regimes in power, that the great decisions and the great revolutions of the first half of the twentieth century have come. Russia, with its 200 million people, China, with its 600 millions, could not fail to achieve power, to be sure. But what was China twenty years ago? Swiftness of change stems from the extreme influence that states exercise on their societies. But the primacy of politics is determined in the same way. Men in power and their regime impose a style, objectives, and a distribution of resources on each industrial society. The rivalry between states today dominates the life of each of them. Prosperity will not become the aim, or the economy of well-being the law, until the day that peace puts an end to the war, hot or cold. As long as war lasts, politics will rule and individuals act. How can we ignore the heroes who made history in the time of Lenin, Stalin, Churchill, and Hitler? Thucydides, witness of a tragic war, of the event as it happened, remains our contemporary, we who are not yet ready to look with detachment at accomplished facts or to allow the sufferings and exploits of the combatants to fall into oblivion.

3. Three Forms of Historical Intelligibility

THE QUESTION OF THE *intelligibility* of *history* is itself ambiguous since each of these two terms involves multiple meanings and covers various realities.

If we agree to call history—in the sense of the *object* to be known—the whole past of human societies and history—in the sense of the knowledge to be developed—the reconstruction of the past in its unique development, the question of intelligibility can be raised apropos of any aspect of human existence taken individually as well as collectively. To perceive the past of one's own consciousness, to perceive other lives, and to perceive the relations between minds as they occur at the moment or are reflected in institutions, each of these endeavors contains an element of the problem of historical intelligibility. One cannot claim to have examined this problem completely without having exhausted each of these endeavors and brought out the consequences of their interaction.

The definition of intelligibility is just as prone to controversy. We are referring not only to the distinction, as classical as it is controversial, between *explaining* and *understanding* (in one case revealing a unique succession within a regular framework; in the other, discovering the significant relation, intrinsic to what is given). The specific difficulty of historical intelligibility results from the plurality of levels on which the questioning must be repeated. Where is one seeking intelligibility: in the soldier's action on the battlefield, in the decision of the war leader, or in the sum total of thousands of actions and thousands of decisions taken by leaders large and small? The example is a crude one: depending on the historical realities considered, the dimension and character of potentially intelligible totalities vary. Nevertheless, it remains true that in historical matters the problem of intelligibility is related first of all to the totalities

"Le trois modes de l'intelligibilité historique." Reprinted from *Methodologie de l'Histoire et des sciences Humaines*, 1972, by permission of Editions Edouard Privat.

one is seeking to understand, from an individual life to a battle, a civilization, and finally the whole of history. In moving from elementary examples to ever vaster ones, intelligibility slips from a practical meaning to a properly metaphysical one, from an intrinsic understanding of man's behavior toward the ultimate meaning of the human adventure, accessible only to God or to those who take themselves to be His confidants.

We will therefore be content in the following pages to give the broad outlines of the problem without justifying the distinctions adopted at the outset. We propose to investigate, in turn, history as a *train of events*, history as a *succession of works*, and finally history as a *series of lives*.

A human act becomes an *event* when it is seen as the result of a choice among several possibilities, as a response to a given situation. It becomes a *work* when it reveals itself as a creation whose end is inherent in the creation itself yet whose meaning is never limited to the one consciously or unconsciously given it by its creator. Just as each life includes acts that are *choices* and others that are *works*, so history, taken as a whole, offers itself to the historian both as a train of events and as a succession of works. But it leaves the historian free to base these two interpretations on the essence of reality or to perceive them as two different forms of the historian's curiosity or inquiry. It also suggests to him the search for a possible reconciliation of these two perspectives at a higher level since although they are not contradictory they are basically different.

☆   ☆   ☆

Human acts, and therefore events related to human beings, involve intelligibility as such. When they lose it, the actors set themselves so to speak outside humanity; they become alienated, strangers to their own and to our humanity. But the intelligibility of human acts does not come under a single heading.

The simplest scheme, the one the historian is always tempted to use, is the relation between ends and means. Why did Caesar cross the Rubicon? Why did Napoleon leave his right flank exposed at the Battle of Austerlitz? Why did the speculator sell francs at the beginning of 1962? Why does the peasant replace his horse with a tractor? In all these cases, the simplest answer consists in connecting the decision taken with the goal pursued: the seizure of power in Rome, military victory, anticipation of a devaluation of currency, superior efficiency of tractors and reduction of farming costs, and so on.

The ends and means pattern usually turns out to be too simple. It bestows on human action only a partial intelligibility; it calls forth other considerations that in any case set the framework within which the act is reduced to a choice of means. Indeed, one must consider (1) the plurality of goals, from short-term to distant, from tactics to strategy; (2) the actor's knowledge of the situation, as well as the relative effectiveness of means (the behavior of a speculator is intelligible only to a person who knows the workings of currency and the stock market, the behavior of a peasant to one who knows the economics of farming, and so on); (3) the nature, lawful or unlawful, praiseworthy or not, of the end or means in relation to religious, mythological, or traditional beliefs; and (4) the duly psychological motivations of the act, which is sometimes appropriate but sometimes apparently irrational with respect to the actor's objective.

The total intelligibility of a historical act requires the progressive exploration of the knowledge, value system, or symbols of the actor. Decisions as to means are rarely the result of a strict plan; rationality, approached but never realized in the economic life of modern societies, seems to be the ultimate end of an always unfinished evolution; economic man, as such, would aim for maximum pecuniary profit without regard to other values. Max Weber, and more recently the American sociologists Talcott Parsons, Edward Shils, and others have attempted a detailed analysis of the basic concepts or the frames of reference (knowledge, values, symbols, drives) necessary for the intelligibility of human conduct. We are not concerned with furthering these analyses but with indicating some ideas that follow directly from our previous remarks.

Human acts can be understood in a variety of ways depending on the aims of the observer. One understands a course of action in depth only after one has laid bare the system of knowledge, values, and symbols that structures the mind of the actor. The meaning the act would have for us, whether or not we were ourselves the actor, does not necessarily coincide or rarely coincides with the meaning it had for the actor and his contemporary. In his first impulse, the historian must therefore go toward others, emerge from himself, and recognize the other in his otherness.

But, at the same time, this discovery of the other as other suggests that he and I have something in common. I can understand the mental universe in which the other lives only if I can discover, at whatever level of formalization or abstraction, the categories of that strange universe. In this way and at this level, the intelligibility of history implies the unity of human nature. No one has demonstrated this thesis more brilliantly than Lucien Lévy-Bruhl himself, inspired at one time in his life by the opposite thesis—which allowed him to extend self-detachment and sympathy for the other to the utmost, thereby, by inference, demonstrating community, the indispensable condition for understanding the other as other.

The real question of historical intelligibility, at this point in our analysis, is thus concerned with the search for the abstract elements—psychological drives, categories of judgment, typical situations, symbols, or values—constituting community among humans and consequently the conditions whereby their acts become intelligible. Another question arises at this point. If it is agreed that an individual act becomes intelligible only when placed in its proper context, can one at a higher level understand the diversity of religions, mythologies, or social organizations? Does *diversity* represent the sum total of responses to a single problem or is it the expression, indefinitely renewed, of creative genius or of tireless imagination?

☆ ☆ ☆

Let us come back for the moment to human events. The action of a general can be understood only with reference to army organization, techniques of weaponry, his knowledge of his own troops and of the enemy, and of course the military rules that have excluded certain maneuvers and permitted others. With the disappearance of these rules, war loses its character as a game, or at least as a regulated social institution, to move closer to natural combat; it becomes more rational in appearance—reduced to a reckoning of ends and means without regard for symbols or values—and less human. Whatever the degree of intelligibility attained by seeing events in their context, any act by an individual considered in itself will retain an element of contingency in relation to the environment and the past. Certainly one has only to invoke the banal formulas of determinism to assert that given the whole of reality at moment A in the history of Rome, the whole reality of moment B would follow. But historical determinism, in the regular meaning of this concept, does not derive from the general principle of determinism. Rather, it would tend to deny it. For, according to the current interpretation of historical determinism, only certain economic or social factors have a decisive effect or necessarily give rise to other historical phenomena (or perhaps to interesting phenomena, but such a concession would lead the determinist further than he would wish).

Let us keep to what can be experienced.

Given a historical situation, no one can prove theoretically and without exception that the act of an individual or a decision taken was inevitable, leaving aside the psychology of the actor; that this psychology was completely determined by economic, social, or intellectual factors in the environment; or finally that the consequences of individual choice do not go beyond a certain point, so that in the end "it would have all come out the same." Phenomenologically, the understanding of history as a train of events obviously implies the retrospective grasp of what was *possible* at the moment of decision but *did not happen*; it implies also the oscillation between massive phenomena tending to push history in one direction and individual acts, minority initiatives, or accidental phenomena (not determined by the whole situation) that straighten or turn back the course of history. History as a train of events belongs by nature to what we have called *probabilistic determinism*. The event, as related to the actor, is defined as such as a decision: no one takes, after having hesitated, one of those decisions that historians will later speculate about, telling themselves it could not have been otherwise for reasons independent of the actor's will; on the other hand, as soon as the historian becomes interested in actors or fragmentary facts, he has to wonder what role individuals and accidents play in relation to what are called profound forces, the massive data of the economic and social structure.

Here it is no more a question of asserting or denying the influence of great men or accidents (fragmentary facts, not made inevitable by the situation). A priori denial of their importance is contradictory, unthinkable; a posteriori denial can be but relative, valid only for this or that particular period in history. Depending on the dictates of their curiosity, as well as their habits, historians are inclined to stress or play down the importance of contingent factors. But this tendency, in one direction or another, does not and must not constitute a philosophy: it is a simple prejudice or mental orientation. Analysis shows that history is inherently made up of events, and it justifies probabilistic determinism by the structure of reality as well as by the goal of retrospective inquiry. As for the conclusions allowed by historical knowledge of the relative importance of massive and fragmentary facts, they do not coincide with the generalization of results reached by causal analysis in a small number of cases. Indeed, there is no reason why the possible margin of effectiveness of individuals should be the same in all periods—always broad, always narrow, or even the same in different sectors.

Explanation in terms of contingency, as opposed to deterministic explanation, has been thought to block intelligibility under the notion that the latter would seem to imply and the former exclude understanding the whole at a higher level. The victory of Austerlitz does not become mysterious or impenetrable if the historian attributes part of it to Napoleon's genius. There is the objection that the victories of revolutionary armies become intelligible only by reference to massive evidence (numerical superiority, popular conscription, revolutionary enthusiasm, novel tactics, etc.); similarly, the triumphs, and later the final downfall, of Napoleon can be understood, it is argued, only by supposing or detecting a connection at some higher level. But why should this connection deny a role to individuals and accidents?

The intelligibility of the whole does not imply a determinism other than the one we have called probabilistic. The relationship between two events, fragmentary or total, remains equally *comprehensible* if it appears, on the causal level, contingent or necessary. The relation between popular conscription, numerical superiority, and tactical maneuvers and the success of revolutionary troops is neither more nor less intelligible than that between the genius of Napoleon and the victory at Austerlitz. The fact that at a higher level one finds a chain of events following satisfactorily one after another does not prove that accidents cancel each other out and that the course of the enterprise, in its broad outlines, was what it had to be, given the profound forces of European society and politics.

This would be a logically false conclusion. Even supposing that the conquests of Napoleon, from a certain time onward, were bound to arouse the unappeasable hostility of England and as a result indefinitely to prolong a war inevitably to be lost against the coalition of a maritime power and one or more land powers, the basic facts of the situation would still not allow one to determine when or at what price the final collapse would come. Nor could one affirm a priori that differences in dates and modalities, once certain broad lines of events had been recognized as necessary, exercised only a limited influence and finally were wiped out. Depending upon the date at which it broke out, the war beginning in 1914 could have taken a very different course, provoked or not provoked European revolutions, and so on.

Let us go further and say that the main lines of history are and can only be, on the causal level, a series not strictly necessary but nevertheless probable to a certain degree and impossible to calculate exactly. After the Battle of Leipzig, the final defeat of Napoleon appears in hindsight to have been inevitable: the disproportion between the forces of the coalition, on the one hand, and those of imperial France, on the other, leaves no doubt about the outcome. Napoleon had no other chance but the breakup of the alliance facing him or the loss of resolution on the part of the allies, a chance that became all the weaker as the likelihood of allied victory came closer and seemed more certain. On the other hand, before the Russian campaign and the destruction of the Grande Armée, one could not have asserted that the collapse of the Napoleonic empire was inevitable or close. One can understand that Napoleon was swayed by the mechanism of the continental blockade and by a conqueror's ambitions toward the immense plains of Russia. One could also understand if he had resisted the temptation. Likewise, several of Hitler's advisers recommended another strategy for 1941, an attack on Alexandria, Malta, and Gibraltar and the intensification of submarine warfare, instead of Operation Barbarossa: even if the same final result had thereby occurred, what should one call the final result—the fall of Hitler or the occupation by the Russian army of half of Europe?

In other words, one can trace, at a certain level, a totality in the chain of events, but the recital does not imply that this history, the only one possible, was determined, in the way it took place, by profound forces, or that accidents or men did not have an effect, or that their effect was quickly erased or compensated for. One confines oneself to ignoring the possibilities that were not realized in order to uncover sufficient causes for what did happen. This is a deterministic view that does not a priori enjoy the presumption of a truth higher than the complementary and opposite view that would stress contingency. The structure of the history of events holds by definition the possibility of these two interpretations—it being well understood that depending on the period and area one or the other seems to come closer to the truth.

This complementarity of necessity and contingency in causal interpretation is enough to define the limits of the various theories that seek to pinpoint, for a society or for the whole of history, a decisive or primordial cause or the various categories of causes and their relationships. It is possible to assert, provided it has first been documented, that certain phenomena—techniques of production, the status of property, or the class struggle—have a dominant influence on all aspects of collective life, including the most subtle creations of human intelligence. When history is seen as a series or totality of human acts, no barrier is raised between the physical and the spiritual, the crude and the refined, the economic and the political, the infrastructure and the superstructure, or reality and consciousness. On this level, there is incessant and undefined action and reaction between the different terms, and it would be impossible to find one that would be either a cause without being also an effect or the very beginning of a series.

Relative and, so to speak, pragmatic distinctions between these fully legitimate terms seem naturally called for. The tools that a society possesses to insure its subsistence have perhaps more important results (who determines importance?) than the conceptions men in this same society have of the origin of the gods or of the powers that be. General propositions, concerning the comparative importance of various categories of causes, should not be excluded in advance. However, as soon as one is dealing with complex civilizations, the interaction among principal causes—tools; the organization of production; the type of power; religious, mythical, or political conceptions—becomes such that one doubts the weight of these general propositions. Does not the relative importance of all these causes vary with each society?

Besides these a posteriori judgments, setting up comparative criteria, one can think of two other kinds of propositions relative to sociohistorical causes. The first, more characteristic of sociology than of history, would be inclined to reconstruct in a comprehensible manner the structure of different societies with a view to determining the different types and, within each type, the *margin of variation.* One might attempt, for instance, to establish the degree to which a given economic organization brings about a particular kind of state or ideology. Perhaps a certain category of phenomena offers the best starting place for this intelligible reconstruction of social reality, though experience seems to indicate that specific techniques of production or types of property status can coexist with different forms of the state or of ideology.

The second kind of general proposition related to causes transcends causal thought itself. If the historian holds social groups, opponents or enemies within complex societies, to be the morally or humanly decisive factors, then he believes in the primacy of class struggle and the economic phenomena that determine or condition it. Such a primacy is no longer causal but philosophical or political. History is *essentially* class struggle not because that struggle entails all the phenomena characteristic of human societies and not because it explains them all but because in the eyes of a person motivated by the hope of suppressing classes, these appear legitimately as primary or fundamental. Let us not say that the goal of a future without classes creates a past dominated by class struggle. Let us say, rather, that from contemporary experience through a constant oscillation between what is and what has been, a historical philosophy of class struggle emerges little by little, along with the present will to transcend that struggle.

☆   ☆   ☆

The history of events is neither progress nor decadence, neither the movement toward a final end nor the endless repetition of the same facts or the same cycles. It is pure continuity, diversity aligned along the flow of time. There is no reason why the historian of events should not note the life and death of empires, the massive increase in our time of the number of men or machines, of the quantity of raw materials consumed. There is no reason why the partial chains of events of which we have observed certain portions should not continue. On this level, predictions with the same probabilistic character as explanations prove possible and legitimate. The meaning of history, in the framework of causal thought, merges with the direction in which partial chains of events seem to be heading. These predictions contain a greater or lesser coefficient of uncertainty: a given chain of events does not always continue in the same direction. The state takeover of the economy witnessed in the twentieth century could be reversed in the twenty-first century by an opposite trend; progress in productivity might give way to regression consequent upon military catastrophe or limitless extension of bureaucracy. The consequences of a series of events whose prolongation seems probable are usually not to be identified with the precision that those who rely on historical providence may imagine. In fact, no one has ever been able to demonstrate that the development of productive forces (whether one means thereby technical equipment or productivity in general) necessarily implies a certain property status. The formula, repeated so often, of the contradiction between the forces and the relations of production has never been subjected to a rigorous analysis or really proved. More generally, the direction in which certain historical sequences seem headed—sequences concerning the more material aspects of societies, human acts most closely related to the natural environment, the more constraining forms of human relationships—does not seem sufficient to determine in a univocal manner the nature of other forms of human relationships. That which in the development of the economy seems predictable for the very near future leaves to politics and human existence a margin of indeterminacy into which extreme values, positive or negative, eventually infiltrate themselves.

A succession of works, as distinguished from a succession of acts, has a meaning philosophically antecedent to empirical observation. The discoveries or conquests of science are organized into a present whole wherein, rectified and made more precise, previous discoveries and conquests have their place. Scientific truth, to its own degree of approximation, remains as pertinent today as the day it was first conceived. By what term should one designate this history of science considered as truth? Accumulation, elaboration, progress? To what extent has the history of truth been necessarily what it was? All these questions go beyond the framework of this brief study.

It is enough to note here a few propositions. Only exploration of the past allows us to determine how, *in fact*, science—mathematics or physics—developed, at what date, through what thinker; how this or that theory was thought out for the first time; how this or that demonstration was perfected; and within what philosophy or theory this or that law was formulated mathematically. The history of science as a succession of acts enjoys no superiority vis-à-vis other types of histories of acts. But the relation between truths discovered yesterday and today's system, or the relation between past science in its intrinsic relation to truth and contemporary science, depends on the very nature of science and is in the domain of philosophic analysis not historical inquiry.

At the level of acts, as we have seen, there is no rigorous separation or barrier, and the interaction of men and institutions, consciousness and economic structures can contribute to the reciprocal elucidation of consciousness and acts crystallized into a sort of social fabric. When the question is science, one can perhaps perceive that the direction taken by research, philosophical interpretations, and the errors of scientists could be made intelligible by outside influences. But the environmental explanation could never exhaust or even reach the true meaning of the work as such. Circumstances explain the search for, or the failure to find, the true solution. One need not appeal to circumstances to explain the discovery of truth since the latter derives from a capacity to form judgments, which cannot be an effect or a reflection of the subject and which the historian, like the historical personage, possesses within himself.

The relationship between works thus depends on the intrinsic meaning of the works, on the immanent end of the activity that creates them and that they express. This meaning can be revealed as the past is explored but, transcending the given historical fact, it can legitimately appear from simple inspection of the works themselves.

Is there an equivalent, for other works, of the distinction between the practical history of scientific development and the history of scientific truth? What are the relationships between art and its history and between philosophy and its history? The equivalent for the art of truth is beauty, or, if you like, artistic quality: the historian uses the milieu to explain the work in its particular details, he does not thus explain the masterpiece as such. The relevance of the masterpiece can be contrasted with that of truth. The masterpiece has meaning throughout the centuries because its meaning is inexhaustible, because it reveals to each generation another aspect of itself; truth has meaning throughout the centuries because it somehow has a unique meaning, acquired definitively. This antithesis is overly simplified: the masterpiece carries within itself certain elements that the spectators of succeeding centuries recognize and that are as intrinsically tied to it as the demonstration to the theorem. The Parthenon appears in a different light in each period, yet the technician finds in it a solution to a problem facing all architects, just as in a great canvas the painter finds an echo or a symbol of his own creative effort.

The identity of research and methods creates between periods of painting and sculpture a deep bond as well as the possibility of multiple meanings, from that bestowed by artists or their contemporaries to that of art historians or visitors to museums. Furthermore, any specific work—sculpture, architecture, philosophy—appears in retrospect as the expression of a community devoted to a particular task. This artistic community in which each creator continues the work of another creator, whether by opposition or by conscious imitation, sometimes becomes conscious of itself. It is not isolated from the society whose desires and contradictions it reflects, but neither is it completely merged with it. The artist as a man belongs to a political society rather than to the community of painting. Picasso, as a creator, is totally unaffected by the political declarations to which he subscribes.

Between the history of works considered as acts and integrated into the whole social fabric and the interpretation of a work in its imperishable significance falls the history of works as works, in other words, specialized histories that seek to grasp the relationships between works, considered as such, while at the same time relating the various moments of this history with the milieu. The history of works in their meaning as works introduces a form of intelligibility that we did not find apropos of the history of acts: a properly rational necessity.

Relating an act to an actor, an institution to a system of beliefs or a society, allows us to understand the act and the institution but not to assert that the relationship could not have been other than it was. Whether this relationship goes back to the psychology of moral philosophers, psychoanalysts, or the disciples of Pavlov, whether it is part of a total attitude toward the world, or whether it belongs to a psychological type, the historian cannot demonstrate that the particular act he is studying had necessarily to be what it was. Max Weber was right, it seems to me, in stating that most of the time the comprehensive relation must be validated in a particular case by a retrospective reckoning of probabilities. Let us say that at least in general the comprehensive relation, whether it connects two acts to each other or a single act to a whole group of them, in no way appears as necessary. It does not imply that the interpretation offered is the only one or that the relation, in the terms in which it is expressed, was necessary in either the deterministic or the rational sense.

The relation between two moments of science does not have to be necessary in the deterministic sense to appear as having inevitably to be what it is. Obviously, one cannot prove that Newton *had* to formulate the law of gravity at the time and in the form in which he did. One can even, strictly speaking, see in this law the characteristics of an invention rather than a discovery and ascribe to it a certain contingency. Nevertheless, with hindsight the historian of science is tempted to see rational development between the known facts and the law that governs them. In any case, one can see that the progress of science does not involve the two categories of necessity and contingency, in the meaning we chose to give these words in the theory of probabilistic determinism, and that it is subsequently intelligible in itself without having to be deduced from a general relation or integrated into a significant social context.

In the history of works, even in that of the arts or philosophy, we find not the counterpart to the necessity of truth but a specific intelligibility—neither that of determinism nor that of the comprehension of acts. The development of a doctrine or school and the transition from one style to another have their own intelligibility perceptible only to those who grasp the specific meaning of the works. At most, this specific intelligibility finds its way to the rational necessity of truth. What occurs could not have been otherwise not because profound forces or weighty facts alone acted and excluded or limited the intervention of individuals or accidents but because it constitutes the projection through time of the stages of a single demonstration or the moments of a demonstration.

The philosophy of history as the interpretation of the whole of history asks two fundamental questions: is it possible to grasp the totality of history at each moment by overcoming the duality of acts and works, the multiplicity of one and the other? What is the texture of this total history, the kind of intelligibility to which it might aspire? Is it closer to the intelligibility of acts or of works? If the latter, does it belong to the category of art or of science?

☆ ☆ ☆

A philosophy of history assumes in fact that human history is not a simple sum of juxtaposed facts—individual decisions and adventures, ideas, interests, and institutions—but that it is, at the moment and in what follows, a totality in movement toward a priviliged state that gives meaning to the whole. History has meaning only if there is a logic of human coexistence that precludes no adventure but that at least, as if by natural selection, finally eliminates those that act as a diversion in relation to the permanent needs of humanity.

It is thus that Maurice Merleau-Ponty defines the fundamental requirements of what he calls the philosophy of history.

Merleau-Ponty takes as a model a philosophy of the Hegelian type and holds that type to be compelling to the point that any other interpretation would not be a philosophy of history in the meaning he reserves for this term. We will limit ourselves to observing that in that case the philosophy of history, a recent phenomenon foreign to most periods, requires an act of faith, more religious than rational: why must we postulate a priori a natural selection, the elimination of adventures that divert us from the fundamental needs of human coexistence? How can we define or even recognize the privileged state that gives meaning to the whole? Let us leave these questions for later and look again at the decisive concept, that of totality. Under what conditions would a moment of history be a totality? To what point can this be so?

The analysis of historical actions or of history as an aggregate or succession of actions has shown us that one cannot set up barriers between the various areas of social reality, between the various activities of men. But it allows us even less to assert that economic and other problems are really only a single large problem. The unity of historical actions precludes strict separations; it does not imply totalization or reduction to unity. The historian seeks to organize the various aspects of a society or civilization in such a manner as to make them appear as different expressions of one and the same existence. We cannot state to what point he accomplishes this organization. Philosophical analysis reminds us that there are limits to the unity of human lives.

I have no trouble admitting that Cézanne's life was both that of a French petit bourgeois of the nineteenth century and that of a painter and creator of new forms revealing a universe unseen before him and that would have remained unseen without him; likewise, I agree not to draw a rigid line between the petit bourgeois and the painter. But who will restore this life to an intelligible whole, unify the problem or the meaning? The specific meaning of Cézanne's painting falls within the history of painting, which has its own particular nature; reducing a work to a historical whole would kill the quality inherent in the works as such. A fortiori, the collective life of a society or civilization does not and could not form a single whole at any moment now or later. Human creations, each having its immanent goal, its own purpose, are linked to each other because in the end the same human being is expressed in any one of them. But when the historian tries to explain the diverse works of a period by reducing them to the social man of a specific time, he explains many features of these works but not the features characteristic of their unique quality as works.

This does not mean that the claim to seize the whole at any moment or later should be condemned as such. It means only that existence as a principle of synthesis between the act and the work cannot be defined empirically. Thus, in this case, existence would be but a combination of acts in the sense in which this term was used in the first part of the study. And combinations of acts always remain precarious, relative, heavy with internal multiplicity. Existence can build into a whole only on condition that it in itself possesses unity. The existence of the human person, human coexistence, do they present a unity, providing foundations for a totality at any given moment or in time?

This unity could not, of itself, suppress the plurality of works and meanings. Comparable to the unity that the problem of salvation gives to the life of a believer, it would involve values, not facts; or again comparable to the will that Kant or Jean-Paul Sartre finds in the origin of the choice that each of us makes of himself. Any unity of existence capable of subsuming the whole of history has to be connected with a problem (salvation) or a principle (freedom) that one recognizes as decisive (in value) or fundamental (as a metaphysical cause behind scattered appearances). Even so, one can doubt that the second hypothesis leads to wholeness either at a given moment or later. Even if we each conceive of ourselves in relation to a constant problem, these choices, Kantian or Sartrean, would more likely distribute themselves in a pure and simple succession or in a dispersal through time rather than in a series oriented toward a goal.

On the other hand, wholeness within the moment obtained by reference to a single problem becomes wholeness through time as soon as the problem involves successive solutions, each necessary in itself and as a stage toward the next solution. When the final stage is reached, the observer recognizes that all the stages have fulfilled an indispensable function. If one grants a parallel between the dialectics of the categories,the development of philosophy and the history of societies confer on a total interpretation the rational necessity characteristic of the movement of concepts, without alienating the plurality of works or leaving out contingencies at the level of secular history.

The philosophy of history thus described, the one postulating that unity at the moment or in time is a privileged state toward which the whole of the human past is moving, logically defines itself with reference to a single problem, basic to human existence, and by the assertion that a radical solution to this problem is in sight. To the extent, indeed, to which historical truth can be revealed only by hindsight, any philosophy of history sees itself as situated at the end of the adventure for otherwise it would exclude the possibility of its own truth.

Thus defined, a philosophy of history appears as clearly religious not only in its origin but also in its structure. A philosophy of history that connects the whole of the past with a privileged condition and that gives its own meaning to what came before is the equivalent of a camouflaged theology of history (or to one interpretation among others that illegitimately asks to be recognized as universally valid). From theology it retains the notion of a final state whereby both to judge and to reveal meanings and human lives, as well as the distinction between sacred and profane history—the first retaining only events that lead to the final state, the second embodying those diversions and accidents whose traces are erased in the eyes of the supreme arbiter, who stands at the end of the adventure. When defined by one basic concept (for example, freedom), sacred history can take on the character of rational necessity, appropriate to the development of concepts.

Does such a construction go beyond the means or ambitions of rational thought? Let us look again at the elements of this construction. Is it possible to determine "the single great problem" in relation to which totalities can be explained? A philosophy that does not imply any transcendent absolutes can nevertheless seize the secular equivalent of the problem of salvation, but if the determination of this problem must be universally valid, it has to be formalized, and how to imagine therefore a single solution? What sort of man represents the fulfillment of man? The sage? Perhaps, but only if he has understood the totality of human experience. Otherwise, how can one choose between him and other exemplars of humanity? Let us assume that this problem has been elucidated. Its solution must be incarnated in a certain order of coexistence. Again, one can conceive abstractly a privileged state—mutual human respect, freedom, consciousness of the world and of oneself—but the passage from abstract conception to concrete representation, necessary to arrive at a philosophy of history of the Hegelian type, brings to the fore opinion and controversy, not rational certitude.

Let us choose the recognition of man by man, outcome of the master-slave dialectic, as the privileged condition. Historical conflicts will end when all men recognize each other. But to determine this privileged condition on the basis of social or historical reality, one must be able to judge different institutions in relation to this privileged condition or, if you prefer, to be specific about the institutions that would faithfully translate it into reality. Now, as soon as the philosopher pretends to judge the merits of private or collective property, the mechanisms of the market or of planning in relation to mutual human respect, he leaves philosophy and rational certitude to enter into political debate and its uncertainties. What form of property favors a humanization of society? What are the strengths and weaknesses of each institution? I do not say that one cannot decide *reasonably*, but certainly one cannot decide *rationally*. There is no institution that does not entail negative features for certain men and in relation to certain values connected with the particular problem in such a way that men of good will arrive, with the same sincerity, at opposite choices even when they share more or less the same universe and the same hierarchy of values.

The idea of reason, the goal of History as conceived by critical philosophy, cannot be identified with a coming period or with particular institutions without creating fanaticism and unreason. The search for an intelligibility higher than comprehension or probabilistic determinism, equivalent at the most generalized level to the intelligibility inherent in the development of works of art, remains legitimate. But this properly spiritual intelligibility does not require the act of faith by which a chain of events *necessarily* comes to realize the decrees of reason. We have no more reason to trust collective history than individual history. Humanity can be carried away by a cosmic catastrophe as can our child by illness. We must desire and hope that our collective adventure will lead to the humanization of society. Nothing compels us to hold this belief. The Christian is not sure of his salvation, humanity without God has even less reason to be sure of its collective salavation.

The intelligibility of the whole preserves distinct forms of intelligibility, each linked to the structure of reality and to the question that has been raised and analyed in the preceeding pages. It does not do away with the contrast between act and creation, or with that between underlying forces and accidents, or with that between comprehension and causality, but it puts each in its place.

The intelligibility of probabilistic determinism characterizes the world in which the life of the man of action unfolds; the intelligibility of psycho-existential comprehension is born of a meeting with others, a discovery and an enrichment of oneself. The intelligibility of works reveals both the meaning immanent in each of them and the law according to which they follow one from the other; meanings that express one aspect of man and his creative capacity, a law that reveals the essence of the search and its progress. Historical totality preserves this plurality, of which the philosopher takes note, an awareness to which is added, with the always provisional discovery of the unique and essential problem, the effort to make sense of a diversity of periods within human society in a drive toward a goal vaguely outlined by reason.

4.   On the Historical Condition
of the Sociologist[1]

. . . INSOFAR AS IT MEANS meditation on the crisis of modern society,
sociology or, if you prefer, the philosophical presociology of the last century has as its origin and subject matter industry and democracy. This
proposition applies to Saint-Simon as well as to Tocqueville or Marx. For
the socialist doctrines of the first half of the nineteenth century are also
responses to the double heritage of the industrial and French revolutions.
The industrial revolution, linked to liberal capitalism, seemed to shield
the major activity of our epoch from any conscious organization. The
French Revolution carried within itself a contradiction: in the name of
the legal equality of individuals, it claimed to eliminate the privileges of
birth and the inheritance of rank but it subjected the majority of citizens
to the yoke of poverty, to the burdens of production, and to a differentiation of prestige that ideologies alone, from social Darwinism to
meritocracy, keep us from mistaking for scarcely altered forms of age-old
inequalities.

Sociology, the science of modern society, thus has as a central category
the social, as distinguished from the traditional concepts of the political
and the economic. Likewise, socialism, a doctrine of action, attempts to
overcome the contradiction between political equality and economic inequality by reforming the very structure of society. The Littré dictionary
still states that the word socialism denotes those systems that, going
beyond political reform, offer a plan of social reform. It cites communism, mutualism, Saint-Simonism, Fouriérism; Marxism is not
included in the list. According to Littré, the social is used, in contrast to

[1] Inaugural lecture to the Collège de France, December 1, 1970; some small sections are
edited out and replaced by ellipses.

"De la condition historique du sociologue." Inaugural lecture to the Collège de
France, delivered December 1, 1970, pp. 14–66, reprinted by permission of the
publisher. Copyright © 1971 Editions Gallimard.

the political, for "conditions that, leaving aside the form of government, are connected with the intellectual, moral, and material development of the masses."

Such second generation followers of Durkheim as Marcel Mauss, François Simiand, and Maurice Halbwachs remained essentially faithful to this inspiration. They would probably have defined socialism, in the Saint-Simon tradition, less by the status of property than by organization, by state control of economic power. Durkheim, Marcel Mauss writes, was profoundly opposed to any war between classes or nations; he wanted change only if it benefited the whole of society and not some portion of it, even if this portion represented large numbers and considerable strength. . . . Even during the war, he was among those who placed no hope in what was called "the internationally organized working class."[2] Mauss himself rejected as "false and dialectical" and excessively rationalistic, the opposition established by revolutionary socialism between "capitalist societies and collectivist societies"[3]; he also refused to set up a radical opposition between reform and revolution; the reform of the inheritance law—for example, the return to the state, sixty years after the death of an owner, of inherited capital—seemed to him a "small revolution." And he concluded: "For those who believe that no revolution exists that is capable of turning society inside out like a glove, and that the idea of the total transformation of society is a false one, revolution can be conceived only as a series, more or less significant and precipitate, of more or less radical reforms of this type."[4]

Spontaneously hostile to violence and to the class struggle, with a tendency to focus on *consensus* rather than on the fruitfulness or inevitability of conflicts, these socialist sociologists remained good democrats and in no way felt the need, perhaps because they were unchallenged, to pursue a dialogue with Marxists. Just after the first war, in the passion of the moment, Mauss, a friend of Lucien Herr's and Jaurès's, spoke of the soviets as institutions "invented out of whole cloth by a society, by a nation, that has never known what a citizen is, or a democracy, or even a law."[5]

Alfred Sauvy's socialism has certain points in common with the Durkheimians: rejection of violence, indifference to the exegesis of sacred texts, absence of dogmatism, and appreciation of individual freedom. But whereas their vague formula of organization led Durkheim and his followers to underestimate the importance of the alternative of a planned economy or the market, our colleague is always hesitating between the market, whose imperfections and iniquities he denounces, and a planned

[2] Mauss, *Oeuvres*, Vol. III, pp. 507–508 (Preface to Durkheim's course on socialism).

[3] Ibid., p. 637 (in a debate with Aftalion).

[4] Ibid., pp. 637–638.

[5] Ibid., p. 619 (in the unfinished essay on the nation).

economy, whose virtues he has sometimes overestimated—the market as it functions, not in the empyrean of pure theory but in the real world of property owners; the planned economy not as led by men uniquely devoted to the common good but by partisans and technocrats, they, too, representing special interests, albeit that of their own power. Thus, Sauvy rejects all models already used or experimented with, yet without losing his faith in socialism. The suppression of social classes, or the suppression of power bestowed by the accumulation of material possessions, such is the well-defined basis upon which he wants to rethink socialism.[6] He is not concerned with fighting today's capitalism, a shameful capitalism[7] that according to him can no longer find advocates and owes its survival only to the fear of communism and the absence of an adequate regime to replace it. Finally, skirmishing more than ever on the margin of political parties, Sauvy freely borrows from all regimes practices and techniques that would combine to produce the perfect mixture—as Plato would have said. It remains to be seen whether statesmen have as much latitude as theorists and whether any society unites the virtues and avoids the defects of the institutions, ideologies, and parties now pitted against each other in dubious battle.

☆   ☆   ☆

I should like to say, without sounding paradoxical, that my quarrel with the second generation Durkheimians rested less on their scarcely subversive socialism than on the serenity of their choice, their irreducible optimism, their indifference to Marx, and their tendency to neglect the struggles, sometimes irreconcilable, among classes, parties, and ideas. Men of my generation did not resist Marxism, or Marxism-Leninism, with the same quiet confidence between 1929 and 1956, between the Great Depression and Khrushchev's speech to the twentieth congress.

Durkheim considered political revolutions superficial, costly, and more theatrical than serious. I am no less shocked by such a judgment than are the Marxists. The revolutions of 1789 and 1917 were certainly costly; yes, in certain respects theatrical: revolutionaries—it has been repeatedly said—reenact the exploits of mythical ancestors while at the same time forging the way to the future. Eighteenth-century revolutionaries wore togas, they donned the buskins of Brutus: historical actors in both meanings of the word actor. But superficial these revolutions certainly were not. Perhaps the events of May 1968 took on an exclusively theatrical character; indeed, there was revolution only in the lecturehalls. theatrical character; indeed, there was revolution only in the lecture halls.

---

[6] Alfred Sauvy, *Le Socialisme en liberté* (Paris, 1970), p. 63.

[7] Ibid., p. 19.

Beginning in 1930, when I was a reader at the University of Cologne and later a resident at the Maison académique in Berlin, I felt, almost physically, the approach of historical storms. *History is again on the move*, in the words of Arnold Toynbee. I am still marked by this experience, which inclined me toward an active pessimism. Once and for all, I ceased to believe that history automatically obeys the dictates of reason or the desires of men of good will. I lost faith and held on, not without effort, to hope. I discovered the enemy that I as well do not tire of pursuing—totalitarianism, an enemy no less insidious than Malthusianism. In any form of fanaticism, even one inspired by idealism, I suspect a new incarnation of the monster.

The rise of National Socialism in pre-Hitler Germany and the revelation of politics in its diabolical essence forced me to argue against myself, against my intimate preferences; it inspired in me a sort of revolt against the instruction I had received at the university, against the spirituality of philosophers, and against the tendency of certain sociologists to misconstrue the impact of regimes with the pretext of focusing on permanent and deep realities. How superficial were parliamentary developments when Hitler's advent to power foreshadowed a world war! How secondary were economic mechanisms when the Great Depression, with its millions of unemployed, was prolonged because of mistakes that today's students, even before graduating in political economy, could easily discern. François Simiand, in his little book on the 1929 crisis,[8] bases his theory on the alternations of high and low prices, alternations he believes necessary for economic progress and whose beneficial aspects he highlights despite the sufferings they cause the masses. Simiand does not seem even to consider the possibility of a regime without crises; likewise, he does not believe that governments have the capacity to acquire mastery over these fluctuations. The Soviet experience held, in his eyes, greater political than economic meaning. The mood of my generation was ill-adapted to this attitude, both resigned and confident, and still susceptible to the positivism of Auguste Comte: the acceptance of social determinism, comparable to a natural determinism, and an ineradicable optimism concerning long-range outcomes.

I sometimes ask myself the reasons for my allergy to Durkheimian thought and for my elective affinity to the thought of Max Weber. Certainly, circumstances explain in part these emotional reactions, whose bias I admit. Thanks to Max Weber, I believed in the possibility of joining, without confusing them, scientific curiosity and political concern, or detached thought and resolute action.

I had begun to study the works of Marx to discover for myself my socioeconomic opinions, with the hope that the predictable course of

[8] *Les Fluctuations économiques à longue période et la crise mondiale* (Paris: Alcan, 1932).

history would teach me what I wanted. Having reached the opposite conclusion, I nevertheless retained as a central theme for meditation the
problems raised by Marxism and restated by Max Weber.

Influenced by Léon Brunschvicg's neo-Kantianism, I found myself in
a familiar universe while reading those philosophers linked to the
southwest German school. The radical distinction between what is and
what ought to be, between perceiving values and making value
judgments, between the willful selection of facts and the universally valid
causal relation—all these classical formulations seemed to me a transposi-
tion to the social sciences of epistemological ideas elaborated through the
analysis of sciences that were more sure of themselves. They consecrated
both the scientific nature and the originality of disciplines attached to the
human universe, external to each of us, and yet constituted by the
meanings we give to beings and things.

Between the sociology of Max Weber—a sociology of the war among
classes, parties, and gods—and the living experience of a doctor of
philosophy, a Frenchman, and Jew living in Berlin during the first
months of the Third Reich, there existed, it seemed to me, a sort of
preestablished harmony, or, in more modest terms, an accord of sen-
sibilities. The struggles within or between nations reached such violence
that we felt we were observing, within our societies, the *other*, of whom
an understanding alone allows us to come to an understanding of
ourselves. Tocqueville understood democratic man with reference to the
aristocrat of the Ancien Régime, upon whom he passed an already
historical judgment without betraying his ancestral loyalties. The
National Socialists and, later, ideologues of all persuasions became my
"Persians" in the absence of a familiarity with archaic societies that books
can never convey.

Lacking any vision of the whole, amid the tumult of events, and
unable to adhere to any faction, I tried to live with full lucidity the
historical condition of man, of which the experience, personal and
philosophical, of Max Weber gave me both an example and a theory. The
dialectic of incomplete knowledge, contradictory values, adventurous
decisions: Europe in the thirties charged these abstract formulas with an
already tragic resonance. In 1938, as I prepared to defend my disserta-
tion, Paul Fauconnet expressed surprise at the emotional tone of my *Introduction à la philosophie de l'histoire* and questioned me on the reasons
for my anxiety. At the time, brooding on the near future, I was surprised
at his surprise, or rather I was indignant at the historical unawareness of
professional sociologists.

☆ ☆ ☆

Ladies and gentlemen, I would not have recalled these old memories,
with an abuse of the first-person pronoun for which I apologize, if the

conflict between Durkheim and Weber did not retain, in my eyes, a contemporary and perhaps exemplary significance. Durkheim was led to sociology by the philosophic question of the relations between the individual and the community; Weber by the question, equally philosophical, of the relations between knowledge and action.

From this initial contrast in conception stem many differences of a scientific nature. Durkheim defined socialism as "state control of economic power," a trait common to all modern regimes. He defined democracy as "the political form by which society arrives at the purest knowledge of itself." A nation is democratic to the extent that deliberation, thought, and critical spirit play a greater role in the conduct of public affairs. "It is not just in the last forty or fifty years that democracy has been in full flood: its rise has been continuous since the dawn of history." Quite to the contrary, Weber defined socialism by the specific traits of a noncapitalist regime, collective ownership of the means of production, and a planned economy. Likewise, he defined democracy by its representative institutions and the organized struggle for power between rival parties, a political form that Durkheim, following Auguste Comte, looked upon with some condescension. Briefly, one stressed the common traits in all modern societies, the other the traits particular to each regime, traits that constitute the stake in political and social conflicts.

Searching for an ethic, and almost for a religion, Durkheim used the concept of society in a manner that has aroused protestations by turns indignant and ironic.

> Everyone remembers the formula: "Between God and society one must choose." I will not here examine the reasons that would militate in favor of one or the other solution; both are coherent. I must admit that from my point of view the choice leaves me quite indifferent, for I see in divinity only a society transfigured and conceived symbolically.[9]

Such a society, the object or principle of feelings comparable to those inspired by God, be it tribe, nation, party, or mankind—the sociologists of today, whether believers or unbelievers, would reject, it seems to me, this assimilation finally reached by the prophet of sociology in his search for intellectual and moral reform.

Max Weber, however, studied social reality not to find in it foundations or justifications for moral or political imperatives but to help the individual become conscious of himself and of his environment. Like Alfred Sauvy, he dreamt of becoming an adviser to the *Prince*. But Sauvy proposed goals—resurgence of the birthrate, regulation of the contingent—that could give rise to unanimous consent. He has thus been listened to, from time to time, by the fickle princes of our successive

---

[9] *Sociologie et philosophie* (Paris: Presses universitaires de France, 1963), pp. 74–75.

republics. Max Weber never advised any *Prince*; he placed himself at the heart of debates that were resolved by violence rather than by words; his fury spared neither Wilhelm II nor the revolutionaries of 1918. He thus remained until the end the Machiavelli of Heidelberg, available and solitary. Perhaps I had a premonition, as early as those times, that my impulses toward action would likewise be checked in the same way.

☆   ☆   ☆

It will be objected, rightly, that the contrast between the two men rests less on the properly scientific aspects of their works than on philosophic intentions or implications. I readily accept this point. It would be wrong to attach too much importance to high-sounding formulas like "God or society," formulas belonging to the reformer rather than the scholar. In depth, the Weberian definition of sociology, arising out of German idealist philosophy and the economic and juridical theory of action, can be reconciled with a definition in terms of the social, as distinguished from the political and the economic, following the double revolution, French and industrial. Both definitions, despite their different language, focus on the socialization of the individual; both overcome the opposition between individual and society, wrongly thought of as separable. Thus, a synthesis between two possible histories of sociology can be sketched, one of them arising from the great classical doctrines, political and philosophical, the other drawn by Paul Lazarsfeld and his students from English economics and German social statistics.

There does not exist, in our time, a sociology that could be taught as one teaches (or perhaps as I imagine one teaches) mathematics or physics; there are, on the one hand, sociologies of work, education, and religion and, on the other, an approach, a way of thinking sociologically, that expresses itself as much in partial studies as in attempts at overall interpretations, in microsociology as in macrosociology. None of the great sociologists of the preceding century would have rejected the methods or results of so-called empirical sociology, neither Alexis de Tocqueville nor even less Karl Marx, always on the lookout for documents and statistics. Only Auguste Comte might perhaps have felt that a strict cognizance of details could hamper one in grasping the whole. As for Emile Durkheim and Max Weber, they both practiced their investigations in a manner that some today contemptuously call microscopic or empirical sociology—Durkheim in *Le Suicide*, Weber in works that Paul Lazarsfeld has recently drawn attention to (an inquiry into the situation of agricultural workers in East Prussia and another on the efficiency of industrial workers).

If a distinction remains between microsociology and macrosociology, it is determined both by the nature of the subject to be studied and by the state of the science. Results obtained in specific areas of sociology do not of themselves fall into a system. The whole of society cannot be integrally explained by its elementary mechanisms and cannot be reduced to the sum or combination of these mechanisms. Present efforts to rebuild, with scientific rigor, the equivalent of the great theories of the past remain partial and disputed.

Does the Weberian critique—critique in the Kantian sense—still retain its long-range significance? Certainly, Weber's language is somewhat outdated. Whether it is a question of understanding, of the relation of values, or of selection, the scientific practice of today calls for another vocabulary or another interpretation of this vocabulary. But the basic themes of the critique—the plurality of social systems and meanings, the construction of scientific models starting from the world of experience but abstracted from it, and the limits of science—all retain their importance because sociological thought, as such, questions the very image we have of ourselves.

Whatever role I play—father, citizen, teacher, journalist, bus rider, tourist—I conform to certain models of conduct; I respect certain customs; I obey certain imperatives: models, customs, and rules slowly internalized over the years of education to become an integral part of myself. If children from Catholic families are brought up from their very first day by Jews or children from Jewish families by Catholics, these same children will become Jews and Christians, respectively. Even if they revolt against the faith of their environment, they will nevertheless remain influenced by what they have received and rejected. The sociologist is not content to repeat the words of Pascal: "Vérité en deçà des Pyréneés, erreur au-delà"—this formula puts the arbitrariness of the social outside of us whereas the sociologist recognizes it in our innermost selves. The hermit in the desert shares with those he has fled the beliefs that propelled him toward solitude, a physical but not a spiritual solitude. We are not unaware that the chance of our birthplace determines the object of our patriotism. We prefer not to know it. For this truth, obvious as it is, cannot help but create within us a sort of malaise. No one willingly confers upon others, human beings or circumstances, the responsibility for his very being. This inevitability of socialization, or, if you prefer another expression, of our accession to humanity through the intermediary of *one* society, one among others, does not only create uneasiness: it also raises philosophic problems whose solution, often implicit, gives to sociology a measure of its meaning.

First of all, depending on the philosophy of the sociologist, the socialization process that makes me what I am, and what from a certain moment onward I want to be, takes on very different meanings: a fall into the *practico-inerte* and alienation if, in the manner of Sartre in the *Critique de la raison dialectique*, one starts with the *pour soi* or *praxis*, transparent to itself, condemned to its liberty and vertigo; repression, but inevitable repression, indispensable to society and civilization, if one follows Freud and allows a fatal contradiction between the impulses contained in our psyche and the requirements of collective life. As for surplus repression—a concept that Marcuse introduced without being in a position to give it an operating definition—it is conducive to the criticism of a particular social order. Socialization—the internalization by each one of us of the culture, one among others, that particularizes our society—remains a neutral concept, describing an observable process, as long as the psychologist or the philosopher has not defined the nature of man. Durkheim emphasized constraint because man, prior to socialization, seemed to him animated by unfocused desires, selfish and anarchic, that is, similar to Hobbesian man. Social constraint plays the part of a categorical imperative as a consequence of an implicit and pessimistic theory of presocial or natural (in the biological sense) man.

Second, the arbitrariness of any social phenomenon[10] constitutes a given fact not a criterion of historical judgment. This fact precludes and should preclude any naive ethnocentrism, any certainty or good conscience on the part of people believing that they hold the only truth. But the whole of history would degenerate into a succession of *ethnocides* if one rejected all value hierarchies between human communities; if one denied any enrichment in the meeting and blending of societies, any meaning to the succession of civilizations. Sociological theory carries within it, implicitly, a philosophy of history.

Third, social reality consists in opinions and ways of thinking, according to the vocabulary of the Durkheimians; in lived experiences and the meanings we give to things and relationships with others, according to the vocabulary of Max Weber and the existentialists. What are the connections between the meanings experienced by the actors and the meanings that the observer, contemporary or retrospective, historian or sociologist, substitutes for experienced meanings?

In his inaugural lecture, Maurice Merleau-Ponty wrote that philosophy

> in principle replaces the tacit symbolism of life with a conscious symbolism and latent meaning with a manifest one. It not only submits to the historical setting (as it itself does not only submit to its past), but also changes it by revealing the historical setting to itself and thus providing the opportunity to forge with other times, other environments; a link in which philosophical truth is revealed.[11]

[10] Mauss, *Oeuvres*, Vol. III, pp. 469–470: "*Any social phenomenon* has indeed an essential attribute; be it a symbol, a word, an instrument, an institution; be it even language, even the finest science; be it the instrument best adapted to the best and most numerous goals; be it the most rational possible, the most human, *it is nevertheless arbitrary*. "All social phenomena are, to some degree, the work of a collective will, and whoever says human will, says choice between different possible options."

[11] "Eloge de la philosophie," Collége de France, January 15, 1953, p.46.

The replacement of latent meaning with manifest meaning? At first glance, I would be inclined to invert this proposition and define the task of the sociologist as the search for latent meanings, that is, the meanings, beyond those immediately obvious to the actors or revealed by their orders. For the transition from latent meaning to manifest meaning to coincide with the apparition of truth, the mediation of an overall philosophy of history is necessary.

In the chapter entitled "Critique de la raison dialectique" in *La Pensée sauvage*, Claude Lévi-Strauss suggests the impossibility of conferring upon an event—the French Revolution—a meaning that would transcend or reconcile the contradictory meanings experienced by the actors. One must thus give up an objective understanding of the event itself and of particular lives and construct the scientific object at another level and by other procedures. This is a fully legitimate step as long as we do not forget that the procedure used or the specificity of the object constructed determines the sort of meaning that will be brought to light. The sociologist engaged in empirical studies of electoral behavior never tires of seeking to find out who votes for whom; he unearths the multiple variables that determine the choice: he will never discover reasonable thought and the honest pursuit of what is preferable since these are by nature impossible to detect by his methods. This limitation is of little consequence in the analysis of millions of social actors, who for the most part respond to each question with the same allegiances or hostilities. But is it the same story if we are looking into the behavior of legislators, government officials, or the sociologist himself?

The sociologist does not much care about the plans of the prophet or the artist as such; as far as their intentions are concerned, he does not hesitate—Weber no less than others—to lump in the same category such charismatic personalities as Christ, Buddha, Hitler, and Huey Long. If, toward the end of the Roman empire, there had been sociologists, they would have carefully analyzed the diffusion of the new faith and the social categories that furnished proportionally the most catechumens and martyrs. Would they have taken seriously the content of beliefs or the specific nature of religious experiences? Would they have understood the cultural revolution they were witnessing and whose consequences are still with us? The sociologist who accepts only the ideas that social actors have of themselves, their society, their faith, and their universe, when they are verified by large statistical samples, why should he have the right not to be just as skeptical when it comes to himself?

In fact, a crisis is enough to transform professional sociological debates into political battles. Sociologists on the Right and on the Left mutually accuse each other of prejudices and run the risk of together weakening their common claims to scientific impartiality.

The "Critique of Sociological Thought," to which I will devote my first course, would aim precisely at both justifying and limiting these claims in order to avoid the alternation or combination of dogmatism and skepticism so characteristic of sociology when it takes up the study of contemporary societies.

☆ ☆ ☆

We have now arrived, or are back, at the theme that I less than anyone else have a right to avoid: the relationship between knowledge and action, or between sociology and politics. The birth of socialism and sociology in the same historical circumstances—the fall of the Ancien Régime and untamed industrialism—has fostered the accusation that sociologists have a professional fondness for socialism. In fact, sociologists and socialists together discovered the social as such; in opposition to the abstraction of economics and the formalism of politics, they imposed an original way of thinking upon scholars and statesmen. This way of thinking, which a minister of education in the Vichy regime deemed subversive, from now on belongs to all, to liberals as well as socialists. Both have learned to distinguish juridical rules from social reality, rights recognized by the law and the capacity to exercise these rights effectively.

Indeed, advocates of this way of thinking are today accused of the opposite sin. Sociologists are said to be the servants, whether they like it or not, whether they know it or not, of the established order.

Sociology has had to endure these contradictory reproaches from its earliest days. You will recall the preface to *The Spirit of the Laws* and the formulas by which Montesquieu in turn conceals and reveals himself: "If only I could find a way for everyone to have new reasons to love his duty, his prince, his country, his laws; if people could better feel happiness in each country, in each government, in each position in which they find themselves, I would believe myself to be the most fortunate of mortals." Is this declaration of principle simply a matter of prudence? Let us think it through: if the sociologist accepts, as a postulate of his method, the idea that social phenomena obey a determinism comparable to that of natural phenomena, will he not be led to demonstrate, by irrefutable reason, that things cannot be other than they are? Thus, to denounce slavery as contrary to the eternal laws of humanity, Montesquieu could have recourse only to rhetoric and eloquence.

A few lines later Montesquieu brings in the counterpart: "I would count myself the happiest of mortals if I could do something to help men rid themselves of their prejudices. I here call prejudice not what makes one ignorant of certain things but what makes one ignorant of oneself." If prejudice is defined as unawareness of oneself, today's sociology effectively fulfills Montesquieu's prescription. But then here it is inclined in the other direction, toward criticism if not subversion. The hostility that authoritarian regimes, of the Right and the Left, display toward sociology is both a proof and an homage. Indeed, all that is needed to depoeticize all regimes is to compare them to the image they wish to offer of themselves. In our time especially, all regimes renege since they propose to fulfill goals so far inaccessible. Between the formula of democracy or of the classless society and the reality of the struggle for power and of stratification, there is significant enough distance for an analysis of what each regime hides from itself to inspire disrespect rather than obedience. "Sociodicies" justify the human condition even less than theodicies.

The contradiction between conservatism, founded on a so-called determinism, and criticism, suggested by the distance between what societies want to be and what they are, was resolved by the philosophies of history of the preceding century, Auguste Comte's and Karl Marx's; each society, in its own time, was what it had to be and it could not have been substantially otherwise; but the movement of history will of itself, or with the help of a class or a revolutionary party, elicit an order in conformity with truth and with the aspirations of mankind. The future will finally eliminate the distance between societies and their ideals.

Unless one believes in these pseudolaws of a completed future, one must risk, despite progress in the social sciences, being in a position comparable to that of Montesquieu and Max Weber, in other words, divided between the search for causal explanations, often valid but always partial, and sociopolitical criticism.

Certainly, macroeconomics, derived from Keynes and using national production statistics, has taught politicians the art of moderating if not eliminating the fluctuations of the economy. All managers, heads of ministries, strategists, and presidents of companies have at their disposal instruments, logical or mathematical, to endow their decisions, at least formally, with rational structure. Since economic growth, over the middle term, benefits directly or indirectly a large portion of the population, he who basically accepts the existing regime easily forgets, when things are quiet, the inevitably political dimension of the administration of public affairs. The sociologist, more readily than the economist, brings us back to reality.

Let us take a fashionable example. Since sociologists have demonstrated that an equal right to education does not eliminate but only camouflages inequality of opportunity, government officials have taken as a theme for their Sunday speeches, and students for their manifestos, this incontestable fact. Depending on the mood, political preferences, and leanings of the scientific community, each sociologist will present the same facts in his own style, ranging from clinical coldness to Montesquieu's indignation toward slavery. In fact, the sociologist is aware that in a society committed to a doctrine of equality the spelling out of inequalities and their perpetuation through time will appear to the public as a critique of the existing order. Thus, it seems to me desirable that the sociologist not limit himself to this implicit criticism but openly ask questions, the very ones to which he still has no answers. Is it possible to define an "optimum of mobility" through the generations in the way in which Sauvy has defined the various optima of population? Up to what point is the transmission of inequalities, from generation to generation, inevitable? Are regimes different in this respect and to what degree? Can governments, and how, modify the mechanisms by which all societies tend to reproduce themselves, the true originality of modern societies being not to reproduce themselves but to proclaim their allegiance to ideologies that condemn these apparently universal mechanisms?

One need ask only whether these mechanisms are universal and to what degree in order to discover the limits of our knowledge as well as the shifting frontier between the improbable and the impossible.

The whole of society constitutes an undefined system over which different conceptualizations give us partial views. So-called holistic views are for the most part ideological metamorphoses of partial views. We are aware that the preference given to centralized planning or market mechanisms has an influence on the entire political, moral, and spiritual existence of society. We are also aware of most of the probable consequences of this choice; we do not know them all with certainty. Moreover, these consequences do not affect the various classes in the same manner. Sociology, in its present state, as do all other social sciences at least in the developed countries, addresses itself to social engineers, to those who try to act, here and there, with partial reforms in mind. It disappoints revolutionaries when it does not make them indignant.

In reality, there is no revolutionary sociology, though sociologists can be revolutionary. Sociology establishes the balance sheet of revolutions, of the past and the present, a positive or negative balance that will convince no one. With the help of what yardstick can one compare the suffering of some and the glorious career of others? How can we determine scientifically that the benefits of revolution could have been acquired at lesser cost? Sociology formulates judgments, not without risk of error, on the more or less probable, more or less desirable, character of a revolution—a violent and sudden change of the political or sociopolitical regime—in this or that country, a revolution desirable if this method alone permits the achievement of certain goals. But then we are dealing, in this case, with a revolutionary pragmatism that must submit, like all pragmatism, to the analysis of ends and means. The real revolutionary, the one we have known in Europe since 1789, dreams of a new man; he wants to change the world. Whereas sociology explores reality and tries to think of what is possible, he reserves for himself the right to aspire to a future without precedent: his project accordingly becomes irrefutable and undemonstrable.

Perhaps we would be mistaken to take too much to heart the political implications of sociology, in one direction or another. What sociological teaching, indeed, does not appear historically ineffective compared to the racist and millenarian follies that have ravaged Europe in the last half century and given it a different face? Certainly, scientific sociology slowly influences our thought and behavior. Scientific civilization rightly prides itself on the formal rationalization of all choices, budgetary, diplomatic, and strategic: the phase that Cournot called historical is not over for all that.

The invisible hand of the liberals, Hegel's cunning of reason, oriented the chaos of passionate actions toward a rational end. Is not our vision today exactly reversed? Many individual actions present at least a sort of rationality, but unreason springs up at the level of the whole, social or historical, a frantic race toward production or armaments. Mankind would be wrong to entrust its future to chance, to which, if we are to believe the scientists, it owes its birth.

☆　☆　☆

In this sense sociology, like all science, though for different reasons, entails what Max Weber called a disenchantment with the world, *Entzauberung der Welt*. Science strips nature of its charms, of all that made it close or familiar, of what touched our sensibility and nourished our dreams. It reveals to us a universe subject to a rigorous or random determinism, which scientists will never finish deciphering, a universe that will never again resemble the cosmos conceived by the ancients, whose harmony was a model and a guarantee of the human order.

Gaston Bachelard, despite his faith in scientific reason as a supreme value, was aware of this disenchantment with the world:

> Ah, no doubt, we know all too well what we are going to lose. In one fell swoop, a whole universe is made colorless, our whole meal is deodorized, our whole natural psychic élan is broken, turned back on itself, neglected, discouraged. We so needed to be whole in our vision of the world! But it is precisely this need that must be conquered. Come! It is not in the full light, it is at the edge of shadow that the ray, by being refracted, reveals its secrets.[12]

And elsewhere in a more lyrical style:

> Yes, before civilization, the world dreamed a lot. Myths rose out of the earth, opened the earth so that with the eyes of its lakes it could look at the sky. A high destiny rose from the abyss. Immediately myths found human voices, the voice of man dreaming the world of his dreams. Man expressed the earth, the sky, the waters. Man was the spokesman of this macro-anthropos that is the monstrous body of the earth. In these cosmic dreams of the earth, the world is human body, human gaze, human breath, human voice.[13]

[12] *La Formation de l'esprit scientifique* (Paris, 1938), p. 241.
[13] *La Politique de la rêverie* (Paris: Presses universitaires de France, 1961), p.161.

Our colleague Jacques Monod finds, starting with microbiology, the same conflict between animistic or mythological explanations, which alone appease the anxiety of man, and objective knowledge, the only source of authentic truth, "a cold and austere idea that offers no explanation but imposes an ascetic renunciation of any other spiritual nourishment." Just like Max Weber and nearly in the same terms, Monod concludes that "the very definition of 'real' knowledge rests in the last analysis on a postulate of an ethical order." Perhaps he would subscribe to Gaston Bachelard's formula: "The world in which one thinks is not the world in which one lives."[14] And in the "one" it is legitimate to include scholars themselves. Here we are at the crux: how can one divide into two without losing oneself?

Sociology also belongs to this secular enterprise, characteristic of our civilization: the conquest for the only authentic truth, a conquest forever incapable of quenching the thirst of men's souls. In a way different from that of the natural sciences, sociology, as we have seen, creates a distance between the world in which one lives and the world in which one thinks. To our customs and beliefs, the very ones we hold sacred, sociology ruthlessly attaches the adjective "arbitrary." For our lived experiences, in their unique richness and indescribable depth, it substitutes indicators. It is concerned only with acts that repeat themselves, with manifest or latent classes; each act becomes one among many, anonymous and uninteresting if it remains alone in its peculiarities, marginal or atypical if it insists on combining features that are normally separate. In the wake of Nietzsche, sociology forces social actors to the light of day and uncovers their hypocrisy. As a millenarian vision, Marxism goes back to those mythologies by which men have wanted to assure themselves of winning in a just war. Insofar as it unmasks the false consciousness of all and the good conscience of the powerful, Marxism, like psychoanalysis, belongs more than ever to our time. In a way, all sociologists are akin to the Marxists because of their inclination to settle everyone's accounts but their own.

Despite these similarities, the existential meaning of sociology is not to be confused with that of physics or biology. It is only to a very slight degree that we succeed in substituting for the society that is experienced a realm of objective truth, of demonstrated explanations. Modern society, and even more that of tomorrow, the system of systems, is beyond our grasp. To what point does a modern society, in its unlimited complexity, constitute a system except in the banal and weak sense of a reciprocal relation among elements? Sociologists are continually wavering between darkness and light, between conscience and the knowledge of our environment.

[14] *La Philosophie du non* (Paris: Presses universitaires de France, 1940), p. 11.

The ethnologist verifies Bachelard's formula in his own way: we think in one world and live in another. As a scholar, he respects all cultures, refusing to establish a hierarchy between them and hoping to save them all from the destruction that threatens them. As a social actor, he has internalized the values of his culture, spontaneously respecting its customs and sharing its ambitions. He lives in the disenchanted world of scientific civilization; he thinks in a world populated by all societies, living and dead, perishable works in which some men, a few hundred or a few hundred million, have found shelter, faith, meaning, and perhaps peace.

Does the duality of life and thought mark the fatal end of the postulate of objectivity? In truth, each of us strives in his own way to transcend this duality. Bachelard sought in poetic surrealism the warmth of a refuge from the icy universe of science, but he remained a spectator of the tumult of history; he psychoanalyzed the dreams of humanity not those of individuals. Léon Brunschvicg asked that the moralist take as example and model the attitude of the scientist, detached from himself, submitting to experience and reason, effacing his own ego in order to be open to truth. To be sure, but what scientist behaves as a scientist as soon as he has left his laboratory or participates in public debate? In any case, how could he? Neither the results nor the inspiration of scientific research enjoins us to feel compassion for the unfortunate or respect for the weak or to acknowledge the dignity of those who will never rise above the darkness. Everything in the biosphere takes place as though individuals did not count. No species knows the equivalent of the socialist plan—mankind as master of its own destiny, real equality between men, all joining in common riches and the collective task.

Max Weber himself held to duality: scientific truth as a value, one value among others, commits only those who have chosen it as a god. But, having taken this step, he became incapable of distinguishing between the demon of Socrates and that of Hitler. Commitment is a necessity, not a value.

The rejection of any hierarchy of cultures is perhaps tantamount, for the ethnologist or the sociologist, to a methodological postulate. But how is one to experience this lack of distinction without condemning oneself to indifference or inaction? Of course, it is still possible to measure each social type in relation to its own goals, as unique, as one among others. This is a partially valid solution, the only possible one in certain areas, but in the last analysis a solution hardly compatible with the universal diffusion of the scientific approach.

I will not be so presumptuous as to try to overcome in a few words the duality to which so many others are apparently resigned. Fortunately, the very thinkers I have quoted suggest implicitly the direction from which a glimmer appears on the horizon. At the moment when Bachelard writes that one lives in one world and thinks in another, to which of the two does he belong? Obviously, he is to be found in a third, the world of philosophic thought, since he seeks a meaning to the quest for truth as well as to our profane existence. This third world in which our lived experience is raised to an awareness of itself is constructed not given, a citadel into which those struck by misfortune retreat, a more or less coherent whole in which we organize the activities among which we are condemned to disperse ourselves, the values suggested by the social environment but slowly recognized by the individual as his own.

Whether he admits it or not, what philosopher has not sought the meaning of his work and life in order to elude the temptation of nihilism, by turns a game and a furor, an unbearable vertigo from which one flees toward fanaticism only to be engulfed?

☆ ☆ ☆

Sociology, civilization, modern: each of these words calls for a definition that in itself would constitute the theme not of a lecture but of a whole course. But I have already taxed your patience. By a stroke of luck, I have found in Marcel Mauss's posthumous study on the nation the sketch for an immense project of which my own covers one sector still too vast for the strength of one man alone.

This text was written just after the first world war; it vibrates with the hopes, fed by ordeals and final victory, to which events were tragically to give the lie. The scientific project remains.

Mauss used as a starting point the distinction between society and civilization. He included in the latter concept "all the social phenomena, customs, manners, words, techniques, beliefs prone to travel, that can be found in many differently organized societies."[15] He noted, in the past, the existence of "areas of civilization," with ill-defined limits, that included societies capable of borrowing from each other a technical or mental tool. From now on, he concluded, the area of civilization is to be equated with the whole of mankind. A global or ecumenical human civilization is in the process of being born.[16]

At the same time he noted other phenomena that seemed to him equally laudable and that led to the formation or reinforcement of nations. A nation, he wrote, is par excellence a society integrated through the elimination of all segmentation by clan, city, tribe, kingdom, or fiefdom. It believes in its language; it wants to have its tradesmen, it lawyers, its bankers, its teachers, its newspapers, and its art; and it wants to create for itself a morality, a tradition, or a set of precepts—a sign of the need

[15] "Sur la notion d'aire de civilisation," Mauss, Oeuvres, Vol. II, pp. 459 ff., and Vol. III, pp. 609 ff.

[16] Ibid., Vol. III, p. 610.

for true independence, or total freedom, to which aspire so many populations thus far deprived of these benefits.[17]

A human civilization, nations more aware of themselves than at any period in the past: a quarter of a century later, in the aftermath of the second war, I had only to glance at the chaos arising from the wars in Europe and Asia to recognize—in Cournot's words—the same two historical series, divergent and perhaps complementary.

Marcel Mauss kept his faith while writing his unfinished essay on the nation. An integrated society, he wrote, "does not even desire to spread, and only the classes representing previous forms of the state push for what is called imperialism. Great democracies or states have always been peaceful and even the Versailles treaty expresses their will to remain within their frontiers."[18] Today we know better the cunning of historical reason: other classes besides those representing previous forms of the state can inspire and animate the will to power even though they conceal their ambitions from themselves. Armed with only the intuition of the philosopher or historian, Nietzsche prophesied: "The time is approaching when the struggle for the domination of the earth will be waged in the name of basic philosophic doctrines."[19]

The men of my generation were trained right after the first war and wrote their first books in the years that preceded the second; after 1945, they asked themselves how to avoid the third. It was not difficult for them to avoid the illusions of their elders and they deserve no credit for it. The sociologists, however, did not return to the study of international relations—a poorly exploited field, as Mauss wrote half a century ago.

Two books, in addition to the direct experience of our times, encouraged me to strike out into this poorly exploited field: the monumental work of Hans Delbrück, *Die Geschichte der Kriegskunst im Rahmen der politischen Geschichte*, and that of Karl von Clausewitz, *On War*. The first sheds light on the integration of the military apparatus with social formations, class relations, means of production and combat, and the nature of power. The second uncovers the implicit logic shared by diplomacy and strategy. One leads to a search for correlations between types of societies and types of conflicts; the other, to the analysis of decisions and actors and to the discovery of contradictions between goals and consequences, between partial rationality and collective unreason. This year's course, "An Imperial Republic: The United States in the World," belongs to the first tendency; the one I hope to give next year, "Strategic Theory from Clausewitz to Mao Tse-tung," to the second. Perhaps the same reason explains my choice and the reticence of many of my colleagues. When the issue is the relation between states, science, in the strict

[17] Ibid., pp. 588 ff.
[18] Ibid.
[19] Quoted by Martin Heidegger (Frankfurt; Holzewege, 1950), p. 236. Text of 1881–1882: *Der tolle Mensch*.

sense of the word, has still not replaced the knowledge of historians or statesmen. It has not yet built, with its own concepts and methods, an object of study radically separated from the lived experiences of those who make or suffer wars and peace.

The quasi-universal vocation of science, of technology, and of the organization of productive units, despite the diversity of cultures and regimes, offers another area, one better explored and in many respects privileged. In the preface to *Capital*, Marx announced, in the tones of a prophet of Israel, that the most advanced economy would point the way that all others would have inexorably to follow and show the sufferings that all nations would know on the road to the Calvary of industrialization. They have all followed a road to Calvary, but they have not all followed the same one. The plurality of ways and means offers the sociologist a theme not yet exhausted. Perhaps I will be able to enlarge and deepen my previous research.

World civilization of European origin no longer displays any unity, either ideological, or political, or moral. The vague terms that designate the transformations characteristic of our time—modernization, industrialization, development—testify both to the various forms of this civilization and to the conflicts by which it is spreading. Perhaps the anxiety in the vocabulary betrays anxiety in thought; despite speculations on the future, how can one grasp the ultimate meaning of upheavals in which nations appear by turns as movers and victims?

Conquering rationalism—man as master and possessor of nature and by the same token of his own destiny—has survived with difficulty the century of great wars. Allow me nevertheless to offer you a profession of faith that still moves me though it does not convince me.

> The history of human industries is properly the history of civilization, and vice versa. The propagation and discovery of the industrial arts, there we have what was, and is, fundamental progress and what permits the development of societies, that is to say, an ever happier life, for increasingly numerous masses, over larger and larger areas. It is this that, through the development of societies, has prompted the development of reason and sensitivity and will; it is this that has made modern man the most perfect of animals. This is the Prometheus of the ancient drama. Let us think of it while rereading the splendid verses of Aeschylus and say that it is industry that has made men, weak ants haunting hovels without sun, children who did not see what they were looking at, did not hear what they were listening to, and who all their life long, confused their perceptions with the phantoms of dreams. . . . It is science and human industry that are superior, not subject to fatality. They constitute the third god that finishes off the gods, those tyrants of heaven and earth . . . it is this, no doubt about it, that will save humanity from the moral and material crisis in which it struggles.[20]

[20] Mauss, *Oeuvres*, Vol. III, pp. 613–614.

No doubt about it—industry serves any end, including rationalizing the putting to death of defenseless men by men in arms. It was against these values or rather against the confidence, which seemed to me naive, in the inevitable realization of these values, that I revolted when fresh out of the university—a revolt against the professional sociologists, who before 1914 announced the decline in the military functions of the state and before 1939 had no presentiment of approaching disaster. Today—who knows?

There are times, yes, when I, too, would repeat: science and technology, the new Prometheus who will finish off the tyrants of heaven and earth. At others, I reread the famous lines of Max Weber, wherein echoes the prophecy of Nietzsche:

> No one knows who will live in this edifice, whether, at the end of this for-midable transformation, entirely new prophets will emerge, if old ideas and yesterday's ideas will take on a new vigor, or if, quite to the contrary, a mechanical petrification embellished with a sort of pompous rigidity will take over. In that case, for the "last men" of this cultural evolution, the saying would become true: specialists without spirit, epicures without heart; this nothingness boasts about climbing heights never reached by humanity.[21]

Fachmenschen ohne Geist, "specialists without spirit," *Fachidioten*, our young comrades say today. Science invents; ideology invents at most, as do mythologies, variations on the same themes.

Between believing in the new Prometheus and desperately awaiting the last man I do not choose—not out of weakness, I believe, but out of ig-norance. Who has the right to state that men will lose or save their souls in the cement, glass, and metal cathedrals they are building for themselves and their descendants? that the combination of man and machine will liberate or freeze initiative and creativity? On the road where upon, for better or worse, humanity is engaged, there is no turning back. Scientific civilization, now universally diffused, protector of individual nation-alities and diverse cultures, providing progressive access by all to material goods available in increasing quantities and to the immaterial goods that each can hold without depriving others—there is no other happy ending to the double revolution, industrial and democratic. As for possible catastrophes, why evoke them: each of us can imagine them without ef-fort.

The liberalism in which I seek and find my spiritual home has nothing in common with a philosophy for tender souls, a formula dear to Jean-Paul Sartre. Tender souls, in fact, are those in fear of being the despair of Billancourt, who, following the bourgeoisie of the last century, believe that the people need a religion, albeit a secular one. The liberal par-ticipates in the enterprise of the new Prometheus; he strives to act ac-

---

[21] Max Weber, *Religionssoziologie* (Tübingen: Von Mohr, 1920), Vol. I, p. 204.

cording to the lessons, however uncertain, of historical experience, in conformity with the partial truths he assembles rather than by reference to a falsely total vision.

"Let us look forward to the future with that healthy fear that keeps us combative and on our guard, and not that faint and idle terror that disheartens and enervates."[22] You have recognized the voice of Alexis de Tocqueville.

☆   ☆   ☆

"In matters of science, one cannot go too slowly; in practical matters, one cannot wait."[23] Sociologists have a hard time following this wise elder's precept as soon as they take their own society as an object of study. The risk is that error will punish their impatience.

Fortunately, whoever has chosen a subject of study too close at hand to tolerate the slowness necessary for science can find consolation either by evoking the errors committed by those greater than himself or by putting himself in thought in the place of those who will come after him. All sociology, in any case all macrosociology, preserves elements of social criticism and philosophic interpretation. It is of little importance here if this authentically scientific nucleus can be isolated by epistemology or not; whatever, in a sociology of modern civilization, eludes science, exceeds its present boundaries, or governs its direction, belongs to the movement of ideas. Tomorrow, historians and sociologists will seek in it an expression of the awareness that the men of today had of themselves, their society, and their future, of their clear-sightedness at times, and perhaps of their blindness.

Research must still be inspired by commitment, without partisan preferences obscuring our perception. While still a student, I feared that a taste for public life would divert me from philosophy. For a quarter of a century I have been trying to reconcile what is perhaps irreconcilable. May your confidence, my dear colleagues, help me to close the gap between the goals I set for myself before 1939 and a destiny for which my own philosophy prevents me from not assuming, despite the circumstances, full responsibility.

[22] Alexis de Tocqueville, Oeuvres, I, De la démocratie en Amérique, Vol. II, part IV, chap. 7, p. 335.

[23] Mauss, Oeuvres, Vol. III, p. 579.

PART II

HISTORY AND POLITICS

POWER, FREEDOM, AND THE DAWN OF UNIVERSAL HISTORY

In the following essays Aron pursues the theme of the historical dimensions of all politics. His discussion of power in "Macht, Power, Puissance" and of freedom in "The Liberal Definition of Freedom" and "Sociology and the Philosophy of Human Rights" emphasizes the present perception of the past as a key to understanding these difficult and fundamental concepts, as well as a precondition for thinking about the future. Political decisions can hardly be understood without taking a historical and philosophical approach to power and freedom. Aron contrasts the thought of Machiavelli and Marx (in "Machiavelli and Marx") and Tocqueville and Marx (in "The Liberal Definition of Freedom") to illustrate the subtle interaction between history and politics, even s and ideologies. In the field of international relations he also stresses the weight of history, which is for the first time becoming universal history. In "What Is a Theory of International Relations?" and in "The Dawn of Universal History" he shows how the use of a scientific methodology can be misleading when applied to the anarchic and historically conditioned materials of international politics. Collective actors and their leaders in the nation-state system are in a "state of nature" vis-à-vis each other. Their decisions can be understood only in terms of a complex of variables, foremost among which are political calculations deeply imbued with past values and traditions. In "The Evolution of Modern Strategic Thought" Aron asserts that the latest techniques in the theory of games, and the most recent developments in computer based nuclear strategy are meaningless without insight into the past, without the wisdom of the historian and the sociologist, who must take into account the unique and the unpredictable, the dimension of human history and irrational human will. The key to understanding the behavior of peoples and their leaders still lies in determining their historical perceptions and subjecting these to philosophic analysis.

5. Machiavelli and Marx[1]

WHOEVER WRITES THE NAME Machiavelli at the top of a blank page cannot avoid feeling a certain trepidation. In the wake of countless others, writers and sovereigns, historians and philosophers, political analysts and strategists, moralists and theologians, he, too, ventures to interrogate the sphinx, Florentine diplomat, Italian partriot, and author whose limpid and, at the same time, totally equivocal language masks his intentions and whose inspired series of insights has resisted the ingenuity of commentators for four hundred years. He, too, must make a choice that he is conscious others have made before him. For whatever interpretation he offers is not exclusively his own.

Whether Machiavelli gave lessons in freedom to peoples or in tyranny to princes, whether he prolonged the tradition of ancient thought or founded modern science, the lecturer of an evening who has not devoted his life to the study of Machiavelli and his heirs, legitimate and illegitimate, will not settle any of the innumerable disputes that scholarship does not so much revive as sustain. Under the watchful eyes not of Machiavelli but of those who keep up the chronicles of Machiavellianism, he feels labeled in advance, classified, placed in perspective or on an index card. No matter what he says or does, he belongs to some family of Machiavelli's followers, imitators, or readers—and he comes too late to found a new family. The honor of founding a separate dynasty is reserved for those who, like the American political philosopher Leo Strauss, endeavor to avoid belonging to any single family by embracing all of them and who, at the same time, read into *The Prince* or the *Discourses* what is not written there, discount the obvious, and look for the mask behind the face instead of perceiving it in front. As in an Edgar Allen Poe detective story, Machiavelli would have disguised himself through his self-exposure and would have revealed his secret only to decipherers of

[1] Lecture given at the Italian Cultural Institute in Paris on November 6, 1969.

"Machiavelli and Marx." Reprinted with permission of the publisher from *Atlantis*, October 1970, no. 2, 14–27.

enigmas or, more precisely, to those who intuitively divine the existence of enigmas not accessible to ordinary minds—I would indeed be foolish to cherish similar ambitions.

In my uncertainty, I have sought escape through the time-honored strategy of drawing a parallel between famous men. And with whom to establish such a parallel if not Marx? Certainly, a century and a half after his terrestrial birth and less than a century after his death, Marx is still a newcomer to the Elysian fields. Machiavelli can teach Marx patience in indulgently tolerating abusive commentators or disciples unfaithful by dint of ignorance, passion, or even sometimes their fidelity.

A Parisian lawyer whose hatred for Napoleon III sometimes reached sublimity and always preserved its vehemence once composed a curious tract, a dialogue in the underworld between Machiavelli and Montesquieu, of which the czarist secret police made use in drawing up one of the most famous forgeries of the century, the Protocols of the Elders of Zion. . . . No Parisian lawyer in our century has felt the hatred or possessed the talent necessary to write an underworld dialogue between Machiavelli and Marx. I will not even offer you this evening the outline of such a dialogue, which would be tempting to a philosopher-novelist. Instead, I will content myself with thinking aloud about some of the elements of a possible dialogue.

The old Machiavelli and the young Marx have had remarkably similar posthumous fates. For a long time now, every historian of Machiavelli has had to become willy-nilly a historian of Machiavellianism, especially when he proposes to strip away the successive layers of commentary with which passing generations have overlaid the elliptical and provocative writings of the Florentine chancellor. The path to Machiavelli winds through the literature on Machiavelli, though in the last analysis his thought, the thought that can without anachronism or paradox be attributed to the actual man, can be understood only in the light of the past that formed him and to which he considered himself the heir and also in the light of the present in which he lived and which he, in interpreting it, defined.

Similarly, how can we get back to Marx except via the Marxists, and how difficult it is to draw a demarcation line between Marxists, Marxians, and Marxologists! Certainly, scholars of Marx are not all Marxists and, conversely, many Marxists know almost nothing about Marx. But the successive and contradictory interpretations by those who claim as their authority the founder of the First International insinuate themselves into the most objectively scientific commentaries and inevitably influence them.

No student of Marx can fail to make, even if only implicitly, a judgment on the relation of Marxism to Marxism-Leninism. In doing so, he cannot help entering that closed field whereupon Marxists, anti-Marxists, and non-Marxists confront each other, most of them wishing to claim for themselves a glorious godfather—this is true in France at least and, I believe, in Italy, too. Elsewhere such a relationship is rejected as dangerous. Galbraith, whom I once, imitating his own style, dubbed an "American Marxist," was subjected to a barrage of questions during his lectures in Italy. What did he think of this description? Did he accept this recognition of a connection? The descendants of both Machiavelli and Marx are as numerous as they are cumbersome, but the work of these two men differs so profoundly that their respective disciples and adversaries have almost nothing in common. How many writers and even statesmen have refuted Machiavelli and his detestable maxims—for example, Frederick II before he ruled Prussia and founded the grandeur of the Hohenzollerns by the might of the sword. Later he was to be reproached for having applied too well in action the teachings of the Florentine whom he had previously condemned in a conventional manner and with doubtful sincerity. But no one will accuse Böhm-Bawerk in his rejection of *Capital*, his revelation of the contradiction between the first and the third volume, between the theory of value and the theory of profit, of playing a part. Some reject the political lessons they suspect Machiavelli of having taught; others reject an analysis of capitalism and its foreseeable development.

Machiavelli, more than any other, has known the posthumous fate of an *auteur maudit*. When Rousseau rehabilitates him, he strives to rescue him from both Machiavellianism and from the accusation of being its sponsor. Machiavelli escapes moral obloquy only on the condition of having wished to say the opposite of what he seems to say openly, at least in *The Prince*. Thus, Rousseau, in *The Social Contract*, asserts:

> I admit that if we suppose the subjects always perfectly submissive, the interest of the prince would then be that the people should be strong, so that this strength, being his, would make him formidable to his neighbors. But as this interest is only secondary and subordinate, and as the two suppositions are incompatible, it is natural that princes prefer the maxim most immediately useful to them. This is what Samuel vigorously demonstrated to the Hebrews; it is what Machiavelli revealed with clarity. Pretending to give lessons to kings, he gave great lessons to peoples.

Spinoza, too, in his *Political Treatise*, declares:

> Machiavelli wished perhaps to show how a free community must beware of vesting its safety exclusively in one man, who, if only from being full of vanity and believing himself capable of pleasing everybody, must every day be in fear of ambushes, obliging him to look ceaselessly to his own security and to be busier laying traps for the multitude than in looking after its interests. I incline all the more, therefore, to read the thought of this clever man as having always been for freedom and given salutary advice for the means of its defense.

Marx, at least at the present time, enjoys an incomparable prestige among the intelligentsia. If some economists, sociologists, and ideologists are pleased to denounce his "errors," others, probably more numerous on the continent, take pride in having him as godfather and referee. Authentic Marxists against Marxist-Leninists, faithful disciples of Marxism-Leninism against revisionists and dogmatics, scholars of Marx and Marxists, thinkers and men of action—they all yearn for the prestige of orthodoxy. The quarrels among the descendants of Marx are not like those among the descendants of Machiavelli. No one wants to be known as Machiavellian; a few confess an admiration for Machiavelli; many declare themselves Marxists.

Why should there be this contrast in spite of the resemblance between their mixed and quarrelsome descendants? Machiavelli and Marx remain equivocal and mysterious but for quite different reasons. Rousseau and Spinoza, in trying to rehabilitate Machiavelli and make him an exponent of republicanism and a defender of freedom, are not entirely wrong. But they simplify and caricature an otherwise rich and subtle body of thought. Machiavelli did not display a sham admiration for Cesare Borgia.

Removed from power by the fall of Soderini, reflecting on his failure and on the fate of cities, Machiavelli wrote his two major works in the role of an adviser to the *Prince*, whoever this might be, one man or all men, a monarchy or the republic. Scholars discuss the feelings he had at different phases of his career for Cesare Borgia, but he would have been able—he was able—without contradiction or denial, to admire this high-flying adventurer while detesting him and while putting his hopes in a different world, a virtuous city, in which the beasts of prey would have neither a chance of success nor functions to fulfill.

As a political thinker, Machiavelli said repeatedly and with absolute candor that we must see reality as it is and not as we would wish it to be. In this elementary sense, he proclaims what some call realism, others cynicism, and others the scientific spirit. At certain periods and in certain circumstances, the scientific spirit, if it involves or demands the use of practical means to attain certain ends, leads to a certain degree of cynicism. Rationality in the choice of means, proceeding from the objective observation of casual connections, no more guarantees the morality of means than it does that of ends. In troubled periods especially, experience suggests much rather the inevitable immorality of action, the outcome of an amoral study of political and historical reality. The mystery of Machiavelli—his intentions, the state of his soul at any moment—exists only outside the limits of this elementary and basic problem.

In what does the mystery, or supposed mystery, of Marx consist? At first one is inclined to give a variety of answers. Marx wrote a lot and his philosophical journey stretches from the writings of his youth, in particular, the *Economic and Philosophic Manuscripts* of 1844 to *Capital*, and beyond *Capital* to the *Anti-Dühring*, the work by Friedrich Engels for which Marx wrote a chapter. The relationship between the early and the mature works, between the profound thought of Marx and the books, devoid of depth, by his friend, the relation of the philosophy to the economics—so many questions still remain unresolved over which commentators, interpreters, partisans, and adversaries conflict.

But let us place ourselves at the center of Marx's thought, the analysis of capitalism, its evolution and inevitable self-destruction. It seems to me difficult to deny that the necessary advent of socialism as a result of the internal contradictions of capitalism constitutes, for men of action, the essential theme of scientific socialism. Socialism becomes the very movement of history and no longer a utopia to conceive or an ideal to realize.

By the same token, the fundamental problem in Machiavelli—the relation between the way in which men in fact behave and the advice Machiavelli or his followers give to princes—reproduces itself in another form. This time it is a question of the relation between the necessary future announced by Marx and his followers and the advice they give to princes or to ordinary mortals. In both cases, the moralist questions the relation between what is and what should be, between the effectiveness of the means and their conformity to ethical standards.

The fundamental problem in Marx does not become confused with that in Machiavelli any more than the moralist's question has the same meaning for both of them. Marx, as much as Machiavelli, belongs to the family of thinkers who are more aware of what divides men than of what unites them. Through the centuries, regimes follow upon one another, all of them torn by contradictions, all finally victims of their contradictions, and all characterized by the exploitation and domination of man by man. This would be a philosophy of desperation if humanity's Way of the Cross did not coincide with the development of the forces of production and if socialism did not put an end to prehistory and open a new era, that of social progress without political revolution.

Marx's realism, unlike Machiavelli's, thus forms part of a philosophy of history that, despite everything, deserves to be called optimistic. It is a philosophy of progress as well as a dialectical philosophy. We can say progress since the growth of the forces of production gives a meaning, at once a direction and a value, to the course of the future and since the successive changes, the death of condemned systems and the birth of new ones, will lead, beyond the next and last crisis, to the reconciliation of men with each other and with their destiny. In this twofold meaning—the accumulation of the forces of production and the resolution of conflicts at the end of prehistory—Marx's thought, whatever its recent interpreters may say, arises out of evolutionary and progressive conviction.

On the other hand, it is true, as certain contemporary reinterpretations emphasize, that this progress and evolution expounded by Marx the man is combined with a theory of capitalism and its functioning that does not necessarily imply paralysis and the inevitable explosion. One need only modify certain hypotheses of *Capital* to show that capitalism, despite its intrinsic injustice, can survive or that, at the very least, it need not perish except at the hands of men, by the action of the exploited or of revolutionaries, an action encouraged but not determined by the growth of a capitalism given over to itself.

One of the neo-Marxist schools of today, in order to reconcile the experience of our century and the revolution of 1917 with Marxist doctrine, has substituted the theory of the self-reproduction of capitalism for the theory of its self-destruction and has elaborated a theory of revolution in which the maturation of capitalism and its contradictions plays only a subordinate role. With that, the prophetic element becomes secondary, almost foreign to the authentic or authentically scientific spirit of Marxism. The banal refutation produced by comparing the predictions of Marx with the actual future loses its essential importance. It matters little that the standard of living of the wage earners increases absolutely or relatively instead of diminishing; it matters little that the crises become less and not more numerous and serious.

As a theory of social formations, Marxism bases its claim to be scientific on its concepts and on its method of analysis; as a theory of revolution, it teaches that one should watch for the opportunity to be created by the interaction of a variety of circumstances, an opportunity that it will then be up to men to seize. A science of social formations and revolutionary practice—this combination defines one possible Marxism among others. Only one more step in this direction is needed to strip Marxism of what I have called its "catastrophic optimism." Why should the regime that will succeed the capitalist one escape the curse that throughout the centuries has blighted all socioeconomic regimes, regimes founded on the domination of some exploiting the work of all? Why should the planned economy not offer a minority the opportunity of setting aside for its own profit a fraction of the social surplus value? Would not the collective ownership of the means of production be transformed, in fact, over the heads of the producers, on the authority of the directors named by the state or by the party? And management of the economy by the producers combined? This is a formula empty of meaning or a badly defined utopia.

Thus Pareto amended Marx to accommodate him to his own pessimism and to bring him into line with Machiavelli. Indeed, if we compare Machiavelli and Marx as philosophers of history, in what essentially are they opposed? I have elsewhere answered this question by proposing the following antithesis: Machiavelli is and wishes to be adviser to the *Prince*; Marx thinks of himself as a confidant of providence. Machiavelli believes he can say to the *Prince, hic et nunc*, at this time, in this place, what must be done to gain such and such a goal. Marx claims to know in what direction, toward what conclusion, the tumult of events is drawing a humanity unaware of its own history and rebelling against its pointless suffering.

Thus characterized, Machiavelli and Marx each represent a typical way of considering history, politics, and action. The first sees in the terrestrial world only the constancy of human inconstancy, the essential precariousness of ever temporary regimes, the permanent struggle of princes anxious to found their power where new principalities are concerned and to maintain it where it has traditionally held sway. Marx, with no illusions about what socioeconomic regimes may think or be, keeps his eyes fixed on a radiant future, radically new with respect to the past. History does not develop in cycles, as had been supposed by the ancient philosophers, witnesses of the vicissitudes afflicting city-states, of democracies degenerating into demagoguery from which only tyrants provided an escape, a tyranny that the inextinguishable needs for freedom would slowly undermine until the day of the liberating revolution—shining dawn of a new day promising in its birth the sadness of its close. History, according to Marx, carries in itself the promise of redemption—a promise that Machiavelli did not perceive.

Why did Marx perceive this promise, which escaped Machiavelli? Marx concentrated on social formations or, in ordinary language, on institutions; Machiavelli concentrated on men. Marx traced the development of the forces of production; Machiavelli described the unending struggle of princes among themselves and with their subjects. One defined history as the creation of humanity by its own effort, and the other defined it as the ever changing expression of a humanity always basically the same. One established a sort of transition between Judeo-Christian eschatology and the method, so popular today, of predicting possible futures; the other, perhaps less assured of his atheism than the son of a converted Jewish lawyer, denounced the Catholic church as responsible for the ruin of divided Italy. One dreamt of a society lucidly aware of its own nature in which the citizens would reject all transcendence and submit themselves to a rational collective discipline without having recourse to ideological illusions; the other did not abandon the hope of a virtuous people like the people of the Roman republic. But political (rather than ethical) virtue passes according to the unforeseeable caprices of fortune from one people to another; it does not linger for long in the same place. There is, of course, hope of a respite, of a perfect moment, of a resounding but ephemeral success—but no hope of a new era that would indefinitely prolong this victory of a few men over themselves and the common fate.

Let us translate these contrasts into a more abstract language. On the one hand, we have an economic philosophy of history, on the other, a political philosophy; in one case, long-term progress, in the other, the inevitable repetition of historical cycles, the result of a permanent and essential instability; with Marx, the growth of social formations or regimes created by the very men whom they shape and imprison; with Machiavelli, the efforts of heroic individuals, ever renewed and in the end always vain, to overcome chance, to triumph over their enemies, and to earn for themselves the good graces of fortune and the goodwill of peoples. Men, according to Marx, make their history but hitherto without knowing what they make; history impelled by the development of the forces of production will end by creating men capable of making their history in full consciousness. Men, according to Machiavelli, bear responsibility for their history but are in no position to be proud of it. Only the virtue of free peoples would permit princes to rule candidly—a rare virtue and one eroded by time. The degraded virtue of heroes takes the place of that of peoples but must submit itself to the ruthless demands of efficacy. Unarmed prophets perish but—to paraphrase Machiavelli a little—prophets do not always have time or good reason to boast of their rarely pure and never durable successes. He who has no sword available will die by the sword. All the same, Machiavelli would not have denied a measure of truth to the gospel's dictum he who lives by the sword will die by the sword.

Thesis and antithesis. Thesis: Machiavelli and Marx are comparable for their innumerable and divided following and for an underlying problem in each case related if not identical: once the overriding necessity of studying reality as it is has been stated, how then can we refuse the lessons this reality teaches, knowledge of the frequent immorality of effective means? Antithesis: Machiavelli and Marx represent two ways of thinking, two visions of the world, two opposed figures, two exemplary and contradictory masters. Adviser to the *Prince* or confidant of providence, politics or economics, action in a specific context or the perspective of the long-term view; man never satisfied, always changing but never to change to the point of finding satisfaction or, quite to the contrary, dissatisfied man, who, in creating the means of production and social formations, will finally achieve a social formation in which he will find satisfaction or in which his dissatisfaction will at least manifest itself other than through the ultimately sterile yet necessary expressions of deceit and violence.

Thesis and antithesis assuredly call for, or at the worst tolerate, a synthesis. The first one comes to mind so readily that I have no doubt you have thought of it even before I formulate it. The Marxist, who knows the end of the human odyssey, opposes the Machiavellian (or the man disposed toward a Machiavellian attitude), who wishes to know what the immediate situation is and who, on the basis of experience and precedents, by reference to comparable situations and causal relations more or less consistently observed, suggests to the actor what he should do to attain his goal.

But the Marxist, *hic et nunc*, even if he keeps his eyes fixed on his distant goal, must make a decision. Long-range realism, linked to a deterministic view of history, becomes logically combined with a short-range realism implied by a philosophy of inexpiable conflicts. The very grandeur of the distant goal gives a supplementary justification to the ruthless rigor of methods and means. If the future regime does not differ essentially from that of today, logic demands that the cost and the profit be compared, that boundless sacrifices be refused if they are to bring only limited or mediocre benefits. On the other hand, the expectation of a total and qualitative change dissipates doubts, awakens enthusiasm, and sustains faith. No longer is it a question of counting the number of victims.

The Marxist, *hic et nunc*, has two reasons for acting in a Machiavellian manner. He lives in a ravaged world wherein violence, domination, and exploitation reign. He sees on the horizon another world purged of these age-old evils. It is but one more step for him to arrive at Gramsci's theme, the "party" as collective *Prince*. Exposed to the risks of war and to the uncertainties of popular passion, the "party," like the armed heroes of Machiavelli, must conquer fortune not for the glory of one man but for the safety of all. The collective *Prince* musters the will of the masses in a small number of leaders, a general staff or politburo. These leaders, on occasion a single leader, clarify the passions of thousands of militants and of millions of sympathizers. The party officials do not flinch from the use of force and guile against class enemies. In the eyes of their following, they act as any prince does in the conquest of a kingdom, heavenly or earthly. The *Prince* relies on the devotion of the faithful, without whom he would be able to do nothing; he knows that devotion alone does not always survive the test of experience and that the threat of ruthless punishment, in case of treason, provides an indispensable guarantee of loyalty. To borrow an expression from Sartre's *Critique of Dialectical Reason*, let us say that terror cements the fraternity of comrades engaged in battle.

To liken the "party" to a *Prince* does not appear to me contrary to the spirit of Machiavelli. The "party" represents in our century the armed prophet. It owes its strength to the number of those who listen to its message, but all the more to its concentrated power of decision. Go back to the early years of the century or even to 1917: there were only a few in the political section of the Bolshevik faction of the Russian Social Democratic party. Lenin prevailed over this tiny group by the confidence he inspired. Events always proved him right. Later, another man came to incarnate the Russian proletariat, itself the vanguard of the world proletariat, in *its* turn pledged to the redemption of humanity. This man helped events to vindicate him by reserving to himself the exclusive right to interpret them, by silencing his enemies, or, better still, by forcing them to acknowledge that only their victorious comrades, now their executioners, were in possession of the truth and the whole truth. At that moment, with the cult of personality, the *Prince* "cloaked in his deceit," again became comparable to certain heroes whose fate Machiavelli had, with mixed feelings, analyzed. An army or religious order, the "party" does not merge in a genuine communion with the man who embodies it. It obeys him as soldiers obey, as those obey who have parted with their free will to put it at the service of a faith higher than their own individuality.

The "party," nevertheless, does not become a sixteenth-century *Prince* in search of power and glory; it stays on the road to a sublime goal. If it were to stop believing in this goal, if it contented itself with the sound objectives, contained in and not transcending history, that its enemies devote themselves to, then the conversion of Marxism to Machiavellianism would be complete. The *Prince* is Machiavellian when he, prone to use any means at any moment, sincerely transforms the necessities of battle because he never doubts that he is working for the truth even as he is lying and for the happiness of mankind even as he is imposing a reign of terror. In this sense, perhaps one could say that Lenin remained more Marxist than Machiavellian, whereas Stalin relied more on weapons than on prophecies. Trotsky, when he lost his weapons, preached in vain. The tiny unarmed groups that reappropriate the original prophecy in opposition to the embodied prophecy manage only to quarrel among themselves on the periphery of world history, which they claim as their own and which rejects them.

The liberal disciple of Machiavelli finds in the fate of twentieth-century Marxism many confirmations of the Florentine's teaching. Are we dealing with the permanence of the power struggle and the primacy of politics as defined by this struggle? Those who deny these propositions in theory have verified them in practice.

The revolutions of the twentieth century did not emerge from the contradictions of capitalism brought to the point of disintegration. Overdetermined—to use a fashionable word—they appear in societies torn by disputes, when the governing power can no longer command and the masses refuse to obey. Revolutionary situations are created not by the development of the forces of production or by the discrepancy between collective production and individual appropriation but by multiple and diverse factors—the unsettling of traditions, the deterioration of regimes, and the weakness of ruling minorities. In such circumstances, as in the Italian cities, the active minorities, led by extraordinary personalities, become the decisive actors. They mobilize the disaffected masses; they inspire confidence; they seize power; and they ruthlessly eliminate their enemies until the day comes when these comrades launch among themselves the struggle for the highest position, for the undivided glory. When one man alone rules, without principle and unrestrained by law, is there any reason why he should not imitate the conduct of Duke Valentino as Machiavelli recounts it in Chapter VII of *The Prince?*

> After taking the Romagna . . . he thought it necessay, in order to bring the country back to peace and obedience to the royal and secular arm, to give it a good government. To this end he appointed Messer Remirro de Orco, a cruel and efficient man, to whom he gave the fullest powers. To his great credit, this man in short time restored peace and unity. Afterward, the duke considered that it was not advisable to confer such excessive authority, for he had no doubt but that it would become odious. So he set up a civil tribunal in the center of the province under a wise president, and where each city had its representative. And because he knew that past severity had earned him some hatred, in order to purge the minds of the people and win them over completely, he desired to show that, if any cruelty had been practiced, it had originated not with him but in the harsh nature of his minister. Seizing the opportunity when it came, he had him cut in half and placed one morning in the piazza in Cesena with the block and a bloody knife at his side. The ferocity of this spectacle caused the people to be at once appeased and dumbfounded.

The followers of our *Princes* in the West no longer risk such a cruel fate, but they do suffer the unpopularity that, in all Machiavellian justice, strikes scapegoats, those responsible for necessary and unpleasant measures, indeed for measures initiated by the hero himself, measures that his admirers prefer to impute to others rather than to the object of their worship. On the other side of Europe, the chief of the Soviet police was one of the last victims of the great purge in 1936. Beria, in his turn, knew the same fate. And as Stalin himself was dead, he could not be cut in pieces on the public square: no other symbolic act remained to appease and dumbfound the people but the transfer of his corpse, at the request of a worthy Soviet woman citizen who had been visited by a dream of justice.

Since Machiavelli, the techniques of conquest and of the exercise of power have gained in subtlety and rational refinement. What once depended on individual improvisation and spontaneity is now the object of scientific studies that form the basis for well-considered strategies. The rape of the masses or hidden persuasion, the organization of enthusiasm or brainwashing, offer *Princes* an arsenal of incomparably rich psychological weapons. So the partisan fighters of former times, the Spanish peasant facing Napoleon's soldiers or the French sniper who lay in wait for the Prussians in 1871, become today, thanks to the technical methods of communication and still more to the organization of parallel hierarchies, a troop both regular and irregular, capable under favorable circumstances of victoriously resisting a force of vastly superior mobility and firepower.

The follower of Machiavelli can still support his argument by referring to the way of governing of the "party"-*Prince*. As Machiavelli thought obvious, and Pareto never tired of repeating, minorities overturn established regimes in the name of the people; they invoke a new formula, but the distinction between the small number holding power and its privileges and the large number that obeys out of conviction or fear is not erased. Marxists have not been content, in Marx's famous phrase, to understand the world—they have changed it. But they have not changed it in such a way as to refute Machiavelli's skeptical irony or Pareto's pessimism. Their rule resembles that of many other elites whose corpses mark the course of history—history, the graveyard of aristocracies, as Pareto called it.

In other words, Marx changed the world more than Machiavelli did because he believed more than Machiavelli in the possibility of change. But the Florentine reserves the right to reply, "Plus ça change, plus c'est la même chose." In a sense he still has the last word in the argument, even though, in a Soviet regime, his Marxist opponent would oblige him to end this dialogue and savor his dialectical victory in a less pleasant place than the public square, the halls of the university, or the Italian Institute in Paris.

Here, then, is the first synthesis—the Marxist, strategist of the class war, or revolution, of guerrilla organization, of primitive accumulation, acts by force and guile, like a Machiavellian, persuading and compelling. Once master of the state, he does not govern according to methods essentially different from those used by former elites in those principalities that Machiavelli would have called new.

This first synthesis raises, it seems to me, two questions. Machiavelli does not know progress and he enjoys the analysis of extreme situations, situations that oblige the politician to make cruel decisions governed solely by the laws of practicality. But between the here-and-now decisions, those of strategy in the midst of a battle, and the future oriented toward a radical transformation of history, the prophetic vision of Marxism, lies the analysis of regimes, each having its own nature and mode of operation and thus in turn a particular type of ruler and of ruling methods. But how can we compare our two thinkers on this point, one having served his city without neglecting the study of books, the other having spent more time in the British Museum than in the organization of the First International and who knew politics from below, as a militant revolutionary, without country or party?

I will answer this by returning to the texts and their innumerable commentaries, and I will limit myself to some brief remarks. Machiavelli, like all other classical political philosophers in the West since Plato and above all Aristotle, distinguishes between forms of government, and one can draw from *The Prince* and especially from the *Discourses* a theory of various forms of government, of their respective advantages and inevitable defects. There is no good reason to doubt that Machiavelli prefers a republic to a monarchy, freedom to tyranny, a legal regime to an arbitrary one. In this sense he does not profess the odious opinions that his opponents foist upon him. Indeed, let us say for good measure that Machiavelli, the Italian patriot, hates the foreigners who trample the soil of his country and hates the Italians (above all the church) who bear the responsibility for the nation's misfortunes.

Marx, on his side, contemplated from the outset a quite different historical experience. Social formations take the place of political regimes. Social formations are defined by the forces and relations of production and Marx, in his theoretical formulations at least, does not distinguish very well between forms of government. Each social formation is characterized by the volume of surplus value appropriated by the privileged minority, by the mode of appropriation, and by the method of distribution. Just as in the works of Machiavelli, the struggle for power occupies the foreground even though the rivalries of social groups and the competition for wealth are neither ignored nor misunderstood, so Marx conversely brings to light the social and economic roots of the conflicts within all social structures without ignoring the fact that citizens of antiquity, medieval lords, or modern bourgeoisie do not exercise power according to the same procedures.

There is nothing, therefore, to keep a Machiavellian-Marxist of today from elaborating a complex theory of social formations and political regimes, a theory that would endeavor to discover the more or less consistent connections between one and the other without denying the partial anomalies of particular instances—the diversity of powers in a formation of a given type, the progressive or sudden change of formations through reforming or revolutionary action on the part of elites or masses. In other words, the adviser to the *Prince*—the man who knows what must be done here and now—and the confidant of providence—the man who knows what the future will be at an undetermined date but does not know the road that leads to the end of prehistory—both need the sociologist and the political scientist. Between the event confronted by the man of action and the qualitative change or conversion conceived by the prophet lies the objective study of systems, regular elements, preponderant tendencies, and probable extrapolations.

The specialist in futurology seems to me inclined to reject the double paternity of Machiavelli and Marx. He puts the mishaps that upset the life of cities between parentheses; even the world crisis of the thirties leaves a scarcely perceptible trace on the line of long-term growth of the GNP per capita in the United States. He likewise leaves out by hypothesis, not so much as impossible but as unforeseeable and almost unthinkable, the "qualitative changes" that would mark a break in development. Or

perhaps one ought to say that this qualitative change is accomplishing itself each day to the degree to which the growth of the forces of production contributes to this miracle, which is so obvious that we almost fail to notice it: man works less and less and he produces more and more. The hippies offer us one early image among several possible images of man liberated finally from the age-old curse of work.

But let us leave the futurologist to enjoy his serenity in peace, the dubious privilege of all those who raise themselves so far above living people and a world not yet freed from work and violence. Let us ask our second question and return to the followers of our two thinkers. Which deserves to be condemned by the moralist?

Which governs in the Florentine manner, to use an expression common during the past few centuries? Who subjugated trust to policy? Who manipulated crowds? Who plots in the shadows the overthrow of Number One? Who teaches crowds to burn from one day to the next what they once idolized? Who scorns the rule of law and knows no morality but that of the collective *Prince*, who is freed by the sublimity of his mission from the scruples of weak souls? Machiavelli never approved these practices, no more than he ever explicitly condemned them. "What is necessary, is necessary."

How can the man of action be forbidden to use practical means? And how can it be denied that on certain occasions practicality requires morally detestable means? One never tires of studying Machiavelli because he explored to the end an insoluble contradiction: to forbid the politician the means of success not only smacks of hypocrisy but is intrinsically absurd; to allow him to use methods in themselves execrable is no more satisfactory. There is no way out and the politician must accept the tragic element in his condition. Still, it is up to him to do everything to avoid extreme situations that leave no choice except between two kinds of defeat: to win while losing the reasons for winning or to renounce victory in the hope of saving his soul.

Now Machiavelli, as a doctrinaire of a desirable politics if not as a theoretician of an actual politics, wishes to reduce the frequency of situations that provide no escape except through Machiavellianism in the vulgar and pejorative sense of the word. To found a state, to restore a corrupt regime, or to give a constitution to a decadent people—in these cases extreme measures prove inevitable. But the ideal remains the republic, law, a virtuous people, the tumult of the public forum. Because he does not believe any man is capable of not abusing absolute power, Machiavelli, like the liberals, recommends the balance of powers and prefers the instability of regimes that live by acknowledged disputes to the deceitful order of the tyranny of one or a few men. In a century during which so much blood has been spilled by those who hope for too much from politics and humanity, the Machiavellians sometimes appear as the defenders of freedom. Pessimism protects one from illusions and there is no prophet without illusion.

Similarly, by a logical reversal, it is the Marxist who becomes the exponent of a Machiavellianism unjustly attributed to Machiavelli. To trust the collective *Prince* is to give full powers to a Cesare Borgia who would like, into the bargain, to enjoy the pleasures of a good conscience, inseparable from his conviction of serving humanity. Freedom flourishes in temperate zones; it does not survive the burning faith of prophets and crowds.

Need it be said that it is Marx and not Machiavelli who becomes the *auteur maudit*? In Stalin's time, the Machiavellians preached as much. They did not and they will not convince. Not that they were entirely wrong: "qui veut faire l'ange fait la bête." Those who wish to change the current of human affairs are frequently merciless, closer to the tyrants of the past than to man the master of his fate, of whom scholars dream in the silence of libraries.

But let us not forget either that pessimists also resign themselves to the unjustifiable, that they sometimes protect societies against the transports of futile passion but rarely restrain the privileged from the temptations of conservatism. It is dangerous to give men too high a conception of their possible goal; it is scarcely less so to convince them of their indignity and impotence. Between Machiavelli, the observer without illusions, and Marx, the prophet, it is better not to choose but rather to let them pursue, in our own minds and beyond, an inexhaustible and unlimited dialogue.

It is a dialogue for our century but also for all centuries. Marx stands as the prophet of our time, in which economics, the forces of production, takes on the form of fate. Machiavelli remains our contemporary not so much for his teachings as for the questions he raises and which do not admit of answers.

Whom should we admire the more—the one who prefers the safety of the city to the safety of his soul or the one who, one day, cried out, "Hier stehe ich, ich kann nicht anders" ("Here I stand, I cannot do otherwise")? Denial by fidelity, or fidelity to oneself in and by revolt—let everyone remember, put a name to each of these symbolic attitudes and choose if he can.

Personally, I have no trouble choosing, but I have paid the price for it or gained the reward: I did not cross the threshold of political action and I remain, not like the people of the Romagna, appeased and dumbfounded, but, like all those who speculate on action without acting, frustrated and secretly satisfied—perhaps.

6. Macht, Power, Puissance: Democratic Prose or Demoniac Poetry?

THE WORDS *power* AND *Macht* IN English and German and *pouvoir* or *puissance* in French continue to be surrounded by a kind of sacred halo or, if one likes, charged with mysterious and rather frightening echoes. The demoniac nature of power *(die Dämonie der Macht)* suggested the title of a book written after the Hitlerian madness. Specialists in international relations use the term *power politics*, the equivalent of *Machtpolitik*, not without some ambiguity as to the meaning of this concept, which at times defines the essence of relations between states and at times a doctrine (usually condemned) about these relations. Across the Channel and the Atlantic people untiringly quote Lord Acton: "Power corrupts, absolute power corrupts absolutely." And before him Montesquieu had written: "It is an everlasting experience that any man who has power is led to abuse it, he will do so until he encounters limits. What can one say? Even virtue has need of limits." When C. Wright Mills wished to expose the hidden minority ruling the United States he coined the expression *power elite*, borrowing one of these terms, *elite*, from the Machiavellian tradition and combining it with *power*, a word disavowed by Marxists and radicals. For power, bad in itself, is doubly bad if possessed by an elite, and in the American ideological climate a small group by definition will not include the best since power corrupts those who hold it.

Let us set aside the emotional echoes of these fears and quarrels and

---

"Macht, Power, Puissance: prose democratique ou poesie demoniaque." Translated from the French and reprinted with authorization from *European Journal of Sociology*, V (1964), 27–51.

address ourselves to contemporary sociologists and political scientists. A Dutch sociologist,[1] after passing in review a variety of definitions, arrived at the following formula: "Power is the possibility, on the part of a person or group, to restrict other persons or groups in the choice of their behaviour, in pursuance of his or its purposes." Similarly, C. J. Friedrich writes that power is "a relation between men that expresses itself in the behavior of those who follow (or obey)." And again: "When the behavior of a certain group of men conforms to the wishes of one or several of them, the relation between them shall be called the power of L over A, B, C."[2]

These definitions are not identical and each presents difficulties. The first claims to eliminate psychological factors such as "conscience," "will," and "motivation." But reference to the goals of the powerholder, as well as to the restricted choice of those subservient to him, precludes explanation of the subject-object nature of power except in terms of what is happening (or is supposed to be happening) in the consciousness of one or the other. Also this definition is, so to speak, indirect: it does not raise the point that some command and others obey or that some lead and others follow; it does not even suggest that the "freedom" of those who are the objects of power is suppressed or curtailed. "The possibility of taking initiative remains completely unimpaired; only the range of choice is restricted."[3] C. J. Friedrich's definition, on the other hand, is direct or positive: the power relation is defined in customary fashion by the fact that "certain individuals follow others." Yet since they do not follow them always or in everything, the difference between the direct or positive definition, on the one hand, and the indirect or negative one, on the other, is not of decisive importance.

In the last analysis, modern sociological concepts of power all originate in an operation that we can define equally well as formalization or abstraction. Society as we know it contains a multiplicity of relationships of the command-obedience kind, the same individual being in turn a giver and a follower of orders not only by virtue of the hierarchy inherent in complex organizations but also by virtue of the multiplicity of social systems to which each person belongs. Thus, if we decide to find a concept that applies to all command-obedience relations, public and private, de jure or de facto, in all areas of collective life, without taking into account the means used by the one who commands and the emotions felt by the one who obeys, we will necessarily arrive at a relation both *interpersonal* and *asymmetrical,* whose nature would be: "Someone moves ahead or speaks or takes the initiative, and others follow and listen." Or again, in order to rid the command-obedience relation still further of concrete con-

[1] J. A. A. van Doorn, "Sociology and the Problem of Power," *Sociologia neerlandica,* I (1962–63), pp. 3–47.

[2] *Man and His Government* (New York: McGraw-Hill, 1963), p. 161.

[3] Van Doorn, "Problem of Power," p. 13.

tent, one could say that "freedom of choice for some is restrained by the voluntary action of an individual or group."[4] At this point power will have ceased to be mysterious, fascinating, demoniac. How could a society exist without subjects and objects of power, without, at every moment, the freedom of choice of A, B, and C being restrained by the power of X? Or again without A, B, and C following the initiative taken by X? To create the fiction of a society without "the power of men over men" F. A. Hayek must propose a radical antithesis between the rule of laws and the rule of men. He has to argue that the generality of laws leaves the individual free to contrive means in pursuit of his ends whereas the clear rule of one man makes the *other* his tool. But why exorcise the demon? Purified by a process of scientific abstraction, power no longer spreads enthusiasm or terror. It has become neutral, pale, and flat. There is no longer any objection to comparing it to money—as Talcott Parsons does: power is henceforth the most widely shared thing in the world, shared unequally, of course, some possessing much, others very little. But it would be a mistake, according to Parsons, to assume that there is anyone with *no* power. A man with only a dime has very little money, but he still cannot be said to have none at all. Likewise, no one is radically deprived of power (should one add: in the political regime of the United States?), meager as the portion he enjoys may be.

I have no wish to cast doubt, personally, on the validity of formal conceptualization, with its suprahistorical tendencies, so long as two conditions are met: that such conceptualization does not lead to a disregard for the specificity of historical or social problems or situations; and that one does not erroneously equate the political order with the economic order, or power with money, as though the inequality in resources or income at the disposal of each individual could be compared with inequalities in power.

☆　☆　☆

So far we have followed general usage and used the term *pouvoir* as the equivalent of *power* and *Macht*. But French has two words to translate *Macht* and *power: pouvoir* and *puissance*. Both words have the same root, the Latin verb *posse* (to be capable of, to have the strength to). The first word is the infinitive, and according to the Littré dictionary, "it simply denotes action"; whereas *puissance* (the participle) designates "something durable, permanent." One has the *puissance* to do something and one exercises *pouvoir* to do it. This is why one speaks of the "*puissance* of a machine" and not its *pouvoir*. The distinction would be about the same as that between the potential (also called *puissance*) and the act. It is well to remind oneself that power, depending on circumstances, refers to a potential or to an act. Or rather that it represents a potential whose ac-

---

[4] If this restriction is the result of the involuntary action of another, the latter has no power.

tualization brings forth its nature and scope. For this reason sociology that aims at an empirical and operational approach sometimes questions the usefulness of the term *power* insofar as it means a potential only known through acts (decisions). At first the duality between *puissance* and *pouvoir* is that of potential and action but usage has introduced other shades of meaning. It has become common in French to use *Pouvoir* for the individual or rather the minority that decides in the name of the community or takes decisions calculated to affect it. In this meaning—which I dare not call popular, since the word is used in this way by many political scientists—*Pouvoir* is equated with the state's ruling minority. One could also say that *Pouvoir* is the human incarnation of the state. An author who ponders the raisons d'être, the foundations, of power is really asking why all societies, except perhaps a few primitive ones, have known a concentration of power, the bestowal upon one or a few of the capacity (recognized as legitimate) to establish rules for all, to impose respect for these rules upon all, or finally to take irrevocable decisions, de jure or de facto, for all. *One* man sets the community at war with another: the other members of the community bear the consequences of this decision to the point of risking or sacrificing their lives in combat.

The word *puissance* is not used in France in this sense. One says *prendre le pouvoir* or *arriver au pouvoir* (expressions translated in German by *Macht*, in English by *power*), one does not speak of arriving at *puissance* or losing *puissance*. Reaching *puissance* or attaining it does not suggest taking possession of the state or the right to command. On the other hand, one speaks of *grande puissance* (great power), not of *grand pouvoir*, when it is a question of the principal actors on the international scene. It is the opposition between the two expressions *arriver au pouvoir* (that is, taking possession of the state or of the legal right to command) and *les grandes puissances*[5] that led me, in *Peace and War*, to retain *puissance* as the more general concept—the potential for command, influence, or coercion possessed by an individual with respect to others—*pouvoir* being only a form of *puissance*, one characterizing not some exercise of *puissance* but a certain kind of potential and the translation of this potential into action.

Let us provisionally retain from these analyses this distinction between participle and infinitive, potential and effective, since it is found in other languages and is justified by semantic analysis: to *have* the power to do something, to *exercise* the power to do it. Whoever possesses firearms or atomic bombs has the *puissance* to kill a man or millions of men, but he does not necessarily exercise his *pouvoir* to do so. The preceding example points the way to another distinction. The *puissance* of a gun or a bomb is completely physical, and though the same word is legitimately used to

[5] It is not possible in French to use *politique de pouvoir* to translate *Machtpolitik*, which suggests once more that *pouvoir* is not only action in relation to potential but potential or the partly legalized act in relation to potential or the pure and simple act.

describe the potential of both a machine and a man (or a group), the *puissance* discussed by sociologists and political scientists is endowed with a special character: the power of man over man, in other words, the capacity of a man to restrict the freedom enjoyed by another or to obtain from one or several that they follow or obey him. *As a political concept,* puissance *indicates a relation between men; however, since at the same time it indicates a potential and not an act, one can define* puissance *as the potential possessed by a man or a group to establish relations with other men or groups in conformity with the former's wishes.*

Let us take henceforth as the more general concept not the term *pouvoir,* as sociologists usually do today, but that of *puissance.* This word has the double advantage of being usable in most cases in which the Germans say *Macht* and the Americans or British say *power.* Furthermore, since according to Littré *puissance* describes something permanent and lasting, and not only an action or exercise, it has a broader range of meaning than does *pouvoir.*

The choice of vocabulary, by the way, is of little importance. The important thing is not to introduce a philosophy or an interpretation of reality by means of a choice of terms. What in this respect seems decisive to me are the stages through which one passes to reconstruct society, concrete and total, from the minute, elementary relationship of power. I discern two principal paths leading to completely different conceptions.

In addition to power (*Macht*), a second, fundamental concept, that of *Herrschaft,* is used by Max Weber. An individual has power, in a social relationship, when he has the opportunity to impose his will on another or several others, even over their resistance, whatever the reason for this opportunity. As for *Herrschaft,* it implies command (*Befehl*) and obedience to this command by those involved. I would translate *Herrschaft* by "domination" because of the common roots (*Herr*) master, *Dominus.*[6] The concept of domination (or *Herrschaft*) tends to circumscribe, within the vast field of power relations (the conduct of A, B, and C is determined positively or negatively, in certain circumstances and from certain perspectives, by the will of X) a narrower domain within which the person aspiring to power exercises it and expects to be obeyed. The dominant person is not just anyone with power. The power relation must be stabilized for the dominant person to command. He must feel assured of his prerogative or of his capacity to exact obedience. In this general framework the casuistry of power relations reveals itself—depending on whe-

[6] This translation is adopted by one of Max Weber's best translators, J. Freund. Italian translators have chosen *potenza* for *Macht* and *potere* for *Herrschaft.* The distinction between *potenza* and *potere* corresponds to that between *puissance* and *pouvoir,* that of the participle versus the infinitive. I will use this distinction in part in that the dominant person will be said to have a *pouvoir* rather than a *puissance* when he exercises his domination (act in relation to potential) and that he exercises it in conformity to legality or legitimacy.

ther these are accidental or regular, customary or legal, simply effective
or legitimate. One goes from *puissance*—a formal and abstract concept—
to *Pouvoir* (in the sense that this word takes on when the governed are
contrasted with the governing) by various stages of stabilization, institutionalization, legitimation, concentration, and domination.

It is striking, and nearly amusing for the historian of ideas, that Parsons should have translated *Herrschaft* by imperative control. Here is an
American sociologist whose knowledge of the German language is
assured, whose effort toward objectivity is obvious, and yet who could not
help translating a perfectly clear concept by a term that has neither the
same meaning nor the same ring but is in closer accord with Parson's own
mental universe.

From Aristotle to Max Weber the command-obedience social relationship has been recognized. The notion of imperative control, barely
translatable into French (unless one uses *contrôle* in the English sense of
control and speaks of *contrôle social autoritaire*), eliminates the face-to-
face relationship involved in command and obedience and merges it with
a *system of imposed order* (or imposed discipline). Now, institutionalized
power and domination relationships do not make up the whole system of
socially imposed behaviors. Mores, laws, prejudices, beliefs, and collective passions also help to determine the social order. Thus, by eliminating
the master-servant relationship and replacing it by an *imposed order*, the
way is paved for eliminating specifically political relations long pondered
by Western philosophers.

C. J. Friedrich, not a sociologist but a political scientist, is adamant on
the subject; he criticizes the translation of *Herrschaft* by "imperative control," which, he says, "amounts to a gloss and lacks clarity,"[7] and he proposes to use the word *rule*, which he defines as "institutionalized political
power" (thus, the *ruler* would be the *Herrscher*). This translation is obviously better than Parsons's, although *Herrschaft*, as defined by Max
Weber, has a greater range of meaning than "institutionalized political
power." Domination implies a degree of institutionalization (otherwise
the ruler would not dare issue orders), but the word *domination* evokes
the direct relationship between master and servant rather than the relationship between ruler and ruled.

Whatever the different shades of meaning among *Herrschaft*, domination, and rule, as soon as this concept is involved, the sociologist, even if
he is concerned with power in its broadest and vaguest connotations, will
necessarily come to the properly political dimension, to the notion of "integral power" in accordance with Thomas Geiger's expression, the power
of society as a whole *over* its members, or the concentrated power of one
or a few over the rest, and not the reciprocal relationship of dependency

[7] *Man and His Government*, p. 180n.

between the directors and members of an organization, party, or trade union. On the other hand, as soon as one makes the leap from the elementary power relationship, with its countless forms and expressions, to "imperative control," one runs the risk of misconstruing the specifically political per se.

Let us look upon the whole of society as a system in which individuals and groups are integrated. Each of these individuals or groups tends to reserve for itself a certain power in the broader meaning of *capacity to act* or in the more restricted one of *capacity to influence the behavior of others*. None wish to be purely the object of an outside power; each wants to be also, to a certain extent, the subject. Suddenly, competition for power seems comparable to competition for money and the realm of politics similar to a marketplace.

This general picture reflects an aspect of reality, especially in certain regimes (for example, the American). Trade unions, political parties, and pressure groups come on the scene as rivals, each seeking a maximum of power (capacity to determine the behavior or decisions of others) without any of them *completely* lacking this rare commodity, which is never monopolized, always divided, though in a very unequal manner, among them all.

Nevertheless, a deeper analysis is sufficient to reveal the flaw in the argument. Competition for the foundation or instruments of power allows the comparison with economic competition. Whoever seeks the most capital, prestige, or guns so that his will may prevail over other men's wills acts in the manner of *Homo economicus* seeking a maximum of profit or production. But maximizing the instruments or the means of power does not amount to *power itself*. Being a relationship between men or groups, power does not lend itself to quantification as readily as goods or things: relative, not absolute, power, extends over some men or groups and not others; it controls some behavior, not all. If so many authors are prone to confuse the struggle for power with economic competition, it is primarily because having identified the struggle for the means (or instruments) of power with the struggle for power itself, they have substituted for the human relationship of power, this or that attribute of that relationship.

If one compares power and money, or power and wealth, the differences are inescapable. The analogy remains superficial and the distinction radical between the distribution of wealth and the apportionment of power. Whoever owns a given quantity of currency can obtain in exchange a given amount of merchandise. Perhaps he is in the position to *buy* the services of certain individuals, but the behavior of a host of others cannot be bought. Money is the means, normally effective in a modern society, to reach the natural goal of economic activity, to satisfy one's desires or rather minimize the disparity between desires and resources.

However, the economy henceforth constitutes a differentiated subsystem: money allows the certain acquisition only of goods supplied in the marketplace. It also endows someone owning a vast amount of it with the capacity to determine to an extent the behavior of particular men: there is no ratio between economic power, defined as the capacity to acquire goods on the market, and political power, defined as the capacity to determine the behavior of others.

Whoever acquires wealth inevitably deprives others. Since the volume of wealth is limited at any moment, it is true in *one* sense (the proposition was virtually true without reservation in traditional societies) that others are deprived of what one person accumulates. At the commercial level, in theory and practice, this does not hold true since in an ideal-typical exchange each participant prefers what he is receiving to what he had and gave in exchange. But if society is considered as a unit, the wealth of the rich automatically lessens what is left for the other members of the community to dispose of. The modern economy, however, insofar as it is progressive, seriously challenges this age-old conception. The volume of goods, limited at any moment, also increases from moment to moment. If the time dimension is taken into account, it is no longer true that the enrichment of one individual automatically brings about the impoverishment of others. Economic growth allows for wealth simultaneously reaching all or nearly all members of a community without, however, removing the element of conflict (*agon*) from the world of economics.

The exchange relationship tends, according to the ideal type, toward equality; the power relationship appears in its essence asymmetrical and unequal. If L makes A, B, and C obey and follow him, or if L limits the freedom that A, B, and C have to select their goals and opportunities, L cannot be the subject of power without A, B, and C being its objects. A fortiori, if we go from power to domination, to institutionalized domination, to legitimized power (*pouvoir*), the lack of symmetry becomes obvious, even glaring. The normal manifestation of stabilized power is for one to command and the other to obey. When one commands the other obeys. In this sense, power can never be shared as wealth can be. Instead of the image of a marketplace with its competitors, there arises that of a hierarchy, of relations between superiors and inferiors, masters and servants.

Of course, the power of L over A, B, or C is not total in that although L prohibits certain behaviors or actions on the part of the objects of his power, A, B, or C can in turn restrain L in his freedom of choice. The plurality of areas wherein power is exercised leaves room for reciprocity: no one is pure subject or object. Furthermore, the foundations or instruments of power—wealth, prestige, strength, or position in the hierarchical power structure—do not necessarily all accrue in the same hands. The sociology of power makes an essential contribution to political science insofar as it permits the integration of the study of legitimate power with a broader analysis of the multiple structures of power.

Again, one must not be deceived by the resemblance between the distribution of income and the dispersion of power. The dispersion of power has many meanings. First of all, it designates what I would prefer to call the differentiation of social subsystems, from which the separation of the instruments of power normally results. The ruler (*Herrscher*) is no longer simultaneously king and high priest. He does not possess both arms and money. The holder of supreme power, in a legitimate social order, has to subordinate his will to constitutional laws. Second, leaders of a given sector—those who manage the means of production—must confront the leaders of another sector. The head of General Motors or of the United States Steel Company must discuss working conditions with union leaders and runs the risk of presidential intervention if he raises prices at an inopportune moment. Third, within complex organizations, authentic power relations do not correspond exactly to formal charts of authority (let us here define *authority* as the power possessed by an individual by virtue of his position in a social organization, without this organization necessarily being public: the head of a firm commands obedience but he holds political authority only in a broader sense, not in the specific meaning true in the political subsystem that culminates in legitimate power exercised by one or several in the name of all or over all). The sociology of organizations, industrial enterprises, public or private bureaucracies, and unions or political parties will seek to discover how decisions are actually taken, up to what point the official distribution of authority converges or diverges from the effective distribution of power (a distinction usually expressed by contrasting formal and informal power).

Without a doubt, power differentiation characterizes the structure of power as well as the entire social order. Differentiation, in the final analysis, just like the elementary relationship, at its outset, deprives power of any poetic quality. But does power, centralized and legitimate, exercised by some over all in the name of all, still deserve to be looked upon with a mixture of anxiety and respect if it becomes the stake of a competition carried on according to rules and exercised in conformity with written laws and with customs that sometimes restrict arbitrariness even more than laws? Furthermore, does not the citizen or observer of American society ask himself what he needs to fear more—the excess or the absence of power? If no one can decide against a few in the name of all, will not society be doomed to a fatal conservatism in a period of rapid change?

Must one take C. Wright Mills seriously when he condemns the power elite or give credence to political scientists who see the United States (or the Western democracies) paralyzed by a dispersion or absence of power?

Are theorists of international relations leading us back toward a soothing prose or a demoniac poetry of power?

☆ ☆ ☆

H. J. Morgenthau is commonly thought of as *the* realistic theorist of international relations; better than anyone else, he would seemingly have uncovered the power stakes that determine the rivalry between nations. The subtitle of his major work *Politics among Nations* is *The Struggle for Power and Peace*. At the beginning of the first chapter, Morgenthau writes: "The concept of political power poses one of the most difficult and controversial problems of political science," a difficulty brilliantly brought to light in the early pages of the book. His theory opens with the following proposition:

> International politics, like all politics, is a struggle for power. Whatever the ultimate aims of international politics, power is always the immediate aim. Statesmen and people may ultimately seek freedom, security, prosperity, or power itself. They may define their goals in terms of a religious, philosophic, economic, or social ideal. They may hope that this ideal will materialize through its own inner force, through divine intervention, or through the natural development of human affairs. But wherever they strive to realize their goal by means of international politics, they do so by striving for power. The crusaders wanted to free the holy places from domination by the Infidels; Woodrow Wilson wanted to make the world safe for democrary; the National-socialists wanted to open Eastern Europe to German colonization, to dominate Europe and to conquer the world. Since they chose power to achieve these ends, they were actors on the scene of international politics.[8]

In this paragraph, *power* is first the *immediate* goal of any actor on the international scene. At the end of the same paragraph, *power* has become the *means* chosen by these actors to reach their goals. What is meant by this notion (or reality) of *power*, simultaneously the *immediate goal* and the *universal means* of international politics? The definition comes a few lines later: "man's control over the minds and actions of other men." As for political power, it is the "mutual relations of control among the holders of public authority and between the latter and the people at large."

How can political power be the specific feature of international politics if it consists in a psychological relationship between those who exercise it and those upon whom it is exercised? Power, indeed, in these definitions, is tantamount to the influence or domination of one man over another, a characteristic of all societies rather than all politics. On the

---

[8] H. J. Morgenthau, *Politics among Nations: The Struggle for Power and Peace* (New York: Knopf, 1949), p. 13.

other hand, political power, defined as the relation between holders of authority and those upon whom it is exercised, is even less suitable for describing international relations since these do not involve a duality between holders of public authority and the people: each of these actors, within a territory, holds "public authority."

Morgenthau shortly recognizes that reference to power does not help to distinguish the specific nature of *international* politics. Thus, he writes: "The aspiration for power being the distinguishing element of international politics, *as of all politics*,[9] international politics is of necessity power politics."[10] No one will doubt, it seems to me, that international politics are power politics, if this concept, translated into English, means simply that international actors, like national ones, seek to acquire domination or influence over each other and that this universal aspiration entails struggle or competition. Indeed, no one has denied that all politics involve an agonic dimension though most authors have also pointed out the complementary dimension of agreement (or, to cite Auguste Comte's concept, of consensus). And when Morgenthau adds, "Would it not be rather surprising if the struggle for power were but an accidental and ephemeral attribute of international politics when it is a permanent and necessary element of all branches of domestic politics?"[11] one is tempted to answer, certainly, but do not those who reject, rightly or wrongly, the expression *power politics* give it another meaning? Can power be simultaneously the *immediate goal*, the *universal means*, and the *constant stake* of international politics without an inextricable confusion being introduced into our language and thought?

Political power as a psychological relation between those who exercise it and those who submit to it obviously does not constitute the "universal means" of actors on the international scene. Power, a relation between a dominating mind and another that experiences its ascendancy would seem to be the "universal means" of man acting upon man but not the specific means of politics, even less the specific means of politics between nations. Is power at least the immediate goal of all politics? One may recall the Japan of the Tokugawa era: it certainly did not have as its goal the exercise or the capability of exercising increased influence on the other actors on the international scene.

In fact, H. J. Morgenthau is clearly aware of the specific difference involved in international politics: "In international politics in particular, armed strength as a threat or a potentiality is the most important factor making for the political power of a nation."[12] And yet he would seem to be trying to convince his readers that international politics are power

[9] Italics added.
[10] Morgenthau, *Politics among Nations*, p. 15.
[11] Ibid., p. 18.
[12] Ibid.

politics, using an argument just the opposite of that used for centuries by all theorists; namely, "the essence of international politics is identical with its domestic counterpart."[13] And this identity grows out of the notion of the struggle for power, which can be traced back to the family: "The conflict between the mother-in-law and the child's spouse is, in its essence, a struggle for power."

Now, I believe that traditional thinkers—and Bergson in *Les Deux Sources de la morale et de la religion* continues the tradition—would have acknowledged, like Hobbes and Morgenthau, that the *struggle for power* is universal if one sees in this struggle the expression of a vital urge of human nature, but they would have maintained that the relations between members of a community are *essentially* different from relations between communities considered as a whole. Philosophers formerly contrasted the *state of nature* with *civil society* in the juridical meaning of this expression: nations have not given up their independence or their sovereignty to an institution with lawmaking or law-enforcing powers. Lacking courts and a police force, state live in the state of nature and the famous formula *Homo homini lupus* continues to apply to relations between these cold monsters.

At the same time, it is easy to see how the notion of power politics can be interpreted either as a definition of relations between states or as a doctrine of international politics (what they are or what they should be). To stress the specific differences involved in international politics is to reiterate that in the last analysis states remain the sole judges of their supreme interest and are free to draw the sword; whereas violence, that of the criminal or revolutionary, violates the legal order within states. It is true—and Morgenthau is correct on this point—that power is not to be confused with force and even less with the use of force. But the more the theorist of power politics disguises the real object of his study by comparing the struggle between states to the conflict between a mother-in-law and a daughter-in-law, the more the listener or reader must try to pierce the camouflage of such a formal conceptualization and to grasp, beyond the "relations between consciences," the struggle to maximize the means of power or the struggle that proceeds by the use of force.

Present circumstances, as a matter of fact, seem in turn to provide arguments to theorists of power politics and their opponents. Never before has it seemed so true that each state or bloc desires the death of the other. Never has the Hobbesian description of the state of nature between states so faithfully reflected reality.

> Yet in all times, Kings, and Persons of soveraigne authority, because of their Independency, are in continuall jealousies, and in the state and postures of Gladiators, having their weapons pointing, and their eyes fixed on one

---

[13] Ibid., p. 17.

another; that is, their Forts, Garrisons, and Guns, upon the Frontiers of their Kingdomes; and continuall Spyes upon their neighbours, which is a posture of War.[14]

However, at the same time, never have states been so solemnly committed to not resorting to force. Never have they concluded so many pacts apparently similar to those setting up the states themselves. Finally, never has the discrepancy seemed as startling between the capacity of the big powers to impose their will on the small ones and the instruments of power within the reach of each. The ratio tends to disappear between power—the relation between wills—and strength—the instruments of physical coercion. Each of the great powers must tolerate being flouted by a small power, the Soviet Union by Albania and the United States by Cuba.

Nothing, in this situation, contradicts the essential nature of relations between states as it has been expressed over the centuries. Today more than ever before the security of a state, its very existence, depends on its will and the means of force at its disposal: when the Soviet Union wished to install middle-range ballistic missiles in Cuba and the United States said *no*, two wills confronted each other, each armed with terrifying instruments of destruction, each threatening the other, neither accepting the verdict of a moderator or a tribunal. The relationship remained in essence what it had been: a Hobbesian state of nature, ballistic missiles replacing fortresses and cannons.

The relationship between wills or between states should never have been confused with the relationship between effective forces. The distinction is accentuated in our time by a development actually more logical than paradoxical because of the enormity of the means of force. The symbolic gunboat of the nineteenth century cannot be replaced by thermonuclear bombs: the United States has never attempted to coerce nonnuclear states by threatening to use nuclear arms. Around 1959-1960, at a time when the Soviet Union pretended, and the United States let it be believed, that the "East wind was prevailing over the West wind" and that missiles would give the so-called socialist camp a military superiority, Mr. Khrushchev did, in a vague fashion, brandish weapons of massive destruction. Finally, however, he, too, rallied to the American doctrine: nuclear weapons are reserved for defensive diplomacy and, militarily, could be contemplated only as a last resort.

Thus, mutual neutralization of thermonuclear devices consecrates the unchanging nature of the relations between states—no one knows what would happen if one state alone possessed such weaponry—but, at the same time, *this neutralization tremendously enlarges the diplomatic field, in which the ratios of military forces do not dictate the relationships be-*

[14] *Leviathan*, I, 13.

tween sovereign wills and do not determine the course of either diplomacy or history. Hegel, apropos of Napoleon, coined the striking expression *die Ohnmacht des Sieges.* Perhaps one should speak of *die Ohnmacht der Macht* if by *Macht* one means weapons of destruction.

These relations between states do not for all that become similar to social relations within states. The semiparliamentary debates in the United Nations add a new instrument to traditional diplomacy; yet, they do not signal a conversion to the rule of law. What is new is a clearer differentiation between levels of force. In the preatomic age diplomatic relations between states depended more on ratios of military strength since the use of such strength seemed less unlikely. But states by no means are giving up fighting nor are they submitting their struggles to rules of non-violence. They incite or encourage revolts, send weapons to opposing sides, with the so-called socialist states claiming as allies those who rise up against a capitalist regime and the United States, not without qualms, taking its chances here and there in the game of insurgence and counterinsurgency (a game for which it is not gifted because of very nature of the American political system).

Are international politics, as presently conducted, terrifying or reassuring, prosaic or demoniac? Depending on the moment, public opinion seems to swing from anxiety to serenity. One day it listens to Lord Russell or Sir Charles Snow giving humanity a few decades at most—from now to the end of the century—to choose between thermonuclear apocalypse or the promised land of a universal state (or peace on earth for states of ill will). This attitude is particularly widespread in Great Britain, where pacifism, popular in the period between the two world wars, is fed at the moment by the horror inspired by nuclear weapons. In France the opposite attitude predominates, a combination of two feelings: a sort of refusal to believe in the possibility of a monstrous war and awareness that in any case decisions of war and peace do not depend on individuals, perhaps not even on France or Europe.

Temporarily, since the Cuban crisis at the end of 1962, humanity is going through a period of calm.

The fundamental elements have not changed. What is new is the destructive power of armaments, the material strength at the disposal of those who hold power. What is not new is the fear the man in power inspires when one thinks of the consequences that *one* decision he takes might have. How else to dissipate that fear than to refuse to give one man the right and capability of taking decisions whose consequences would affect millions of people? It is thus that philosophers and legal scholars have reasoned while elaborating doctrines of the separation of powers. When sociologists observe a dispersion of social power, they are gratified, so much is the fear of man natural to man.

However, on the international scene, it seems that the concentration of power is reassuring and that the very idea of dispersion is terrifying. Pacifists join the leaders of the United States and the Soviet Union in condemning what all call "dissemination of atomic arms." The international system has always been oligarchic or, if one prefers, unequal: certain actors, called great powers, have dominated the scene and set the unwritten rules of competition. But the secondary actors have usually been irritated by their own subordination and have aspired to independence. Why do these secondary actors, more numerous than ever, seem reconciled to a dyarchy?

I see two reasons: the first is what I earlier called *die Ohnmacht der Macht*, the impotence of force, or again the disproportion between the potential for thermonuclear destruction and power politics (in other words, the two great powers are not able to impose their will by using their military strength diplomatically); the second is the widespread and rather superficial conviction that the risk of accident remains slender as long as two states alone are in possession of such monstrous instruments. If these two states have forbidden to all the use of regular armed forces and abstain from using nuclear weapons except to paralyze each other, this situation would seem after all to offer the least possible evil. Power is concentrated in a strictly limited area. It continues to inspire a certain anxiety because no man deserves to control such deadly weapons. It would seem as though the temptation to use them could only grow with the number of states possessing them. In this sense, the present dyarchy tends to conceal the fact that power is already dispersed in the full measure compatible with the essence of international politics.[15]

☆   ☆   ☆

Power politics, or rather the *Machtpolitik* of German thinkers, as a *doctrine* of diplomatic action was inferred from the *theory* of international relations. Since these relations were beyond the law, each actor kept the responsibility for his destiny and the freedom to draw the sword in defense of his supreme interests. *Machtpolitik* does not imply imperialism or the will to enlarge one's sovereign space or enslave foreign people, but the concept does have a nationalist ring and it inspired a pessimistic philosophy: states, in the throes of permanent competition, by turns peaceful and bloody, survive only through a "will to power" and prosper only in the arrogant affirmation of their independence.

The same concept in English, *power politics*, expresses the same theory yet teaches a completely different doctrine. The theory stresses the originality of international relations with respect to other social relations (the absence of a tribunal or police), but the doctrine that emerges goes, so to speak, in the opposite direction from that of the German doctrine.

---

[15] It is true that certain states reject this dyarchy, but the motive for this refusal seems less to be fear than independent will.

These American theorists stand in opposition to moralists and jurists who dream of submitting state sovereignty to law; they remind us of the eternal essence of these sovereignties (or, if they are theologians like Reinhold Niebuhr, of corrupt human nature) in order to warn theorists and statesmen of the dangers of saintliness, of ruthless wars, and Carthaginian peace under the guise of punishing states guilty of aggression and forever securing democratic values. American theorists of power politics tend usually toward moderation, realism, and pessimism; they recommend a return to the tried and true methods of diplomacy and condemn all crusading impulses: reversing the order of values of nationalist ideology, R. E. Osgood, a disciple of Morgenthau's, writes that any use of force for any other goal than defense of the national interest should be condemned.

In other words, *Machtpolitik* and *power politics* can, according to circumstances, suggest the romantic "grandeur" of states fighting for the domination of the world or the subtlety of a Talleyrand or the bourgeois wisdom of diplomats who would also say that a bad compromise is superior to a good court case (a bad agreement to a victorious battle).

If we move from international relations to power within states, power becomes both diffuse (who does not possess some?) and indeterminate (at most, each time A determines an act by B it reflects A's power over B). Used as a principle of analysis, in the case of American society, such a concept leads inevitably to a picture of reality relatively congruent with the democratic ideal. If one studies a complex organization (a large industrial corporation), a political party, a city, the army, Congress, or the presidency, the difficulty lies less in discovering the limits of power of those officially in charge than in singling out those responsible for decisions taken. In other words, the theory currently accepted goes in a direction of what one would call dispersion of power. Thus, simultaneously, more and more individuals have a feeling of impotence—they feel unable to influence the course of events—and are convinced that their destiny is being decided for them by obscure forces that no one controls or that are controlled only by cynical and hidden minorities. The violent reaction of a C. Wright Mills can therefore be understood—a reaction that attributes supreme power to an elite controlling the means of production, to generals, and in addition to politicians, all of this hidden by the game of politics and the clamor of the public arena.

Orthodox sociologists did not take Mills's book seriously, and their reaction would probably not have been different even if the theory of the power elite had rested on a broader factual basis and if its conceptualization had been less primitive. Not that the sociological theory of the *ruling class* is so contrary to facts, even in the United States, that it cannot be granted a certain credibility. But one must first grant the thesis of the dispersion of power its *obvious* component of truth (in view of the meaning of the word power).

The sociology of organizations or the sociology of local politics, at this level of investigation, arrives at results that no one can challenge (unless they proceed, with equal attention to detail, to investigations leading to opposite results). Power is not, in the sense here offered, a total, undifferentiated potential that someone might possess in all circumstances, with respect to everyone, whatever the area involved. If one wants to know "who governs" in the large corporation, in the municipality, in the factory, in the army, or in the state, one must set aside the metaphysical conception of power (*puissance*) as well as the juridical concept of power (*pouvoir*). When analyzing an organization, it is obviously not enough to know, on paper, the formal hierarchy in order thereby to know the distribution of power. The degree of autonomy—the number of decisions that an individual can take—is not necessarily proportional to the level at which each is situated in the hierarchy of the organization. Furthermore, the personality of an individual who has this or that position can increase or diminish the power normally reserved for the holder of that position. In other words, a certain dispersion of power results from the very nature of complex organizations. This dispersion could be questioned only by refuting the very hypothesis necessary to this type of analysis, namely, the *interchangeability of various decisions.*

Likewise, at the municipal level, R. Dahl has shown in a convincing manner what went on in New Haven, in what way some citizens were able, by taking initiatives, to favor some projects and cause others to fail, despite the passivity or indifference of most voters. He did not, at least in this fairly small community, uncover anything like a *power elite:* the same men are not powerful in all areas; those who hold the various reins of power do not form a coherent group; they do not plot conspiracies at night; they do not take over the city or the will of its citizens behind a democratic facade. But the decisions that have to be taken in New Haven are rarely the kind to revolutionize individual habits or the common destiny.

Would the same picture emerge if one studied under a microscope a town in the American South in which problems of segregation are acute? if one followed the decision-making process in the army, the State Department, or the Congress? Two factors are likely to affect any conclusions: the dispersion of power favors the resistance of the privileged just as much as it protects against the mythical tyranny of legislators feared by the founding fathers. At a certain level of social organization what counts is not the number of decisions taken by this or that person, or the number of cases in which A prevailed over B or B over C or C over A. What counts is the man who takes major decisions, irreversible ones, whose consequences can go on almost indefinitely and be felt by all members of the community. In the last analysis, the power of supreme authority, as Maurras would have said, is absolute and restricted. It does not reach out into all areas, but in its sphere it belongs to one alone and must not be divided: the president of the United States—commander in chief of the army, architect of war and diplomacy.

Western societies seem characterized by a dispersion of power when compared to Soviet societies. The latter inspire fear because of the apparent total power concentrated in the ruling authorities. The same men direct foreign policy and economic planning, interpret doctrinal truth, and decide on the distribution of incomes. Society is absorbed by the state and the state belongs to a more or less coherent minority. As long as this minority responded to the fear generated by a supreme tyrant, power reached a sort of grandiosity, demoniac and almost demented. It is well to wonder what an honest citizen can do to encourage or prevent the construction of moderate income housing on public lands, but it would be foolhardy to forget the demoniac power held by a single individual either when the decision taken at the top sends millions to their deaths or when there are persons endowed with the mysterious gift of carrying along their fellows, inspiring both fear and devotion, mesmerizing opponents and partisans, set apart by charisma and born to command. When such individuals succeed in taking power, humanity trembles with anxiety and hope.

The sociology of decisionmaking inevitably leaves in the shadow three aspects of the problem of power.

1. Any complex organization, private or especially public, from time to time makes historic decisions if one agrees to define these by the following traits: they are unique and irreversible and involve long-term consequences whose effects will be felt by all members of the organization.

2. These historic decisions are usually taken by one man (or a small group). However limited in its area of application, established power (*pouvoir*) remains absolute in the field of historic decisions (diplomacy and strategy).

3. The individual in power (of a stabilized, institutional, legitimate sort) sometimes has no other authority than that attached to his function. But authority also embraces the quality thanks to which one personality impresses itself upon others and obtains acceptance, fidelity, and obedience not by the threat of sanctions but by the very spell cast by his will. The merging of legitimate authority and personal authority lies at the beginning of great destinies, those who feed dreams of glory and memories of horror.

In the absence of these prestigious rulers, even historical decisions are taken or seem to be made according to democratic—therefore, prosaic and predictable—procedures. In this situation the individual in revolt against the regime or diplomacy of his country cannot help blaming a *power elite* for the persistence of an action he disapproves of. Actually, in the United States, the dispersion of power at the federal level will paralyze stray impulses for reform without shaking the principles of social order or modifying diplomatic action, whoever holds the principal executive positions. But what Mills attributed to an elite, and in the end to a conspiracy, could just as well have been ascribed to the dispersion of power and to the democratic nature of the regime.

A society such as the American remains faithful to its traditional ideologies and passions, to *free enterprise* and *anticommunism*, to the very extent that no one possesses an exceptional *authority*. It takes special circumstances such as the crisis of 1962 or the war of 1941 for the man in power, legitimately and legally, to become again, in the eyes of all, the man of destiny, the one who, by saying yes or no, by choosing the landing in Normandy over a landing in the Balkans, will decide for decades the destiny of tens of millions of men. In quiet times, pluralist societies and democratic regimes lean toward conservatism and preserve the rights (called privileges by those who oppose them) of a few minorities. Is conservatism the work of a *power elite* or the result of the *dispersion of power?* Is the question even meaningful? In a society wherein the ruling circles are in agreement on the principles of the political regime and the broad outlines of diplomacy, the rebel sees himself as the victim of a plot; whereas the empirical sociologist, a solid citizen, simply observes the complex interplay of ideas and interests. The conspiracy exists only through the resentment of the rebel, who refuses to see that the normal functioning of the regime is sufficient to guarantee the preservation of what he detests. One could speak of a conspiracy if the mass of the people shared the revolt of the heretic. But the heretic pledges himself to solitude as long as the hour of the revolution has not sounded. Revolution, like war, gives a chance to leaders whose potential power goes beyond the limits of democratic authority. As long as power remains bound by ties of tradition and legality, only great events make it prestigious or poetic. Subjected to rules and habits, it lacks the capacity to upset everyday life by the very fact of its dispersion.

☆   ☆   ☆

As long as humanity is divided into a multiplicity of sovereign units, one or a few men, here and there, will determine by irreversible decisions the lives of millions of their fellows. This power of life and death is expanded beyond measure by thermonuclear armaments. The more power is dispersed, the more individuals feel helpless to influence the social order and see it as frozen (it matters little whether this condition is believed to be caused by the dispersion of power or the conspiracy of the privileged classes). On the other side of the Iron Curtain, power terrifies because it embraces the whole community and is reserved for a minority. On our side, it is reassuring because it seems limited in its sphere of action and fought over by many claimants. But do not the masses preserve a nostalgia for personalized power, men of destiny who command and are obeyed because they have the vocation to rule and not because they have been invested according to a legal procedure? According to Hayek, in a free society laws and not men rule over men. If such is the definition of freedom, do men aspire to freedom?

7. Sociology and the Philosophy of Human Rights

In 1968, THE UNITED NATIONS celebrated the twentieth anniversary of the voting, by the United Nations General Assembly, of a universal declaration of the rights of man. *The United Nations*—the organization that gathers together almost all of the states of the world (with the exception of China and various fragments of divided countries) but not humanity itself. The declaration, now twenty years old, was not accepted by member states as a basis for either legislation or judicial principles; it remains, today as it was yesterday, a simple, solemn—and perhaps vain—enumeration of the rights that states judge theoretically desirable to grant to individuals but that they shun considering as imperatives: intentions or objectives, perhaps; higher commands to a positive right, before which the leaders of states themselves must bow, certainly not. No state, not even the United States, has given the rights of man, as proclaimed in 1948 by this assembly of states, a status equivalent to that of the amendments to the American Constitution on the basis of which the U.S. Supreme Court makes its decisions. This anniversary—the year of the rights of man—cannot fail to arouse mingled emotions in all of us. Is it an occasion for sadness or for joy? Remembrance of a lost hope or of a work in progress? Is the century of concentration camps, genocide, and the atomic bomb rendering the homage of vice to virtue when it evokes or invokes the rights of man? Or must we go still further: do the rights of man appertain to the philosophy of our time? In the eighteenth century, they were intrinsically linked to the rights of the citizen; personal and political rights were expressed in a liberal and universalist conception of the social order. In the twentieth century, they have been enlarged by economic

"Sociology and the Philosophy of Human Rights." Reprinted from *Ethics and Social Justice*, edited by Howard E. Kiefer and Milton M. Munitz, by permission of the State University of New York Press.

and social rights. Does this represent a progression, in conformity with the logic of the philosophy of the Enlightenment? Or perhaps, on the pretext that carrying bourgeois statements to their completion by including in them the rights legitimately claimed by socialists, have the drafters of the 1948 declaration confused incompatible ideas, brought together desirable objectives and categorical imperatives, without distinguishing between them, and, finally, emptied the concept of *right of man* of its content and significance by giving it an undefined extension?

These are the questions to which the following pages attempt to give an answer.

I shall take as a point of departure a comparison between the first French declaration of the rights of man (voted by the Constituent Assembly on August 23, 1789, accepted by King Louis XVI on October 3, and promulgated on November 3) and the universal declaration of the rights of man voted by the General Assembly of the United Nations in December 1948. In such a comparison, two propositions stand out very clearly: *in essence, individual, political, and intellectual rights have not changed in the period from 1789 to 1948;* jurists or statesmen continue to formulate them in the same terms (though not without some important exceptions). The 1948 declaration, however, devalues certain rights (such as property) that lie between political rights and economic rights, *and it includes a section on social rights to which the members of the French Constituent Assembly gave no thought.*

I shall distinguish four categories of rights in this French declaration—or perhaps it would be preferable to say four kinds of articles.

1. The first category proclaims the *egalitarian* principle. Thus, in article 1: "Men are born and remain free and equal in rights. Social distinctions can be founded only on common utility." Or again, in article 6: "The law must be the same for all, whether it protects or whether it punishes. All citizens, being equal in the eyes of the law, are equally admissible to all public dignities, places, and functions, in accordance with their capacity and without distinction other than that of their virtues and their talents." Pareto or an analytical philosopher would have no difficulty in demonstrating that "common utility," for lack of a precise definition, does not make it possible to determine what "social distinctions" are justified. By the same token, there must be a standard of measurement for "virtues and talents" in order for society to reconcile equality and social distinction in accordance with justice.

The egalitarian principle finds an equally strong and more precise expression in the 1948 declaration: "All human beings are born free and equal in dignity and rights." The term "dignity" belongs to the language of the twentieth century. It would be interesting to seek out its origin, the date on which it was incorporated into the classic terms (equality, liberty, and fraternity). Article 2 reinforces the egalitarian principle: "Everyone is entitled to all the rights and freedoms set forth in this declaration, without distinction of any kind, such as race, color, sex, language, religion, political or other opinion, national or social origin, property, birth or other status." Article 7 goes on to affirm equality before the law and explicitly proscribes all discrimination; whereas article 16 sets down the equality of man and woman in matters of marriage or divorce. And article 23, in paragraph 2, offers the following rule: "Everyone, without any discrimination, has the right to equal pay for equal work."

Obviously, formulas such as "Men are born free and equal in rights" cannot stand up under analysis ("to be born free," in the proper sense of the term, signifies nothing), but they draw their inspiration from a philosophy we will follow Parsons in terming *universalist*. Equality before the law excludes privileged classes and inherited status even though it does not forbid the transmission of fortune or prestige from one generation to another. In 1789, of course, this egalitarian or universalist principle took on a revolutionary dimension against the estates of the Ancien Régime since it included the "admissibility of all to all functions" and called for reform of the tax structure, of which article 13 ("A common contribution is indispensable to the maintenance of public authority and the expenses of administration. It should be equally shared among all citizens, in proportion to their abilities.") suggested changes that would bring about the liquidation of the fiscal privileges of the nobility and the clergy.

2. The articles that specify what I shall call, in Gaetano Mosca's phrase, *the democratic formula*, belong to a second category. Representative of this, in the 1789 declaration, are articles 3 ("The source of all sovereignty resides essentially in the nation") and 6 ("The law is the expression of the general will. All citizens have the right to contribute to its formation, personally or through their representatives."). Article 21 of the 1948 declaration echoes this position: "Everyone has the right to take part in the government of his country, directly or through freely chosen representatives. The will of the people shall be the basis of the authority of government; this will shall be expressed in periodic and genuine elections which shall be by universal and equal suffrage and shall be held by secret vote or by equivalent free voting procedures."

Even though both these declarations affirm the democratic idea, they differ in many respects. The 1789 declaration is manifestly directed toward limiting the action of the state (article 5: "The law has the right to prohibit only those actions prejudicial to society") and draws its inspiration from a philosophy enunciated both by Rousseau ("The law is the expression of the general will") and by Montesquieu (article 16:"No society in which the guarantee of rights is not assured nor the separation of powers determined can be said to have a constitution."). The 1948 declaration seems more precise in its categorization of the democratic idea and in its reference to free elections. The latter represent another institutional translation of the democratic idea—more democratic, from some points of view—than separation of powers. But article 12 of the 1948 declaration, which tends toward conservation of the rights to private life (". . . no one shall be subjected to arbitrary interference with his privacy, family, home, or correspondence") does not suffice to conceal the gap between the *nomocratic* state envisaged by the members of the Constituent Assembly of 1789 and the *modern* state, in which achievement of social and economic rights is accorded a higher place than respect for individual rights.

3. Individual and intellectual liberties belong in a third category. They are summed up in articles 10 and 11 of the French declaration ("No individual shall be molested because of his opinions, even religious opinions, provided that their manifestation does not disturb the public order established by law. . . . Free communication of thoughts and opinions is one of the most precious rights of man; every citizen, therefore, may speak, write, and print freely, with the exception of being answerable for abuse of this liberty in cases determined by the law."). Even the drafters of the 1789 declaration did not accept religious liberty without some difficulty and reticence ("*even* religious opinions"). By invoking disturbance of the public order brought on by a manifestation of opinion, the authorities of the time found a facile argument for limiting or prohibiting such manifestations. And in the same manner, the expression "abuse of liberty" authorizes all of the abuses of repression.

The 1948 declaration has a more liberal sound: freedom of thought, of conscience, and of religion (article 18); freedom of opinion and expression (article 19); freedom of peaceful assembly and association (article 20); and freedom of movement and residence within the frontiers of the state, freedom to leave one's own country or to return to it, and freedom to find refuge from the persecution of a foreign state (article 14). The representatives of the communist nations were among those who signed this declaration: should this be considered a cause for rejoicing or indignation; should it be regarded as an expression of their ideal—extending beyond the despotism of the present time—or of their contempt for these bourgeois rituals?

4. Last, the administration of justice forms the subject of a fourth category of rights: articles 7, 8, and 9 of the French declaration; articles 9, 10, and 11 of the universal declaration: "No man may be accused, arrested, or detained except in cases determined by the law, and in accordance with forms prescribed by the law"; nonretroactivity of laws (article 8 of 1789; article 11, paragraph 2, of 1948); and presumption of innocence until a verdict of guilt (article 9 of the French declaration; article 11, paragraph 1, of the 1948 declaration). The universal declaration adds more of a supplementary formula than the element of a new idea: "Fair and public hearing by an independent and impartial tribunal."

The historic, social, and political import of the French declaration was not lost on the most farsighted and most implacable of critics of the revolution, Edmund Burke. *Analytically*, the article stating that men are born free and equal in rights presents nothing of significance. *Historically*, it excludes hereditary distinctions of classes or estates. And, in the same way, other articles postulate the fact that functions prohibited to anyone by reasons of birth, fiscal exceptions inherited through tradition, and, in the final analysis, monarchy by divine right no longer exist. The author of *Reflections on the French Revolution* was therefore not mistaken when, in a certain sense, he encroached on the Marxist critique—though on a basis of judgments of value in only a contrary sense—and passionately denounced the revolutionary principles expressed in abstract language by the declaration of the rights of man. This declaration delivered the coup de grace to the hierarchic order of the Ancien Régime by stripping it of all legitimacy. The relative permanence of individual, political, and intellectual rights, between 1789 and 1948, can also be explained by its context of history. The Ancien Régime, as Burke conceived it, with its reciprocal obligations, from above as well as from below, the rights and the duties defined by the place of each individual in the fabric of society, had been carried away with no hope of return by the revolutionary agony, though traces of it remained in Europe and in France throughout the nineteenth century and even during a part of the twentieth.

In terms of *ideas as power*, individual rights triumphed and destroyed institutions founded on contrary ideas. To what extent did they triumph in a positive sense, favoring or permitting the construction of a society in conformity with their demands or their logic? Marxists and democrats of liberal inspiration give contradictory answers to this question. They reached agreement, sincerely or hypocritically, in drafting a declaration that adds economic and social rights to those rights whose four categories we have just summed up. But the democrat-liberals deny the fact that the democrat-socialists respect the individual rights of bourgeois tradition, and the democrat-socialists deny the idea that the society termed capitalist, whether bourgeois or liberal, achieves the economic and social rights that the authors of the universal declaration placed on the same level as those rights I shall call traditional.

Before attempting to interpret or comment on the dialogue between liberals and socialists relative to economic and social rights, I shall offer a few remarks on the changes that took place between 1789 and 1948 in the matter of the traditional rights whose four categories were previously summarized. The first such change concerns the right of property, and its significance must be readily apparent to any observer. In 1789, property formed a part of article 2, between liberty, on one side, and security and resistance to oppression, on the other. In 1948, it did not appear until article 17, following an article relative to the family and to marriage and preceding an article relative to freedom of thought, of conscience, and of religion. The right of property is expressed in ambiguous terms, acceptable both to the Marxists of the East and to the liberals of the West: "Everyone has the right to own property alone as well as in association with others. No one shall be arbitrarily deprived of his property." Even in a socialist regime, certain goods may be the object of individual appropriation: the Soviet representatives were thus able to subscribe to such an article without violating their own principles. But in spite of everything, the moral devaluation of the right of property between 1789 and 1948 emerges clearly from the comparison of the two texts. Even a text drawn up exclusively by the Western powers and intended only for the use of the West would have marked more or less sharply a decline of the right of property in the hierarchy of values.

Even more than this devaluation of one right, it seems to me that a comparison between the two declarations makes clear the decline of *all* rights, of the very notion of the rights of man. The French declaration termed the right of property an inviolable and sacred right, which the drafters of the 1948 declaration would never have written. But neither would the latter have written that the aim of all political association is the conservation of the natural and unalienable rights of man. Such a formula in effect implies a philosophy of *natural right* and *individualist finality*: in other words, a philosophy by whose standards reason is called upon to determine the principles of the social order, valid everywhere and at all times; a philosophy that states, as its final goal for the collectivity, a guarantee of the rights of individuals, with the individual appearing as the sole reality of which a society is composed and, simultaneously, as the ultimate finality of the collective organization. This individualist philosophy of natural right survives here and there, but it no longer receives the assent of either legislators or influential thinkers, even in Europe or in liberal America. It is true that in the United States the amendments to the Constitution resemble a statement of the rights of man and give form to abstract principles in the light of which the Supreme Court decides the questions submitted to it. It seems to me, however, that even in the United States the amendments, like the rights of man, are considered as the supreme rules of a particular constitution and not as universal principles. Even the members of the American Congress would hesitate to take up again the French formula by which the goal of all political association is the conservation of the natural and unalienable rights of man. Moreover, if we suppose that they were to consider such an article, it would not have the meaning it assumed in the eyes of its authors at the end of the eighteenth century: those authors, in fact, did not entrust to the state the responsibility for promoting what we call today economic and social rights. They were far more concerned with limiting the established power, that of the monarch at first and that of the state in whatever form it might later take. The rights of man have not disappeared but they have changed in character: henceforth, they define or characterize the condition considered proper for all members of the collectivity, to be assured if necessary through the intervention of the state. Obviously, it is a logical step from traditional rights, restated from declaration to declaration, to the rights termed economic and social.

Before taking up the significance and status of these economic and social rights, I should like to pose a question that inevitably provokes contradictory replies. Were the socialists, by which I mean the representatives of regimes of the Soviet type, sincere in their agreement to traditional rights or were they not? When half the drafters of the 1948 declaration rendered only lip service to traditional rights and the other half was unresolved as to the meaning of the new rights, is there any cause for astonishment at the fact that it remains, twenty years later, what it was on the first day, a sort of appeal to the leaders of governments, an exhortation to conduct themselves in a decent manner?

Of the four categories of traditional rights that we have surveyed, the Soviet regimes accept the first—that which translates into abstract language the idea of nondiscrimination and of equality before the law—without reserve. Not that the Soviets do not sometimes violate the rules of what Parsons calls *universalism;* but, then, Western nations do likewise. The claims of racial, ethnic, or religious minorities invoke violations, both overt and covert, of the universalism proclaimed as a maxim for any modern society.

The second category, that which translates the *democratic formula,* is not foreign to the authentic philosophy of the Soviet leaders and the peoples of Eastern Europe. The Marxist-Leninists claim to express and interpret the will of the masses. They organize ceremonies of acclamation and dub them elections, as if to symbolize their respect for a formula they do not apply but do not wish to repudiate and that they probably hope to apply some day, after having long held it in contempt. The Soviet leaders offer multiple justifications for the rule of the single party, sometimes as the vanguard of the proletariat, which is itself invested with a historic mission, and sometimes as the guide and representative of the entire people. Occasionally they put forth other arguments, such as the futility of elections in a country in which there no longer exists a class conflict or the greater importance of other forms of participation in the collective life, within the trade unions or the factories and farms. But no matter what the justification finally adopted may be, the spokesmen for the socialist regimes—of tomorrow if not of today—do not reject the democratic formula, the origin of sovereignty in the people.

The attitude of the Soviet regimes with regard to the rights of the third and fourth categories—personal liberties and guarantees of impartial justice—seems to me more ambiguous. At the present time, full and complete freedom of expression has not been granted to the citizens of any of the countries of Eastern Europe. At the very moment in which I write these lines, the liberalization toward which the leaders of the Czechoslovak government are striving is spreading terror in Warsaw and Moscow to such an extent that the men of the Kremlin are talking of a counterrevolutionary movement and of eventual action on the part of "fraternal countries" to reestablish or restore socialism. In the sense given to it by the Marxist-Leninists, socialism therefore seems to exclude liberty in the sense given to it by liberals of the entire world and even in the sense given to it by intellectuals and ordinary men formed under socialist regimes.

Marxist-Leninist socialism does not, however, reject freedom in the way fascism did. It does not deny personal and intellectual freedoms—which the Stalin constitution of 1936 itself solemnly recognized and promised to all—any more than it denies the sovereignty of the people, as amended by the guiding role of the Communist party. *Ideologically*, how is the reconciliation between principles and reality brought about? The arguments employed by the leaders of the regime oscillate between the old formula—no freedom for the enemies of freedom—and the pure and simple affirmation that the citizens of the Soviet Union effectively enjoy freedom of expression but have no desire to express anything that contradicts orthodox doctrine. To conclude on this point, let us say that the socialist regimes, which at first are ambitious to enrich formal freedoms by real freedom, have not, a half century after the October Revolution, succeeded in reestablishing the formal freedoms whose insufficiency Marx proclaimed but whose decay he would have indignantly denounced.

The same contradiction exists to an even greater degree with regard to the exercise of justice in the socialist regimes. Concentration camps, condemnation and execution of innocent people by the hundreds of thousands, confessions by individuals and groups accused of imaginary crimes: no regime before Stalin's had violated the rules of civilization relative to the administration of justice with so much brutality, so much cynicism, and such enormous, Kafkaesque lies. These violations of legality were attributed to the "cult of personality"—an expression devoid of meaning except in the sense that it imputes to a single man the responsibility for all of these crimes (and such an imputation, coming from Marxists, is not lacking in involuntary irony). The fact remains—and the evolution of the socialist regimes proves this every day—that here again adherents of the Soviet system subscribe to the fourth category of the rights of man without hypocrisy and without illusion. Without hypocrisy, since they are not actually opposed in principle to an administration of justice in conformity with the ideal of the bourgeois West of the eighteenth century. Without illusion, since they are well aware of the enormous gap between the reality and the ideal. Perhaps for that matter, I am wrong in according them such an ideal. Despite all else "socialist legality," which they invoke more and more frequently, differs in one essential point from liberal legality: the tribunals, even in theory, have no status of independence with relation to the state, which is itself in the service of the party. Insofar as minor offenses or common law crimes are concerned, socialist tribunals may come fairly close to tribunals of the liberal type; they are not, however, similar in matters of crimes against the state—and this concept remains curiously elastic.

Such then, avoiding all polemics, is the manner in which I see the dialogue between a Marxist-Leninist and a liberal philosopher of the rights of man; rights that even if he does not apply them, the Marxist does not deny. The Marxist respects the principle of universalism, common to all modern societies; he admits the democratic formula while asking a translation for it other than that of free elections; he does not definitively exclude intellectual or personal freedoms although he refuses the benefit of them to the citizens of today; and he preaches socialist legality but shows no sign of resigning himself to the independence of tribunals.

Does the dialogue between a philosopher of the rights of man, as they have been formed by tradition, and a champion of economic and social rights, take on a character comparable to that of the preceding dialogue? I do not think so. The liberal does not reject the majority of economic and social rights, either in principle or in fact. The crux of the debate seems to me essentially theoretical: can or should economic and social rights be placed on the same level as the rights I have termed traditional—those that express universalism, the democratic formula, and personal or intellectual freedoms?

Let us first recall the principle economic and social rights enumerated in the 1948 declaration: the right to marriage without "any restriction due to race, nationality, or religion." The declaration evens adds to this the equality of rights of male and female with regard to marriage and divorce by requiring the "free and full consent of the intending spouses." The declaration goes on to accord to each individual the right to social security (article 22), the right to work with the free choice of employment and an equal wage for equal work, the right to form a trade union or to belong to one, the right to repose and to leisure, the right to a "standard of living adequate for the health and well-being of himself and of his family," and the right to an education (and even to an obligatory and free primary education). And finally, in article 28, the declaration includes the following formula: "Everyone is entitled to a social and international order in which the rights and freedoms set forth in this declaration can be fully realized."

Does there exist a difference of nature or only one of degree between economic and social rights and the rights I have called traditional? In a little book entitled *Human Rights Today* (London, 1962) the English writer Maurice Cranston devoted some pages to this problem and concluded there is a difference in nature. Economic and social rights, he wrote, constitute, so to speak, the "lofty ideals" of societies; they cannot be assimilated to categorical or unconditional rights. Two criteria permit and justify the distinction between *rights* and *ideals:* the criterion that Cranston terms *practicability* and that of *paramount importance.*

In order for one person to have a right, it is necessary that another have a duty—that of respecting or of carrying out that right. Any state can normally assure the right to life, to freedom of expression, and to a trial of its citizens by a jury; however, the picture changes when it comes to the right to work, to social security, to paid vacations, to a decent standard of living, to obligatory and free primary education, and so on. The second criterion, which Cranston considers less decisive than the first, is easily applied to certain cases: "Holidays with pay are excellent too; they contribute to the greatest happiness of the greatest number. But they are not a matter of paramount importance, like freedom of speech or equality before the law."

Does this second criterion, which is obviously valid for the example mentioned, have general significance? Is there a distinction of decisive importance in whether criminals are subject to the decision of a jury rather than to that of a professional judge? And if so, for whom? There are fewer criminals than workers. If importance is measured in terms of the number of individuals affected, the jury has less importance than holidays with pay. But is it not true that since *anyone* may be called before a tribunal, *everyone* is interested in the administration of justice? Remembering the situation of Russia under Stalin, let us admit this to be true. Yet even in this hypothesis, it is a matter less of a difference of nature than of degree unless we are to define *importance* in moral and not in material terms. The equitable administration of justice concerns us all because it calls into question *values* that are essential in our eyes. It is no longer a question of happiness but of morality. But in this hypothesis, the criterion supposes something that remains in question: the radical distinction between the *universal rights* of man and the *objectives* that a social order should set for itself.

The first criterion, that of practicability, of a duty correlative to rights, is also applicable at first estimate once a choice has been made of economic and social rights, expressed with excessive precision, and personal or intellectual rights, expressed in vague and abstract terms. The governments of the poorer nations do not have the material means to assure a decent standard of living to all or to guarantee a free and obligatory primary education to all children. How can we accord to all men a right to which there is no corresponding duty since no one can be *held* to the accomplishment of what he *cannot* accomplish?

The argument loses something of its force if economic and social rights are formulated in other, less precise, less restrictive terms. In order for the concept to seem less sharp, it would suffice to suppress rights such as those to paid vacations (a desirable objective but not a universal right of individuals or an unconditional duty of government leaders or private businessmen) or to suppose that the right to work, to social security, or to a decent standard of living is understood with a reserve of common sense "in terms of the resources available to the collectivity." Why should the state not have the same obligation to assure to all the standard of living compatible with the wealth (or the poverty) of the nation as to guarantee freedom of expression or equitable administration of justice? In what manner does the capacity or the power to accomplish these goals differ from one case to the other?

The question may be raised that the rulers of the state do not manipulate the distribution of incomes in accordance with their own will since such distribution is probably subject to a determinism that economists strive to understand and that the government leaders find difficult to control. The objection is just, but are the leaders of governments any more capable, at all times and everywhere, of achieving the rights of man relative to freedom of expression and to the democratic formula? As soon as one attempts to measure the real capacity of the effective leaders of the regime, or the multiple pressures to which they are subjected, there no longer exists any radical difference between the economic order and the political order: the leaders do not completely control either the one or the other.

According to Maurice Cranston, "A human right by definition is a universal moral right, something which all men, everywhere, at all times, ought to have, something of which no one may be deprived without a grave affront of justice; something which is owing to every human being simply because he is human." In other words, Cranston is here taking up again, purely and simply, the philosophy of natural right, of the rights of man as men. It is in terms of this philosophy that he sets up a discrimination of principle between political and individual rights, on the one hand, and economic and social rights, on the other. The two criteria on which he supports his attempt to establish this discrimination are theoretically open to criticism. They are applicable to the simplest cases, to the most pronounced oppositions; they suppose essential discrimination but do not establish it.

The distinction between universal and categorical rights, on the one hand, and noble ideals, on the other, marks a return to the very philosophy whose particular character, in spite of its claim to universality, has been brought to light by all sociological thought and not simply by Marxism.

The French declaration of 1789 draws its significance less from its alleged universality than from the historic content that was both expressed and concealed in abstract formulas. Two centuries ago, the right to property was considered sacred; in our time, it has become relative, precarious, and revocable—a universal right on the condition that it is expressed in terms that condemn neither Soviet nor Western practice. Each regime determines what may be the object of individual ownership. Generally speaking, one could state the dilemma in the following terms: either rights attain a certain sort of universality because, thanks to the vagueness of their conceptual structure, they allow of any institution whatever; or they retain some preciseness and lose their universality. The accused has the right to be judged according to fair procedures, but in every period and in every society the definition of fairness of procedures is subject to substantial variations. And in the same manner, participation in the government of the nation remains a universal right only on the condition that the institutions through whose intermediary such participation becomes effective are no longer specified. The principle of nonretroactivity of laws was violated at the Nuremberg trials.

The radical discrimination between *universal rights* and *lofty ideals* is vulnerable to the criticism that, from Nietzsche to Pareto, by way of Marx, brings to light the ruses of the will to power and of personal (or collective) interest. The Marxist seeks to *unmask* the predominant concern for personal freedoms, which are vital to some, in the refusal to place economic and social rights on the same level as the rights of liberal tradition. Do those rights decreed as universal and categorical and that act primarily to the profit of some present a greater importance than social security or the standard of living, which are profitable to all? Is not the inequality of the statutes attributed to these two kinds of rights the conscious or unconscious expression of a policy, legitimate but not evident as such? A liberal policy is not a universally valid philosophy.

Last, the radical distinction between categorical rights and lofty ideals is open to a final and more serious objection. Whether it is a matter of universal suffrage, freedom of expression, or guarantees of impartial justice, the rights of man demand an established order. They have not been gained without violence and they are not respected in a period of violence. Revolutionaries forget or scorn them and they cannot always do otherwise. In certain circumstances, the transformation of the social order with a view toward achievement of *lofty ideals* demands a resort to force. In such a case, the means judged necessary—rightly or wrongly—to attain the objectives fixed by economic and social rights exclude respect for personal or intellectual rights, for a period of uncertain duration. The rights of these two categories are not *essentially* incompatible, but they become so under specific conditions.

Obviously, the experience of the twentieth century has taught us the perils of sacrifice of traditional rights in the hope of realizing the lofty ideals of economic and social rights. Formal freedoms—the right to the vote, personal freedoms—do not suffice to guarantee a decent existence to all; they can expand only in a climate of real freedoms or, if you prefer, on condition of assuring security and a decent standard of living to the greatest number. The Marxists are right to remind us of this point. But there is available to us in this respect a pertinent reply: the suppression of traditional rights, though proclaimed at the beginning to be provisional, may remain in effect for a long time, and the producer does not always gain in real freedom what the citizen loses in formal freedom.

However pertinent this reply may appear to me, it leaves intact a system of reasoning most often attributed to Marxism but renewed in one form or another by all sociological thought. Once the achievement of economic and social rights becomes the first order of business on the part of the state, individual rights, far from retaining their sacred character, become, or are in danger of becoming, obstacles to be surmounted in order to attain the true goal: reconstruction of the social order. Let us once again cite article 2 of the declaration of 1789: "The aim of all political association is the preservation of the natural and unalienable rights of man. These rights are liberty, property, security, and resistance to oppression." If the men who govern, even in the West, were to seek to define "the aim of all political association," what terms would they employ? Probably they would refer to equality (nondiscrimination), to economic security, and to the standard of living but certainly not to the preservation of the natural and unalienable rights of man. Thus, we return to the opposition already mentioned between a philosophy of rights, that tends to limit the power of the state, and a philosophy of rights confused with lofty ideals, which assigns to the state the crushing, perhaps unrealizable task of transforming the condition of man in society in compliance with certain requirements that were never manifested in the course of preceding centuries.

This ambitious, sociologically inspired philosophy prompts a refusal to hold strictly to the formal or the legal. Whether individuals are formally equal before the law signifies nothing so long as custom ignores this equality. In the United States, civil-rights legislation tends not only to compel the states or the schools to put into practice the equality that is an integral part of the American credo but also, on occasion, to curtail certain traditional rights—that of the landowner, for example—by prohibiting discriminatory practices. In this sense, legislation endeavors to alter custom.

Another example of this movement extending from the formal to the real can be found in the realm of education. The right to education signifies nothing if the family does not have the financial resources without which it would be unable to exercise this right. This necessity has already resulted in free primary and even secondary education and in the multiplication of scholarships. But, in a later stage, we might question the advantages derived from their environment by the children of privileged families. Might it not be advisable to reestablish real equality by doing away, insofar as possible, with advantages that are reflected in a certain correlation between educational results and the social origin of students? Until the present time, it seems that no government anywhere has given supplementary points to candidates coming from the lower classes of society. But such a project has nonetheless been evoked. Carried to its logical end, it could imply, in a case in which the number of places available for higher education was limited, a *numerus clausus* for the children of the upper classes, in order to augment the degree of social mobility.

But let us set aside these projects, which are utopian at the present time, and which we have evoked here solely to shed light on the passage from the formal to the material. In poor societies, particularly in Africa, even a primary education for all is probably beyond the resources of the states. Thus, it will be the responsibility of these states to select those who are to receive a basic education. Of course, such a process of selection has also been at work in the past, but within and by society. Experience of the exclusion of the majority has not, in the common conscience, threatened the principle of the right of all to education. An unexercised right remains a right. Neither society nor the state was held responsible for furnishing to all the material means of exercising their rights. Sociological thought dispels this illusion of good conscience. And at the same time, it is concerned less with limiting the intervention of the state in order to protect the individual than with strengthening the public powers in order that they may permit every individual to exercise his rights.

If we follow this line of thought, society or the state becomes, so to speak, the parties responsible for individual failures. American experts are already discussing formulas for a negative income tax: a contribution, by the state to taxpayers situated below the line of poverty, of a sum that would raise the lowest incomes to the level estimated to be the social minimum. Such a formula can be justified by reference to the classic conception of welfare payments or of social security. It seems to me, however, to have a more profound and richer significance: sociological thought has conferred on economic and social rights a status equivalent to that to traditional rights; it has transformed lofty ideals into unconditional imperatives. Some will conclude from this that the theory of the rights of man has become obsolete; others, that it has become richer. In both cases, the state appears as the victor since neither traditional rights nor economic and social rights restrict it or conceivably condemn it.

If necessary, the wealthy societies can move through the successive stages of this dialectic without sacrificing either the freedoms of the liberals or the ideals of the socialists. It is not the same in poor societies. So long as legislators and philosophers refrain from establishing a hierarchy between civil and political rights, on the one hand, and the conditions of existence of the masses, on the other, what reason is there for astonishment that the latter should be considered more important than the former? Can the underdeveloped countries make the passage from the formal to the material without recourse to violence? In a revolutionary age, do the rights of man represent something more than a luxury of wealthy nations?

What conclusion is suggested by this brief analysis? Should we rejoice at the extension of the traditional idea of the rights of man into the political and social realms? Or should we deplore the fact that these rights have lost or seem to have lost their unconditional, almost sacred character? Probably we should accept both conclusions at the same time: our period has the merit of having enlarged the number of subjects and the scope of objects of those rights that are stated to be universal, but this enlargement has been accompanied by a compensating depreciation.

In a certain sense, sociological thought has consecrated Nietzsche's, Marx's, or Pareto's criticism of eighteenth-century philosophy. It accepts historic relativism: every society organizes itself in accordance with a certain system of standards or values, which are termed culture. So-called universal rights merit this description only on condition of being formulated in a language so vague that they lose all definite meaning. Of what significance is the right to property so long as the nature of the property open to individual ownership remains undetermined? Of what significance is political liberty so long as, from one period to another, there are constant changes in the institutional translation of participation of all in the government of the nation? This historic relativism now becomes an integral part of the common conscience and, profoundly marked by the sociological mode of thought, entails the technique of "debunking," of bringing to light the interests or passions concealed behind these supposedly disinterested, passionless resolutions. But at the same time, the rights of man, stripped of their false universality, recover a historic significance, indeed a historic efficacy. The 1789 declaration cannot be separated either from the particular and nonuniversal philosophy that inspired it or from the bourgeois revolt against the Ancien Régime. Logico-experimental thought, to use Pareto's expression, has no difficulty in bringing out the nonlogical character of the rights of man, the variation of formulas between an abstraction too vague to authorize any judgment and a preciseness too great (separation of powers) to safeguard the claim to universality. But the analysis of historic origins restores dignity to the rights of man by stripping them of their illusory universality. Any declaration of rights appears finally as the idealized expression of the political or social order that a certain class or a certain civilization is attempting to realize. It at least permits condemnation of certain institutions (class distinctions) or affirmation of certain principles (non-discrimination), if not definition, on the basis of imperatives, of the precise composition of social organizations.

It is in this manner that the ambiguity of the universal declaration of rights of 1948 can be explained. That statement borrows from Western civilization the very practice of a declaration of rights; whereas other civilizations, though not ignorant of collective standards or of individual rights, are unaware of the theoretical and allegedly universal expression of such standards or rights. The Western origin of the declaration manifests itself, for example, in the articles relating to the family: nowhere is the free choice of a spouse or the equality of rights of male and female fully realized; in a strict sense, perhaps, Westerners play out for themselves the comedy of subscribing to such an ideal of the family. It is not the same thing for the men or women who belong to other cultures. If so many delegates from five continents did, in appearance, subscribe to this article relating to the family, it is because it, too, expresses, in an extreme form, the philosophy of individual rights or of the equality of all—a Western philosophy granted lip service as an exemplary pattern. Another ambiguity of the 1948 declaration stems from the attempt at synthesis between a Marxist-Leninist conception and a liberal conception. The juxtaposition of traditional rights and economic and social rights was and remains acceptable both to the representatives of the Soviet Union and to those of the Western nations. Both camps in effect have set themselves the objective of accomplishing these two forms of rights. But this reconciliation leaves unanswered the real question, that of the relative importance of the two forms of rights.

Among the liberals, some, like Cranston, would reserve for the traditional rights a status different from that of economic and social rights. Others accept the theoretical equality of status but maintain the decisive importance of traditional rights on the level of political strategy. Still others—and I am among these—reject both the one and the other of these discriminations, even if they personally accord a higher place to traditional rights; even if they judge that, for the moment, the regimes of political democracy offer the least defective synthesis between the double ideal of bourgeois liberalism and socialism.

Interpreted thus, the 1948 declaration, through its very ambiguity, fulfills the historic function of any such declaration: it criticizes modern society in the name of the ideals that this society has set for itself. According to sociological thought, all philosophy of natural right expresses and denies at the same time the society from which it emanates. It borrows its values and reproaches it for having betrayed them. The 1948 declaration, sometimes overly concrete, sometimes falsely universal, takes its place in the line of earlier declarations in spite of the defects natural to a collective work; it enjoins modern societies to maintain the traditional rights of individuals and to give to all the material means to make use of these rights. The drafters of the 1789 declaration wanted to limit the state in order to liberate the individual. The drafters of the 1948 declaration, without being fully aware of it, were prepared to give all powers to the state in order that it might guarantee security and a decent standard of living to all.

The declaration of rights criticizes positive right in the name of the ideal to which the society subscribes. The 1948 declaration criticizes liberal society in the name of the socialist ideal and socialist society in the name of the liberal ideal. Which of the two societies offers the greater resistance to this criticism? This is a question that each individual must decide for himself. In any event, to the pessimist who rightly deplores the excessive gap between proclaimed rights and respected rights, the optimist may reply that men have never before been so ambitious: they wish to conciliate the ideals of enemy regimes; simultaneously or at intervals, they grant their confidence to the state or they mistrust it. Through impatience or through necessity, they often prefer violence to reform. In a revolutionary age, is there cause for astonishment that states so often violate the rights of man or that the representatives of these same states pretend to retain both the memory of and the respect for these rights?

8. The Liberal Definition of Freedom

TOCQUEVILLE'S VOCABULARY IS NOT unambiguous and the two words he is most apt to use are neither rigorously defined nor always taken in the same sense. His thought, however, seems to me easily grasped.

In the majority of cases, Tocqueville uses the term democracy to signify a *state of society* and not a *form of government*. Democracy is opposed to aristocracy. The Ancien Régime was founded on the inequality of social conditions, on a nobility rooted in the soil; all true aristocracy is ultimately territorial because only the ownership of land assures the necessary continuity. It is true that in *Democracy in America* (vol. II, 2, chap. XX), Tocqueville conjures up an aristocracy that might arise out of industry: "Thus, as the bulk of the nation turns to democracy, the particular class that is engaged in industry becomes more aristocratic. Men become more and more similar in the one and different in the other, and inequality increases in the little society in proportion to its decrease in the larger one." But if it is true that, in the world of industry, a few very rich men are set against a very wretched multitude, Tocqueville scarcely believed that very rich men were capable of forming a true aristocracy or that the contrasts visible in the small manufacturing classes were the sign or symbol of what society as a whole would become. There are rich men, he wrote, but the class of rich men does not exist,

> for these rich men have no common spirit or aims, no common traditions or hopes. There are thus individual members but no body of membership. . . . Not only are the rich not solidly united among themselves, but one can say that there is no real link between the poor and the rich. . . . The manufacturer asks nothing of the worker but his labor, and the worker expects nothing from him but his wages. . . . The territorial aristocracy of past centuries was committed by law, or felt the obligation through tradition, to come to the rescue of its servants and alleviate their misery. . . . Between the worker and the master there are frequent relations

---

"La définition liberale de la liberté." Translated from the French and reprinted with authorization from *European Journal of Sociology*, V (1964), 159–89.

but no true association. I believe that, all things considered, the manufacturing aristocracy that we see rising before our eyes is one of the harshest that has ever appeared on earth; but it is at the same time one of the most restricted and least dangerous.

Democracy, as it is usually conceived by Tocqueville, is thus essentially a negation of aristocracy, the diasppearance of privileged orders, the elimination of distinctions between estates, and, little by little, a tendency toward economic equality, a uniformity in ways of living. The master-servant relationship disappears along with the aristocracy, as does the authority to command combined with an obligation to protect those who obey. Power and wealth tend to become disassociated. Work becomes a normal, honorable activity for each and all. Aristocracies disdain profit motivated work. In democratic societies the two ideas of work and gain are visibly united. Servants and the president both receive a salary. "He is paid to command as they are to serve."

If this is the most usual, as well as the most obvious, meaning that the term democracy takes on in Tocqueville, he is nevertheless conscious of the distance between the definition of democracy as a *state of society* and the traditional definition of democracy as a *type of regime*. Monarchy, aristocracy, democracy—according to the age-old classification, do they not mean the sovereignty of one, a few, and all? A text, discovered in Tocqueville's papers and published by J. P. Mayer in the second volume of *L'Ancien Régime et la Révolution*, reveals how hesitant Tocqueville was to break the link between the *social* and the *political* definition of democracy.

> It will be claimed that a country governed by an absolute prince is a democracy because he will govern through laws and amid institutions that are favorable to the condition of the people. His government will be a democratic government. He will form a democratic monarchy. Now the words democracy, monarchy, democratic government can mean only one thing according to the real meaning of the words: a government in which the people play a more or less significant role. Its meaning is intimately linked to the idea of political freedom. To give the title of democratic government to a government in which there is no political freedom is a palpable absurdity in terms of the natural meaning of the words. What has brought about the adoption of false or in any case obscure expressions is: 1) the wish to provide the multitude with illusions, the words democratic government having always enjoyed a certain success with it; 2) the genuine difficulty of finding a word to express an idea as complex as the following: an absolute government, in which the people have no part in running affairs but in which the upper classes enjoy no privileges and laws are drawn up in such a way as to favor as much as possible the people's well-being.[1]

---

[1] *Oeuvres complètes*, vol. II, 2, p. 199; hereafter cited *O.C.*

This fragment appears in the chapter that Tocqueville had planned to devote to the work of the Constituent Assembly. And, he writes, "I never examine the system of laws of the Constituent Assembly without finding the twin characteristics of *liberalism* and *democracy*, which brings me back bitterly to the present." At the time he wrote these lines, he was self-exiled from French officialdom because of the coup d'état by which Louis Napoleon restored the empire. An imperial regime is neither aristocratic nor democratic. It is a despotism superimposed on a society with democratic tendencies. Ernest Renan as well, after the defeat of 1870, was to raise the issue of democracy or of a false conception of democracy. As against the abuse of the word democracy by spokesmen of a despotic regime, Tocqueville recalls that the society to which the Constituent Assembly aspired would have been free as well as democratic, "not a military society but a civilian one." The chapter entitled "Les Idées de 1789," on the Constituent Assembly, exalts "the soundness of its general views, the true grandeur of its purposes, the generosity, the loftiness of its sentiments, *the admirable union of a taste for freedom and for equality that it revealed.*" Thus, the fragment itself is integrated into Tocqueville's general scheme of things.

In any case, yesterday's aristocracy is condemned and, even in a despotic regime, laws could be made in such a way as to favor as much as possible the well-being of the people. But if modern societies, even despotic ones, preserve certain democratic traits, the profound inspiration of the French Revolution as well as the American is to join *democracy* and *liberalism, equality* and *freedom*.

But what meaning does Tocqueville give to the word freedom, a word so widely used and so equivocal, since in the name of freedom men in every period have claimed powers they feel unjustly deprived of and have protested against real oppression? The clearest definition of freedom that Tocqueville provides can be found, it seems to me, in his essay "L'Etat social et politique de la France," published in 1836.

> According to the modern notion, the democratic notion, and I dare say the correct notion of freedom, it is assumed that each man has received from nature the gifts necessary to conduct his affairs and carries at birth an equal and indefeasible right to live independently from his peers in everything that relates only to himself and to regulate his own destiny as he sees fit.[2]

Thus defined, freedom is both negative and undetermined—negative in the sense that it is expressed through independence, the choice by each of his own destiny; undetermined in the sense that it remains to be seen how far that which "relates only to himself" goes for each. This freedom with relation to others—what, in English, is called *freedom from*—also has, according to other texts, a positive content: it is *freedom in view of* or

---

[2] *O.C.*, vol. II, 1, p. 62.

freedom to. Independence-freedom, what Montesquieu would have called security or absence of the arbitrary, can be genuinely realized only in properly political freedom, that is, participation by the citizen in the administration of local affairs and the care of public matters. Now, political freedom, which despotism, even when it claims to be democratic, eliminates, is in Tocqueville's eyes the supreme value. This passionate attachment to political freedom can certainly be seen as personally motivated. But he himself gives a properly sociological justification to the value he attaches to political freedom, specifically in democratic societies.

In democratic societies,

> the desire to become rich at any cost, the taste for business, the love of profit, the quest for well-being and material joys are thus the most common passions. These passions easily spread to all classes, penetrate into those very ones that had hitherto been most inhospitable to them, and would soon enervate and degrade the whole nation if nothing were to stand in their way. Now it is of the essence of despotism to encourage and extend them.

And, a little further, in this same preface to *L'Ancien Régime et la Révolution*, he writes again:

> Only freedom is capable of tearing them away from the cult of money and the petty daily cares of their personal affairs to make them aware at all times of the nation above and beside them; it alone replaces from time to time the love of comfort with higher and more energetic passions, gives ambition greater goals than the acquisition of wealth, and creates the light that makes it possible to perceive and judge the vices and virtues of men.

And finally:

> I am not afraid to state that the common level of hearts and minds will never cease to degenerate as long as equality and despotism are joined in them.

Though Tocqueville speaks of freedom in the singular, and not freedoms in the manner of the counterrevolutionaries, he clearly enumerates, here and there, the various aspects of freedom: "the ability of a nation to govern itself, the guarantees of the law, freedom of thought, speech, and writing"—in other words, intellectual and personal freedoms, the protection the law provides against the arbitrary, and finally the participation of citizens, through their elected representatives, in public life. It is the sum total of these freedoms that constitutes, in his eyes, *freedom*, alone capable of raising egalitarian societies, mainly concerned with material well-being, to greatness.

In this passion for freedom, it is not only the sociologist who is speaking, it is also the man, and if I may say so, the aristocrat, the descendant of a great family. In the essay "L'Etat social et politique de la France avant et depuis 1789," from which we took his definition of the modern notion of freedom, Tocqueville also analyzes the aristocratic notion of freedom:

> One can see in it the use of a common right or enjoyment of a privilege. To seek to be free in one's actions or in some of one's actions not because all men have a general right to independence but because one possesses in oneself a particular right to remain independent, such was the manner in which freedom was understood in the Middle Ages and the way in which it has nearly always been understood in aristocratic societies. . . . This aristocratic notion of freedom produces in those who have inherited it an exalted opinion of their individual value, a passionate taste for independence. It gives to selfishness a singular power and energy. Held by individuals, it has often led men to the most extraordinary actions; adopted by a whole nation, it has created the greatest peoples that have ever existed. The Romans believed that they alone of the whole human race had the right to enjoy independence, and it was much less from nature than from Rome that they believed they derived the right to be free.[3]

This freedom, privilege of the aristocracy, belongs to an irretrievable past, and in 1836 Tocqueville used the word *juste* for the modern notion of freedom—the rights of all. In 1856, twenty years later, without going back on his historic judgment, he permitted the nostalgia for aristocratic freedom that survived in his soul to appear[4] and in addition revealed the link, in his very person, between the aristocratic tradition and a passionate attachment to democratic freedom.

> Nearly all the guarantees against abuses of power that we possessed during the thirty-seven years of representative government are highly prized by [the aristocracy]. One feels, in reading its *cahiers*, amid its prejudices and failings, the spirit and a few of the great qualities of the aristocracy. It is forever to be regretted that instead of bending this nobility to the service of the law, it was lopped off and uprooted. By this action the nation was deprived of a necessary part of its substance and a wound was inflicted on freedom that will never be healed.

This text should not be interpreted as an admission of fidelity to his class, inadvertently made by the sociologist of democracy. It is the sociologist who adds to independence-freedom and participation-freedom a third term, more difficult to define in depth, perhaps, but still more indispensable to the precise understanding of freedom: the nature of the relations between he who commands and he who obeys.

> However subservient the men of the Ancien Régime were to the will of the king, there was a sort of obedience that was unknown to them: they did not

[3] *O.C.*, vol. II, 1, p. 62.
[4] In chapter XI of Book II of *L'Ancien Régime et la Révolution*, entitled "De l'espèce de liberté qui se rencontrait sous l'ancien régime et de son influence sur la Révolution," *O.C.*, vol. II, 1.

know what it was to submit to an illegitimate and contested power, one scarcely honored, often despised, but accepted because it is useful or can inflict harm. This degrading form of servitude was always unknown to them.

And a little later:

For them, the worst evil of obedience was constraint; for us, this is the least. The worst is the servile feeling that creates obedience.

One can speculate, reading this text, about the foundation of freedom in America, where society was so to speak spontaneously democratic. In fact, there is no contradiction. The privilege-freedom known to the Ancien Régime gave rise to "profound audacious geniuses," but it was in itself "unregulated and unhealthy, it prepared the French to topple despotism, but it made them less capable than any other people, perhaps, to form in its place the free and peaceful empire of laws." On the contrary, in America, free institutions were born with society itself and had as a foundation not the privileged and arrogant spirit of the aristocracy, but a religious spirit. Accepting the laws, the citizen obeys a power he respects, whoever may hold it temporarily. If he opportunistically obeys an illegitmate regime, the citizen is degraded into a subject. Or again, as we would say today, he is a consumer, anxious about his well-being, not a citizen, concerned about and responsible for public affairs.

Between the obedience of the aristocrat to a sovereign he venerates and the obedience of the citizen to laws he has helped make, the gap is enormous. Each of these two kinds of obedience characterizes a society. But both are compatible with freedom because they are consistent with recognized legitimacy. Obedience is servitude when power is illegitimate and despised and has no other principle,[5] as Montesquieu would have said, than fear or conformity.

Thus emerges the theory of liberal democracy, in many respects different from the ancient republic that Montesquieu had taken as a model of democracy. Work, commerce, industry, the desire for profit and well-being, and the pursuit of happiness are thus no longer in contradiction with the principle of democracy.

The Americans are not a virtuous people, and yet they are free. This does not prove absolutely that virtue, as Montesquieu believed, is not essential to the existence of the republic. Montesquieu's idea must not be construed narrowly. What this great man meant is that republics could continue only by society acting upon itself. What he meant by virtue is the moral power that each individual exercises upon himself and that prevents him from violating the rights of others. When the triumph of a man over temptations is the result of the weakness of the temptation and calculated self-interest, it does not constitute virtue in the eyes of the moralist; but it enters into the idea of Montesquieu,

[5] In Montesquieu's sense, that is to say, the sentiment by which a particular regime is able to prosper.

who was speaking of the effect much more than of the cause. In America, it is not virtue that is great, but temptation that is small, and this comes to the same thing. It is not altruism that is great, it is self-interest that is well understood, and this again comes nearly to the same thing. Montesquieu was thus right though he was speaking of ancient virtue, and what he says of the Greeks and Romans applies to the Americans.[6]

Perhaps a few passages, borrowed from the second part of *Democracy,* will serve as a useful commentary on this analysis of American virtue:

> The passion for material well-being is essentially a middle-class passion and grows and spreads with this class; it becomes preponderant with it. It is from there that it enters the upper reaches of society and descends to the mass of the people.[7]

And, in the following chapter, the thought is completed:

> This particular taste that men of democratic times have for material joys is not naturally opposed to order; on the contrary, it often needs order to be gratified. Neither is it an enemy of regular habits since good habits are useful to public tranquility and encourage industry. Often it even comes to be combined with a kind of religious morality. One wants to be as well off as possible in this world, without renouncing one's chances in the other.[8]

This middle-class society, opulent, democratic in spite or because of a universal concern for work and well-being, inspired mixed feelings in the descendant of the old nobility. But he saw in it the inevitable future, and it remained in his eyes worthy of respect as long as it respected freedom, which was its origin, its foundation, its very soul, not

> the sort of corrupted freedom whose use is common to animals and man and that consists in doing whatever one pleases. This freedom is the enemy of all authority; it cannot accept any rules; with it we become inferior to ourselves; it is the enemy of truth and peace; and God felt it necessary to rise against it! But there is a civic and moral freedom that finds its strength in unity and that the mission of power itself is to protect: it is the freedom to do without fear everything that is right and good.[9]

Logically, this definition is so to speak a "vicious circle." We must be free to do what is "right and good." But who determines what is right and good? These formulas take on precise meaning only in the historical con-

---

[6] This fragment, found in Tocqueville's notes, was published by J. P. Mayer in the *Nouvelle Revue française* of April 1, 1959, and in the *Revue internationale de philosophie* (1959), number 49.

[7] *O.C.*, vol. I, 2, part 1, chap. X, p. 135.

[8] *O.C.*, vol. I, 2, part 1, chap. XI, p. 138.

[9] Speech by the magistrate Winthrop, as cited by Tocqueville, *O.C.*, vol. I, 1, part 1, chap. II, p. 41.

text in which each person knows what the state has a right to demand or forbid and, by the same token, what the individual has a right to claim as the private sphere that he alone rules.

Among sociologists of the past century—for he deserves this title as much as Auguste Comte—Tocqueville offers a triple originality. He defines modern society not by industry, in the manner of Auguste Comte, or by capitalism, in the manner of Marx, but by *equality of conditions*, that is, by democracy in the social sense of the term. On the other hand, in contrast to Comte and Marx, he is, with regard to history and the future, a *probabilist*. He does not predict an irresistible movement toward a specific regime, positivist or socialist. Tocqueville states, as obvious, that certain movements will prolong themselves, that certain institutions are dead (the landed aristocracy), others inevitable (the equalization of conditions). But there is no adequate way of determining, in Max Weber's words, the political regime from the democratic state of society. The political superstructure may be despotic or liberal; multiple circumstances, traditions, and living men determine which of the two alternatives will carry the day. Finally—and he has been criticized many times for this originality—*he refuses to subordinate politics to economics*, either to prophesy, in the manner of the Saint-Simonians, that the administration of things will replace the rule of men or, in the manner of Marx, to confuse the socially privileged class with the politically dominant one. Not that Tocqueville was unaware of social classes. It is enough to reread *L'Ancien Régime et la Révolution* to discover a class analysis of French society on the eve of the revolution: "One can no doubt object to what I am saying by bringing up individuals; I am speaking of classes; they alone must occupy history."[10] And, just as clearly, in a fragment from the second part of *L'Ancien Régime*, this description of the Third Estate that could well illustrate the Marxist conception of classes:

> We see in this entire first part that a complete unity exists in the whole body of the Third Estate because class interests, class relations, conformity of position, uniformity of grievances in the past, and the discipline of the guild hold strongly together and carry forward in unison the most dissimilar minds, those very ones who least of all agree on the further road to follow and on the goal to achieve in the future. One is first and foremost of one's class before being of one's own opinion.[11]

But these texts relate to the France of the Ancien Régime, whose tragedy, in Tocqueville's eyes, was precisely the separation and inequality of classes.

> The division into classes was the crime of the old monarchy and became later its excuse. . . . When the different classes that formed the society of ancient

---

[10] *O.C.*, vol. II, 1, chap. XII, p. 170.

[11] *O.C.*, vol. II, 2, chap. I, text note 8.

France came into contact, sixty years ago, after having been isolated so long by so many barriers, they touched at first only at their most sensitive spots and met only to tear each other to pieces. Even in our day, their jealousies and hatreds survive.[12]

In other words, it is the Ancien Régime rather than modern society that appears to Tocqueville to be divided into classes. The rich, in the United States, do not constitute the equivalent of an aristocracy; a manufacturing aristocracy will never be a true aristocracy. It is to the extent that the distinctions of the Ancien Régime survive that inequalities of wealth take on the appearance of classes in modern society. In this sense, Tocqueville had, it seems to me, a premonition of the ambivalence in the Marxist conception of classes, the synthesis between the orders of the Ancien Régime and the inequalities characteristic of any industrial society. The middle-class society of prosperity is assuredly stratified. But is it divided into classes as the capitalist society observed by Marx at the start of the last century seemed to be and in which inequalities in economic functions and income reproduced, while accentuating them, the distinctions between the former estates?

☆   ☆   ☆

Tocqueville elaborated his system of thought between 1830 and 1840, if one dares apply the term system to an author whose fundamental ideas were few, simple, and profound and who multiplied their illustrations and applications by the observation of facts. It is in the following decade, 1840–1850, that Karl Marx went through the stages of an intellectual journey that was to lead him to a doctrine today hailed by a third of mankind—a billion human beings—a doctrine that it is fair to say has shaken up the world, inflicting on itself a glaring contradiction inasmuch as it has denied the influence of ideas, an influence of which its own destiny offers a shining example.

Marx himself was convinced, from the start, that democracy is the truth of our time and even the definitive truth, one that illuminates itself just as it illuminates whatever is opposed to it.

> Democracy is the solved *riddle* of all constitutions. Here, not merely *implicitly* and in essence but *existing* in reality, the constitution is constantly brought back to its actual basis, the *actual human being*, the *actual people*, and established as the people's *own work*. The constitution appears as what it is, a free product of man.[13]

---

[12] *O.C.*, vol. II, 1, chap. X, pp. 166–167.

[13] Karl Marx, "Contribution to the Critique of Hegel's Philosophy of Law," Karl Marx and Frederick Engels, *Collected Works* (London: Lawrence & Wishart, 1975), vol. 3, p. 29; hereafter *C.W.* Aron's French quotation is from the French translation of Karl Marx, "Kritik des Hegelschen Staatsrechts," MEGA I 1/1 *Oeuvres philosophiques* (Paris: Costes, 1935), vol. 4, p. 67; hereafter *O.P.*

Outlining a comparison that holds a primary place in his thought during his formative years, Marx wrote:

> Just as it is not religion which creates man but man who creates religion, so it is not the constitution which creates the people but the people which creates the constitution. In a certain respect the relation of democracy to all other forms of State is like the relation of Christianity to all other religions. Christianity is *the* religion, the *essence* of religion, deified man as a *particular* religion. Similarly, democracy is the *essence of all state* constitutions—socialised man as a *particular* state constitution. Democracy stands to the other constitutions as the genus stands to its species; except that here the genus itself appears as an existent, and therefore as one *particular* species over against the others whose existence does not correspond to their essence.[14]

Is there any need to underscore the difference in style between Tocqueville and Marx and also the difference in meaning given by the one and the other to the same word, democracy? Equality of conditions, representative government, personal and intellectual freedoms, this is liberal democracy, the full realization of modern society according to Tocqueville. Democracy, according to Marx, is the secret truth, the resolved enigma of all constitutions because the people are the source, the creators of all political superstructures, and because man arrives at the truth about himself, at a consciousness of that truth, only by seeing himself as master and possessor of all the institutions within which he has, over the centuries, allowed himself to become alienated. But if the end of history is, in this sense, democracy, the sovereignty of the entire people, it is also the end of the duality between society and the state, between private and public life. Real democracy, true democracy, will not exhaust itself in episodic participation in public life through elections or elected representatives; it will be achieved only when the worker and the citizens are one, when the life of the people and the political empyrean come together.

> Up till now the *political constitution* has been the *religious sphere*, the *religion* of national life, the heaven of its generality over against the *earthly existence* of its actuality. . . . *Political life* in the modern sense is the *scholasticism* of national life.[15]

Let us try to translate this Hegelian language into a language accessible to nonphilosophers. The man of civil society, involved in work, industry, and commerce, remains locked in himself, in his particularity. As a citizen he participates in the universality of the state, but this participation remains marginal to his private, concrete life as a worker. Political citizenship is, in relation to the activity of the worker, like the destiny of the immortal soul in Christianity in relation to our miserable life on this earth. These two separations, these two alienations are

[14] *C.W.*, vol. 3, pp. 29–30; *O.P.*, pp. 67–68.
[15] *C.W.*, vol. 3, p. 31; *O.P.*, pp. 70–71.

parallel: the duality of the profane and the sacred, like that of the private and the public, has as its origin man's failure to accomplish his humanity.

Two famous texts, taken from Marx's youthful works, will illustrate the theme of these two dualities, this double alienation:

> The *political revolution* resolves civil life into its component parts, without *revolutionizing* these components themselves or subjecting them to criticism. It regards civil society, the world of needs, labour, private interests, civil law, as the *basis of its existence*, as a *pre-condition* not requiring further substantiation and therefore as its natural basis. Finally, man as a member of civil society is held to be man in *the proper sense, homme,* as distinct from the *citoyen,* because he is man in his sensous, individual, *immediate* existence, whereas *political* man is only abstract, artificial man, man as an *allegorical, juridical* person. The real man is recognised only in the shape of the *egoistic* individual, the *true* man is recognised only in the shape of the *abstract citizen.*[16]

In other words, a purely political revolution, one that does not modify the social infrastructure, does not allow man to realize himself because it confuses the genuine man with the worker locked into his particularity and because man is in conformity with his essence; that is to say, socialized man, a participant in universality, appears only in the form of an abstract citizen. The *civil society*[17] of workers will never be reconciled to the empyrean of politics as long as it is given over to the arbitrariness of desires, the anarchy of selfishness, the struggle of all against all. Similarly, the duality of the profane and the sacred, of society and religion, will last as long as man, failing to realize his essence on this earth, projects it into an illusory transcendence.

> This state, this society, produce religion, an *inverted world consciousness,* because they are an inverted world. . . . It is the *fantastic realisation* of the human essence because *human essence* has no true reality. The struggle against religion is therefore indirectly a fight against *the world* of which religion is the spiritual *aroma.*[18]

To free man from religious illusion, to free man from the separation between the worker and the citizen, this double liberation is impossible as long as the "weapon of criticism" and the "criticism of weapons" do not reach to the roots, that is to say, to the economy. Religion is the image of a topsy-turvy world and politics is separated from the real life of one and all because work itself is alienated since the private ownership of the means of production makes the worker the slave of a master and the master himself the slave of things, of merchandise and the market. Human eman-

---

[16] Marx, "On the Jewish Question," *C.W.,* vol. 3, p. 167 ("Zur Judenfrage," *O.P.,* pp. 200–201).

[17] In German, *bürgerliche Gesellschaft.*

[18] Marx, "Contribution to the Critique of Hegel's Philosophy of Law," p. 175 ("Zur Kritik der Hegelschen Rechtsphilosophie," *O.P.,* p. 84).

cipation, beyond religion and politics, can be accomplished only by an economic and social revolution thanks to which

> the real, individual man re-absorbs in himself the abstract citizen, and as an individual human being has become a *species being* in his everyday life, in his particular work, and in his particular situation, only when man has recognized and organized his *"forces propres"* as *social* forces, and consequently no longer separates social power from himself in the shape of political power.[19]

That Marx does invoke freedom and is truly intent on the liberation of man is beyond dispute. He radically criticizes religion but

> the criticism of religion ends with the teaching that *man is the highest being for man*, hence with the *categorical imperative to overthrow all relations* in which man is a debased, enslaved, forsaken, despicable being.[20]

The young Marx did not renounce the aspirations and ideals of the liberal movement, of which the Revolution of 1848 was both expression and failure. But the radicalism of his critique and the goals proposed by this radical critique take us into a world profoundly foreign to that of liberal democracy. Wherein lies the originality of the revolution dreamed by the young Marx?

> Communism differs from all previous movements in that it overturns the basis of all earlier relations of production and intercourse, and for the first time consciously treats all naturally evolved premises as the creations of hitherto existing men, strips them of their natural character and subjugates them to the power of the united individuals.[21]

What is new is not so much the idea of an upheaval of economic conditions, of the means of production and exchange, as the refusal *to hold any of the given facts of the social order as fatal, eluding human control.* It is through Promethean arrogance, through confidence in the capacity of united men to become masters of nature and society, that Marxist inspiration differs in essence from liberal inspiration and that it is still today, as much or more than the latter, the soul of industrial societies, on one side or the other of the Iron Curtain.

From the very start, Marx did not want to return to the conquests of the French revolution; he wanted to complete them. Democracy, freedom, equality—these values appeared obvious to him. What made him indignant was that democracy should be exclusively political; that equality should go no further than the voting booth; that freedom, proclaimed by the constitution, should not prevent the enslavement of the

---

[19] Marx, "On the Jewish Question," p. 168.

[20] Marx, "Contribution to the Critique of Hegel's Philosophy of Law," p. 182; *O.P.*, p. 97.

[21] Marx, "The German Ideology," *C.W.*, vol. 5, p. 81 ("Die Deutsche Ideologie," *O.P.*, p. 231).

proletariat or the twelve-hour workday for women and children. Though the texts we have cited are written in a philosophic idiom, their meaning is as precise as the indignation is sincere. If Marx dubbed political and personal freedoms "formal," it was not that he despised them, it was because they seemed to him ludicrous as long as the real conditions of life barred most men from the authentic enjoyment of these subjective rights. To create a society in which *all* men would be in a position, for *their entire life*, to accomplish *effectively* the democratic ideal, this assuredly was the utopia toward which the thought of the young Marx tended.

But what, concretely, is the significance of inserting the democratic ideal into civil society or, to state it more clearly, how can the worker reach a freedom comparable to the formal freedom of the citizen? One interpretation, rather trite, has long been adopted. The worker is deprived of his freedom because he is under the orders of an entrepreneur, just as the latter is enslaved to the anonymous mechanisms of the market. In this case, it is through the suppression of private ownership of the means of production that civil society—or the socioeconomic infrastructure—will be "democratized," brought under control of the combined producers. According to another interpretation, which can also be based on a number of Marx's texts, the first condition for liberation is the development of the productive forces, the making available of all the resources necessary for a decent life, in the end, a reduction of the working day. A famous passage in the third volume of *Capital* points out that work will always be in the realm of necessity. It is outside, beyond work, that the realm of freedom begins.

These two interpretations, both of them valid, do not take into account certain essential elements of Marx's thought. It is easy to expose the contrast between the servitude of the proletarian and the abstract freedom of the citizen: in England in the first half of the last century this contrast was glaring and scandalous. But through what actual institutions could civil and political society, economic and political activity, be merged? And what would be the outcome of this merger? The day the worker is directly at the service of the community and no longer at the service of the owner of the means of production, he is a citizen in the manner of a civil servant who, in his very work, participates in the public realm. But does this politicization of economic life, the public character given to an activity today private, spell liberation or servitude for individuals? It will be liberation if one decrees, by definition, that freedom is obedience to necessity and that, in a humanity in control of its destiny, each accomplishes the part that universal reason attributes to him. But if freedom begins beyond necessity and is realized in the margin of choice and autonomy reserved to the individual, what Marx calls emancipation can, in fact, become degraded into servitude.

Let us not forget: Marx himself always recognized the risk of servitude involved in the refusal to discriminate between civil society and political society. After all, in the Middle Ages this nondiscrimination existed:

> In the Middle Ages there were serfs, feudal estates, merchant and trade guilds, corporations of scholars, etc.: that is to say, in the Middle Ages property, trade, society, men are *political;* the material content of the state is given by its form; every private sphere has a political character or is a political sphere; that is, politics is a characteristic of the private sphere too. In the Middle Ages the political constitution is the constitution of private property, but only because the constitution of private property is a political constitution. In the Middle Ages the life of the nation and the life of the state are identical. Man is the actual principle of the state—but *unfree* man. It is thus the democracy of *unfreedom.*[22]

Certainly, Marx, when he wrote these lines, did not doubt that the return to a merging of society and state would be realized in the democracy of freedom: men would be equal and not, as in the Middle Ages, locked up in a class or corporation: the state would be the business of all and not a few. At the limit, according to the Saint-Simonian formula, the administration of things would replace the government of men and, by the same token, in a merged society and state, it is society that would survive and the state that would wither away. But on what is this liberal optimism founded if not on a utopian picture of "administration by the combined producers"?

Later, having replaced philosophic language with socioeconomic language, Marx gave another expression to this same danger of total emancipation degenerating into total servitude. The Marxist classification of economic regimes is based on a unique criterion, in his eyes, decisive: the relation between men at work, which determines the method of extracting and distributing surplus value. The slave is the property of his master, who takes care of him but keeps for himself all value produced beyond the cost of upkeep. Similarly, the serf is bound to the soil and the lord owns the means of production and keeps for himself the value produced beyond what the worker and his family need to survive. Capitalism conceals exploitation under the appearance of freedom (the proletarian is neither a slave nor a serf; he offers himself on a labor market where he negotiates with the buyer of his labor power) and the appearance of equality (wages are the apparently equitable counterpart of labor furnished by the worker). But the exploitation has not disappeared; it has, so to speak, realized itself by camouflage: wages are but the equivalent of the goods necessary to the life of the worker and his family. The rest—that

---

[22] Marx, "Critique of Hegel's Philosophy of the State," *C.W.*, vol. 3, p. 32 ("Kritik des Hegelschen Staatsrechts," *O.P.*, vol. 4).

is to say, surplus value—belongs to the owner of the means of production.

The elimination of the capitalist class opens up the way for an economy without exploitation, or an economy in which the community itself would distribute, according to needs and justice, the resources necessary to the development of the means of production and incomes for consumption. But this elimination of private exploiters could also restore what Marx called the *Asian mode of production,* in other words, the separation of society into two parts (that it is best not to call classes): the huge majority of workers on one side, the state apparatus on the other, with its army of civil servants organized according to a strict hierarchy, surplus value being extracted by the state apparatus and distributed according to the will of the masters of this apparatus. From this angle also, Marx had a premonition of the potential for enslavement contained within the drive to overcome the duality characteristic of liberal democracy between the worker and the citizen, between society and the state, between the private sphere and the public realm.

Marx, it is true, from 1848 on, once he had reached the end of the intellectual journey that had led the young Hegelian to the materialist conception of history, no longer stressed the will for radical revolution but the inevitable character of that revolution. The Promethean ambition was no longer that of an individual or of all humanity or even of the proletarian class to the extent that its only mission was to realize a destiny determined in advance. Capitalism is condemned by its internal contradictions and, if the timing and form of the catastrophe remain unknown and perhaps undetermined, the catastrophe itself, terrible and beneficial, is inevitable. Thus, it would seem that Tocqueville left men the responsibility of choice, within the democratic world, between freedom and despotism, whereas Marx condemned that world either to submit passively to the dialectic, or to try to oppose it in vain, or finally to accelerate its development.

In fact, the dialogue of the two men is the opposite of what it seems. Marx invoked historical determinism not as an alibi for cowardly resignation but as both justification and dissimulation of a truly demiurgic will. To reconstruct society, from its socioeconomic foundations, so that freedom and equality would be given to all at all times, such will be the revolution of the *fourth estate,* a continuation and a completion of the French Revolution, which was the revolution of the third estate. Thus, when Lenin and the Bolsheviks, at the beginning of the century, tired of leaving to recalcitrant history the task of crushing capitalism and building socialism, placed their trust in the party to replace the dialectic and the proletariat itself, they assuredly betrayed the doctrine that had become official in the Second International and sacrificed certain elements of the Marxist heritage, but they rediscovered one element, and an original and vital one: faith in the capacity of united men to liquidate the relics of past centuries and with supreme authority to construct a social order upon new foundations.

☆   ☆   ☆

It would be easy to analyze the dialogue between Tocqueville and Marx that we have just sketched according to a sociological and so to speak Marxist method. One was an aristocrat, who rallied to democracy by reason and not sentiment, but who, though sometimes demonstrating the coming of a radically different order, remained the defender of the existing structure and was passionately hostile to socialism. The other was by origin a bourgeois but, in revolt against a bourgeoisie that betrayed its own values, became the representative of the working class, denouncing the injustices it was subjected to and announcing the revenge the future would bring. One, out of social conservatism, made himself, against his private preferences, the theoretician of liberal democracy, that is to say, bourgeois democracy; the other wanted to be, with total commitment, the theoretician as well as the leader of an organized working class.

Though they were contemporaries, they so to speak ignored each other. I doubt whether Tocqueville even knew of the *Communist Manifesto*. Marx had certainly read *Democracy in America*, but if he suspected and sometimes suggested that the course of history could be different in the Old and New Worlds, the example of American democracy did not suffice to modify the picture he had formed, once and for all, of the inevitable and catastrophic future of capitalist societies. One explicitly placed above all else the safeguarding of individual and political freedoms, but liberal democracy also seemed to Tocqueville the most effective protection of the social hierarchy and of economic inequalities. The other judged ridiculous any reforms that allowed the survival, along with private ownership of the means of production, of the ultimate cause of social contradictions and the plight of the workers.

The two men shared a distaste for opportunism, a total fidelity to themselves and their ideas. Tocqueville retired from politics the day Louis Napoleon violated the constitution and reestablished the empire. Karl Marx, until the end of his life, remained a rebel, committed to the struggle against a cruel society and for a class that bore the whole brunt of social injustice. Both believed in freedom, both had as a goal a just society, but one would leave industry and commerce to themselves, to be spontaneously run by individuals under the control of laws, and feared that the individual might come to lose independence-freedom and participation-freedom all at once. The other held the free activity of individuals in industry and commerce to be the cause of the servitude of all. Thus, for one the major condition of freedom was representative government and for the other, economic revolution.

This contrast can easily be explained by the origins, careers, and temperaments of the two men, yet not without a paradox that deserves to be stressed: it was a Norman aristocrat who became the doctrinaire of liberal democracy, the son of a Rhenish bourgeois who became the prophet of the fourth estate. It was in the United States that the descendant of European nobility studied the model of the future society. It was in Victorian England that the young Hegelian completed his economic studies and borrowed from Ricardo concepts and methods thanks to which he tried to give scientific form to his hopes and indignation.

Whatever the partial truth of these sociobiographical interpretations, the fact remains that, at a decisive point, the contrast turns on a fact or an evolutionary tendency. Does an economy founded on the private ownership of the means of production set up a trench between the rich and the poor or not? Does it create enemy classes, incapable of cooperation and by this very fact doomed to fight each other mercilessly until the death of one and the triumph of the other? It is possible to contend that Tocqueville guaranteed himself a certain intellectual comfort by predicting that the society of the future would be dominated by the middle class. This peaceful waiting and optimistic prediction absolved him from the effort to struggle against present injustices. What he had in mind for a future Europe was a society as mobile as the American one, and he was easily resigned to the persistence on the old continent of class discrimination and the powerlessness of the poor. But, this said, his vision in the long run was nonetheless true and Marx's false, without the latter's short-term view being correct either, since from the middle of the last century on, he counted on the salvationist upheaval from year to year.

Why was it that the man who reasoned in political terms and not the one who had read all the economic books foresaw the diffusion of prosperity? One answer would be to claim the superiority of naive observation and historical experience over the unilateral and imperfect arguments of specialists. Tocqueville, as we have seen, reasoned from social equality to political equality and from political equality to an egalitarian tendency in the distribution of income. The passage from the one to the other seemed to him likely in the long run and governed by the deep forces that determine the destiny of societies. As for the development of productive capacity and technical revoltions, he knew no more and said no more than any other educated man of his time. But he believed in all simplicity that the combination of increased resources and a democratic climate would probably lead to an improvement in the destiny of most and not to the contrast between an excess of misery at one extreme and an excess of wealth at the other.

As an economist Marx questioned, and to a certain extent rightly, this complacence. In an economy founded on private ownership of the means of production, it was not inconceivable that wealth would be concentrated in the hands of a minority without the masses profiting from it (as has happened many times). Nevertheless, a paradox remains. No economist of his time was as attentive as Marx to the dynamism of the modern economy; none repeated so stubbornly that a static model is remote from reality and that capitalism is defined by the accumulation of capital, therefore by the development of productive forces, and indirectly by greater productivity. Now, why does Marx draw the conclusion that a dynamic model with strong capital accumulation will lead to the impoverishment of the masses in spite of growing productivity?

A complete answer would require a detailed study of Ricardo's system and the manner in which Marx used it for his own ends. But a few elementary observations will suffice. Having taken work as the unit of measure for value, and for measuring wages (or the value of the labor force) the goods necessary for the life of the worker and his family, Marx could arrive at one of two conclusions. If, thanks to the rise in productivity, the hours necessary to produce goods representing the value of wages go down, then either the rate of exploitation increases or wages, without representing added value, must represent a greater quantity of goods. Marx did not assert that the rate of exploitation would rise; he said that the rate would remain stable. He should have recognized that with the same part of the day being devoted to producing a value equal to wages, and with productivity having risen, the standard of living would tend to rise or poverty to diminish. To avoid this conclusion, Marx, unlike many economists of his day, did not introduce the effect on the birthrate, and therefore on the supply of work, of an increase in wages, but cited instead the industrial reserve army, in other words, the pressure permanently exerted on wage scales by the availability of unemployed workers, unemployed because of changes in technology.

If Marx had approached the study of the economy as a pure observer without knowing in advance what he wanted to demonstrate, he would not have insisted with so much force on *absolute pauperization*, which does not obviously result from his analysis of capitalism, any more than he would have concluded from the increase in constant capital in relation to variable capital—therefore, of the fall of the rate of profit[23]—the progressive paralysis of an economy whose driving power is private investment.

In the prosperous West of 1963, Marx seems to have been wrong in economic matters, precisely an area in which he was one of the most learned and erudite men of his times, and Tocqueville seems to have divined the future despite his ignorance (a relative ignorance, of course)

---

[23] Surplus value *(s)* being drawn exclusively from variable capital *(v)*, the increase in constant capital *(c)* in relation to variable capital *(v)* obviously entails a decrease in the ratio

$$\frac{s}{v + c}$$

and perhaps thanks to it. Propelled by his common sense or by his intuition, he admitted without solid proof or deep analysis that a society obsessed by the concern for material well-being will assure to the majority the moral status and economic conditions of the middle class. Such a society will be agitated by incessant demands and conflicts of interest, but little prone to revolutions. Too many individuals will have something to lose for endemic dissatisfaction to result in revolt: "What if I don't own today, I may own tomorrow, and my children will own it if I don't." Thus, without too great a paradox, one can credit Tocqueville with having had a premonition of the anxious and peaceful society in which Westerners live fifteen years after the second world war.

At the same time it is impossible not to attribute to Marx a cardinal error: that in a regime of private property and a market economy the condition of the masses would worsen fatally and that, paralyzed by its contradictions and torn by class war, capitalism, incapable of self-reform, would perish. It is tempting to proceed still further in this line of thought and see, in the very successes achieved by Marx's doctrine, the confirmation of Tocqueville's alternative.

A probabilistic thinker, the latter left two roads open to mankind's future: liberal democracy or despotic democracy. Do not the Soviet regimes represent one of the alternative terms and the Western regimes the other, so that the persistence of capitalism in the West would refute Marxist prophecies whereas despotisms claiming to be Marxist confirm rather than refute Tocqueville's thought? Did he not, in a passage we quoted earlier, conceive of despotisms without aristocracies, in which the laws would aim at the well-being of the masses?

Let us take care, however, not to be carried away by an interpretation that is both easy and seductive. If in the course of these past years sociologists have paid more attention to politics, to constitutions in the wider meaning of the term (ways of selecting leaders, methods of exercising authority), it is assuredly because of the striking contrast between the two greatest powers in the world, both committed to industrial growth, one claiming to be liberal democratic (in Tocqueville's sense of the term), the other having as its ideal the suppression of classes, the merging of society and state, according to the dream of the young Marx. We call Soviet society despotic but the spokesmen of this society return the accusation and denounce the enslavement of Western proletarians to the private owners of the means of production, the enslavement of the state itself to the monopolists, that is to say, to the socially dominant minority, which is consequently capable of manipulating those representatives whom the citizens have the illusion of having chosen to govern in their name.

Is this exchange of accusations the symbol of an irreducible dialogue? Does the same word have two different meanings depending on which side of the Iron Curtain it is uttered? Or do the facts themselves allow us to decide between rival claims?

Marx's cardinal error, as we have said, was to believe, or to write as though he believed, that only radical revolution can liberate the worker, in the double sense of improving his standard of living and allowing him to participate in collective life. The other cardinal error, not of Marx but of the Marxists, was to draw a false conclusion from fair criticism. The personal freedoms or subjective (political) rights to which Tocqueville was passionately committed are not sufficient to give a feeling of freedom, much less a freedom that will effectively create a future for those who live miserably on ever uncertain wages. This critique is true but the conclusion—that formal freedoms are a luxury for the privileged—is false. For the Soviet experience is a glaring demonstration that the "combined producers," under the direction of the proletariat organized as a ruling class, can be experienced by individuals not as the architects of total liberation but as those responsible for total servitude.

I am thinking of the Hungarian revolution of 1956, the only anti-totalitarian revolution of the century that could be called victorious even though the intervention of a foreign army finally "reestablished order in Budapest." Now this revolution is the one, to my knowledge, that most resembles the one Marx dreamed about in 1843 in the name of revolution. "Philosophy," he wrote, "is the head of this emancipation, the proletariat its heart." In Hungary, it was the intellectuals, united in the Petöfi circle, who launched the popular revolt, by taking a stand against established lies, against the mystification of which they themselves had been victims. The workers went into the street and overthrew the Rakosi regime, in their eyes the incarnation of despotism, at the appeal of writers or artists, in order to realize the values of which intellectuals are the custodians: the right to truth, the simplest and deepest of subjective rights that liberals, in the nineteenth-century European meaning of the word, hold to be the essence of freedom.

Let us reflect a moment on the meaning of this inversion, this paradox that conceals an authentic logic. What do formal freedoms mean? cried Marx—the right to speak, to write, to choose one's representatives, and to adhere to one's god—if real life, the everyday life of work, is imprisoned by the ruthless necessity created by the power of the boss and the tyranny of need? Against a certain complacency of the privileged, who are disposed to accommodate themselves to the misery of the majority as long as formal freedoms are respected, Marx's protest has lost none of its freshness. But the day when, under the pretext of real freedom, the authority of the state spreads to the whole of society and no longer tends to recognize a private sphere, it is formal freedoms that intellectuals and the masses themselves demand.

No revolution, in its aspirations and watchwords, is as close to the

Revolution of 1848 as the Hungarian revolution of 1956. And yet it confronts not a traditional despotism but a regime claiming to be one of the proletariat and intellectuals, a regime of the future, and which to hide from itself the true nature of its adversaries attempts to disqualify them by labeling them counterrevolutionaries. Nothing could be a greater lie. Neither the Petöfi circle nor Imre Nagy is counterrevolutionary or aims at bringing back the dead Hungary of the Ancien Régime or returning to the large landowners their former holdings, to the capitalists their banks and factories. They do not question the public ownership of the means of production and in a certain way this subject interests no one (at least if it is a question of vast concentrations of capital: the peasant remains interested in his land, and nationalization of trade and handicrafts cannot be justified on the level of technique). In brief, intellectuals and popular masses, in 1956 as in 1848, cry "freedom" and they are thinking of subjective rights, of participation-freedom through elections and many parties, and finally of national, collective freedom, of which each one feels the lack since the citizen has the sense of being reduced to a ridiculous role if those he chooses to govern are themselves the toys of an outside and all-powerful force.

One could object that the Hungarian revolution was above all a national one and that we falsify its meaning by interpreting it as a dialectic between formal and real freedoms: formal freedoms, despised by the Marxists, are from now on the stake of popular movements in a country wherein, with the whole of society submissive and seemingly integrated with the state, protest can become only immediately political. But the case of Hungary is an extreme case. Even in the Soviet Union, what is constantly at issue is how much (formal) freedom it is appropriate to allow intellectuals. During the years of monolithic Stalinism, the question apparently did not arise. The discipline imposed from above, by one man alone ruling through terror, was such that speech itself was in bondage and the changing version of the ideology was at each moment repeated by millions of voices and echoed to the four corners of the universe. When men in white jackets were decreed to be assassins, the apparatus of all parties and all propaganda machines echoed the master's decree, and the indignation spread to Parisian doctors, ignorant of everything but won over, sometimes by humanitarianism, to Marxism-Leninism. Since Stalin's death the discipline of lying has disintegrated and the regime seeks a compromise between respect for state orthodoxy and the freedom of expression to which writers and artists aspire.

Why refuse to painters the right to formalism and to musicians the right to dodecaphony? But if art is no longer at the service of the party and socialist growth, if ideology no longer dominates the whole of social existence, then the unity of a classless society, the merging of this nonantagonistic society and the state that wills itself the expression of the whole, is in turn compromised. A distinction emerges between the public sphere and the private ones, between the area in which public will rules and those in which the individual can be left to himself. But then, on that day, on what will the monopoly of the party be based? How can it justify its claim to absolute power? Why would it alone have the right to proclaim absolute truth and to interpret it, at every moment, against the constant perils of dogmatism and revisionism? It is not chance but logic that causes Marxist-Leninist regimes, in search of real socioeconomic freedoms, to experience the opposition of the heirs of all those who throughout the centuries have fought orthodoxies and refused not to obey Caesar but to worship him—the eternal protesters who have never definitely won the game but have never resigned themselves to considering it lost.

It will be objected that the dialogue of Khrushchev and the intellectuals, and the Hungarian revolution of 1956, has nothing to do with Marx's Marxism and that the latter did not aim at suppressing but completing the formal freedoms of the bourgeoisie. I do not deny this point. But a doctrine of action such as Marx's is responsible not only for its intentions but also for its implications even if they are contrary to its values and goals. Now I agree that an all-powerful party, such as the Bolshevik party, does not conform to Marx's thought; as early as 1917, a great number of Marxists refused to allow that public ownership of the means of production and a planned economy constitute the achievement of socialism in the absence of political freedom; it nevertheless remains difficult to conceive the elimination of class antagonisms, the end of the duality between society and state, without an absolute authority, without something like what is called the dictatorship of the proletariat. The proletariat, that is to say, millions of workers, cannot itself exercise a dictatorship. Thus, it is not historically surprising that Marxism—rejecting the method of progressive reforms, refusing to admit the permanence of distinct economic and political spheres, and aiming at a liberation of all through mastery by the combined producers over their destiny—should end up with the total enslavement of all to one party, even to one man. Because how could the "combined producers" reorganize society from its foundations if their "combination" does not show itself capable of command, in other words, if the combination of producers itself does not form a party, with a hierarchy, a general staff, a chief?

Must one say that, by an irony of history, the governed are seeking formal freedoms there where the philosophy of real freedoms rules? And that, on the other hand, formal freedoms are being belittled in favor of real freedoms there where the former are guaranteed, at least for the most part, but where there continue to exist, along with private ownership of the means of production, social power and perhaps political power among a minority in the private sphere? This dialectic, which contains a part of the truth, expresses despite everything an otherwise complex historical reality.

In Hungary the revolutionary élan came from intellectuals, but the popular masses would not have followed if they had not felt themselves to be downtrodden and thus exploited. And since there were no more private exploiters, only the Hungarian Communist party or the Soviet Union could be responsible for the exploitation. In any case, economic policy, as practiced throughout Eastern Europe in the postwar years, resembled on one essential point what Marx considered typical of capitalism: "Accumulate, accumulate, that is the law and the prophets." This famous formula can be translated, in the language of socialist construction, by the primacy of investment, in particular, in heavy industry over consumption. A revolution against poverty, despite the development of the means of production—is this not the revolution that Marx anticipated and that the rise in living standards in the West has forestalled?

On the other hand, it would be a mistake to believe that in the West formal freedoms can be considered assured or that real freedoms are the only ones demanded. What characterizes Western regimes, as compared to those of the Soviet bloc, is pluralism—a plurality of spheres, private and public, a plurality of social groups among which certain form classes by becoming conscious of their own mission and their opposition to the existing order, a plurality of parties in competition for the exercise of power. Depending on countries and circumstances, it is formal freedoms—as during the McCarthy period—or real freedoms—as in the eyes of workers devoted to the Marxist-Leninist doctrine—that seem in peril and constitute the stake in conflicts. Sometimes it is society that seems tyrannical rather than the state (in the eyes of American blacks, for example); sometimes it is the state that, by refusing wage increases or being thought to be under the influence of plutocratic minorities or a conspiracy of the military or the industrialists, seems to escape the will of those who, according to the law of democracy, should provide its inspiration if not its management.

The dialectic of formal and real freedoms, of Soviet regimes and Western ones, thus cannot be reduced to an ironic reversal of for or against, with men setting out on the conquest of real freedoms having destroyed formal ones without increasing the standard of living or broadening people's participation in the community, which would have been the authentic content of real freedom, while the masses, in societies faithful to formal freedoms, continue to aspire to more real freedom, that is to say, to more material well-being and to increased participation in the administration of industry or the state. For thts oversimplified antithesis, I would substitute the following one: wherever a single party maintains a despotic regime and forbids intellectuals, writers, or artists to work according to their talent, the demand for formal freedom, silent or public, regains luster and in certain cases its past virulence. As for the masses, they do not seem, even if dissatisfied, to question the dogmas of the government, that is to say, public ownership of the means of production and planning. But, at least in the countries of Eastern Europe, they do question the one-party state, and left to themselves, Poles, Czechs, and Hungarians would reestablish party rivalry and parliamentary deliberations. In other words, economic and social grievances, on the other side of the Iron Curtain, are of course multiple and diverse but they do not become organized into a rival ideology when in the political sphere a substitute ideology or even institutions are available.

In the West, the principles of formal freedoms and liberal democracy are not seriously challenged, except by minorities devoted to the doctrine of Marxism-Leninism or again in circumstances in which the regime reveals itself incapable of resolving urgent problems. As for social and economic dissatisfactions or demands, they are many and diverse, but they no more readily become organized in an ideology, or a system or doctrine of substitution, than on the other side of the Iron Curtain. Depending on the case, the protesters blame the state or the monopolies, the big corporations that spearhead technical progress or the small firms that are prisoners of anachronistic methods. Setting aside once again the minority that puts its faith in a Soviet-type regime, the intellectuals in the West, like the masses, are neither contented nor revolutionary, neither free nor enslaved.

The prevailing mood is such that dissatisfaction is incapable of inspiring a revolutionary will, liberation is incomplete, but the causes of this semiservitude are so numerous and so obscure that no total theory can encompass them all, no action eliminate them. Western dissatisfaction rejects both despair and hope.

☆   ☆   ☆

If these analyses are correct, what answer should we give the question raised earlier: are today's industrial societies the heirs of *liberalism*, concerned primarily with subjective rights and representative institutions, or of the *Promethean ambition* of the Marxists, concerned with freedom in their own way but with a freedom that would come about through the fundamental reorganization of society beginning with its existing socioeconomic infrastructure?

One answer is that, from one perspective, all industrial societies are heirs of the Promethean ambition in the sense that they all lay such trust in the mastery achieved through the technological control of nature and the organization of social phenomena that no government, no theorist, would admit as inevitable certain forms of human misery, and none would accept passively the undeserved disasters that here and there befall individuals. Among the freedoms proclaimed by the Atlantic Charter there are two that would have been ignored by traditional liberalism—*freedom from want* and *freedom from fear*—because want and fear, hunger and war, were inherent to human existence throughout the centuries. That poverty and violence have been as of now eliminated, no one believes: that one day they might be, why not hope? That the ambition to eliminate them is new and shows an arrogance that the founding fathers as well as Tocqueville would not have shared or approved is beyond doubt. For this ambition emerges from equating the tyranny of things with the tyranny of men or, again, to put it perhaps more precisely, from the assertion that a man deprived of bread and education is not a victim of things but of men. Only men can deprive other men of the right to select a government and worship a god. But what men are responsible for, and what men can conquer want and fear? *No social condition must be accepted as independent of the rational will of men.* This is nearly a textually Marxist formula but it expresses the *common faith* or *univeral illusion of modern societies.*

From the moment this equivalence is raised or this ambition asserted, industrial societies, even of the Western type, even if they continue to quote Madison or Jefferson and to reject Marx and Marxism, even if they in fact remain liberal democracies, are permeated with a spirit fundamentally different from the one that inspired the framers of the American Constitution or the actors in the French Revolution. As long as the only despotism one fears is that of a government without checks or a man corrupted by excess power, it is against the power of the state or the arbitrariness of governments that one multiplies one's precautions. From the day when poverty and misfortune are no less imputable to society itself than abuse by the police or the injustice of kings, must the major concern be to limit the government or, quite the contrary, to give it means commensurate with the tasks that one expects of it, that is to say, almost unlimited means? Liberalism, because it was suspicious of men, was stingy in granting them authority to govern. The confidence we feel in science, technology, and organization becomes as irritated with the slow pace of deliberations as it does with the paralysis that can be created by checks and balances, in which the drafters of constitutions once saw the supreme art and guarantee of freedom. What was yesterday the pride of legislators is today the despair of technicians.

Let there be no mistake: Western type industrial societies and, more than all others, the more advanced among them, remain liberal democracies in Tocqueville's sense. The author of *Democracy in America* saw correctly. The union has endured, having been threatened only once and, as he predicted, by slavery. Institutions that in his eyes were the expression and guarantee of freedom—the role of citizens in local administration, voluntary associations, the mutual support between the democratic and religious spirit—have survived, in spite of the advance of centralization and the strengthening of the presidency, a strengthening that Tocqueville had furthermore declared to be inevitable from the day when the republic would have to face enemies and be engaged in an active foreign policy.

It would therefore be absurd to suggest that the effort to assure to all individuals material resources sufficient to realize themselves, that is, to be really free to determine their destiny, is contrary to the eighteenth-century ideal of liberalism, the fear of despotism and the arbitrary, and proper constitutional procedures. It is even obvious at first glance that liberal democracies have taken root and prospered today especially, if not exclusively, in countries that have reached a standard of living sufficient for the mass of the population to feel its benefits. In particular, in the United States, why should a contradiction be felt between subjective rights or formal freedoms and real freedom (distribution of material well-being and social participation) since it is within the framework of a liberal constitution that the republic raised itself to the first rank of economic power and abundance?

It is therefore not so much a matter of suggesting any sort of contradiction; but how can one not recognize that fear of the arbitrary and Promethean arrogance belong to two spiritual universes, express two very different attitudes toward society? It may be that the Americans will be the first to arrive on the moon and thus demonstrate that the endless Senate investigating committees, survivals of bourgeois traditions, in no way weaken the will that Spengler would have called Faustian and the efficiency of collective organization. I do not deny that the United States can maintain intact its original values since each nation remains, sometimes unconsciously, faithful to the ideal that presided at its birth.

Is what is true for the United States true to the same degree of the other countries of the West? Is it true for the rest of the world? Let us not try to settle the issue but to give it a radical expression. Half a century ago, a constitution and formal freedoms still represented, if not the whole, at least an essential element of modernity. Japan, whose deliberate Westernization, a conscious response to external danger, is one of the most extraordinary events of history, tried to introduce a constitution and a parliament at the same time as the science and technology of Europe and America. The young Turks, too, were no less anxious than the army to modernize politics, and political modernization was symbolized by a parliament. Today a blast furnace symbolizes modernity better than a parliament.

It is fair to object that the very opposition of Soviet and Western societies has made this ambiguity of modernity inevitable. Since the Soviet Union rose to the summit of political power and technological efficiency without a plurality of parties, without respect for formal freedoms, without even a constitutional mechanism, why should these survivals of a preindustrial age, these procedures invented by republics of landowners or the bourgeoisie, be surrounded with a halo? Why should nations desiring rapid growth, rightly anxious to give individuals the material means to live their lives, be encumbered by these subtle mechanisms, better designed to brake than to promote public action? In all of the new nations, the ambition is to construct or reconstruct the social order from its foundations, that is to say, it is the Marxist ambition, and not liberal modesty, that corresponds to the sentiments of the elites even more than to those of the masses. Even the merging of society and the state, the worker and the citizen—much protested by men on the other side of the Iron Curtain and repugnant to Westerners—seems, in the form of the single party, to be a useful method to rally a people, force it to change its traditional ways of life, and unite social and political forces in a common thrust. Liberal freedoms require the separation of spheres and respect for forms. Out of impatience and perhaps an illusion of efficiency, single parties are multiplying over the planet, even without reference to Marxism-Leninism, and denying individual freedoms in the hope that the "combined producers" will first build a new social order to free men from want, if not from fear.

☆   ☆   ☆

Let me repeat in conclusion: I do not doubt the compatibility of the old ideal of liberal democracy with the renewed ideal of Promethean mastery over nature and society itself. Western societies, American society, are proof not only that formal freedoms and real freedoms are not contradictory but that, in our time, it is in the same societies that both are least imperfectly realized.

What I should like to express from this historical dialogue between Tocqueville and Marx, between liberal democracy and socialist construction, is that the industrial society in which we live and which the thinkers of the past century divined is democratic in essence if one means by that, as Tocqueville does, the elimination of hereditary aristocracies; it is normally, if not necessarily, democratic if one means that no one is excluded from citizenship and the spread of material well-being. On the other hand, it is liberal only by tradition or survival if by liberalism one means respect for individual rights, personal freedoms, and constitutional procedures.

Western societies today have a triple ideal, *bourgeois citizenship, technological efficiency,* and *the right of every individual to choose the path of his salvation.* Of these three ideals, none should be sacrificed. Let us not be so naive as to believe that it is easy to achieve all three.

9. What Is a Theory of International Relations?

FEW WORDS ARE USED as often by economists, sociologists, or political scientists as the word "theory." Few words are as ambiguous. A recent book developing two ideas—the virtues of nonalignment and the influence that the priority of economic considerations in modern societies allegedly exerts in favor of peace—has as its subtitle *A General Theory*.[1] A hypothesis that alliances are founded on calculations of national interest and do not withstand a conflict of those interests is christened "theory" in the current language of political science.[2] As a matter of fact, the distinction is rarely made explicitly among related but separate concepts such as "models," "ideal types," "conceptualizations," and even empirically observed, regular occurrences. What authors call "theory" belongs more or less to one or the other of these categories or may contain elements borrowed from one or the other in varying proportions.

This lack of rigor in the use of a key word can be explained and perhaps justified by the desire for progress. Political scientists feel that their discipline appears underdeveloped compared to economics, not to mention the natural sciences. This desire for progress has the unfortunate effect of making it seem more important to do than to know what one is doing. The accumulation of information matters more than the critical understanding of it.

The quarrel, however, between proponents of the "classical" and "scientific" approaches to the study of international relations, a quarrel I

[1] J. W. Burton, *International Relations: A General Theory* (Cambridge, Eng.: Cambridge University Press, 1965).

[2] Raymond Dawson and Richard Rosecrance, "Theory and Reality in the Anglo-American Alliance," *World Politics*, Vol. XIX, No. 1 (Oct. 1966), pp. 21–51.

deplore because it has increased the confusion, shows that scholars in the field are not indifferent to the theoretical basis of their discipline. Thus, it will perhaps be not entirely useless to pose the question: what is a theory of international relations?

☆   ☆   ☆

It seems to me that in the Western world the concept of theory has a double origin or, if you prefer, two meanings, each derived from a different tradition. Theory as contemplative knowledge, drawn from ideas or from the basic order of the world, can be the equivalent of philosophy. In this case, theory differs not only from practice or action but also from knowledge animated by the will to "know in order to predict and thus be able to act." The less practical a study is, that is to say, the less it suggests or permits the handling of its object, the more theoretical it is. At most, it changes the one who has conceived it and those who are enlightened by it through his findings.

The other line of thought leads to authentically scientific theories, with those of physical science offering the perfect model. In this sense, a theory is a hypothetical, deductive system consisting of a group of hypotheses whose terms are strictly defined and whose relationships between terms (or variables) are most often given a mathematical form. The elaboration of this system starts with a conceptualization of perceived or observed reality; axioms or highly abstract relationships govern the system and allow the scientist to rediscover by deduction either appearances that are thereby fully explained or facts that are perceptible through devices, if not through the senses, and that temporarily either confirm the theory or invalidate it. An invalidation necessitates a rectification; a confirmation never constitutes an absolute proof of the theory's truth.

We shall entirely discard the first meaning—theory as philosophy—and restrict ourselves to the second meaning, the meaning preferred by the "modernists" among sociologists and political scientists.

Aside from the special case of linguistics, economics, of all the social sciences, has probably developed theoretical elaboration to the greatest extent. Pure economics, in the style of Walras and Pareto, constitutes the equivalent of a hypothetical, deductive system; it is expressed in a set of equations. But it is well known, as Walras and Pareto were the first to point out, that pure economics sets up a simplified representation of reality. In place of actual economic life, the economist substitutes an artificial market in which men of flesh and bone are replaced by subjects with specially defined characteristics. They have perfect information at their disposal and a single objective, the maximization of a certain quantity (the intervention of money makes this calculation easy).

It is not our concern here to enter into a classic controversy over whether economic models are comparable to the theory of rational mechanics or whether they should be considered as "ideal types" according to Max Weber's conception, that is, as rationalized and stylized reconstructions of certain types of behavior and situations. Though I personally prefer the second interpretation, it is not necessary to choose between them; indeed, both lead to the notions I should like to restate.

The models of pure economics provide indispensable insights (the reciprocal solidarity among all the elements of the system, the need for economic calculation in order to decide on a rational allocation of resources, the dependence of each price on all prices, and so on). Those without some theoretical training always run the risk of committing great errors if they limit themselves to empirical description or research. For example, they might predict a wave of unemployment with each spectacular technological innovation. But, in the opposite sense, theorists do not have the right to derive a doctrine of action from their models. The fact that the perfect market assures an optimum distribution of resources does not authorize the doctrinaire to claim that science demonstrates the superiority of free enterprise over socialism. Even if we ignore the fact that this distribution is optimum only for a certain distribution of income, the fact remains that pure theory carves out a clearly defined system (the economy) within an undefined system (the global society) and defines an imaginary actor (*Homo economicus*) far removed from real actors. (It is not true that all behavior that deviates from that of the imaginary actors disappears in the mass and that average behavior or the final outcome of real behavior corresponds to the expectations based exclusively on behavior as defined by the theory, that is, on behavior aiming at a maximum gain.)

Progress in economic science results from a ceaseless dialectic between theory and experiment. The theory in operation today has been profoundly marked by the influence of Keynes, whose "general theory" diverged sharply from classical theories in several respects: it was directly macroeconomic; it set up six variables, some independent and some dependent (at the same time, it suggested a technique of manipulation); it considered equilibrium at the level of full employment as a special case; it set up an entrepreneur different from the economic subject of traditional theory, an entrepreneur who would make investment decisions based upon expected profit (individual psychology, the psychological climate of the community—in other words, sociopsychological data—were thereby introduced into the system); and finally, it postulated, so to speak, the nonelasticity of nominal wages, thereby integrating additional social data into the system.

One could debate whether Keynesian theory is a general theory or just a model valid for explaining short-term fluctuations and their control for a historical period characterized by certain extraeconomic factors. I shall not undertake this discussion, which would be an excessively long digression in view of the aims of this short essay. Indeed, the preceding discussion should suggest the following propositions that have implications for the study of international relations.

1. In order to elaborate the theory of a social subsystem, we need a definition of this subsystem that indicates both its limits and its specificity. What are the true characteristics of the interconnected actions that constitute a relatively defined whole, whose implicit logic the theory tries to elaborate?

2. Scientific progress requires shuttling back and forth between simplified systems and renewed observations. Keynes's system involves actors who are less remote from actual actors than those in Walras's system. At the same time, Keynes postulates certain historical and social facts outside the specific field of economics (external variables).

3. Even the Keynesian system assumes the constancy of data that, in reality, are not constant; focusing on short-term fluctuations, Keynes does not take technical progress into consideration.

4. Progress in the economic field over the past thirty years has been largely the result of empirical, statistical, and descriptive studies. Empirical and statistical studies have led to an awareness of essential phenomena, such as long-term growth and the transformation of price relationships among goods of different sectors owing to unequal rates of growth in productivity. National accounting, much more than theory, has given governments better control over economic fluctuations. Models of crisis—the configurations of variables considered as crisis indicators—have been misleading; indeed, it has not yet been proven that "crisis situations" are all alike. It is possible that each crisis is unique or, if you prefer, has its own particular story and that the structure of the system itself contains possibilities of a crisis.

5. Progress in economic knowledge has not eliminated doctrinal conflicts, uncertainties in short- or middle-term forecasting, or the political (in other words, partisan) dimensions of the decisions taken by governments (decisions affecting the interests of various social classes in various ways). In short, neither theoretical knowledge nor empirical findings authorize the economist to dictate, in the name of science, a specific action to a ruler, though he can often advise the ruler on how to avoid evils dreaded by the whole community and sometimes predict the probable consequences of the ruler's actions. We cannot go directly from theory as a science to theory as a doctrine for action.

From these propositions emerge the problems I should like to raise about the theory of international relations.

1. Is it possible, and if so how, to define and delimit the subsystem of international relations?

2. What is the relation of this theory to empirical study, of the sub-

system to the social context? Is this theory historical or metahistorical? (This question was debated by the marginalist and historicist schools of economic thought at the end of the nineteenth century.)

3. What are the connections between theory and doctrine or, to use a word that shocked so many American readers, between theory and praxeology.[3]

Thus we rediscover the classical antitheses that define the meaning of theory: reality and theory, empiricism (historical and sociological) and theory, practice and theory.

☆   ☆   ☆

We can determine the true field of international relations in two ways. Either we try to grasp what distinguishes this field from other social fields, what differentiates relationships among politically organized communities from all other social relationships, or we start with concepts that can be applied to areas other than international relations. This difference in approach in no way corresponds to that between traditionalists and modernists. Hans Morgenthau is a traditionalist and Kenneth Boulding a modernist, yet both begin with general concepts not unique to international relations: *power* and *conflict*. International power politics or international conflicts are treated as species belonging to a genus, as illustrations or special cases of universally human phenomena. The first pages of the classic *Politics among Nations*[4] offer an equally classic example of conceptual confusion arising from the use of a term such as "power," which, depending on the paragraph or even the sentence one is reading, means either the end or the means of politics and is finally of no use. If "power" is defined in Weber's way, which is moreover the common way, as the ability of agent A to get agent B to submit to his will or to obey his orders (or, more precisely, the good fortune of agent A to achieve submission and obedience), then all social life is a question of power to some extent; power is obviously essential for collective action in any field whatsoever. Setting up power, thus defined, as the unique and highest goal of individuals, parties, or nations does not constitute a theory in the scientific sense but rather amounts to a philosophy or an ideology. In any event, it is not a proposition that can be proven false; thus, it cannot even be considered a scientific hypothesis.

I chose the other alternative in my book *Paix et guerre entre les na-*

---

[3] May I say, without being impertinent, that the reaction of American critics to the word *praxeology*, including that of my friend Henry Kissinger, who was in other respects so kindly disposed, seems typically parochial to me. Recalling the awkward jargon found on every page of sociological studies, one is amazed that a correctly composed word (praxis-logos), which has no equivalent (the science of practice) and is in current use in Europe (Professor Kotarbinski, of the Polish Academy of Sciences, wrote a well-known book bearing this title), should offend a linguistic purism so rarely in evidence.

[4] Hans J. Morgenthau, *Politics among Nations* (New York: Knopf, 1949).

tions.[5] I tried to determine what constitutes the distinctive nature of international or interstate relations, and I concluded that it rests in the legitimacy or legality of the use of military force. In higher civilizations, these are the only social relationships in which violence is considered normal.

This conclusion was not at all original: it was obvious to the classical philosophers and to the jurists who developed European international law (*jus gentium*). It has been confirmed, if I may say so, by the experience of our century and by the failure of American statesmen. The latter, prisoners of the contradiction between a national ideology (that war is a crime and that the rule of law must prevail in the relations between nations) and the nature of international society, have appeared to others as cynical, naive, or hypocritical. Never was the contradiction so glaring, and in a way both tragic and comic, as at the time of the double crisis in Hungary and Suez. To justify the stand taken against the British and French, President Eisenhower made the memorable remark, "There should not be two laws, one for friends, another for enemies" (the British and French were the friends), at the very time when he was passively witnessing the crushing of the Hungarian revolution by Soviet troops. American friends told me later that they had felt moral pride upon learning that President Eisenhower was joining the Soviets and the Third World against the British and French "in the name of law." They did not want to admit that President Eisenhower,[6] in allowing the Soviet Union to do as it pleased in Eastern Europe, was devaluing the legal or moral significance of the U.N. censure of the Anglo-French expedition and was applying the old rule of the international jungle: there are two laws, one for the strong, another for the weak. The strong have not yet found a better means of avoiding conflict and imposing something approaching order than by defining spheres of influence.

In short, neither the Kellogg-Briand Pact nor the United Nations has as yet eliminated the basic characteristic of the international system that philosophers and jurists of previous centuries designated the "state of nature." They contrasted the international system with the civil state, which possesses a tribunal and a police force. There is no equivalent of a tribunal in international society, and if the United Nations tried to compel one of the great powers to submit against its will, the police action would degenerate into a major war. Furthermore, the U.N. charter explicitly recognizes the "sovereign equality" of states, and diplomats have

---

[5] Translated into English as *Peace and War: A Theory of International Relations* by Richard Howard and Annette Baker Fox (Garden City, N.Y.: Doubleday, 1966).

[6] It goes without saying that these remarks are not meant as either an attack on or an approval of American policies in 1956. Maybe there was nothing better to do, but the moralizing speech, perhaps necessary for American public opinion, camouflaged a diplomacy that the European disciples of Machiavelli would not have repudiated.

never succeeded in defining the "international crime" par excellence—aggression.

The Cuban missile crisis of 1962 provides the same lesson. Frederick II gave his lawyers the task of justifying, ex post facto, the conquest of Silesia. President Kennedy found lawyers to formulate the "quarantine" of Cuba in apparently legal terms. But all the legal subtleties could not hide an undeniable fact: the United States itself has continually applied the principle that every government has the right to request the stationing of armed forces of another state on its territory if it judges this outside assistance necessary to its security. According to this principle, Cuba had as much right to set up Soviet medium-range missile bases as Turkey had to set up American bases. Fortunately, President Kennedy was not dissuaded by legal considerations. As Frederick had done, he consulted his lawyers for the apparent legitimization of a necessity. And the whole world is grateful to him for having strengthened the effectiveness of deterrence more in a few days than hundreds of books or speeches could have done in a dozen years. At the same time, that crisis, settled without the loss of human lives, marked a turning point in the postwar era; it hastened the liquidation of the Berlin affair and gave a new content to "peaceful coexistence" between the two superpowers. World opinion was grateful for the priority given to the exigencies of the balance of nuclear forces over the sovereign rights of a small country. Wiser than the ideologists, it took into account the circumstances and intentions rather than the law.

Can that essential characteristic—the absence of a tribunal or police force, the right to resort to force, the plurality of autonomous centers of decision, and the alternation and continual interplay between peace and war[7]—serve as a basis for a scientific theory even though it is obvious to the actors themselves and belongs to their own intuitive "sociology" or "political science"? Should not science substitute for everyday notions those concepts that science itself elaborates? It seems easy for me to answer that nothing prevents us from translating the preceding idea into a word or a formula more satisfactory to the "scientists." As we know, Max Weber defined the state as a "monopoly of legitimate violence." Let us say that international society is characterized by "the absence of an entity that holds a monopoly of legitimate violence."

A theoretical definition of this kind cannot be proven in the same way as an equation in theoretical physics: by showing its agreement with experimental data. Nor can it be invalidated. Even if a monopoly of legitimate violence in international society should be established in the future, we would merely say that the specific domain of interstate relations, as it had existed for a few thousand years, had disappeared as such. Yet a theoretical definition of this kind entails several direct and indirect

[7] The formulas are not equivalent but can easily be deduced from each other.

confirmations. To simplify matters, I shall say that these confirmations will be brought forth by answering the following questions: (1) does this definition permit the delimitation of the subsystem that is being considered? (2) does it allow us to deduce or include other elements of the subsystem? and (3) does it permit us to rediscover (and to explain) the original data that served as a starting point for the theoretical elaboration?

The answer to the first question seems, on the whole, affirmative. I do not deny the difficulties involved. The real delimitation is often more difficult than the conceptual one. In primitive societies, it is sometimes hard to find the effective power that holds the highest authority. In the absence of politically and territorially organized entities, distinctions between various types of more or less violent conflict and between groups are vague. The collective actor that reserves for itself the right to use violence against other collective actors is more or less large: a village, a clan, or a tribe. But the difficulty in defining subsystems in primitive societies by using concepts derived from complex societies exists in economics as well as in international relations. Why blame the theory for what can be imputed to the very nature of its subject matter? Likewise, it would be easy to object that feudal societies, owing to the dispersion of means of combat, make it difficult to distinguish between violence within the state and violence between states. Civil wars, such as the American Civil War, are also often hard to distinguish from foreign wars. Moreover, international law has taken these marginal cases into account. When a state loses the "monopoly of legitimate violence," and two parties have organized military forces at their disposal, the nonbelligerents tend to treat the two camps as if each one formed a separate state. Such marginal cases, however, do not constitute a valid objection to the rigor of the initial definition.

I believe that the answer to the second question provides the best justification for our chosen point of departure. Indeed, by postulating a society without a monopoly of legitimate violence, composed of collective actors, each of which confers the monopoly of legitimate violence on an entity within itself, we also implicitly define the main variables necessary to explain the systems and the events. As a matter of fact, the plurality of collective actors implies geographical space in two respects: the area in which each of the collective actors is established and the area within which the relations between the actors take place. Actors whose mutual relations are such that each one takes all the others into account in the calculations preceding its decisions belong to the same system. In the absence of a monopoly of legitimate violence, each actor is obliged to provide for its own security, either with its own forces or by joining forces with its allies. Consequently, the configuration of forces (bipolar or multipolar) is one of the main variables of any international system. Since each actor is controlled, in its relations with the other actors, by the entity that possesses a monopoly of legitimate violence, and thus by the handful of men who are responsible for that violence, the internal regimes of the collective actors constitute one of the variables of the international system: the homogeneity or heterogeneity of the system depends upon the kinship or opposition between the internal regimes of the different actors.

Should such an analysis be called a *theory* or a *conceptualization?* Is it an outline of a theory or an admission that a general theory is impossible? It all depends on what we expect of a theory, of the model of a theory (in physics or in economics) to which we refer. Such a conceptual analysis seems to me to fulfill some of the functions that we can expect from a theory: it defines the essential features of a subsystem; it provides a list of the main variables; and it suggests certain hypotheses about the operation of the subsystem, depending on whether it is bipolar or multipolar, homogeneous or heterogeneous. It has an additional value: it makes it easier to distinguish between theory and ideology or, if you prefer, between pseudotheories and theories. For example, let us take the formula, sometimes presented as theoretical, whereby states act according to their "national interest." The formula is just as meaningless as that of La Rochefoucauld, who discerned selfishness behind behavior that was apparently the most unselfish. It is enough, indeed, to postulate that Meredith's character Beauchamp, who drowns while trying to save a child, finds more satisfaction in sacrificing his life than in saving it at the expense of someone else's death. Likewise, whatever the diplomacy of a state may be, nothing prevents one from asserting after the fact that it was dictated by considerations of "national interest," as long as "national interest" has not been strictly defined.

Indeed, the so-called theory of "national interest" either suggests an idea as undeniable as it is vague—that each actor thinks first of itself—or else tries to oppose itself to other pseudotheories, for example, that the foreign policy of states is dictated by political ideology or moral principles. Each of these pseudotheories means something only in connection with the other. To say that the Soviet Union conducts its foreign affairs on the basis of its "national interest" means that it is not guided exclusively by ideological considerations, by its ambition to spread communism. Such a proposition is undeniable, but to conclude from it that the rulers of a noncommunist Russia would have had the same diplomatic policy between 1917 and 1967 is simply absurd. The purpose of the empirical study of international relations consists precisely in determining the historical perceptions that control the behavior of collective actors and the decisions of the rulers of these actors. The theoretical approach we have adopted throws light upon the diversity of the stakes involved in conflicts between collective actors, of the goals that they may have in view. The obsession with "space," characteristic of Japan's and Hitler's ambitions between the two world wars, has disappeared. The Marxist-Leninist ideology of an implacable conflict between the capitalist and socialist camps, which if it has not dictated the day-by-day decisions of the Kremlin leaders has at least molded their thinking, is in the process of erosion. The Kremlin's diplomacy is being transformed at the same time as its image of the world.

This theory can be presented as a failure or as a limitation of theory. Indeed, if we refer to the pure economics of Walras and Pareto, there can be no "pure theory of international relations" any more than there can be a "pure theory of internal politics" because we cannot endow the actors, either through the centuries of within a given system, with a single aim: the conscious or unconscious desire for a certain maximum gain. Those who presuppose the will to "maximize power" are not even aware of the ambiguity of the term they use.

If we refer to the Keynesian model, the gap between economic theory and the theory of international relations is less wide, but it still exists. There is no equivalent in the international system either for accounting identities (investment = savings) or for the distinction between independent and dependent variables. The international system is even less homeostatic than the system conceived by Keynes: though the latter contains equilibria without full employment, automatic or manipulated mechanisms tend either to reestablish equilibria or to induce alternating movements of expansion and contraction. No international system, whether homogeneous or heterogeneous, bipolar or multipolar, has a mechanism guaranteed to restore equilibrium. Innumerable are the factors, within states or in their relations, that tend to modify the nature of the system or to bring about a shift from one system to another.

Only a halfway affirmative answer can be given to the last question, but this does not condemn our theoretical choice. Systems and social events are *undefined* in the epistemological sense of the term: as they are experienced by their subjects and observed by historians or sociologists, neither do they parcel themselves out into neat and definite subsystems, nor can they be reduced to a small number of variables that could be organized into a body of interconnected propositions. The definition we have adopted allows us to set up such a body, but we could not deduce the industrial murder of millions of Jews by the Nazis as a necessary consequence of any theory. An analysis of the European state system of 1914 helps us understand the unlimited nature of the first world war. Indeed, a hypothesis to the effect that "a conflict between two alliance systems involving an entire international system, whose outcome will determine the hierarchical position of all the principal actors, will naturally tend to be carried to its conclusion, that is, until the complete victory of one of the two camps" seems probable. But such a hypothesis, assuming that its wording is precise enough for it to be applied to many other cases, should be confirmed by historical studies. Besides, it could have been contradicted if the course of military events had been different in the summer of 1914. For that matter, the decisive factor between 1914 and 1918 seems to have been what I have elsewhere called "the technical surprise."[8] (None of the military high commands had been prepared for a long war and none had foreseen the relentless mobilization, which was the work of civilians on both sides.) On the other hand, the period of revolutionary wars between 1792 and 1815 can be attributed to the ideological factor much more than to other elements of the international situation. Clausewitz wrote that there is a theory of tactics but not of strategy because the strategist must base his decisions on a particular situation, and each situation presents too many special features for us to be able to substitute deduction from certain generalizations for the intuition, common sense, or intelligence of the military leader. It is not always ignorance but sometimes the very nature of the subject matter that determines the limits of a theory.

On the other hand, from the theoretical definition we have adopted, one cannot deduce all of what I shall call "peaceful commerce between communities," whether it concerns relations between individuals (buyers and sellers belonging to two political entities) or relations between states (scientific, economic, intellectual, tourist, and so forth). There is no prohibition against attempting to define international society on the basis of the state of peace instead of the risk of war or against considering tests of strength and military competition as exceptional situations rather than essential features of international relations. It might be objected that we have confused international and interstate relations and that our definition can at most be applied only to the latter, and even then solely during times of crisis. Transnational (or transstate) society would thus be presented as the true international society, which supranational organizations would progressively regulate, military competition between states gradually losing its virulence and narrowing its scope.

I wish it would be so tomorrow. But considering the long history of complex societies, the theoretical definition I have chosen seems to me to be closer to reality, more in keeping with experience, more instructive, and more productive. Any definition that fails to take account of the basic characteristic of international relations, which is rooted in the legitimation of the resort to force, neglects both a constant factor in civilizations, one that has had tremendous effects on the course of history, and the human meaning of military activity. Statisticians such as Lewis Richardson who count acts of violence or homicide without differentiating between murderers and soldiers provide an opportune reminder that figures in themselves are meaningless. The theoretical definition offered here coincides with actual experience; statesmen, jurists, moralists, phil-

[8] *The Century of Total War* (Boston: Beacon, 1955), chap. 1.

osophers, and military men throughout the ages have perceived the essence of international relations to be just what I see as the starting point for a theory. Perhaps some modernists will condemn me for this. On this matter, I am a traditionalist.

☆ ☆ ☆

The relationships of such a theory to the social context (or, if you prefer, to global society) cannot be the same as those of economic theory (whether of Walras, Pareto, or Keynes) to that same context. To be sure, economists are far from agreeing upon the best way to combine economic and sociological conceptualization. We cannot easily move from a theory of the distribution among factors of production to a theory of the distribution of income. The historical school in Germany and the institutional school in the United States have sought to define, more or less rigorously, the social contexts (an inevitably vague expression) in which actual economic mechanisms come into play. It is easy to assert that war is a factor external to the economic situation. But is the view of the economic system that prompted the leaders of Europe and America to seek budgetary equilibrium in a period of deflation an external factor or not? Are monetary or budgetary decisions external? The present quarrel about the international monetary system and the ability of the United States to have an annual balance-of-payments deficit of one to three billion dollars for eight years without being forced to modify its internal expansionist policy illustrates, if need be, the way in which the economic subsystem impinges in its daily operations on the whole social system and particularly on the political system. Power relations (which does not mean military force) affect production and trade relations.

The theory of international relations differs from economic theory in that the distinction between internal and external variables, even in the abstract, is impossible. Indeed, the distinctive feature of the behavior of actors in relation to one another is that, in the absence of a tribunal or police force, they are obliged to calculate forces, especially military forces, available in case of war. No actor can rule out the possibility that another is harboring aggressive designs against it. Each must therefore estimate which forces are reliable in view of what Clausewitz called the outcome of credit transactions: payment in cash, the test of strength.[9] This calculation of forces in itself requires a reference to the area controlled by each actor, to its population and economic resources, to its military system or mobilization coefficient, and to the types of weapons available. Military systems and weapons are in turn the expression of political and social systems. Every concrete study of international rela-

[9] In the atomic age, "payment in cash" is perhaps no longer war but a crisis. At least it has been so up until now. I analyzed this transformation in *The Great Debate: Theories of Nuclear Strategy* (Garden City, N.Y.: Doubleday, 1965), chap. 5.

tions is thus a sociological and historical study since the calculation of forces refers to number, space, resources, and regimes (military, economic, political, and social), and these elements in turn constitute the stakes involved in conflicts between states. Once again, theoretical analysis itself reveals the limits of pure theory.

I have purposely used two adjectives, *sociological* and *historical*. The first term, *sociological*, can be contrasted, as the case may be, with *economic*, *theoretical*, or *historical*. Pareto referred nonlogical actions back to sociology, while distinguishing different levels of abstraction or schematization within the area of logical actions, the true goal of economic science. The greater its schematization or simplification, the more theoretical economic science would be. At the same time, sociology, the science of nonlogical actions, can be contrasted with history because it is searching for general relationships and does not aim, as history does, either to understand peculiarities or to narrate events.

Any concrete study of international relations is sociological, as I see it, in the sense in which Pareto contrasted sociology with economics (i.e., it is not possible to isolate a system of international relations because the actors' conduct, controlled by calculations of force, is determined by economic, political, and social variables). In *Paix et guerre entre les nations*, I contrasted sociology with history as the difference between seeking regularities and understanding unique situations. Henry Kissinger considered it paradoxical that I called the part of my book devoted to an analysis of the global system in the thermonuclear age "History." Perhaps I had an ironic intention in choosing that title. I certainly did not imagine that Weber's classical antithesis between sociology and history would seem paradoxical or unintelligible to my readers.

The historian's intention can be defined in four different ways. Either he is interested in the past and not in the present, or he is interested in events rather than in systems, or he narrates rather than analyzes history, or he sticks to peculiarities rather than generalities. In the end, the first definition seems meaningless to me because the subject we are discussing already belongs to the past at the time we speak about it. The global system, as I described it, had already changed by the time my description was published. It is true that the historian of the present lacks archives, the perspective that loosens the bonds between the observer and his object of study, and especially knowledge of the consequences. A history of the present[10] will serve as a document for the historian of the future. Historical science proceeds by the accumulation of knowledge, yet also by a constant reinterpretation of preceding interpretations. From the history of the present written by a contemporary to the history of the same period written in the next century, the amount of reinterpretation will probably

---

[10] A history of the cold war is already possible.

be greater than from Mommsen's *History of Rome* to a history of Rome written in the middle of the twentieth century. The difference appears to me as one of degree rather than of kind.

The second definition does not seem to me to be valid either. To be sure, the professional historian, because of his training and his tradition, pays more attention to accidents than the sociologist or the economist. But the present-day historian who is interested in demographic, economic, or social data also strives to reconstruct the meaningful wholes that have marked out the course of human development. If indeed the historian is more interested in events than the sociologist, it is to the extent that he relates what happened: he puts events or systems viewed as events into place, into their order of succession, and discerns a meaning immanent in this order, a meaning that would be lost in any other method of reconstruction.

Thus we arrive at two legitimate definitions. The historian either narrates events or tries to comprehend the uniqueness of a culture, a society, or an international system. Thucydides narrates the events of the Peloponnesian War, but Jacob Burckhardt, who tries to grasp and convey the unique whole of the century of Constantine or of the Italian Renaissance, is also a historian. My analysis of the global system in the thermonuclear age is historical although it does not narrate events. After seeking generalities or peculiarities, it has a special aim: the extension to the whole globe, for the first time, of a single international system, a system distinguished by its heterogeneity and dominated by the thermonuclear duopoly of the United States and the Soviet Union.

In *Paix et guerre entre les nations*, I wrongly gave the impression that sociological research does not lead to any result. But that was not my thought. I tried to refute the geographical, demographic, and economic single-cause explanations of peace and war; but taking space, numbers, and resources into account is obviously indispensable to any explanation of international relations, as is a consideration of the character of political regimes or of nations. Furthermore, by refuting the demographic or economic "theories" (in the sense of causal explanations) of wars, one makes a positive contribution to knowledge by shedding light on the constant data of international society, and even of human and social nature, that form the structural conditions for hostility. One dissipates the illusions of those who hoped to put an end to the reign of wars by modifying a *single* variable (the number of men, the status of property, the political regime). Above all, one gains a deeper understanding of the historical diversity of international systems by discriminating between variables that have a different meaning in each period and variables that, at least temporarily, remain unchanged despite technological upheavals (for example, the concern for autonomy and the desire for power on the part of collective actors who constantly vie with each other for their security, their glory, or their ideas, through alternately violent and non violent means).

Within an international system that is historically unique there is room to set up models (all analysts of nuclear strategy set them up).There is also room for the equivalent of what Robert K. Merton calls "middle-range theory." The hypotheses we find in the writings of various authors (for instance, that alliances and nuclear weapons are incompatible or, in a more sophisticated form, that the major nuclear powers will refuse to back up their guarantee to those of their allies who insist on having their finger on the nuclear trigger) can be called theoretical. They constitute forecasts that will be confirmed, invalidated, or more likely amended by historical experience.

The theory of nuclear strategy is in certain respects more like economic theory than the general theory of international relations. Indeed, it relies on implicit axioms: that a "rational" *Prince* will not intentionally unleash a thermonuclear war or will not even risk thermonuclear war except for a vital stake. The "rational" *Prince* of nuclear strategy resembles the economic man of game theory more than that of Walras. But it is not possible to make an exact calculation of either the stakes or the risk. The theory of nuclear strategy is nonetheless a theory, albeit restricted to a particular phase of history and a special problem. It could not arise before the weapons whose implications it seeks to explain. It applies to only a single aspect of the conduct of states in our time. Moreover, it takes account of its own limitations: the greater the stability at the higher level of nuclear weapons, the more the danger of escalation diminishes and the less terrifying are the nonnuclear military conflicts. These hypotheses are theoretical because they do not take into account the whole reality. The United States and the Soviet Union, for many reasons, can either agree to impose *their* peace or clash here and there without fearing mutual destruction. For the time being, they seem to have chosen the first alternative. Rulers of other states are secretly pleased with this: it is good that the concern to avoid a thermonuclear war prevails over other considerations. This concern also dictated the American attitude during the simultaneous crises of Hungary and Suez. It could be expressed by the familiar saying: "Injustice is better than the risk of nuclear war."

Can the theorist approve or condemn? Certainly not. We thus arrive at our final antithesis: practice and theory.

☆   ☆   ☆

Many authors are severely critical of political science or of the science of international relations because it permits neither prediction nor manipulation.[11] A science that is not operational is no science. Economic

[11] Cf. Oscar Morgenstern, *The Question of National Defense* (New York: Random House, 1959).

science is at least partially operational since it shows statesmen how to tax a definite portion of individual incomes without jeopardizing the growth of production; it teaches them to control economic fluctuations at all costs and to limit the extent of deflationary and inflationary movements. It seems undeniable to me that, in this sense, political science or the science of international relations is not operational and will perhaps never be so, at least not until the time when politics per se, that is, the rivalry between individuals and the community to determine what is good in itself, will have disappeared.

Let us consider only the field of international relations. There is no lack of partial studies of a purely scientific character, in the strict sense of that term as used in physics or chemistry. How vulnerable are the silos in which nuclear missiles are stored? Given the explosive force of thermonuclear warheads, the average deviation in range, and the "hardness" of the sites, how many missiles are needed on an average to destroy an enemy device? The method of analysis, in such a case, is no different from that used in the natural sciences. The nature of the new weapons has given an unprecedented rigor and technical precision to the traditional calculation of the relations between forces. But these calculations are not yet sufficient to dictate a *scientific strategy*, whether it concerns a single decision (such as the "quarantine" of Cuba), or a whole political program (such as preventing the proliferation of nuclear weapons and refusing to assist allies anxious to develop their own nuclear industry), or a vision of a desirable international order. The science of international relations (and especially the analysis of the relations between nuclear powers) has had an effect upon the outlook of the *Princes* (the president of the United States and the men of the Kremlin) by turning strategists into the equivalent of what were called advisers to the *Prince* in Machiavelli's century. The theory of nonproliferation is not a scientific theory. It is a doctrine for action that coincides almost exactly with the interests of the United States and the Soviet Union and perhaps with those of all states (which, for the time being, are not sure of this).

During the Cuban crisis, President Kennedy applied one of the lessons suggested by theoretical analysis: since the major danger, in case of a confrontation between two nuclear powers, is a total war that would be disastrous for everyone, wisdom compels the state that wants to impose its will upon the other to act gradually. It is advisable to begin at a lower degree of violence and, through actions that are messages and messages that are actions, to make known one's inflexible determination to go as far and as high as necessary to obtain satisfaction. Thus, the duelists allow themselves time to reach a settlement without letting the irreparable take place. The winner—the one who has finally achieved his goal—will not cause his rival to lose face and will have left the path open for an honorable retreat. He will voluntarily create the illusion of a compromise even though he has won a victory.

On the whole, opinion in the United States, as in the world, approved of the conduct of the crisis, viewing it as the perfect expression of diplomatic skill or of the strategy of the nuclear age. Only a few cynics have stood apart. They have argued that even if President Kennedy had not taken so many precautions to spare the Kremlin leaders' pride, the latter would not have allowed themselves to be provoked. They would have adhered to Lenin's rule of taking two steps forward and one back, a rule that assumes additional validity in the nuclear age. I am raising the argument of the cynics not because I accept it myself but in order to show that, even in such a critical situation, science proposes and the *Prince* disposes.

Another example will illustrate the limitations of a doctrine based only on the lessons of abstract analysis. Such analysis clearly shows that the more monstrous a total nuclear war is, the less plausible is a threat to unleash it. The doctrine of all or nothing, of massive retaliation, becomes more and more unreasonable and, in the end, ineffectual. The result is that deterrence by nuclear threat requires the existence of conventional forces sufficient to prevent a would-be aggressor from gaining easy victories at small cost and to give the defender the means of increasing his stakes until the time when the use of nuclear weapons becomes plausible or even inevitable.

Passing from the doctrine of massive retaliation to the doctrine of flexible response is in keeping with the logic of strategic thinking. All countries possessing nuclear weapons will accept the abstract value of this reasoning as soon as they have the means to apply its conclusions, that is, when they will no longer be compelled, consciously or unconsciously, to pretend to be irrational because they lack the resources to adopt another strategy. But the doctrine of flexible response does not necessarily justify America's insistence, since 1961, on increasing NATO's conventional forces, on accumulating stockpiles for battles to be waged for ninety days without resorting to nuclear weapons, and on planning for a "pause" after a few days or a few weeks of combat before using nuclear weapons.

Finally, it remains true, according to abstract reasoning, that the reinforcement of conventional armaments adds to deterrence by giving the potential victim of aggression an additional margin of maneuver. But this freedom of maneuver belongs only to the holder of atomic weapons, that is, in the West to the United States; moreover, restricting the battle to Europe and to conventional weapons would consequently spare the United States and the Soviet Union the horrors of war. Once this is realized, the objections or suspicions of Europeans, and of the Germans in particular, cannot be attributed solely to a lack of understanding, as American analysts want to believe. Depending on the language used, the interpretation suggested, and the extent of preparation, the accumulation of conventional forces will appear destined either to make the threat of escalation plausible (that is, to maintain the threat of resorting to nuclear weapons) or to permit prolonged, costly combat on European soil (that is, to delay, if not eliminate, the threat of resorting to nuclear weapons). In the latter case, the policy fosters European skepticism ("the United States will not sacrifice New York City or Boston to save Frankfurt, London, or Paris"); in the former, it dispels this skepticism. But if the *Prince* does not understand the various possible interpretations of his nuclear policy, if he goes too far in one direction, if he does not tailor his preparations to the extent and foreseeable duration of conventional battles, he will upset the alliance he wished to consolidate. That is what has been done since 1961 by American leaders, who started with sound ideas but became the victims of the capital sin of diplomats and strategists: single-mindedness.

The same is true of the doctrine of nonproliferation. Let us assume that the chiefs of state all agree that the avoidance of a nuclear war is their highest objective. Let us further assume that they all believe that the risk of such a war increases with the number of states possessing these weapons. It still does not follow that they should rationally adhere to the doctrine of nonproliferation, which the Russians and Americans preach and strive to put into practice. This doctrine implies a discrimination between states, with some deemed worthy and others unworthy of holding such weapons. This discrimination may endanger the security of nonnuclear states. At any rate, it assigns them to the status of protectorate, which *Princes* traditionally have considered incompatible with dignity and sovereignty. Not to have to depend on any protector is a value in itself even if dependence does not jeopardize security.

Do not misunderstand me: I am not saying that the Russians and the Americans are wrong to subscribe to the doctrine of nonproliferation. It is possible that an implicit or explicit agreement between the two major powers is desirable. But I want to show that the doctrine, drawn from a simplified model and presuming that all actors have a single or ultimate goal, has no claim to validity or scientific accuracy. Whether the doctrine is inspired by unselfish motives or by an unconscious desire for power, it appears to be cynical since it tends to sanctify the reign of the two superpowers. In any case, the doctrine conforms to the essential nature of the system of international relations I have analyzed: it endeavors to substitute the rule of the strongest for the still nonexistent tribunal and police force. Far from having modified the asocial nature of international relations, nuclear weapons have given rise to new expressions of that nature: solidarity of interests between ideological enemies, conflict of interests among allies. Because resort to force is still possible at any moment, the two superpowers subordinate their rivalry not to a rule of law but to a common concern for their security.

If we expect a theory of international relations to provide the equivalent of what a knowledge of construction materials provides the builder of bridges, then there is no theory and never will be. What the theory of action is able to offer, here as elsewhere, is an understanding of various ideologies—moralism, legalism, realism, and power politics—through which men and nations think out problems in international relations, establish their goals, or assign themselves duties. The theory of practice, or *praxeology*, differs from these ideologies insofar as it considers them all and determines the full implications of each one. As long as international society remains an asocial society whose law, in serious cases, is left to the interpretation of each actor and that lacks an authority holding a monopoly of legitimate violence, the theory will be scientifically valid to the extent that it does not provide the equivalent of what noble-hearted people and lightweight minds expect, that is, a simple ideology guaranteeing morality or efficiency.

This theory, as objective a study as possible of the conditions under which foreign policy develops, is not irrelevant to the morality or efficiency of action. For moralism, if it leads to Max Weber's *Gesinnungsethik*, by failing to take account of the probable or possible consequences of the decisions made, turns out to be immoral. As for realism, it would be unrealistic if it considered the moral judgments men pass on the conduct of their rulers as negligible, if it disregarded the interest of all actors in maintaining a minimum of legal order in their reciprocal relations, or if it ignored the yearning of humanity, now capable of destroying itself, to reduce interstate violence. The more the theorist of practice bears in mind the multiplicity of aims pursued by actors in the international system, the less he will be a prisoner of an oversimplified representation of *Homo diplomaticus* and the more chance he will have of understanding his allies and enemies by understanding the diversity of perceptions that govern their conduct. The *hic et nunc* decision, about Cuba or Vietnam, can never be dictated by the theorist. Nor will he be able to dictate, with assurance of scientific validity, the strategy that would lead humanity beyond "power politics" toward a monopoly of legitimate violence.

The course of international relations is eminently historical, in all senses of the term: its changes are incessant; its systems are diverse and fragile; it is affected by all economic, technical, and moral transformations; decisions made by one or several men put millions of others into action and launch irreversible changes, whose consequences are carried out indefinitely; and the actors, citizens or rulers, are forever subjected to apparently contradictory obligations.

It would be unreasonable to decree in advance that modern methods of investigation will not teach us anything we do not already know. Long live computers, the "prisoner's dilemma," and experimental research on the probable results of confidence or suspicion in interpersonal relations!

But until machines and technicians instruct statesmen, let us take care not to forget the lessons of experience brought to light by the effort to conceptualize.

Is it a failure or a success for the theory of practice to rediscover the paradoxes of human existence as they have always appeared to philosophers, both ancient and modern, without resolving them? Whether failure or success, the fact is that the scientist has not yet been given the means to transform man's historical condition.

☆　☆　☆

Perhaps, having made this circuit, we can again take up that meaning of the concept of theory we put aside: theory and philosophy as one and the same. Not that we have in some way found in conclusion what we decided not to seek at the outset, namely, a philosophical truth of a higher order than scientific knowledge. But the whole approach, which proceeds from the determination of the international system as a specific social system to the prudence of the statesman through the analysis of sociological regularities and historical peculiarities, constitutes the critical or questioning equivalent of a philosophy.

No technique of inquiry, no traditional or modern method, should be accepted or rejected a priori so long as the investigator remains aware of the whole into which his individual undertaking is placed or integrated. The different levels of conceptualization—a definition of the asocial society of sovereign states, a theory or pseudotheory of the demographic or economic causes of wars, models of typical situations between nuclear powers, an enumeration of the main variables of all international systems—are distinguished from each other to suit the needs of clarity. Understanding of a single system—for example, the global system from 1949 to 1960—must take all levels into account; it calls for the simultaneous use of all available instruments. It is not even a paradox to suggest that theory alone makes it possible to incorporate the personal relationship between two men, Khrushchev and Kennedy, into an interpretation of the development of the Cuban crisis of 1962. In the opposite sense, this crisis adds something to our theoretical knowledge, reminding us that the historian has to be a philosopher and the philosopher has to be aware of what we shall never see a second time—at least when the object of knowledge is not only the logic of systems but also the logic of action.

10. The Evolution of Modern Strategic Thought (1945–1968)

No ONE WOULD CLAIM to be acquainted with *all* the literature on strategic problems published in the United States since 1954, still less that published throughout the rest of the world. The latter, though nearly always dependent on the American literature, nonetheless in several countries still shows a certain originality.[1] In reading the American literature, what I am really concerned with is its content, analyses, and conclusions, never with its actual history—that is to say, the origin of each idea, the order in which the various theories or doctrines have been elaborated, or the influence of a given analyst on his colleagues and the statesmen of the time.

I will therefore limit myself to a historical outline, to distinguishing the principal phases in strategic thought insofar as I believe I have experienced them directly, with the aim of giving a diagnosis of the present situation. Let me briefly recall a few commonly acknowledged facts, which will serve as an introduction. At the end of the second world war[2] there emerged an unprecedented situation in international relations. Nuclear weapons were certainly one factor, but there were also the expansion of diplomacy to the entire planet and the rise to dominance of a country, the United States, whose diplomatic tradition ran counter to that of European cabinets and which six short years earlier had still been trying to safeguard its neutrality. Other factors were the decline of the great colonial powers and the proliferation of national liberation movements. In short, historical reality was confronting the strategists

---

[1] The literature of socialist countries, which I will come to later, derives from another philosophy.

[2] I will use the word "modern" in its narrowest sense—to refer to the period since 1945.

"Remarques sur l'evolution de la pensée strategique (1945–1968)." Translated from the French and reprinted with authorization from *European Journal of Sociology*, IX (1968), 151–79.

with a series of problems. (1) How to make room within strategic thought[3] for the doctrine governing the use of nuclear arms, qualitatively different from so-called classical or conventional weapons? (2) Once these weapons are given an essentially deterrent function (i.e., diplomatic use designed to prevent military use), how does this affect the distinction between peace and war in the first instance and between the various forms of armed conflict in the second? (3) The overall course of events has gradually refuted, at least for the time being, the two extreme hypotheses, the one according to which nuclear weapons would lead to peace through fear, the other that they would exclude the possibility of the continuation of power politics even in another form or by other means. At the same time, numerous questions concerning relations between allies, relations between enemies, and the use of force commanded the attention of the strategists, now no longer able to restrict themselves to the narrow meaning of the term strategy.

The classical sense, that of strategy as opposed to tactics, is defined with perfect clarity in Clausewitz: "Die Taktik ist die Lehre vom Gebrauche der Streitkräfte im Gefecht, die Strategie die Lehre vom Gebrauche der Gefechte zum Zwecke des Krieges."[4] Sometimes modern authors contrast strategy not with tactics but with policy. In this case, the words "strategic" and "military" tend to be confused: by the strategic aspect of the Czechoslovakian affair one really means the military aspect, the way in which the presence of Soviet forces on the western borders of Bohemia modifies the European situation.

The term strategy has been extended to its utmost in the social sciences and even in everyday speech. One speaks of the strategy of a firm, the strategy of development, the strategy of devaluation. In all these cases it strikes me that by strategy one means a series of decisions more or less foreseen by the protagonist and formulated in a more or less fixed and coherent plan—provided, of course, that he is faced not by inert matter but by individuals or groups whose reactions, rational or irrational, he must guess in deciding on the broad outlines of his action.

In this sense, there is no difference between what was once called a "policy" and what one now calls a "strategy." The substitution of the latter word for the former can probably be explained by the new awareness of the confrontation or dialogue of the actors. The action, in the broad sense of the word, does not confront an actor with mere matter but with one or several enemies, allies, or spectators; consequently, the actors adopt a strategy, rather than a policy— the former concept suggesting the constraints to which they are subjected, the uncertainties to which they

---

[3] The term "thought" embraces *theory*, or abstract and scientific study, *doctrine*, prescriptions relative to action, and finally the historical or political study of theories and doctrines.

[4] *Tactics* is the concept of the use of armed forces in battle; *strategy* is the concept of the use of battles to forward the aim of the war (Clausewitz, *On War*, Book II, chap. I).

are exposed, by the reactions, appropriate or otherwise, of those with whom they are playing or fighting.

If I were to adhere to the term strategy in its broadest sense, I would have to consider the conduct of states toward other states, indeed even their conduct toward their subjects or citizens, to the extent to which a mode of government affects both the mode of action in external matters and the influence it can exercise by its example, be it admirable, odious, or fascinating. Instead, I will opt for something halfway between the narrow interpretation, say, of Clausewitz, and the unlimited sense of the word as used by the press. By strategy I mean the action in cases in which the rules actually observed do not exclude recourse to armed force. By European tradition, such was moreover the specific nature of diplomatic action: each state reserves the right to use force to defend its vital interests and it is the state, if it has the means, that defines what it considers to be its vital interests. Strategic thought (in the narrow sense) was concerned first of all with the implications of nuclear weapons; as these implications gradually emerged, it expanded to include diplomacy to the entire extent that diplomacy is influenced by arms and, in particular, nuclear arms. I might roughly summarize the evolution of strategic thought as I see it with the phrase *"from the narrow to the broad sense of the concept of strategy."* Analysts of nuclear problems[5] have become the diplomatic advisers of the *Prince,* to the glory or misfortune of *Princes* and analysts.

This development seems to me to be divided into three periods—possibly two main periods, with the first broken up into two subperiods. In 1961 the analysts arrived at the White House with President Kennedy; at that time they worked out various deterrent schemes and heatedly discussed the strategic or diplomatic doctrines that can be derived from theoretical elaboration. For the first time the secretary of defense, though he comes from private industry, has a taste for ideas and the capacity to understand the most subtle of analysts. The latter are living their "finest hour," and most of them approve, in essence, of the McNamara doctrine. The early postwar years perhaps constitute a subperiod, that of nuclear innocence, during which the United States alone possessed nuclear weapons[6] and the military chiefs stuck firmly to the simple alternative: peace or atomic war (or perhaps one should say atomic peace or total atomic war). Nuclear arms had provided the rulers of America with a justification for disarmament, which the country, unaware of its new responsibilities and faithful to its tradition, had embarked upon immediately after victory had been won and which it had pursued too fast and too far.

The Korean campaign and the establishment of NATO made govern-

---

[5] Currently one says—and I have said it, too—*nuclear strategy.* In fact, this term can refer either to a doctrine of the use of a particular weapon or to global strategy in the nuclear age.

[6] One could also say that they exercised a unilateral deterrent.

ment leaders and public opinion aware of what the analysts had probably already grasped: a state, even if it is alone in possessing nuclear arms, cannot deter anyone from doing anything by the threat of using these weapons. This incapacity, which the Korean campaign clearly revealed, is not a material but a psychological and moral one. The 1950s saw the emergence of the sum total of concepts, schemes, and doctrines that have since been an integral part of the lessons in international relations given to students and statesmen alike.

There is no need to expound these schemes and concepts—they have long been common knowledge: first- and second-strike strategy (it might be better to say attack) against the cities and resources or against the opposing retaliation force; vulnerability or invulnerability of nuclear installations; massive reprisal or flexible response; and reinforcement or weakening of the deterrent by the substitution of flexible response for massive reprisal. Toward the end of the 1950s all the main ideas had been worked out, all the theories constructed, and all the doctrines set forth.

The whole can be divided into four categories. I will call the first "conceptual elaboration": deterrent, first and second strike, attack on cities or military targets, and massive retaliation or flexible response, escalation (or increase to the extreme). This elaboration we tend to accept by virtue of its ideological and doctrinal neutrality. It is the result of the mental tools that analysts necessarily use for reasons of convenience.

A second category covers scientific or technical studies, often concealed from the layman (classified material), that end by indicating or demonstrating the vulnerability or invulnerability of such and such a retaliation force. Everyone will remember the famous article by our colleague Wohlstetter entitled "The Delicate Balance of Terror" (*Foreign Affairs,* January 1959). It remains true that a state is not assured of second-strike or retaliation capability as soon as it possesses a few dozen nuclear bombs with suitable means of delivery (supersonic planes or ballistic missiles). It also remains true that no one can predict with certainty what would happen if one of the two superpowers were to try, by a sudden act of aggression carried out with all the resources at its disposal, to disarm and force the capitulation of the other. And it remains still more true that technical research continues to improve shells and armor, bombs, and the means of delivery: the balance of terror is thus never completely stabilized. Rational analysis intervenes at this point to determine, as rigorously as possible, in economic and strategic terms, the cheapest method of attaining a given objective. Is it better to respond to an antimissile system with a similar system or to increase the penetrability of the missiles? When confronted by a new form of armor, would equilibrium be best reestablished by similar armor or by an improved shell? In these controversies analysts with access to secret studies easily and mysteriously overwhelm their less fortunate colleagues, condemned to the uncertain status of amateurs enlightened only by their common sense.

So-called cost-efficiency methods were introduced into the Pentagon by civilian specialists in nuclear problems, in particular, by economists from the RAND Corporation. These studies, though technical and scientific in their origin and development, nonetheless contain an element of what I below call doctrine. The quantitative value attributed to various weapons or weapons systems depends to an extent on the degree of probability that those making the calculations attribute to various eventualities and on the importance assigned to the functions or objectives of the military means.

A third category covers plans (more or less comparable to theoretical economic plans) in which states are likened to strategic actors and take supposedly rational decisions in abstractly defined contingencies. Let us imagine a state with nuclear arms that are vulnerable to an enemy's first strike. If, in the event of a crisis, it is afraid of being attacked and disarmed, it will be tempted to strike first in anticipation. The greater the advantage of striking first, the greater the temptation for an anticipatory (preemptive) strike. Similarly, let us suppose that two enemies wish to avoid escalation; they will have far more chance of doing so if, without any explicit agreement, they stick to some rule that each can understand and respect—the nonuse of nuclear arms, for example. The desire to limit violence finds expression in one side's acting with a degree of moderation or restraint that the other cannot fail to notice.

The fourth category embraces two kinds of debate: doctrinal and ethical.[7] Taking into account theoretical plans and sometimes also scientific data (in other words, depending on the results of the two previous categories), what doctrine ought one to adopt? Or, more precisely, what doctrine should a given state adopt in a given contingency? The distinction corresponds to the one recognized by everyone in economics, between the pure equilibrium theory of Walras or Pareto, on the one hand, and liberal policy, on the other (in fact, neither group preached liberalism). Similarly, though in slightly different form, Keynesian plans inspire rulers with certain ways of conceiving the responsibility and the capacity for action of states; they never dictate, as such, the decision to be taken *hic et nunc*.

Let us look again at the example of the anticipatory strike by a state fearful of being disarmed by reason of the vulnerability of its forces. What conclusion should one draw? First, Robert McNamara advised the Russians to conceal their ballistic missiles in underground silos so as to remove from them the temptation of an anticipatory strike, then he comforted the members of the U.S. Congress by guaranteeing American counterforce

---

[7] I am steering clear of the ethical debate that one finds in the well-known books of Anatol Rapoport, P. Green, and R. C. Tucker.

capability (even in a second strike). Clearly, one must choose: an actor cannot reinforce his deterrent by making himself capable of disarming his nuclear enemy and at the same time escape the risk of an anticipatory strike by an enemy possessing only a vulnerable force. Which alternative should one prefer? The reply probably depends on the circumstances. Certainly, the whole question could never aspire to the dignity of a scientific proposition and the use of the term "rational" is merely a vain camouflage either for uncertainly of choice or for the legitimate recourse to reasonable intuition.

Massive retaliation or flexible response, the deterrent value of a modest force in the hands of a medium-sized state, acceptance of parity or a quest for superiority on the part of the United States, the advantages and disadvantages for various states and for all humanity of the nonproliferation of nuclear arms, disarmament or arms control—all these doctrinal debates are generically the same. They make use of scientific research but end in conclusions based on abstract reason rather than concrete evidence. They can be compared to debates on economic policy in the sense that all economic policies involve disadvantages for certain individuals or groups in the community, that the process of measuring advantages and costs can never be absolutely precise, and that every decision has an inherent coefficient of uncertainty. Perhaps the greatest good for the greatest number imposes sacrifices on some: there can be little doubt that nonproliferation is in the interests of the Soviet Union and the United States; and it may also be in the genuine long-term interests of those states that renounce nuclear weapons, but there is no secret file in the Pentagon to prove this point.

The first period of postwar strategic thought came to an end between 1961 and 1963 with the McNamara doctrine, the controversies between Europe and America, the first applications of the idea of arms control (the hot line and agreement on the partial suspension of nuclear tests), and the agreement, at first implicit and then increasingly explicit, between the two superpowers both to slow down the qualitative aspect of the arms race and to practice their rivalry in such a manner as to reduce to a minimum the risk of a direct confrontation.

Since about 1963 a shift of interest has taken place. There is not really much more to be gained from the study of what is wrongly called nuclear strategy (here one should, for instance, talk of the changes that nuclear arms impose on traditional strategy). It is a state's diplomatic activity taken as a whole that, in the nuclear age, holds our attention and for a twofold reason: first, analysis has shown the link that exists between the nuclear threat and the everyday course of international relations; second, events brought to light a certain kind of neutralization of nuclear arms (at least a partial neutralization)—the impossibility (for the time being) of forcing a nonnuclear state to capitulate by threatening it with the use of nuclear arms. Putting the matter more simply, let us say that the second period, in which we now find ourselves, began when the conclusions from the first became the basis for the strategy (in the broad sense) of the United States and the Soviet Union. Or one can simply look at it in terms of the *rise and decline* of nuclear strategy, or rather of the civilian analysts. If they lived their "finest hour" with Kennedy, the Vietnam war—for which they are not responsible—represents their epitaph.

☆   ☆   ☆

This shift of interest, like the whole history of strategic thought, can be explained both by the general course of events and by progress in analysis.

The impassioned debates of 1961–1963 came to an end not through a lack of combatants but *through a lack of interest in the combat.* Here, without making any claim to a complete list, are what I consider to be some of the reasons for this transfer of research activity to other fields.

1. Conceptual elaboration can hardly be called intrinsically complex, nor does it lend itself to infinite refinement. Compared to economic elaboration, it remains in reality primitive and crude. To quote Napoleon, "Strategy is a simple art; it's all in the execution."

2. Even today, only two states possess the complete thermonuclear apparatus with the whole range of bombs from the least destructive, with an explosive power equal to or less than that of the most powerful conventional bombs or shells, right up to the monster bombs of seveal dozen megatons. But so far, in their relations with each other, these two states, these duopolists, have stuck firmly to the most elementary rule of prudence: they have steered clear of all armed confrontation. The nuclear threat allows and perhaps favors limited wars, but so far it has prevented (or helped to prevent) *limited wars between the states that hold the supreme weapons.* It is as if the two superpowers feared that a clash between a Soviet and an American battalion would provoke the ultimate escalation. Russian cargo vessels unload war material at Haiphong yet even American "hawks" do not clamor all that vigorously for the port to be bombed since they know it would involve hitting Soviet ships. Likewise, careful analysis showed the vulnerability of the position of West Berlin or even, generally speaking, of any position where an overwhelming superiority of conventional forces allows one of the superpowers to burden the other with responsibility for recourse to nuclear arms. Admittedly, the Russians could have gone forward by stages, first signing a peace treaty with the German Democratic Republic and then nibbling away at Western rights to Berlin, without setting off a nuclear response (and they know it). They refrain from doing so, in spite of loud declarations, as though out of respect for a simple law, one that predates the nuclear age and conforms to diplomatic tradition: not to interfere with what the other—their only rival and only equal—considers to be a vital

interest.[8] American diplomacy or strategy also obeys this law. Where a clear line of demarcation has been traced by explicit agreement, the old practice of spheres of influence, condemned by American ideology and by President Roosevelt himself, comes back into its own and offers statesmen a convenient substitute for a refresher course at the RAND Corporation.

3. The Russian and American leaders have come to understand, either by themselves or through their analysts, *one* of the lessons that everyone can draw from weapons of mass destruction. Whereas in the past the leading state of a bloc or coalition could gain the maximum advantage from a victorious war—Machiavelli advised small states not to link their fate to that of a state more powerful than themselves—a war waged with all available arms and directed at the nuclear armament of the enemy, far from sparing the leading states, would strike them first. The common interest of the United States and the Soviet Union not to give themselves up to a war to the death, not to exchange nuclear bombardments, seems so obvious that a commentator of the historical school suggested that a *Russo-American alliance against total war* existed as early as 1956, the time of the Suez crisis, as the sign of this relationship. Our American friends keep reminding us—and rightly—that they do not invade a country that nationalizes some investment by one of their corporations and invoke the U.N. Charter. The Europeans, molded to skepticism or cynicism by centuries of history, will not be any more indulgent of the collusion between Russia and America in 1956 than the Americans themselves are of the collusion among Israel, France, and England.

Since then, discussions on the extent of "unacceptable damage" (ten, twenty, or forty percent of resources), on "limited nuclear war," and on the volume of military operations carried out with conventional weapons that should be taken as "critical" (meaning that they would lead to escalation)—all these debates inevitably have become academic. Statesmen for the most part have drawn from Keynesian theory a mode of economic vision, a new perception of the state's responsibilities and rules of action, based on simplified models or approximate propositions. The same holds true in matters of nuclear strategy. From the third category, statesmen have deduced principles that common sense should have been able to teach them but for which analysts have given a rational justification. They have gained insight into the relations between states and an understanding of the role of the armed forces. But this understanding, the result at least in part of the work of the analysts, has, it seems to me, also removed some of these analysts' ardor for research. So long as only the United States and the Soviet Union merit the name of nuclear powers and go on playing the same game they have been playing for twenty years, formerly disguising it under martial language but for the last half dozen

[8] Naturally, each of the superpowers tries to make the other aware of what it regards as its vital interest. But the other is not obliged to let itself be convinced and an error in communication always remains a possibility.

years playing it almost openly, the construction of more and more complex forms of deterrence, in accordance with conventional and first- and second-strike nuclear capacities, gradually assumes an academic character. These models do not display even the character of economic models of the same type, nor do they require any uncommon intellectual subtlety.

4. The debate between the United States and Europe on the value of the American guarantee and on the respective merits of the threat of massive retaliation as against a flexible response has, for the time being, quietened down. Not that it has ended in unanimous assent: most Europeans, especially the Germans, are convinced that the doctrine of flexible response expresses the desire, legitimate on the part of the Americans but dangerous for the countries in the front line, to make a war possible that would be limited for the two superpowers and disastrous for the countries in the battle zone. Certainly, in abstract terms, the reply given by the analysts on the other side of the Atlantic remains irrefutable: the Europeans cannot at one and the same time declare that the threat of massive retaliation has lost all credibility and yet claim that the American leaders, by substituting the threat of responses adapted to the nature of the provocation or aggression, are weakening the deterrent. On an intellectual level, the dialogue tends to favor the Americans, but the fact remains that they quite naturally reserve the right to make decisions and that, in all circumstances, they alone maintain contact and continue the dialogue with whoever is officially designated the potential enemy. The leading state of a coalition does not always measure its allies' losses and its own on the same scale.

The endless debate has lost its acuteness, its actuality. It is not as if by dint of continuous dialogue the speakers had reached sincere agreement: they have the feeling, rightly or wrongly, that debate, too, has become an academic matter. France has withdrawn from NATO; she possesses a strategic nuclear force that, in the present situation, inspires the French with neither excessive pride nor terror and that the Russians and Americans for the moment regard with more indifference than anxiety. As for the other members of the Atlantic pact, they accept the American doctrine, with discussion beforehand and a promised share, to the extent possible, in the decision-making process at the moment of the crisis. Since in the present situation they hardly fear a serious crisis and cannot, in any case, get better terms, they stick to what they have.

5. The war that for three years has aroused the passions of the masses and the interest of experts is still being fought in Vietnam. On one side there is an American expeditionary force of half a million men and the South Vietnamese army; on the other, the south Vietnamese partisans and the divisions of the North Vietnamese regular army. For twenty years wars described sometimes as "revolutionary," sometimes as "wars of national liberation," have multiplied but never before have they reached

such proportions and never before has the United States, with its immense resources, the unprecedented mobility of its troops, and its anticolonial ideology found itself, in the eyes of an important section of world opinion, playing the same role as the old colonial powers, France in Vietnam and Algeria, and the Netherlands in Indonesia.

Strategic thought draws its inspiration, in each century or rather at each moment of history, from the problems posed to it by events themselves. Clausewitz puts into theoretical form, after all, the battles of regular armies such as were offered to him by his experience of the wars of the French Revolution and of Napoleon. But his philosophical mind allows him to formulate certain propositions relative to the very nature of conflicts between states, propositions that have such permanent validity that strategic thought can successfully integrate the consequences of nuclear arms in a theory that retains the basic essentials of Clausewitz's concepts. Nor did he forget guerrilla warfare (he had visions of a popular uprising in 1813, but it never took place), and everyone is familiar with the chapter on "Arming the Nation"[9] and with the reference to the partisans of the *Vendée*, who, he says, were capable of constituting the equivalent of an army.

The Vietnam war calls for a *theory* (the expression in conceptual form of the manner of fighting both of the partisans and of the forces of order or repression) as well as a *doctrine* (a collection of precepts valid for the partisans or for their counterinsurgent adversaries). But I wonder whether these same analysts, trained in their various academic disciplines, are having as much success in this new area as they did in the old. Certainly, there are more or less general rules governing insurgency and counterinsurgency. But at the risk of appearing discourteous, I will ask myself aloud whether a single member of the Hudson Institute, unable to speak the language of the country, knowing little of the Vietnamese people, their customs, or history, can claim the title of expert. I can only admire professors who undertake fact-finding missions in Vietnam and bring back analyses and suggestions.

The example of the theory of guerrilla warfare or of the struggle against insurgency is by way of a general comment not only on the strategic thought of today but also on the study of international relations and the influence of the so-called scientific school. I have no wish to rekindle the controversy between the traditionalists and the innovators (these last work in the areas of categories 2 and 3; category 1 belongs to all schools of thought and category 4 to no one and everyone). The integration of partisan warfare, or of war waged by regular armies in the manner of partisans, within a general theory of conflict presents no great difficulty.

In all conflicts one must distinguish between the trial of strength and the test of will, a duality expressed in the well-known adage: only those

[9] *On War*, Book VI, chap. XXVI, and Book V, chap. II.

are beaten who admit themselves beaten. When a partisan army, or a regular army adopting partisan methods, fights against a regular army obliged to maintain and defend a large number of fixed points, the attitude of the civilian population becomes one of the principal stakes in the struggle, as well as one of the main factors in its success or failure. And victory sometimes seems impossible for the forces of order or the regular army. Certainly, the press often rather flippantly and without proof suggests that victory is impossible. The "impossibility" theory is the result of the counterinsurgents' (the United States in this case) limiting the forces they are willing to engage and imposing, or having public opinion impose on them, a time limit in which to emerge triumphant.[10] In any case, the two factors of the stake involved and the degree of resolution shown are effectively extending the psychological or moral dimension of the conflict at the cost of the actual military aspect of the operation. But what expert has pointed out this dimension? Certainly not the mere analyst of strategic contingencies, or those who construct simulated models, or the mathematician calculating the relation between cost and yield. Not that these men of science are disqualified as such, but they owe their eventual qualification as much to their political, historical, and human judgment as to their scientific training in the strict sense of the term.

In other words, the example of guerrilla warfare brings us back to the central thesis of this lecture: that the partial neutralization of nuclear arms, and the temporary absence of armed conflict between nuclear states, serves to focus our attention once more on traditional problems of a strictly military nature at the same time that strategic thought is extending its scope to include all forms of relations between states in wartime. The strategy of North Vietnam and the United States also involves the use of nonmilitary (i.e., psychological and administrative) means, but it comes very close once again to the classical concept of the use of all means, and in the first instance of arms, to attain the military objective *and* the political goal, with the relationship between this objective and this goal varying according to the circumstances and sometimes also the parties involved. Briefly, strategy remains an entity in the sense that it cannot be reduced to the movement of armies or the conduct of military actions, but it is only indirectly influenced by what one used to call "nuclear strategy" or the doctrine of the deterrent use of nuclear arms. As both sides have rejected actual use, it is within the framework of this refusal that the two superpowers, insurgents, and counterinsurgents fight their battles and must find the secret of victory.

One should hardly be surprised that today more than ever before both the analysis of the present situation and the suggested courses of action should take into account concrete situations in their specific historical

[10] This notion of the "impossibility of a military victory" is by no means unequivocal. It may be impossible with the means that the state consents to use or in the period of time allowed to the rulers.

context. Perhaps theory, inasmuch as it has a physical or economic aspect, will allow a *rational* distribution of budgetary resources among the different arms systems. When it is a question of Vietnam, or the use of force or escalation, the analyst who wishes to be the *Prince's* adviser must dirty his hands; I mean he has to come down from the ethereal level of models and plans and get to know in their totality the elements that make up the situation and in terms of which the statesman will have to make his decision.

Of course, all analysts, that is, all those who since 1945 have devoted the whole or part of their time to the study of strategic matters, would subscribe to these general statements. They would agree that a decision or piece of advice, valid *hic et nunc,* can never be derived from theoretical propositions or plans. One must still know how most effectively to clarify an action, which always unfolds within a particular context.

Let us take the problem of what is called escalation. This concept is already present in Clausewitz's book although the phrase he uses is more striking from a literary point of view: *"Steigerung biszum äussersten,"*[11] rise to the extremes. It appears in the course of the analysis of the dialectic of hostility: enemies by definition are so to speak prisoners of each other; neither can trust the other; neither has the power utterly to determine the volume of forces he will engage since the other can always outbid him; neither can achieve security except by disarming the other, that is to say, by gaining absolute victory. The rise to the extremes, as described in the abstract logic of hostility, does not always take place in reality for several reasons that can be summed up in the formula: real belligerents are not to be confused with the enemies that figure in the abstract theory of the dialectic of hostility; should the occasion arise, they aim at limited objectives and inform each other of their intentions. Though Clausewitz does not express himself as I have just done, his writings can be taken to suggest that historical conflicts differ from perfect hostility as a consequence of the dialogue between enemies that continues throughout the combat and does not end in a pure and simple trial of strength.

By reflecting on nuclear arms and on the necessity of preventing their use, American analysts have come back to the concept of escalation. Once the seductive but illusory conception of peace through fear had been dismissed, once the bitter truth had been admitted that nuclear arms do not prevent all armed conflict, the strategists resolved—to use an expression that is becoming current—to save humanity from nuclear arms by saving war. By the same token, they went back to the old idea of matching the volume of the violence to the importance of the stake, that is, of not pushing all armed conflicts to their limit, or always aiming at absolute victory, of being satisfied sometimes with peace without victory. The

[11] *On War*, Book I, chap. I. The related concept of the reduction of violence or deescalation appears in Book VIII.

historical turning point in this century occurred at the time of the Korean war: for the first time the misleadingly obvious motto of certain generals, "There is no substitute for victory," appeared equivocal if not false and in the final analysis anachronistic.

The concept of escalation translates into military language the political notion of limitation, of diversification, of progression in the use of force. So the risk of escalation in our age, of the recourse to nuclear arms, remains an ever present reality influencing all levels of conflict and all forms of diplomacy. It not only restricts the bidding but also obliges the strategists to show imagination, to invent for each given situation the means of action that suit the circumstances and will allow the actor to reach his goals without excessive expenditure and without committing the whole system. Finally, this same risk of escalation establishes the progressive use of force, defensively and offensively—defensively, within the framework of the doctrine of flexible response, since deterrent action at a lower level depends for its effect on the potential aggressor's fearing both the effectiveness of the initial response (the classical means of defense, for example) and escalation should this response prove insufficient; offensively, in cases in which the strategist endeavors to multiply the effectiveness of a limited force by the implicit or explicit threat of climbing further rungs on the ladder of violence if the enemy refuses to yield or proves capable of resisting the dose of violence that has been administered to him. The widely read books *On Escalation* and *Arms and Influence* are devoted to a deep and subtle analysis of the innumerable forms of conflict, of the dozens of rungs on the ladder of violence, and of the diversity of punishments (or chastisements) that can be inflicted on the territory or population of an enemy state little by little to persuade or compel it to negotiate, if not actually to lay down its arms.

I confess that in spite of the intellectual satisfaction it often gives me this literature makes me uneasy. Here, in a few words, are the reasons I give myself for feeling as I do.

At the beginning of his book on escalation, Herman Kahn quotes a sentence[12] from one of my books that expresses the following idea: there is no deterrent in a general or abstract sense; it is a case of knowing *who* one can deter *from what, in what circumstances, by what means* (by threat or by organizing defense). This perfectly ordinary and so to speak innocent statement is the result of placing the doctrine of the diplomatic use of nuclear arms within the general doctrine of strategy (or of total diplomacy) between states. Herman Kahn quotes this statement and immediately adds that he does not study specific historical problems of the kind that confront statesmen. He imagines, invents, and describes with a

---

[12] See Herman Kahn, *On Escalation: Metaphors and Scenarios* (London: Pall Mall, 1965), pp. 23–25.

minuteness bordering on unreality, dozens of situations of conflict reduced to simplified schemes[13] and the decisions that suit these situations. Failing science fiction, what other name but "strategy fiction" could one give to this form of literature?

Everyone has his own way of amusing himself. I wonder, however, whether this type of literature—neither abstract theory nor historical analysis—does not bring with it as many disadvantages as advantages. Does it endow statesmen with imagination—supposing they read it? Is there not a risk of worsening rather than curing the spontaneous faults of the leaders in Washington: overestimating the technical aspect of diplomatic or military problems; underestimating the importance of given psychological, moral, and political factors, *which are different in each situation;* and allowing their decisions to be influenced by people acquainted with strategy but not with Vietnam?

Certainly, neither Herman Kahn nor Thomas Schelling commits the intellectual errors of presenting these imaginary cases as real and deriving from strategy fiction a course of action valid for a specific case. In his preface to *Arms and Influence* Schelling makes the explicit distinction on which I insist, though it is self-evident: "I have used some historical examples, but usually as illustration, not evidence."[14] But he adds a little later: "The several pages examining the 1964 bombing in the Gulf of Tonkin do not mean that I approve of it (though, in fact, I do); the several pages on coercive aspects of the bombing of North Vietnam in 1965 do not mean I approve of it (and, in fact, I am not sure yet)."[15]

The reader cannot fail to establish a relationship between the analysis of "punishments" inflicted on the enemy, his territory and population, and the present conduct of the Vietnam War. But such analyses remain deliberately partial; they fall somewhere between abstract plans and concrete situations. The notion of rationality (or of the rationality of irrationality) is put between quotation marks, as though to acknowledge that it does not lend itself to scientific definition. Doubtless Schelling considers rational any conduct of a war that maintains a certain proportion between its cost and the stakes involved, between the means used and the eventual benefits of victory. But he writes in his preface: "Principles rarely lead straight to politics; politics depend on values and purposes, predictions and estimates, and must usually reflect the relative weight of conflicting principles."[16] Such a proposition should put the statesman on his guard against all advice given by an analyst who is not fully ac-

---

[13] "Much of the seeming artificiality and abstractness of this book comes from the fact that I will necessarily tend to ignore or deemphasize the who–when–why aspects" (ibid., p. 25).

[14] *Arms and Influence* (New Haven, Conn.: Yale University Press, 1966), p. vii.

[15] Ibid.

[16] Ibid.

quainted with the *values and purposes* of the enemy, whose conduct will seem rational or irrational according to the *values and purposes* attributed to him.

Schelling also takes great care not to confuse the considered conduct and the rational conduct of the conflict:

> It would be a mistake to think that conducting war in the measured cadence of limited reprisal somehow rescues the whole business of war from impetuosity and gives it "rational" qualities that it would otherwise lack. True, there is a sense in which anything done coolly, deliberately, on schedule, by plan, upon reflection, in accordance with rules and formulae, and pursuant to a calculus, is "rational" but it is in a very limited sense. It helps if we can slow down a war, induce reflection, and provide national leaders with a consciousness that they are still responsible, still in control, still capable of affecting the course of events. This is different from saying that there is some logical way to conduct a war of limited reprisal or that a decisive intellect can prove sure guidance in such a war on what to do next.[17]

Thus, no analyst has ever confused "considered" conduct and "rational" conduct of the war or derived from strategy fiction an effective strategy for use in an individual case. Nonetheless, the fact remains that the second Cuban crisis—the one involving ballistic missiles—marked the triumph of the analysts and that the Vietnam war points to their decline and undermines their prestige. Why? Because the so-called escalation method, used in each case, seems to have succeeded in the first and failed in the second.

In November 1962, President Kennedy threatened to go to extremes and yet had no need to resort to any form of force. The fact of putting the army, the air force, and the navy on alert was enough of a signal to "persuade" the men of the Kremlin. Three years of bombing have not "persuaded" the Hanoi leaders.

Opposition cannot be thought of simply in terms of "rationality" or "irrationality." Bombing, as everyone knows, runs as great a risk of hardening the resolution of a people as of unsettling its courage. Between North Vietnam and the Viet Cong, on one side, and the United States, on the other, there exists a double dissymmetry, acting in the opposite direction, that makes calculation almost impossible: the United States possesses immense resources, far beyond those of North Vietnam (despite Chinese and Soviet aid) but, per contra, the stake—the government of South Vietnam—means much more to Hanoi than to Washington. The American president makes the stake appear more significant by including in it the credibility of American involvement and the unity of Southeast Asia (the domino theory).

Last and most important, the United States is up against a nonnuclear

17 Ibid., p. 183.

state that is determined to ignore the threat of escalation. Indeed, the war is being fought as if only one state—the one possessing nuclear arms—understood this threat. North Vietnam in no way relies on the deterrent exercised by Soviet strength vis-à-vis the United States; what it relies on is American self-deterrence. No one in the United States envisages recourse to nuclear arms to break the resistance of the North Vietnamese; no one explicitly recommends it. The progressive use of force has not yielded psychological results to compensate for its military ineffectiveness.

At the same time, one implication of the doctrine of limited war is becoming increasingly apparent: victory does not necessarily come to the strongest party. The U.S. expeditionary force in Vietnam does not run the risk of a *military defeat,* but if the *political goal,* a South Vietnamese government capable of independently holding its own against the Viet Cong, remains unattainable and if Hanoi, through the intermediary of the Viet Cong, gains control of Saigon, the United States will have lost the war even if it wins most of the engagements.

In short, to repeat what I said earlier, limited wars are won or lost within frameworks (theater of operations, nature of the weapons used, volume of resources, resolution or patience of the population) *that strategists cannot extend at will.* Or, putting it another way, the strategist should not nurture the illusion that he can climb the rungs on the ladder of violence at will and that superiority, or a higher rung, guarantees him victory at the level at which a specific conflict actually takes place.

☆　☆　☆

Soviet literature (which I know only through English translations) does not seem to me to make any contribution to the first three categories of studies. Military writers in the Soviet Union reiterate the concepts elaborated by American analysts. Soviet technical services may also have undertaken research projects, comparable to those carried out by the RAND Corporation, on the number of missiles required for the assured destruction of protected or unprotected enemy ballistic missiles. But, even more than in the United States, the results of these projects are restricted to narrow official circles. As for abstract plans and models, whenever the authors of the classic *Soviet Military Strategy*[18] refer to them at all, they borrow from the Americans. The Soviet contribution belongs essentially to the fourth category, that of doctrines. And, there again, one has difficulty distinguishing between propaganda and science, between ideology for use at home or abroad and authentic concepts.

The language of the Soviet leaders has, it seems to me, gone through a number of relatively distinct phases. In the first, when the United States

[18] I refer to the English translation by the RAND Corporation (Englewood Cliffs, N.J.: Prentice-Hall, 1963).

enjoyed a monopoly in nuclear arms, Stalin and his comrades belittled in words the revolutionary importance of atomic weapons—all the while organizing the Stockholm movement to ban weapons of mass destruction. The "five permanent factors," the principles determining the course and outcome of wars, figured at the head of all strategic theories. But, quite clearly, Stalin himself immediately understood the importance of nuclear arms and put all necessary resources at the scientists' disposal. The fact that the first Soviet thermonuclear bomb was exploded only a few months after the first American one is proof enough that Stalin left no stone unturned to "overtake and surpass" capitalism and its most advanced exponent, the United States.

Nuclear weapons, which scientists and technicians were working day and night to manufacture while party leaders were calling for their condemnation on moral grounds and striving to prohibit even their use in diplomacy by the West, became, after Stalin's death, the subject of an ideological debate during the struggle between Malenkov and Khrushchev. Would a nuclear war result in the destruction of mankind and civilization or only of capitalism? Malenkov was the first to formulate the apparently heretical doctrine that nuclear war would no more spare socialist countries than it would capitalist ones—a doctrine that precluded the final victory of socialism by means of a general war and that Khrushchev at first rejected out of hand in order to eliminate his rival. Then, without clearly and explicitly subscribing to this doctrine, Khrushchev himself, harassed by the Chinese, suggested that it was at least partly valid. The atomic bomb does not distinguish between social classes. The hundreds of millions of deaths and the enormous destruction that a total nuclear war would cause would make the building of socialism more difficult, assuming, of course, that such a catastrophe would not actually prevent it. Though neither Marshal Sokolovsky's treatise of 1963, nor the letters of the central committee of the Soviet Communist party to the central committee of the Chinese Communist party, reassert this radical formula (that nuclear war would destroy civilization itself), by quoting the estimates of Western writers and adding that these still fall below the true figure, the Soviet writers are indirectly suggesting the immensity of the eventual disaster—unless, of course, the enemy is disarmed by a first strike. But, as the Soviet authors deny that the United States possesses the capacity to disarm the Soviet Union, the reader can and should, it seems, understand that the Soviet Union no longer has the capacity to destroy the American retaliation forces.

In the years immediately following Stalin's death, the Kremlin leaders claimed to have reached a sort of parity. They were insistent about the destruction they could inflict not only on Western Europe but also on the United States, thanks to their nuclear bomber strike force. With the launching of the first Sputnik in the autumn of 1957, the language changed and, in place of parity, the Russians gradually began to claim superiority ("the East wind prevails over the West wind"). It was a claim we know today to have been unfounded (it amounted to "nuclear bluff") and that ultimately brought no substantial gain to the Soviet Union: Berlin and Cuba, two verbal offensives that tested the moral and nervous powers of resistance of the American leaders, both ended in failure.

Beginning in 1963, the tone changed again and the Soviet leaders resigned themselves both to the rupture with Peking and to an explicit accord with the United States (Moscow treaty on the partial suspension of nuclear tests, hot line, nonproliferation treaty) on arms control. Despite the Vietnam war, cooperation between Russia and America in this sphere, the common effort to avoid direct confrontation (for example, in the Middle East in 1967), still continues. Might one then say that the American leaders have succeeded in convincing the Soviet leaders and that both parties have finally retained the lesson of the analysts and now see the world as these men have taught them to see it—that it is in the interests of both superpowers to close the atomic club and to keep their rivalry within narrow limits?

In one sense I would be tempted to reply in the affirmative. Everything is, in fact, turning out as if, given a few years' time lag, the Russians were thinking and acting in the same way as the Americans. Toward the end of the 1950s, they, too, toyed with the theory of massive retaliation and Khrushchev seems even to have entertained the notion of using it offensively. And like John Foster Dulles in the United States and Duncan Sandys in England, Khrushchev experienced the temptation of considerably reducing conventional forces and relying on missiles and thermonuclear weapons. Having, in their turn, concealed their missiles in underground silos, the Russians for some years now have shown themselves no longer content with the doctrine of the *minimum deterrent*. Instead, they are tending toward parity in the number of missiles and, at the same time, are providing themselves with the means for limited wars and for intervention outside their continental land mass. The presence of a large Soviet fleet in the eastern Mediterranean and the development of a corps similar to the United States Marines provide two more examples of the way the Soviet Union and the United States vie with and imitate each other.

Is Russian strategic thought then really so similar to that of the United States? Certainly not, at least if one restricts oneself to the form in which it is expressed in the book by Marshal Sokolovsky. Several differences strike me:

1. On certain questions of vital importance Soviet authors are careful not to take a categorical position. How will a massive attack by ballistic missiles affect the duration of a war? Will the missile attack be accom-

panied by the action of ground forces? How decisive would the results of a sudden missile attack be? Can, or should, the Soviet Union launch an anticipatory attack ("preemptive strike") if the enemy himself appears to be on the point of striking? On all these points discussion remains so to speak open. In some cases the uncertainly reflects a debate between opposing pressure groups (in spite of opposition from the leaders of the armed forces, Khrushchev wanted to bring about massive reductions in the total strength of the armed forces of millions of men). In others the uncertainty seems as genuine in the Soviet Union as it is in the United States (what would happen after an exchange of ballistic missiles?). Finally, in a few cases (the moral question of the victory of socialism in a third world war), the uncertainty arises from the difficulty of reconciling new technological data with Marxist-Leninist ideology.

2. The strategic or scientific analysis of the situation seems at each moment to be mingled with ideological considerations, to be influenced or distorted by the dogmas of Marxism-Leninism. By definition, the socialist countries want peace and the capitalist countries of NATO are plotting aggression. The American theory of limited war or flexible response becomes, in certain situations, the hypocritical camouflage for aggressive aims. For example: "Under the guise of discussing local war, feverish preparations are being made for unlimited nuclear war against the socialist countries. Many telling facts indicate that the imperialists have not discarded the strategy of a surprise nuclear attack."[19] However, on closer examination, this difference tends to disappear or, more precisely, to take us back to the first or lead us to the third.

In fact, American analysts also suppose, by definition, so to speak, that the aggression will come from the Soviet Union, which they see as aggressive as such (the Russians dub capitalist states imperialist). As a result, the Russians interpret all American or Western doctrines, which we claim to be defensive (i.e., as deterring aggression) as being inspired by offensive intentions. When it comes to the question of a surprise or an anticipatory attack, the Russians adopt the same basic line of reasoning as the West. The latter no longer thinks that Russia is going to unleash a sudden ballistic missile attack in order to eliminate the American means of retaliation, but it is an eventuality that still comes to mind. The Soviet analysts do the same in attributing to the United States, more by ideological tradition than by actual conviction, the plan for such an act of aggression, which only Soviet might can deter them from carrying out.

Even on the subject of local or limited wars,[20] Soviet authors, while rejecting the subtle distinctions of their American counterparts, arrive at reasonable propositions.

---

[19] RAND, *Soviet Military Strategy*, p. 382.

[20] The two notions are not interchangeable: a local war can be waged with all the means at the belligerents' disposal. For the two superpowers, however, a limited war must be local.

While preparing for a decisive struggle with the aggressor in a world war, the armed forces of the socialist countries must also be ready for small-scale local wars which the imperialists might initiate. The experience of such wars, which have broken out repeatedly in the post-war period, is that they are waged with different instruments and by other methods than world war. Soviet military strategy therefore must study the methods of waging such wars, too, in order to prevent their expansion into a world war and in order to achieve a rapid victory over the enemy.[21]

Certainly, above all the authors emphasize the danger, the probability, sometimes the inevitability, of a rise to the extremes, of any limited war becoming total war. But, according to more recent commentaries, this fatal tendency[22] operates only when states possessing nuclear weapons directly confront each other. What the Russians do not accept are the subtleties of the American analysts when it comes to the tactical and strategic use of nuclear weapons or the progressive use of conventional or nuclear arms in the European theater of operations. In this respect, they remain closer than the Americans to traditional concepts or to the doctrine of massive retaliation. But there is no way of telling whether, in a crisis, the Kremlin leaders would apply or quite ignore their own principles.

The fact remains that so far the two superpowers have conducted their foreign policies in the spirit of the crude or primitive Russian doctrine rather than drawing their inspiration from the subtleties of the American analysts. Moreover, the latter are now showing a tendency to return to ideas current some ten years ago: around 1957, leaders and public opinion in the West were inclined to believe that nuclear parity was about to be, or would inevitably be, reached. The Sputnik led to the anguish of the "missile gap," which never actually become a reality because the Russians lacked the means or the will to produce the largest possible number of ICBMs in the shortest possible time. In 1962, after a massive effort, the Americans considered themselves assured of superiority for several years, and Mr. McNamara went so far as to introduce the doctrine of flexible response into Europe itself. Even in a second strike he envisaged the use of missiles against enemy military forces (and not against the cities), which amounted to a limitation of nuclear war between the two superpowers. Gradually, he abandoned these pretenses, came implicitly to accept parity with the Soviet Union in the number of missiles, and returned to the simple distinction between total war in certain areas of the planet (Europe) and, in the event of the involvement of the two superpowers, limited and local wars as a possibility elsewhere.

[21] RAND, *Soviet Military Strategy*, p. 288.

[22] "One must emphasize that the present international system and the present state of military technology will cause any armed conflict to develop, inevitably, into a general war if the nuclear powers are drawn into it" (ibid., p. 299).

There are many explanations for the insistence on the risk of escalation: real uncertainty, an implied threat to the United States ("You will not dictate to us the conditions under which conflicts are to take place: we can compensate for our eventual inferiority in a given area by resorting to superior means"), a refusal to go into distinctions in their eyes unreal or academic, and, last but not least, the fact that, *for reasons of national and ideological self-interest*, those who formulate Soviet doctrines have been *partly converted* to the American way of thinking. Marshal Sokolovsky's book mentions wars of national liberation from time to time, but he does not clearly relate such wars to the risk of escalation or to the question of nuclear arms. Traditional ideology is expressed in the formula: "And as long as imperialism and colonialism exist, *wars of national liberation and revolutionary wars are unavoidable.*" But a few pages later: "The Communist Party of the Soviet Union and the Soviet government regard the prevention of nuclear wars as their main task.[23] These two statements, in no way contradictory, bring us to the third difference between the American and the Soviet literature as well as to the debate between the Russians and the Chinese.

3. Marshal Sokolovsky's book does not separate strictly military or strategic problems from a Marxist-Leninist sociological interpretation of the phenomenon of "war" or, for that matter, of international relations in all their integral complexity. Certainly the American authors also refer to Clausewitz, to the primacy of politics over war, to relations between classes, to the nature of the internal regime of states, and to the influence of the regime on diplomacy. But, generally speaking, the same authors do not deal simultaneously with the sociology of war in our age and the dialectic of first and second strikes.

In short, drawing their inspiration from Marxism-Leninism, Soviet authors present their ideas in the language of positive (or what claims to be positive) science; they evoke the laws of war and relate the class struggle to wars between states. Rarely do American analysts ask themselves, "Why war?" An antianalyst like Anatol Rapoport looks for the psychological causes of wars while the analysts give themselves hypothetical examples of sovereign states whose interests oppose each other one moment and coincide the next. The Soviet authors take as their point of departure a sociological theory of modern warfare, making room in it for what they take to be the aims of the American analysts.[24] For example:

> Wars between states with different social systems are particularly decisive, inasmuch as they are a higher form of the class struggle. . . . The subordination of

[23] Ibid., pp. 281, 285.

[24] For the reader who has not read *Peace and War: Theory of International Relations*, I will say that the Russians take as their point of departure a *form of sociology* that they regard as scientific and also that they subordinate what I call *theory* to a science of the laws of war. Marxists use a similar method in economics with the sociology of the capitalist system representing the cornerstone of their theory.

military strategy to state policy not only determines the nature of the strategic aims, but also the general nature of strategy. . . . For example, the policy of imperialism as an outmoded social system is to attempt to forestall its inevitable downfall and to prevent the historically determined development of socialism in the world. Being reactionary and adventuristic by nature, the policies of imperialist countries also produce a military strategy founded on adventuristic calculations.[25]

The strategic doctrine of a Marxist-Leninist state, taking into account as it must the class struggle within regimes, *logically* oscillates between two extreme forms. One maintains the primacy of *politics* and of *prolonged conflict* between the two camps, the other, which draws its inspiration from the American way of thinking, takes as its point of departure the technological revolution brought about by nuclear arms and refuses to admit that the contradiction between capitalism and socialism would be resolved by a war to the death. The Russians and the Chinese have different views on the risk of escalation, the danger of a war of national liberation turning into a general war, the modification of the laws of warfare by nuclear weapons, and the probability of the use of these weapons. The Russians accuse the Chinese of failing to recognize the destructive potential of these weapons (which is certainly false), of underestimating the nuclear peril (which is doubtful), and of wanting a nuclear war that would destroy both superpowers at one blow (a possible ulterior motive; but does not the United States possess the means to devastate the territory of both China and the Soviet Union at the same time?). As for the Chinese, they accuse the Russians of overestimating the danger of escalation in order to justify both their collusion with the forces of imperialism and the fact of their not supporting wars of national liberation. These two strategic doctrines, Russian and Chinese, are but aspects of two overall views (both deriving from Marxism-Leninism) of the historical world of today. The one, dominated by the nuclear peril, though it does not exclude wars of national liberation, nevertheless accepts the idea of lasting peaceful coexistence between the two camps; the other, dominated by the concept of prolonged conflict between social systems, recognizes the nuclear peril but thinks that it can be eliminated by avoiding "tactical adventurism" and relies on wars of national liberation and guerrilla activity progressively to undermine the imperialist position and gain the final victory—whether it takes decades or centuries to do so.

☆ ☆ ☆

Does the difference between the philosophies of the Russian and Chinese Marxist-Leninists on the one hand and the Americans on the

[25] RAND, *Soviet Military Strategy*, p. 100.

other prevent their communicating with each other? I do not think so at all. Neither faction will ever give the same name to the same realities, but each, provided it knows the intellectual system of the other, will be able to translate what its enemy says into its own vocabulary. The Russians call "the guiding role of the Communist party" what the West calls "the political monopoly of the Communist party" or "the banning of all opposition whether open or disguised." And what to the Russians is "the use of the means of the press and propaganda for the building of socialism" is to us "censorship" and "toeing the party line." But the Russians know as well as we do that they are forcing the Czechs to speak a language contrary to their feelings and convictions. In short, the Russians are forcing the Czechs to lie, and they know it.

In strategic matters the respective philosophies of the Russians and the Americans sometimes also need translating: what the Russians (or the Chinese) call "the aid given by socialist countries to a war of national liberation" becomes, in American terminology, "indirect aggression." But, between the two world wars, the treaties concluded by the Soviet Union with its neighbors made the organization of partisans or the sending of supplies to them seem like a form of aggression. The Americans tend to see in any assumption of power by a communist party a threat to their interests and therefore claim for themselves the right to help established regimes, of whatever kind, to combat any revolution that threatens to slide toward communism. American intervention to prevent the takeover of power by a communist party, the strategy of containment in American terminology, becomes the manifestation of American imperialism in the language of Marxism-Leninism. The uncommitted observer, however, uses a neutral language: each of the two opposing camps, in its own style and using its own methods, is doing its utmost to stop the progress of the other. Moral judgment on these acts of intervention depends as much on one's own ideology and one's view of the future as it does on the present characteristics of the opposing regimes.

As far as strategic doctrine goes, communication seems to me to be easier still. In fact, American analysts, obsessed as they are by the nuclear peril, have on the whole attained their immediate objective—"to save humanity from nuclear war by saving war," which is a step in the direction of Mao Tse-tung's thought. The Chinese are no more unaware than the Russians of the fact that "the paper tiger has atomic teeth." Debate rests on the strategic role of nuclear arms within the framework of a prolonged conflict. But the American analysts have influenced public opinion and statesmen toward thinking in terms of neutralization of these arms, of banning their first use or using them otherwise than as a deterrent, to repulse a possible attack. The Russians have let themselves be convinced of the nuclear peril; they have rejected the subtleties of the flexible response or of limited nuclear war and have maintained their almost fatalistic belief in escalation in the event of a direct clash between nuclear states. As a result of this belief, the absence, so far, of nuclear war between the Soviet Union and the United States has meant the absence of all war. In the Third World, however, the absence of nuclear war or of the recourse to nuclear weapons is creating the sort of situation envisaged by Mao Tse-tung. The Americans are now devoting as much attention to the theory and doctrine of counterinsurgency as Mao Tse-tung devoted, over a period of many years, to the philosophy and practice of wars of liberation and guerrilla action.

Perhaps all this provides another reason for the feeling of unease that I get from reading American strategy fiction, falling as it does halfway between a theory and a model, on the one hand, and historical analysis, on the other. I cannot say that I have ever seen the equivalent of this intermediate stage either in Clausewitz or in the work of economists.

Not that the economists and sociologists do not do their utmost to conceptualize the data of a socioeconomic situation lying somewhere between an abstract theory and an entirely historical analysis. And economists and sociologists are also equally avid to define one or all of the strategies of development that take these conceptualizations as their starting point. Perhaps the results, equivocal to say the least, of these researches are in part the product of the formulation of the problem in terms that appear soluble by only those means that the American strategist can effectively employ (that is, without a revolution in policy). The strategies of conflict run an even greater risk than the strategies of development of being as much misled as clarified by abstract formulations.

The threat of increasing escalation should "give the enemy pause." Also, the enemy must take the threat seriously; in other words, he has to think that the actor brandishing the threat of escalation *can* put it into execution. It is not a question of material or physical capacity; the North Vietnamese know that the United States can wipe out almost the whole population of North Vietnam in a few minutes using nuclear weapons, but they also know that the United States will not do it. Even if the North Vietnamese or the Chinese do not exclude the possibility of a recourse to atomic weapons, when it comes to the point they prefer death to surrender—a decision by no means irrational since wise men have never suggested that one ought to prefer life to the reasons for living. The strategy fiction of escalation presupposes that the American strategist can act freely without reference to public opinion and that threats of escalation are credible—both the freedom and the credibility are equally unreal.[26]

The diplomatic situation has changed in the last few years.[27] Though they continue to oppose each other in many ways (the North Vietnamese

---

[26] Schelling noted, in the course of the ISS Oxford conference, that the bombing of North Vietnam had done more harm to the United States than to North Vietnam—what the strategist *can* do depends on what public opinion will *morally* accept.

[27] It is still too early to know whether the Soviet intervention in Czechoslovakia will put an end to the developments that preceded it.

are not short of Soviet arms; Warsaw Pact troops occupy Czecholovakia under the pretext of combating counterrevolution and capitalism; the United States wants to halt communism in Vietnam), the two super-powers appear not only to be acting in collusion over nuclear armament but also to have reached agreement on a clear allocation of spheres of influence. A situation of this kind, with its inherent ambiguity, with its partial hostility and implicit alliance, can hardly be said to lend itself to abstract formulation. The more the observer substitutes schemes or conceptual simplifications for the situation in its singularity, the more he risks becoming a poor adviser.

Strategic thought is never separate from political thought. But, whereas in the early postwar period nuclear arms, the arms race, and arms control constituted the most compelling subject, the one that promised the greatest number of new ideas, the present period opens other avenues of research. Perhaps the debate between the traditionalists and the innovators expresses genuine opposition—albeit in a confused form as befits conflicts between academic factions. It is as though, theory having brought out the consequences of nuclear weapons and these weapons having indeed been partially neutralized, strategic thought had ended by absorbing the innovations and was resuming, in a modified but not radically different form, the course of tradition: no amount of conceptualizations, schemes, or scientific studies of quantifiable decisions (arms systems) are a substitute either for historical analysis of actual situations or for decisions clarified but not determined by the results of science. Have the innovators anything better to offer us to assure peace, to win the cold war or to bring it to an end, to take just decisions, or to change the nature of relations between states than prudence nurtured by history at least as much as by laboratory experiments on the psychological effects of confidence? Does make-believe teach us more about the reality of a situation or the development of a crisis than historical and sociological analysis?

Perhaps the antimissile defense and the progress of the Chinese nuclear force will again set off speculations on models of relations between nuclear states. For the time being, strategists are pondering the lessons of Vietnam and seeking the true doctrine, the effective means for combating guerrillas. More generally, they are devoting their attention to international relations in their entirety—the logical consequence of their rediscovery of a truth as old as it is often disregarded: the real strategist is the leader in war or peace and thus the chief of state. At the top level, strategy merges with the conduct of a state's activities abroad. Nuclear arms have modified but have still more sanctioned the true nature of foreign policy, which is always carried out with reference to the force of arms.

For twenty years the West has been reading or rereading Clausewitz.

For a few years it has been reading Mao Tse-tung. To the first it owes the notion of escalation or the rise to the extremes, the import of which has been changed by nuclear arms. To the second it owes the notion of prolonged conflict. All doctrines, in our age, are defined by relation to these two concepts, and they all seem to lead to a paradoxical conclusion. To guarantee that *wars* remain limited, must we not learn to accept permanent *war?* Will not the limitation of means bring about a boundless extension in time?

11. The Dawn of Universal History[1]

A FEW WORDS OF EXPLANATION are called for, I think, to justify the title of this lecture and to dispel the unfortunate impression that it has undoubtedly created. My choice of subject—a subject that I shall deal with only sketchily—is attributable to my English publisher. A year or two ago, this publisher, who has brought out a series of books dealing with different periods of civilization, asked me to write a history of the world since 1914. I replied immediately that no serious historian would undertake such a task. We have lived through only part of the history of these years. We have followed it from different places and under the influence of our different passions and prejudices. None of us has a complete picture, or has mastered the immense mass of scattered material, or has been able as yet to achieve a rational understanding of events so crammed with human suffering, unprecedented crimes, and immeasurable promise.

On reflection, I qualified my objection that no serious historian would have the temerity to accede to such request by pointing out that I was not a historian. And I asked myself whether as a philosopher, perhaps, or as a sociologist, I could not write a brief study of the history of our time, bringing out its originality and emphasizing what I have called the dawn of universal history. For the first time, the so-called higher civilizations are in the act of living one and the same history. For the first time, we can perhaps speak of "human society."

I shall include in this lecture a few of the ideas that will form the introduction and conclusion to the book I agreed to write. I am fully aware that this study will probably be judged severely by many philosophers and historians among my university colleagues. In the more traditional English universities, sociology is not yet a fully accepted subject, or else it disguises itself under some less Americanized name, such as anthropology.

[1] Third Herbert Samuel Lecture delivered on February 18, 1960, under the auspices of the British Friends of the Hebrew University of Jerusalem.

As for the philosophy of history, whether deriving from Bossuet, Hegel, Marx, or Toynbee, it is still, for the most part, held to be less of a scientific than a literary exercise, an exercise to which writers, but not respectable thinkers, may devote their attention. What can I say in my own defense? First, that nobody is more conscious than I of how uncertain and vulnerable what I have to say will be. I say it in advance: this will not be a narrative like that of Thucydides (the events to be dealt with are too numerous and too incoherent), nor will it be a synthesis like Burckhardt's work on the Italian Renaissance. It will be an essay and nothing more, limited in its perspectives by the inevitable personal limitations of the author and marked by the experiences and hopes of a man committed to a particular country, a particular generation, and a particular intellectual system.

Can I really be reproached for writing an essay so stripped of all am-bition when, unconsciously or not, we are all helping to write it? The scholar is perhaps able to look at past ages from the viewpoint of a pure spectator. The historian of Athens or Sparta, of Rome or Carthage, of the pope, the emperor, the Holy Roman Empire, and the French monarchy, may not feel personally involved in the passions that moved the actors; he may succeed in comprehending with the same serenity the combatants on all sides, their common beliefs and conflicting interests, the achievements and disasters of which they were the unwitting architects. But when we open our morning newspaper or vote for a candidate in an election, we deliberately situate ourselves in our period and situate our period in time. Anyone who attempts to understand clearly the fate experienced or suf-fered by an Englishman or Frenchman of the twentieth century must also be interpreting "the world since 1914." I will try to make my inter-pretation of the twentieth century less fragmentary, less emotionally sub-jective. Here is the method I propose to adopt.

☆   ☆   ☆

Every European generation since the beginning of the nineteenth cen-tury has believed in the uniqueness of its own period. Does the very per-sistence of this conviction in itself indicate that each time it was unfounded? Or was it rather a kind of premonition, whose falsity as regards our predecessors and truth for ourselves have been borne out by our experience? And finally, if we hesitate to ascribe error to so many generations, or rather to every generation but our own, does there remain a third hypothesis, namely, that all of them were right, not individually but taken as a whole and not always in the ways in which they thought?

In other words, it would seem to be true, or at least very likely, that the last century has seen a kind of revolution, or more precisely a *muta-tion*, that began before the nineteenth century but whose pace has ac-celerated during the past few decades. Since the beginning of the last century each generation and thinker has tried to define this historical mutation. Saint-Simon and Auguste Comte spoke of industrial society, Alexis de Tocqueville of democratic society, and Karl Marx of capitalist society. If we go back to the great theorists of the first half of the last century—from whom we derive our ideologies, if not our ideas—and compare their diagnoses and their prophecies with what has actually happened between their time and our own, we should be able to reach a tentative definition of what I have just called a historical mutation.

Let us begin with the school of Saint-Simon and Auguste Comte, who are now once again becoming fashionable, for the very comprehensible reason that the growth of large-scale industry on both sides of the Iron Curtain has at last compelled observers to recognize the existence of a certain type of society, of which the Soviet and Western systems represent two different species or versions. Why not call this form of society industrial since its characteristic is the development of industry?

This was, indeed, the central insight supplied by Saint-Simon and Auguste Comte. Both watched a new society forming before their eyes, a society they described as industrial and that Europe had created. The essential characteristics of this new society were more accurately described by Auguste Comte than by either Saint-Simon or even the Saint-Simonians. And though few today read the works of the founder of positivism, and still fewer devote any serious study to them, it is his definition of industrial society that offers us our starting point.

Like Saint-Simon, Comte contrasts producers—industrialists, farmers, bankers—and the political and military elites who, in a society devoted to peaceful activities, represent survivals from a feudal and theological past. Industrial society, like all human society, has henceforth as its first objective the exploitation of natural resources. Wars, conquest, and Caesars belong to the past. Napoleon, for all his genius, was guilty of what in the eyes of philosophers of history is the most serious of all crimes—that of being an anachronism. Roman conquests were meaningful and fruitful because they prepared the way for a unified world in which the Christian religion was to spread and because communities dedicated to war would at some point achieve peace through the victory of the strongest. In our time, however, conquest cannot be justified because it no longer serves any purpose and because the spontaneous resistance and ultimate triumph of the people has revealed the error of Napoleon, who, in reaping the heritage of the French Revolution, transformed into hatred the sympathy once felt by the peoples of Europe for an enterprise that the French people had launched for the advantage of all.

Arguing with a dogmatism that some will see as typical of sociologists, Auguste Comte deduces the consequences, all the consequences, that follow from this change of objective. Henceforth it is labor, not war, that constitutes the supreme good. It is through men's labor that a society's cadres and leaders are formed, that individual prestige is generally recognized, and that one's place in the hierarchy is assured. There must, therefore, be freedom of labor. Instead of the rooting of families in a class or occupation, mobility becomes the rule from one generation to another. Henceforth individuals are entitled to hope that their place in society will be determined on the basis of merit, without reference to the position of their parents. To Comte, the wage earning class represented not a modern form of slavery or servitude but the promise of individual liberation.

Europe, or more precisely the nations of Western Europe—England, France, Italy, Spain, and Germany—constituted the vanguard of humanity in the eyes of Auguste Comte. They were in advance of others in the pursuit of what was henceforth to be the common objective, namely, the exploitation of the resources of the planet, the creation of an industrial civilization, and the unification of all the human societies scattered over the five continents into a single peaceful community. According to the high priest of positivism, Europe's advance did not confer privileges so much as impose obligations, and Auguste Comte warned his contemporaries against the temptation of colonial conquests. Again and again he denounced the occupation of Algeria and even expressed the hope that the Arabs would "vigorously expel" the French should the latter lack the intelligence and virtue to withdraw of their own accord.

It is easy enough to ridicule Auguste Comte's prophecies and many have done so. In proclaiming that the days of colonial wars and colonial conquest were over, he was grossly self-deceived. But if he is regarded not as a prophet but as an adviser of princes or nations, then he was certainly wiser than events. He did not predict the future as it has turned out but as it would have turned out had history developed in accordance with the wisdom of men of good will.

He used to say that the industrial society in process of spreading throughout Western Europe is, and must be, an example to the human race. He was right at least on this point. He was certainly wrong in regarding Europe as the center of the universe, in failing to recognize the singularity of other civilizations, in believing that the forms of political organization and religious belief were rigorously determined by the type of social organization, and in overlooking the endurance of ways of thought that he called theological or metaphysical. But in his perception of the relation between work and war, between the exploitation of natural resources and the exploitation of man by man, he understood, with unquestionable clear-sightedness, the revolution that governments and peoples have today painfully come to accept: wars between industrial societies are both ruinous and sterile, and nonindustrial—or as we call them, underdeveloped—societies cannot help modeling themselves on industrial societies. In this sense, Europe has truly been an example. But

Europe would be wrong, said Comte, to impose this example while using her temporary "advantage" to reopen the era of great conquests. What purpose is served by killing, enslaving, pillaging? Gold and silver no longer constitute real wealth. Wealth consists of rationally organized labor. In the distant past, slavery was necessary in order to impose the habit of regular effort on men naturally prone to idleness or distraction. But Europeans are now so habituated to the concept of the rationalization of labor that coercion is no longer necessary. Wars, like colonial conquests, are therefore anachronisms. Both continue to take place but today they seem irrational, at least if we assume, along with Auguste Comte, that men do not make war for its own sake or simply out of a frenzy to win. If the major objective of industrial societies is to achieve well-being through work—as spokesmen of both Soviet and Western society today vie with each other in stating—then the two European wars of this century were useless and there ought not to be a third.

Let us now consider another great theorist, one generation later than Auguste Comte. Karl Marx also discerned a historical mutation and although he used different words and concepts, he emphasized the same essential fact, namely, that the forces of production had developed more rapidly than in any preceding century and this he saw as the achievement of bourgeois capitalism. Within the space of a few decades, the triumphant bourgeoisie had overturned the conditions and methods of collective labor to a greater extent than the ruling class of any feudal or military society during the previous thousand years.

There is agreement between the high priest of socialism and the high priest of positivism regarding the fundamental difference between modern and traditional societies. Both men consider that the uniqueness of modern society lies in the preeminence of work, in the application of science to the techniques of production, and in the resultant increase in collective resources. The major difference between their two doctrines is that Marx attaches fundamental importance to the conflict between employers and employed, a conflict that Auguste Comte sees as secondary, a symptom of social disintegration that will be corrected as organization improves.

Marx tends to explain everything—poverty in the midst of plenty and despite the growth in the forces of production, the alienation of the workers, the despotism of the property owning minority—as the result of the conflict between employers and employed, the class struggle between the capitalists and the proletariat. His vision of the future of capitalism is thus apocalyptic. The conflict between capitalists and proletariat will be intensified until the final explosion. By the same token, he sketches an idyllic picture of the postcapitalist regime, which he never describes but whose benefits he evokes by contrast. If the specific characteristics of capitalism—private ownership of the means of production, the capitalist minority's possession of economic power and, through intermediaries, of political power—are responsible for social inequalities, the exploitation of man by man, and workingclass alienation, then with the elimination of private property, and with the proletarian revolution, the prehistory of humanity will come to an end and a new era will open in which social progress will no longer depend on violence and political revolution.

On the essential point of difference between Karl Marx and Auguste Comte, the former seems to me to have been right in the short term but wrong in the long term. Conflicts between employers and employed, either within industry or over the distribution of the national income, have not been decisive. On the whole, they have been more serious during the initial phases of industrialization than in mature industrial societies. The working classes, organized in trade unions and protected by social legislation, often represented in the parliament by powerful socialist parties, continue to press their claims, but they have been converted to peaceful and legal methods. They do not want a revolution that would establish a dictatorship of the proletariat, nor are they really clear as to what a proletarian revolution would be. In their view, as in that of most observers, there is clear proof that private ownership of the means of production, as it exists today in Western society, does not prevent either the development of productive forces or a continued rise in the standard of living of the masses. Whatever one's judgment may be of the relative effectiveness of the Soviet and Western regimes, it is obvious that the one does not mean plenty for the masses nor the other poverty. The differences between the two systems are more striking in society than in the factory and in the structure of the state and public administration than in that of society. As Auguste Comte stated, industrial society allows for a technical and bureaucratic hierarchy in which there is a place for free workers.

The conflicts that have dominated the twentieth century and determined its course have been more national and imperial than social. Their role as doctrinaires did not blind Auguste Comte and Karl Marx to the nature of the historical mutation that was taking place before their eyes, but they underestimated the persistence of the traditional aspect of history—the rise and fall of empires, the rivalry of regimes, the beneficial or disastrous exploits of great men.

In different ways, both underestimated the importance of the political factor. Marx wrote as if the political aspect of capitalism were adequately defined by the power of the bourgeoisie and as if a socialist political system were adequately defined by the semimythological concept of the dictatorship of the proletariat. Auguste Comte was content to leave power in the hands of the managers responsible for production, trusting to the resistance of public opinion, that of women and of the proletariat, to soften its rigor and prevent abuse. Both left out of account the possibility of an evolution along the lines suggested by Alexis de Tocqueville, who foresaw the development of a commercial and industrial society with increased social mobility and greater equality. This is, fundamentally, the direction in which modern societies are moving, though they are still free to choose between a system in which a single individual rules despotically over millions, whose individuality is submerged in servitude and uniformity, and one based on freedom for all, perhaps alike in their material circumstances and in a kind of mediocrity, that safeguards rights of individual initiative, opinion, and belief.

Sociological theorists, by failing to take into account the partial autonomy of the political order, have argued as though history, meaning a succession of wars and empires, victories and defeats, was henceforth ended. But the present century seems to me in 1960 to present two distinct faces. It has witnessed an intellectual, technical, and economic revolution, which, like some cosmic force, is carrying humanity toward an unknown future, but in many respects it is very like its predecessors. It is not the first century to have seen great wars. On the one hand, there is the need for progress; on the other, there is *history as usual*,[2] with its drama of empires, armies, and heroes.

The forces of change are clearly revealed in statistics of intellectual and industrial production. At the beginning of the century, the consumption of petroleum amounted to a few tons a year. Today it comes to nearly a billion tons a year—I repeat, a billion tons—and it is increasing at the rate of ten percent or more every year. Fifty years ago, a great power would produce a few million tons of steel a year. Today the same amount represents no more than the annual increase in production. Robert Oppenheimer has quoted some figures that seem to me particularly striking in this context. He states that of all the scientific researchers who have existed since men began to think, ninety percent are still alive. Such statistics illustrate the acceleration of history, the rapidly increasing growth of knowledge and power—to return to the language of Auguste Comte.

Let us turn now to traditional history. At every juncture the mind is baffled. Things happen and, once done, nothing can be undone. But how near some events have come to not happening! If the Germans on the eve of the battle had not sent two army corps to the east, would there have been the miracle of the Marne? If the world crisis had not lasted for years, or if the British and French had used military means to prevent the German reoccupation of the Rhineland, would the last world war have taken

[2] In English in the original.

place? Without Churchill, would England have stood alone against the Third Reich? If Hitler had not attacked Russia in 1941, what would have been the subsequent course of the greatest of all wars? Traditional history is action; in other words, it is made up of decisions taken by specific persons at specific times and in specific places. If a different man had been called on to make the decisions in the same circumstances, or if the same man had had to make them in different circumstances, the results might have been quite different. Yet nobody can determine either before or after the event the extent to which certain of these decisions, taken at particular times and in particular places, have affected the course of history.

Traditional history seems to be governed by chance and there is cruelty in it as well as grandeur. The blood of innocents flows everywhere and the victories of princes are paid for by the sacrifices of the people. The growth of knowledge and power seems to be governed by the law of necessity, and numerical triumphs make the exploits of individuals or of small groups look insignificant. I am tempted to imagine what the history of the thirty years' war—the thirty years from 1914 to 1945—would look like if it had been written by Thucydides. Its first episode was compared by Toynbee and Thibaudet to the Peloponnesian War. (But did they realize, in 1918, that the peace of Versailles would simply turn out to be the truce of Nicias?) It would probably be necessary to fill in the gaps in the dramatic narrative by asking a Marx or a Colin Clark to write not a narrative but an analysis of the irresistible process of industrialization on our planet. In one sense, this process is no less dramatic than the story of the rise and fall of the Third Reich. Like a torrent it carries everything along with it, uprooting age-old customs, causing the growth of factories and sprawling cities, covering the entire planet with roads and railways, offering the masses the prospect of that plenty that privileged nations have shown to be attainable. But it begins by tearing men away from the protection afforded by beliefs and habits that have been handed down for centuries and by subjecting millions of men, bereft of faith and law, to the uncertainties of an incomprehensible system governed by mysterious machines.

I do not know whether, in the book that I have still to write, I shall be able to convey to the reader the twofold feeling of human action and necessity, of drama and process, of *history as usual* and the originality of industrial society. But now that I have emphasized the differences be-tween these two aspects of our century, may I go on to indicate the numerous ways in which accident and necessity, drama and process, have been combined to form the fabric of history as it has actually unfolded? Let us try to discern the law of industrial necessity at work in the drama of wars and empires, and let us see, too, how the action of a few individuals gives shape and form to the process of industrialization. After this double dialectical reversal we can go on to ask whether the process will be able to continue without the drama.

☆ ☆ ☆

As I see it, there are three ways, none of them exclusive, of arranging in logical sequence the succession of events and accidents and discovering the law of industrial evolution in the drama of great wars. The historian can use the state of the industrial system to explain either the origin of wars, or their course, or their results. I do not accept the first method, but I put considerable store in the second and third.

The first method, that of Lenin and the Marxists, sees in the drama merely a spectacular episode in the process. The 1914 war would be not an expression of the traditional nature of human history but the fatal consequence of capitalist contradictions and of rivalry between capitalist states. This is not the place to analyze in detail a theory that I have often discussed.[3] But it will perhaps help to make these remarks more complete if I may be allowed to summarize this classical thesis—which still has more supporters than it deserves—by the three following propositions.

1. Colonial imperialism, it is claimed, is merely the extreme form of capitalist expansion in that part of the world now called underdeveloped, on continents with a traditional economy whose weakness delivered them over to the rapacity of large companies and to domination by European states.

2. In this view, the peaceful division of the world into spheres of influence or colonial empires was impossible. Capitalists and capitalist systems were driven by their feverish search for profits, for markets for their products, for human labor to exploit and raw materials to develop. Capitalist economies were no more able to reach lasting agreements for the division of the planet than individual capitalists within one country were able to agree on the division of markets or the cessation of competition.

3. Though the great war was waged on the old continent and was apparently a specifically European conflict, its real cause, what was really at stake, was the division of the planet. Frenchmen, Germans, and Englishmen unwittingly died to increase the share of their respective countries in other parts of the world.

In my view, the facts do not bear out these three propositions and in some respects they disprove them. Or at least, an impartial examination of the facts renders them suspect. Economic expansion in its different forms (the search for excess profits from the development of rich sources of raw materials or from the exploitation of human labor, the search for

---

[3] See, for example, *War and Industrial Society* (London: Oxford University Press, 1958).

markets for manufactured products, the attempt to reserve privileges for oneself and to exclude competitors), even if we suppose it to be essentially bound up with the capitalist system, does not automatically entail colonial conquest and the establishment of political sovereignty. The latter is useful or indispensable, in the economic sphere, only to keep out competitors and obtain advantages not admissible in conditions of free competition. The African territories, which the Western European countries were able to conquer with ease at the end of the nineteenth and the beginning of the twentieth century, accounted for but an infinitesimal fraction of the foreign trade of capitalist states and absorbed but a small percentage of the capital that the old continent, as world banker, invested abroad. In these circumstances, how can we accept the proposition that colonial conquest is the extreme form, the inevitable expression, of an expansion inherent in capitalist economies?

The second proposition also seems to me arbitrary. It is well known that domestic competitors often succeed in dividing up markets and thus suspending the operation of the so-called inexorable law of competition. A division of the world into spheres of influence, an amicable settlement by the European nations of their quarrels over Africa and Asia, would a fortiori have been easily achieved if these quarrels had had no other origin or stake than mere commercial interest! The European countries were each other's best customers precisely because of their industrial development. The great capitalist companies regarded West or Equatorial Africa, Algeria, or Morocco as only marginal areas of their activity. German banks were less interested in Morocco than the Wilhelmstrasse would have liked them to be. It was the chancelleries that made cooperation between French and German capitalists impossible in Morocco. The diplomats thought in terms of power not because they were concerned about commercial interests or because spokesmen of commercial interests brought pressure to bear on them but because they had read their history books and for centuries power had been the rule of politics.

Finally, I am still waiting for someone to convince me that a war started by German and Slav rivalry in the Balkans, fought mainly in Europe, and seen by the participants, from the day it broke out, as being concerned solely with power relationships within the European diplomatic system had in reality different causes and different aims. It would need a great deal of ingenuity to prove that Africa and Asia were the cause of a war beginning with the revolver shots that killed the archduke of Austria. Why should distant lands constitute a more authentic stake than the political status of Central and Eastern Europe?

To anyone who looks at the past without preconceived opinions, all the facts, indeed, point in one direction and justify a single conclusion. The causes of the 1914–1918 war conformed to historical tradition no less than those of preceding European wars and no less than those of the great war whose history was written by Thucydides and which involved all the city-states forming the Hellenic system, just as the states of the old continent made up the European international system. A system of equilibrium slides by itself toward irreconcilable conflict when it splits into two coalitions or when one of the political units seems on the point of establishing its hegemony over the whole of the historical area.

At the end of the fifth century B.C., Athens was endangering the liberties of the Greek cities. At the beginning of the twentieth century, Germany was exposing the nations of Europe to the same peril. War to the death was not on that account inevitable, but what was inevitable was that in the event of war the other great powers would immediately feel that they were fighting for their existence and freedom. The situation in the Balkans, the immediate cause of the explosion, was neither a pretext nor a mere occasion. Austria-Hungary and Turkey were multinational empires, the one a survival from a time in which provinces belonged to sovereigns, the other built solely on conquest and maintained only by the power of the sword. But the balance of power was disturbed by the ultimate disintegration of these empires and particularly by that of Austria-Hungary. Germany lost its principal ally, and millions of Slavs appeared likely to go over to the opposite camp. It is not incomprehensible that the Reich should have supported the dual empire in an enterprise in which the latter sought salvation and instead found its death. It is no more incomprehensible that, from the beginning of August 1914, Great Britain and especially France should have feared a German victory, which would have meant for them the loss of their independence or in any case of their status as great powers.

The 1914 war broke out in the industrial century but its beginnings were those of an ordinary war. It is in its development and consequences that it bears the stamp of the century to which it belongs and of which it is the tragic expression.

The great war whose history was related by Thucydides was fought from beginning to end with the same weapons, and throughout its countless battles, apart from a few crafty devices during the Sicilian expedition, it is the heroism of the Greeks that stands out rather than their technical or tactical ingenuity. The thirty years' war of the twentieth century began with the revolver shots of Sarajevo or with the bombardment of Belgrade by Austrian cannon, yet it ended with the atomic thunderclaps of Hiroshima and Nagasaki. Between 1914 and 1945, the techniques of production and destruction had gone through several stages.

The first battles were fought with machine guns, light, horse-drawn cannon, and heavy artillery. The continuous front, the trenches, the accumulation and preparation of artillery, requiring ever increasing numbers of cannon and amounts of ammunition, belong to the second phase, that of the bloody and sterile battles in which tens of thousands of men fell in order to hold a few miles of land whose possession or loss meant nothing. The thousands of planes, tanks, and trucks in the last phase of hostilities foreshadow the motorized techniques, the cooperation of aviation and armored might, that assured Hitler's Wehrmacht its spectacular triumphs between 1939 and 1941. The age of petroleum had succeeded that of coal (without, however, replacing it), and light metals were being used along with steel. But the qualitative superiority that one industrial country achieved over another was bound to be precarious. The battle for quantity—the race for men, arms, munitions—which had been the predominant feature of the first phase of this thirty years' war, was intensified during the second phase. With four thousand tanks and almost as many planes, Germany had put first Poland and then France out of action and gone on to win some striking victories during the summer of 1941. But by 1944–1945 the industrial machine of the anti-German coalition was working at full steam and the Soviet and Anglo-American armies were winning, thanks to a numerical superiority comparable to that of 1918.

This was a war waged by industrial societies able to mobilize all their men and all their factories. All citizens contributed to the collective effort either as workers or as soldiers. The *levée en masse* decreed by the convention had become a reality. The effort of organization, including "the organization of enthusiasm"[4] for which the survivors of the massacre later reproached the old men, was incomparable. This industrial war, waged by civilians in uniform, was to inspire the pacifist revolt, which is more a characteristic than a contradiction of periods of war.

It is possible to interpret the second phase of this thirty years' war as belonging, like the first, to the categories of traditional history. The defeated side, which had for so long appeared to be the stronger, retained a keen sense, excessive perhaps but understandable, of the injustice of the conditions imposed by the victors and made a second attempt. There could be true peace only if all the rival states were satisfied. Since they were not, what we had was merely a truce. Whatever government Germany had had, it would have been tempted to break the truce. The ambitions of Hitler's Germany were boundless, and Germany broke the truce cynically.

But this interpretation, traditional and partial, is in many ways insufficient. It is true that Jacques Bainville had predicted most of the events leading up to the catastrophe of 1939, without taking into account the economic consequences of the war or the Treaty of Versailles. The successive stages of the tragedy—German rearmament, the reoccupation of the Rhineland, the breakup of France's alliances with the succession

---

[4] The phrase is Elie Halévy's.

states of Austria-Hungary, the Russo-German alliance for the partition of Poland, the German attack on the West, and the rupture of the Russo-German pact—all these had their precedents and were in line with conventional power politics. All the same, it took the Great Depression of 1929, the millions of unemployed, and the total disintegration of the political and economic unity of Central Europe to convince the millions of Germans that the emotional movement of their National Socialism held out the hope of a future for them. And it took the diabolical genius of a Hitler to transform this desire for revenge into a monstrous campaign and unparalleled crimes.

It was inevitable that a war between industrial societies should take the form of a battle of matériel. The Great Depression, however, was not an inevitable consequence of the nature of such societies—we now know that it would have been a relatively easy task to limit its ravages. But it had been a dramatic accident, made possible at the time by the nature of our society. Thirty years ago, it was possible to blame the authors of the Versailles Treaty of 1918 for ignoring economic necessities. In the period since 1945, an even more irrational territorial settlement than that of 1918 has not, in fact, ruled out prosperity. Meanwhile, the thirty years' war produced consequences on which we have still not ceased to dwell and that we are still endeavoring to explain satisfactorily. Were these developments part of the drama or part of the process? Or had they elements of both? And if so, did they belong more to the process or to the drama?

These consequences—*Weltgeschichtlich,* as the Germans would say—amount to a loss by Europe of its hitherto dominant position. Formerly the center of world politics, Europe is now divided into a zone dominated by Soviet Russia and a zone subject to the influence and protected by the forces of the United States. Its former colonies have become independent. Industrialization, which was responsible for European superiority, has become, or is in the process of becoming the common boon of all mankind. Since all portions of mankind now possess, or will shortly possess, the same tools, will not the ruthless law of quantity henceforth apply in peace as it does in war and thereby reduce the old continent to an importance commensurate with its size on the map?

"The rape of Europe," "the decadence of Europe"—I have no doubt but that the present situtation can be expressed in historical, dramatic terms. For us Europeans, who have lived through two world wars and experienced the worst outrages that man can inflict on the honor of mankind, who have seen the end of empires, nothing is more tempting than to reflect bitterly on the fragility of historical achievement. But is it essential to look at events in this light? The spread of industrial society and the unification of the human race are two realities that were either provoked or accelerated by the thirty years' war, but were they not in any case inevitable? Are they not in accordance with the law of necessity? And has not the entire drama, in the light of this result, been the means for fulfilling a destiny set down in advance, the very one envisaged by Auguste Comte: industrial society, as a pattern for all human communities, forging for the first time the unity of all mankind?

☆   ☆   ☆

Let us now pause and turn our attention to the other aspect of this century, to the process of accumulation of knowledge and power. Economists and sociologists are now used to studying long-term movements of production and productivity. Thanks to Colin Clark's *Conditions of Economic Progress*, calculations of the rate of growth (of either the national or the per capita product) and comparisons of the labor employed in each of three sectors have become the accepted method of estimating the development of different economies. But statistics of the national income or of employment clearly reflect the consequences of dramatic happenings as much as they do those of regular development. The spread of industry over the whole planet has been brought about through wars, revolutions, and disasters.

This is a fact so self-evident as to require no proof. One illustration will be sufficient. Consider how differently China and Japan reacted to the influence and threat of the West. In Japan, a fraction of the ruling class deliberately set out to bring about the historical mutation without which the Empire of the Rising Sun would have been condemned to a kind of servitude. In China, the great majority of the bureaucratic class failed either to grasp the need for or to bring about this necessary mutation, and it took a long period of civil wars and the seizure of power by the Communist party for the Chinese state to acquire the strength or capacity to carry out an accelerated program of industrialization. The whole of Asian history since 1890 has been dominated by the fact that the modernization of the two empires was out of phase. It was the industrial advance achieved by its adoption of Western methods that inspired Japan's insane ambition to conquer China. And it was the Sino-Japanese war that gave the Communist party its great opportunity. In both cases, a dramatic phase of the conflict between past and present, between traditionalism and the West, lies at the beginning of industrialization.

The unfolding of this dramatic phase does not merely determine the moment when industrialization will begin and the pace at which it will proceed; it also helps decide on the choice of possible methods. And it determines which social group will take the initiative and assume responsibility. In Japan it was a class permeated with the spirit of the aristocracy that brought about the mutation and sought to preserve a synthesis of national values and Western techniques. In China, it was ultimately a class formed by Marxist-Leninist ideology and by totalitarian practices that made itself responsible for industrialization and provided leadership for the countless masses. In Russia itself, industrialization had begun during the last quarter of the nineteenth century, when the country was still subject to absolute rule. War and revolution interrupted its progress and produced a new elite, one that adopted a Western doctrine but was opposed to Western liberalism. If the 1914 war had not led to the downfall of czarism and given Lenin and his comrades the opportunity they had long been waiting for, it is conceivable that Russian industrialization might have been achieved in a different manner, under other direction, and at a different pace. But when we look back from our vantage point in 1960, it seems that only the destruction of Russia's imperial unity from within or from without could have prevented that country from becoming the greatest power in Europe. For once all nations have at their disposal the same means of production and destruction, then, up to a point, the situation is governed by the law of numbers. But whatever may be our answers, we are still justified in asking the following questions. What would have happened if Kerenski had eliminated the Bolshevik leaders during the abortive uprising of July 1917? What would have happened if Russia had had two or three decades of peace in which to get over the critical initial phase of industrialization?

Though Russia did not have this breathing space, and China was not spared the consequences of the ambitions of the more advanced countries of Asia, America, and Europe, this does not mean that capitalist economies were inexorably committed to imperialism but rather that industrialization provided both the temptation to conquest and military glory and the means to achieve them. For statesmen and peoples whose thought still ran in traditional grooves, the most important consequence of industrialization was the increase of mobilizable resources. Industrialization did not open a new era, it simply supplied additional cards to be used in an ancient game.

This is, in a sense, the meeting point of history as usual and necessary history. Are knowledge and power to serve power politics or do they, as Auguste Comte prophesied, foreshadow the end of power politics, enabling a united mankind to pursue the only worthwhile struggle, that directed at the mastery of nature and the well-being of all men? The two great twentieth-century disturbers of the peace, Japan and Germany, gave the old-fashioned answer to this modern question. In the view of the leaders of these two empires, nothing had changed except the number of soldiers and the effectiveness of their weapons. Industry was a means to power and the purpose of power was conquest. Does the same hold true for today?

At the risk of being thought naively presumptuous, I would say that the present generation has a better understanding than its predecessor of the world in which we live, a world whose new features had been intuitively foreseen by the thinkers of the last century. This optimism is justified, it seems to me, by certain facts.

The first and best known is the revolution that has taken place in the field of armaments. Between 1914 and 1945, the destructive capacity remained lower than the productive, or constructive, capacity. The armies of 1914 used weapons less effective than those that scientists and engineers might have invented and produced had the best brains been devoted to the task. The infantry of 1914, marching on foot and with horse-drawn cannon, belonged to the age of tradition. Even armored divisions and air squadrons did not decisively effect the reckoning of costs and advantages. The revolution came with nuclear explosives. A war given over to thermonuclear bombs would no longer be a rational one for any belligerent. Since 1945, industry has at last achieved the first condition for peace through fear of war—an eventuality prematurely announced by so many writers. This does not mean that peace is now assured, only that war can no longer be the continuation of a policy by other means. Unless one of the belligerents is almost invulnerable, thermonuclear war can occur only as the result of an accident or a misunderstanding.

In addition, world opinion today understands more clearly than ever before the facts of modern economic life and its potentialities for peace. The possible causes of conflict between classes or nations now seem less important than the reasons for solidarity. Of course, there is nothing fundamentally new in all this. For centuries, liberal economists have been proclaiming that trade benefits both sides, that the essence of the economic system is exchange, and that wars and conquest are always sterile and frequently ruinous for all concerned.

But recent facts have helped to spread these convictions outside the narrow circles to which they were once confined. West Germany, with half the space of France and which has had to absorb some ten million refugees, is enjoying unprecedented prosperity. For Germany the price of defeat has been not poverty, as in the past, but well-being. Western Europe as a whole, including Great Britain, has lost colonies, power, diplomatic prestige, yet never before has it achieved so high a level of production and productivity.

In the thirties, the West, haunted by the Great Depression, thought in quasi-Marxist terms; it looked for outlets and ended by convincing itself that economic growth was or would be paralyzed by the lack of markets. Today the West has realized, almost with surprise, that in spite of recessions and temporary interruptions, expansion creates markets, of itself and for itself, as economists had always maintained. The progress achieved by the Soviet Union through a rigidly planned system, by Federal Germany through a relatively free economic system, and by other European countries through methods combining both principles has discredited so-called doctrinal disputes in many people's minds. The scientific, social, and human requirements of growth—the number of technicians, the incentives to progress of entrepreneurs and administrators, the spontaneous or forced acceptance of change by the masses—these are now considered more important than the forms of regulation. The emphasis is on the factors making for economic expansion in general rather than on the specific characteristics of a particular system.

By the same token, ideologies are also becoming discredited and tending to lose their emotional content. In the West, and perhaps even in the Soviet Union, men no longer think of one regime as imperialist or exploiting, the other as peaceful and just. All regimes are imperfect; none is immune or offers sure immunity to injustice; none is subject to the law of pauperization. The most fervent opponents of communism do not deny the rapid growth of the Soviet economy and the rise in the standard of living of the masses. The most fervent opponents of the liberal West or of capitalism admit that there has been no serious economic crisis since 1945 and that the exploited proletariat live better than ever before.

Does this mean that the industrial society to which Auguste Comte looked forward and which is now in different ways in the process of formation is in reality the pattern and that humanity is now becoming socially uniform as well as diplomatically unified? Such a conclusion would be premature. The dawn of universal history is, I think, about to break and universal history will have a number of original features to offer, as compared with the provincial histories of nations or with the civilizations of the past six thousand years. But nothing indicates that it will cease to be dramatic.

What exactly do I mean by the expression universal history? First, unification within the diplomatic sphere. China and Japan, the Soviet Union and the United States, France and Great Britain, Germany and Italy, India and Ghana—all these states today form part of a single system. What happens on the coasts of China has repercussions on the relations between Europe and the United States or between the United States and the Soviet Union. Never have so many states mutually recognized the rights of others to existence. Never have Europe and Asia, Africa and America, felt so close to each other. What large states formerly did in Europe or Asia, the large states of today—for the time being, the United States and the Soviet Union—do across five continents. It is a commonplace to say that the means of transportation and communication have abolished distances. The accumulation of the means of knowledge and power in continentwide states is also one of the conditions of planetary diplomacy, of the changed scale of power.

With diplomatic unification goes the universal spread of certain forms of technical and economic organization. No community anxious to survive can afford deliberately to slow down the development of what the Marxists call the forces of production—the rationalization of labor and the growth of technical equipment. How can we reject what provides power and prosperity? And so the visitor is struck by the spectacle of the same airports, the same factories, the same machines from Tokyo to Paris, from Peking to Rio de Janeiro. The same words—capitalism, communism, imperialism, dollar, ruble—ring in his ears as soon as he enters into conversation with an intellectual or a politician. A traveler who does not go beyond superficial impressions might be led to believe that mankind lives in a single world of machines and ideas.

Such impressions are largely illusory. Mankind to the very degree to which it is diplomatically unified, is still as divided as were all the diplomatic systems of the past. Two coalitions confront each other at the heart of Europe, and around them more and more states boast of their nonalignment. The relations between the Soviet Union and China are, to some extent, wrapped in mystery. The United Nations offers a symbolic forum to the spokesmen of states in the universal era, but most of the speeches express not the real existence of these states, whose weakness condemns them to impotence, but the ideologies in which they indulge in order to give themselves the feeling of participating in the history of mankind.

It may be that the classic divisions inherited from our provincial past weigh less heavily than the symbolic divisions of a period in which one kind of society has become the norm. For of the two versions of industrial society, the Soviet and the Western, one at least claims sole validity for all men. The great schism created by the embodiment in two states, and in two historical areas, of the two ideologies characteristic of the West has been accompanied by the division—brief on the scale of centuries but long in terms of decades—between rich and poor peoples, between those who have almost everything and those with almost nothing, between those we call underdeveloped and those already reaping the fruits of productivity. For a human race in the process of becoming unified, inequality between peoples plays the role formerly played by inequality between classes. The condition of the masses according to continent and country differs more widely today than ever before. And as their awareness of this inequality grows, people become less resigned to poverty and misfortune.

The causes for hostility between the different portions of this unified mankind are not inhibited by any spiritual union. For unification is henceforth based solely on material, technical, or economic factors. The power to produce, to destroy, or to communicate has overtopped oceans, leveled mountain ranges, and abolished distances. Vague ideologies, derived from European doctrines of the last century, furnish a few common words to men who do not worship the same gods, or observe the same customs, or think according to the same categories. Never before have states belonging to the same diplomatic system differed as they differ today. Never before have the partners in a common enterprise been so devoid of deep solidarity.

For ten years or more we have been obsessed by the gulf that exists between the communist and the free world. How could we fail to be so, with Soviet armies stationed 125 miles from the Rhine and Soviet propaganda claiming that the ultimate triumph of communism is inevitable the world over—in other words, telling the West that it has no other choice but to be killed or die itself.

Nor is this all. The clash between the two blocs is twofold. There is both rivalry for power and ideological competition. There is foreign war with some of the characteristics of civil war. Economic planning by a proletariat in control of the state and aiming at equality and plenty, whether or not it is achieved by the Soviet Union, is a Western dream, a utopia in which reality is denied and which in the West has dominated political if not philosophical debate for decades. It may be that Orthodox Russia, heir of Byzantium and of the monolithic traditions of Eastern bureaucracy, belongs to another sphere of civilization than Western Europe. But the Russia that makes use of Marxism and socialism belongs to the Western sphere of civilization, at least in its vocabulary and its claim actually to have achieved what the best among European reformers have preached as the goal of mankind.

It is possible, however, that the conflict is now becoming less acute. The leaders of both blocs are well aware of the irrationality of a war to the death, waged with atomic and thermonuclear weapons. Even the most doctrinaire are gradually being forced to recognize the resemblances between the techniques of production and the organization of labor in industrial enterprises whose juridical status differs. There is, of course, still plenty of room for genuine controversy. Societies differ in their thinking and way of life depending on the kind of ownership, the methods of regulation applied to the whole economy, and the style of authority. Let us not be guilty of the error of some Marxists who, on the basis of partial resemblances between productive forces and methods of labor organization, refuse to recognize the impact of the economic system on the aggregate of collectivities. This is no less serious an error than the one formerly committed by the Bolsheviks in exaggerating the implications of regimes, one, in their view, the safeguard of peace, equality, and abundance, the other the inevitable cause of imperialism, exploitation, and poverty in the midst of an accumulation of excess wealth. These two conflicting myths are equally false. Let us not yield to the temptation to create yet a third, perhaps less objectionable but with no more truth in it. There is no more reason to believe that mature industrial societies will necessarily achieve moral unity than that they will necessarily come into conflict. Even if, as seems likely, they come more and more to resemble each other, there is no guarantee that they will get on with each other. How many of the great wars of history look, in retrospect, like family quarrels!

Indeed, even if we accept what is now the fashionable thesis that the two great powers will gradually converge, it would still be wrong to conclude that, even in an age of universal history, the problem of unity can be reduced to a mere comparison between the United States and the Soviet Union or even to the mere contradiction between a system of economic planning under the direction of a single party and a semiliberal and multiparty system. The two other decisive factors that I have just mentioned, inequality of development and diversity of customs and beliefs, must also be taken into account. The first is a historic survival and is characteristic of a transition period. But even if we assume that the African and Asian peoples will eventually overcome their backwardness (and this cannot happen in the immediate future), equilibrium between populations and the space they occupy can be achieved only by limiting population growth. And since the natural mechanisms of elimination (famine and epidemics) have ceased to operate, such control can be achieved only by the conscious will of individuals or communities. If nations do not achieve a rational control over their own growth, then numerical disparities and differences in the standard of living will recur perpetually and bring poverty and incitements to violence in their train.

But the second decisive factor may have even greater importance. To the degree that mankind will henceforth live a single history, it will have to learn another form of rational control not only over its biological instincts but also over its social passions. The more men of different races, religions, and customs find themselves living in one world, the more they must learn to treat each other with tolerance and mutual respect. They must mutually acknowledge their humanity and refrain from ambitions of conquest or domination. These are trite formulas to which the reader will have no trouble in subscribing. But let him reflect: they require of man a new kind of virtue. For it is what men hold sacred that divides men most. A pagan or Jew who remains unconverted is a challenge to the Christian. Is a man who knows nothing of the God of the religions of salvation our fellow man or a stranger with whom we can feel nothing in common? It is with him that we will have to build a spiritual community—as the superstructure, or the foundation, of the material community now arising from the scientific, technical, and economic unity imposed by historical destiny on a mankind more conscious of its conflicts than of its solidarity.

It took the tragedy of two world wars to unify the diplomatic sphere. It took successive revolutions in France, Russia, and China to achieve the spread of industrial development. Violence opened a path whose stages lie strewn with millions of innocent victims. The cunning of reason evoked by the disciples of Bossuet, Hegel, and Marx has not been sparing of suffering and human blood. Nothing would suggest that all this is over and that henceforth the process can proceed rationally without drama. It may be that universal history will differ in this respect from the provincial histories of past ages. But this is only a hope based on faith.

☆ ☆ ☆

The above statement, in its very ambiguity, is probably the sole conclusion to which this rapid survey can come.

The philosophies of history to which our contemporaries are drawn place their emphasis on one of two related concepts of historical development. Optimistic philosophies, whether of Marxist or liberal inspiration, prolong the process of accumulation of knowledge and power indefinitely into the future. Through fair exchange or rational planning, mankind will equitably share in the benefits of progress achieved by the genius of scholars or technicians. Pessimistic philosophies, for example that of Spengler, point out the resemblances between the disasters that overwhelmed past cultures and those we have witnessed in the course of the twentieth century. Western civilization is dying, just as ancient civilization died, in the midst of wars and revolutions, sprawling cities and uprooted masses, the overrefinement of impotent elites and the triumph of money or technology. Is not a Europe that has lost its empires already decadent? Does not the transmission to other races of the instruments by which the domination of the white minority has been maintained signify the inevitable decline of Europe?

Whether optimistic or pessimistic, these philosophies disregard certain characteristics of our period and certain potentialities of the universal age. Seen in the light of the past, the present situation of the old continent would seem to justify gloomy forebodings. What will yesterday's great powers—England, France, and Germany, with their fifty million citizens impatient for material well-being—look like beside continent states that reckon their populations in the hundreds of millions? Has not the loss of their empires deprived the European nations of their historical being, so to speak, and must they not therefore renounce their greatness?

This traditional view is perhaps anachronistic. In our century, domination has more often than not been a burden rather than a gain. Rationally organized work in common is both the source and the measure of wealth. As Europe looks at a world now in the process of adopting a type of civilization that it created, it need not necessarily regard itself as the victim of its own triumph. Greatness and military strength are no longer inseparable because the great powers can no longer employ their weapons without risking reprisals that may result in their own destruction and because it is no longer essential for any society to dominate another in order to provide a good life for its citizens.

Europe has two reasons for refusing to regard itself as decadent. It was Europe's achievements, and later its military follies, that brought humanity to the threshold of the universal age. In an age in which men no longer need to tyrannize each other to be able to exploit natural resources, Europe can still be great if it conforms to the spirit of the new age by helping other peoples cure themselves of the childhood diseases of modernism. If Europe can apply its principles at home and still have a task to perform abroad, why should it go on nursing a bitterness that its recent past may explain but that future prospects do not justify?

Never before have men had so many reasons for ceasing to slaughter each other. Never before have they had so many reasons for feeling involved in one and the same undertaking. I do not thereby conclude that the age of universal history will be peaceful. Man, as we know, is a rational being, but what about men?

After a long and circuitous journey, I end with some propositions that popular wisdom would not find unacceptable. Having evoked Hegel and the cunning of reason, I find myself quite close to Candide and the language of Voltaire. But, after all, when philosophy (or sociology) join hands with common sense, is that a tribute to common sense or a proof of the wisdom of philosophy?

PART III

CONCLUSION

12.   History and Politics

POLITICAL THOUGHT CAN BE NEITHER detached from nor a slave to reality. One cannot opt for a certain regime while ignoring the one that exists in a given country at a given time or those that have existed throughout the world in times past; nor can one determine what should be on the basis of what is.

It is doubtless permissible to apply classical logic and to make a distinction between political science, which studies facts relating to government and patterns of authority, and the art of politics, which by combining ethical imperatives and the lessons of experience seeks to proffer advice or prescribe courses of action. But the soundest outcome of any reflection on political thought (as on all the so-called social sciences) is to limit the importance of such a distinction. The knowledge of facts is in numerous ways influenced by our value judgments, and these in turn are defined largely by the milieu—nation, class, period—to which the thinker belongs. In short, political thought is essentially impure, equivocal. When it claims to be scientific it is already moralizing. When it claims to be normative it is influenced by prevailing realities.

It is not impossible to conceive, at one extreme, a politics of pure and simple observation and, at the other, a politics of pure and simple ideals, each of these two terms setting, so to speak, the limits of an effort either toward objectivity or toward utopia. However, raw observation is hardly instructive and utopia of little use in practice.

It is in the middle area that political philosophy can thrive, expressing both the free and conditioned nature of human thought. The situation always allows for a margin of choice, but the margin is never unlimited. A Frenchman in 1949 is not limited to the choice of one social regime or diplomatic orientation, but he is not free to choose any regime or diplomacy whatsoever. More precisely, he can, in the abstract, conceive

"Histoire et Politique." Reprinted from *Revue de Metaphysique et Morale* 1949 by permission of Librairie Armand Colin.

of any regime or diplomacy, but reality will not allow all conceptions to be realized.

This proposition will probably be accepted at face value with no great objection. But difficulties arise as soon as one tries to specify this "margin of choice." Who is competent to say what arguments are suitable to demonstrate that a certain policy is without merit because it is unrealistic and that another one is compatible with the facts of a given situation? The answer, however unsatisfactory, seems to me obvious. It is political thought itself, coming round full circle, that determines the margin of choice as well as its contents. Whoever suggests reforming parliamentary democracies in the middle of the twentieth century must show both the steps that would improve their functioning and the compatibility of such steps with the structure of these regimes.

In other words, political thought is essentially an attempt to elucidate, from the study of societies, the goals one can aspire to and the means most likely to reach them. Clearly, this investigation of what is possible is influenced by prior desires and preferences, desires and preferences that are also modified by the investigation itself. The outcome is never a moral or political imperative but an indication of diverse possibilities (as to goals) and degrees of probability (as to means).

Political thought, whatever the scope of its ambitions, remains basically the same. The here-and-now judgment made by a statesman and the decision he takes involve this consideration of possible objectives, the recognition of compatible elements, and the selection of effective means. The doctrines of theorists are based also on an analysis of actuality and a formulation of values. For the theorist, however, actuality is fused with the whole of history, the multiplicity of regimes that have existed in the past or continue to exist at the present hour. Consequently, the relation between what is and what ought to be is tantamount, at a higher level not so much of abstraction as of scope, to the relation between historical experience and political will.

Among competent observers who have taken the trouble to pursue the necessary studies, a large measure of agreement can quite easily be reached on what is possible within a given political or economic system. If a common political stand does not ensue it is because all concrete steps entail consequences favorable or unfavorable to diverse groups in the body politic. Each one of these is more affected by the inconveniences it suffers than by those suffered by other groups or the society as a whole. No policy simultaneously satisfies *all* the desires of men, none avoids *all* the risks. Everyone establishes differently the priorities to be considered or the risks to be avoided. When history seen in its entirety is at stake these antitheses become basic.

Men's minds are divided between two tendencies: some look to the past to understand the present and draw lessons from precedents; others are inclined to pursue changes throughout time and, by their actions, stress the desire for the new. Of course, a reasonable mind seeks to combine these two tendencies. The same analysis should prevail for history, strategy, or politics. Tactics, as developed by German theory, the geometry of the battles of Cannes or Lützen, retain their relevance in the twentieth century—that is, if proper account is taken of the revolution in the composition and equipment of modern armies. Generalities on the comparative merits of defense and offense have led to disastrous errors when endowed with timeless authority. The defeat of 1945 will not suffice to change the psychology of the German people. It is dangerous to dub as "eternal Germany" the Germany of one set of policies. Great Britain was fiercely opposed, in the nineteenth century, to a union of continental European states. The same concerns, in the middle of the twentieth century, can lead to an opposite point of view.

Specifically, there is not and should not be a contradiction between the search for constant factors or regularities and the search for unique situations or progressive changes. The task of the historian and the statesman is precisely to discriminate, at each moment, between one and the other. But when one envisages general philosophies of history is there not an unbridgeable antithesis? Does one not have to pronounce in one sense or the other? One acknowledges, strictly speaking, partial cycles that would not exclude unilinear progression either by a society toward fulfillment (or collapse) or by humanity as a whole toward unity. But is not the hypothesis of a plurality of regimes, each *immédiatement à Dieu*, incompatible with the hypothesis of a unique history whose result would be either liberal democracy or communism?

☆ ☆ ☆

I call millenarian politics those that endow an objective, one that can be achieved within a fixed period of time, with absolute value, or again that confuse a society in history, actual or to be created, with the ideal society that would fulfill human destiny. Communist politics are a perfect example of millenarian politics.

Originally, Marxism combined fatality and will, reform and revolution. The spontaneous course of history leads to the Russian Revolution, whose agent is the proletariat and from which the reign of freedom will emerge. Reforms within the present system strengthen the position of the working class and lead to the final break. Leninism, in the form it has taken since 1917 (and maybe one should even say since 1903), reduces the role of fatality and of reform while emphasizing the part played by the will to revolution. The supposed inevitability of the Russian Revolution serves only to communicate to the faithful the certitude of final victory.

Anticapitalist revolutions, of Marxist inspiration, have so far succeeded only in predominantly agricultural countries with a precapitalist structure. On the other hand, the full development of capitalism has brought with it profound changes but has in no way numerically increased the strength of the truly revolutionary forces. The development of productive forces tends rather to weaken than to quicken any subversive élan in the masses. The historical pattern—feudalism, capitalism, liberal socialism—that Marx endowed with a kind of inevitability has been denied by experience, with the appearance in Russia of socialism as the substitute for and not the heir of capitalism. The mechanism by which capitalism is supposed to destroy itself—proletarianization, pauperization, concentration, and the like—is refuted by the facts: the rise in the standard of living, the social differentiation in the bosom of capitalism, and so on. I do not mean to say that communism is wrong when it heralds its final victory: it is simply wrong (in the eyes of reason) to declare this success inevitable by virtue of a historical evolution that never took place.

There is no dearth of Marxists who have more or less admitted that the revolution necessary *rationally* may not be determined historically. Marx's formula "socialism or barbarity" (which implies that revolution is not inevitable) is often cited. Trotsky himself, toward the end of his life, was inclined to doubt the coming of socialism, if after the second war the proletariat of the world did not perform its function. Still more clearly Maurice Merleau-Ponty writes:

> Perhaps no proletariat will ever exercise the historical function that the Marxist scheme awarded it. . . . But it is obvious that no other class would be able to replace the proletariat in this role. . . . This would mean that there is no history, if history is the coming of humanity and humanity the mutual respect by men for each other—consequently, no philosophy of history—and that finally, as Barrès said, the world and our existence are a senseless tumult.[1]

Is it possible, philosophically, to separate a rational end to history from a necessary one? The difficulties are greater than is usually believed, at least within the framework of a philosophy that aspires to be truly historical. Whereas it is usually held that historical truth emerges only retrospectively, man is here given the capacity to anticipate the future and find within it an absolute truth. Since the future event cannot be grasped in its concrete features, one is led to an abstract formalization of the goal of history. Thus, Merleau-Ponty speaks of a mutual and universal respect by men for each other, but one may well wonder to what point such a formalization is compatible with an essentially historical philosophy. Are we not led back to a sort of Kantianism and does mankind's mutual respect teach us more than the Kantian maxim to treat man as an end and never as a means?

As soon as rational dialectics and actual dialectics fail to coincide, millenarianism is forced concretely to define the October Revolution,

---

[1] *Humanisme et terreur* (Paris, 1947), p. 168.

alone capable of conducting humanity toward the goal of history. The strength (political) and weakness (intellectual) of Russian Communism are rooted in the definition, disarming in its simplicity, that it gives to the true revolution: the conquest of the state by the Communist party. Lacking such a definition, Merleau-Ponty cannot escape ambiguity.

Marxism, he says, has placed its stamp on a humanism pushed to its limits: no more masters and slaves, respect by man for man, concrete equality and freedom, the formation of the proletariat as a universal class, alone capable of advancing this revolution. But it was not Marx who discovered that humanism would be accomplished only on the day that all men truly participated in humanity and recognized each other as men. It is not possible to determine from this formal proposition the historical mission of the proletariat as long as one does not specify the social relations implied by this mutual recognition. There will always be, in any foreseeable society, governors and governed, employers and employees. Neither the technical nor the political hierarchy excludes mutual respect. The task is to discover in which cases hierarchy and respect are compatible. Otherwise, no one knows what the mission of the proletariat is or whether it has a chance of being realized. Let us assume that mutual respect implies the revolt of the oppressed class (in this instance the proletariat). It is not appropriate, even within this philosophy, to say that history has no meaning unless the proletariat becomes a universal class. Why would the middle of the twentieth century be just the moment in history when the destiny of humanity is played out? One has no right to shift from an end to history, formally defined, to the alternative: now or never (at a time when more than half of humanity still lives in incredible poverty).

A formalized end to history avoids the obvious absurdity of transforming a rather banal fact into an ultimate end. But this formalization entails a kind of rupture with Hegelian thought and imposes the obligation, as with all philosophies of the Kantian type, to refer social systems and political decisions that give rise to uncertainty to the ultimate ends of humanity and history. On the other hand, the confusion of the end of history with a possible or probable event, of limited scope, allows millenarian politics to develop logically (once this confusion is accepted).

Since absolute good is defined in historical terms, the ultimate relationship is no longer that of the soul to God but that of the individual acting for historical ends—that is to say, the militant in the revolution. The spiritualization of human worth, to which all religions of personal salvation tend, becomes impossible: worth is measured only in relation to the revolution and cannot be distinguished in the final analysis from efficiency. If the October Revolution marks the entry into the kingdom of God, the class struggle and the conflict between nations constitute sacred history. All of secular history becomes sacred history to the degree to which it has an influence (and what event has not?) on the progress or set-backs of the revolutionary movement. The interpretation of history rests with the prophet or the pontiff, who at every instant proclaim the given truth, unassailable like all interpretations of dogma.

The interpretation of specific situations can be free of dogma. Such was the case for the Social Democrats before 1914. Only the historical scheme partook of dogma—which explains the condemnation of Bernstein, who had expressed doubts about it: the interpretation of events and the making of decisions depended on the militants and on the parties. The Russian Revolution proved that there is no need to wait for the ripening of capitalism. The sacred act depends less on technical and economic conditions than on the Communist party itself. The mission of the proletariat is transferred to the "party." The "party," much more so than capitalism, is the revolutionary agent par excellence. The "party line" has henceforth the same place in sacred history as that held by the "evolution of capitalism" in the determinist conception of social democracy.

The absolute value of the end justifies cynicism in the means of attaining it. Since nothing surpasses in worth the revolutionary goal, since ethical rules have only a historical basis and are stamped with their class origins, the believer uses with a good conscience any means, however abhorrent to traditional beliefs. The party has no obligation to the outside world, neither toward mankind nor toward national collectivities. Or rather the party has no other obligation than that of liberating the whole of mankind by its victory. It is fair to say that it is engaged, permanently, in a life-and-death struggle from which it must emerge victorious since the dialectic of history demands it and since otherwise history would have no meaning. Such a war eliminates all standards but that of efficiency. To deceive the enemy has always been recognized as conforming to the customs of war. To annihilate or liquidate hostile troops has since Napoleon, and perhaps much earlier, been the supreme ambition of the strategist.

Thus, millenarian politics, dreaming of the kingdom of God on earth or of the respect of man for man, bring mankind back to a stage prior to civilization, to the struggle of all against all. "Qui veut faire l'ange fait la bête."

☆   ☆   ☆

I call conservative politics those that stress the persistence of a basic order, whether historical or eternal, and deny the possibility of a final regime that would overcome the contradictions of previous regimes and be immune to the constituent laws of human societies as such.

This definition is inevitably both complex and rather vague. This is because conservatism, in the meaning we are here giving the word, is above all antimillenarianism. Now, there are many ways to refute the notion of an end to history. People who are loosely called conservative obviously fit into our framework; committed to a certain historical order, they do their utmost to preserve it, either by agreeing to reform or, on the other hand, trying to undo reforms that challenge the integrity of the order they seek to defend or restore.

Since they do not concede an end to history, it cannot in its totality have meaning or unity. Political history is seen as consisting of a plurality of regimes, each with its virtues and defects; or of cycles, different regimes succeeding each other with a more or less obvious regularity or necessity; or of incessant struggle between natural disorder and the will for order, each successful period marking a temporary and precarious victory of the forces of order; or, finally, of variations on a simple theme, with all societies displaying the same fundamental characteristics, whatever the diversity of their concrete forms. Montesquieu, Vico, Maurras, and the Machiavellian tradition (as interpreted by Burnham)[2] can be taken to represent these four possible approaches.

Logically, there are two fundamental kinds of conservatism or negations of millenarianism. One argues that the contradictions within regimes are insurmountable; the other, that there is an eternal order to life in general that survives all revolutions. The theory of insurmountable contradictions and the theory of an eternal order both rest on a certain view of human nature. Millenarianism always implies, in one way or another, that man, by his own creative effort or by grace from on high, is capable of eliminating his imperfections. Conservatism, on the other hand, recognizes a basic human nature that determines the characteristics of man in society.

In spite of logic, conservatives are not always more tolerant than millenarians. Often, a doctrinal relativism propels them into a practical dogmatism. From conservative they become revolutionary.

Let us take, for example, conservatives who in France defend a specific historical order, the Ancien Régime. Once they have endowed this order with an exemplary value all attempts to transform it appear destructive. It is possible to judge the bourgeois order inferior aesthetically, or in terms of stability, to the order of the Ancien Régime, with its division into estates and its multiplicity of intermediary bodies, but one cannot doubt that the bourgeois order is a viable social structure, opposed to the hereditary, hierarchic structure of prerevolutionary France. However, having confused a particular order with eternally valid order, these conservatives become revolutionary in relation to the established one (which they call established disorder). This is why so many conservatives have become fascists.

The transition from conservatism to fascism is psychologically

[2] See J. Burnham, *The Machiavellians:* Defenders of Freedom (New York: John Day, 1943; Chicago: Regnery, 1962).

understandable. The main reason for this is that conservatives and fascists have the same enemies (liberals, plutocrats, Jews, parliamentarians). They have also some common claims (authority, organic coherence) and values (stability rather than social justice, power of the community rather than individual rights). Their ways of thinking likewise hold some similarities: historical consciousness rather than universal principles, opposition to abstract rationalism. But all of these common features should not mask a fundamental contradiction: fascism is a mass movement, a revolutionary movement and, at least in the form of national socialism, thoroughly anti-Christian. European conservatism is antirevolutionary and Christian. The conservative works to save and the fascist to destroy remnants of the traditional and hierarchical order spared by the bourgeois revolution.

Anyone wishing to preserve a historical order has to grapple with a contradiction: how is one to defend or restore, by nonrevolutionary means, a threatened or unsettled order? Conservative theory nearly always thrives when order is challenged. As long as it is taken for granted, no one thinks to curse it or exalt it. Conservatism is a rise in consciousness coinciding with a period in which order, whose guardian it claims to be, becomes the issue at stake. This leads to the constant temptation to suppress criticism, which leads the conservative to sacrifice at least a part of the liberalism he advocates. If a revolution has occurred, the conservative faces yet a more serious contradiction: one cannot restore a vanished order by conservative methods. To destroy the society that has replaced the order he intends to reestablish, the conservative must resort to revolutionary means. He comes closer and closer to the revolutionaries he denounces. Thus, monarchism became Caesarism; waiting for General Monck[3] was transformed into nostalgia for a leader; and finally many conservatives participated in ventures that were to ruin European civilization.

Does the risk of such a fatal slippage disappear if a plurality of social orders is accepted? Does the recognition of the imperfection of man and societies—the basis of Machiavellian thought from Machiavelli to Pareto—lead to an effort to minimize such imperfection or, on the contrary, to an urge to manipulate the mechanism of human and social passions for the sole benefit of personal ambition? Neither empirically nor normatively does the theory of social order based on the theory of human nature imply a predetermined political doctrine.

Let us consider Machiavellianism as presented by Pareto. Any society includes a privileged minority holding key positions and consuming a disproportionate share of the national wealth. The behavior of the masses is determined not by logic or reason but by "residues" (that is to say, emo-

[3] General George Monck, First Duke of Albemarle, was instrumental in restoring the monarchy of Charles II (1660) to the English throne.

tional patterns) more or less rationalized by "derivations." Any elite will do its utmost to guard its privileged position, using a variety of means ranging from force to cunning. The energetic minorities who do not find sufficient outlet for their talents within the existing society excite the masses to revolt with promises to end exploitation and bring about the era of equality. Once in power these minorities govern first of all for their own good and not necessarily for the good of all.

From such a conception one cannot derive an inevitable picture. But one can garner rules of human wisdom: if all elites are tempted to abuse their power, the most tolerable ones are those whose divisiveness deprives them of absolute authority. There is no perfect society, but there are degrees of imperfection. Often the prophets of the perfect society are precisely those who construct the most oppressive one. To attain an absolutely sound end, the prophets of the absolute require unlimited power. They persecute millions of human beings guilty of not recognizing in the new regime the accomplishment of the human vocation. A person with no other goal than to lessen as much as possible the ills inseparable from the human condition, and who does not forget the existence of wickedness, will do more for the welfare of his fellow humans. The breed of optimists produces the likes of Robespierre and Trotsky—the breed of pessimists a Talleyrand or a Louis Philippe.

Unfortunately, the Caesars also belong to the breed of pessimists. A wise tolerance is one of the inferences to be drawn from reflecting without illusions on the eternal order of human societies. It is not the only one. Since, we are told, the masses are the raw material of historical events, the clay that heroes model, should not the supreme goal be to construct one of those empires that arouse admiration throughout the centuries? A perishable empire to be sure: nothing that issues from history can resist history. Elites degenerate, peoples exhaust themselves, states crumble—such is fate. At least Caesar leaves his name in the annals of these great and precarious deeds, and sometimes, on the sand, the mark of his genius. Throughout the generations the monuments to his glory will bear witness to a will that, for a time, brought order to chaos.

In other words, if history has no final resting place, if states and civilizations follow each other, equally transient, equally imperfect, and perhaps also equally glorious, why worry about the lot of the multitudes, inevitably passive and sacrificed? Why be obsessed by the impossible goal of social justice? Man can somehow accomplish his highest vocation only by confronting destiny and overcoming it, at least in the narrow confines within which it is given to a mortal being to create—not for eternity but for a given time.

Theorists of Machiavellianism have perhaps for the most part been defenders of freedom, not its practitioners. They have been especially subject to the glorification of the will to power. Committed to action, the Machiavellians seek to achieve for themselves the advantages of millenarianism, just as millenarianism does not hesitate to resort to the ways of cynicism. All means are good since the end is sacred, say the millenarians. The end must appear sacred since we must convince the crowd to accept any sacrifice to attain it, say the Machiavellians. Thus are born "natural millenarianisms," of which the credo of the Third Reich offers a striking example.

In strict logic, the ideal of the Third Reich cannot be construed as the equivalent of the goal of history. Unless all non-Germans are exterminated, the German race (assuming this term could have a precise meaning) will never be certain that its rule will last indefinitely. The thousand years of the Third Reich were reduced to twelve, but after all the Byzantine empire lasted a thousand years and no one perceives in it an absolute value. Conservatives are able to adopt the language of millenarianism because the masses are just as willing to commit themselves with enthusiasm to a temporal goal as to an absolute one. Those who believe in the eternal struggle of states and races can invite men to die for a lasting good, not for an absolute good. National socialist millenarianism—an answer to communist millenarianism—logically led straight to an apocalyptic catastrophe. It placed a prophetic vision of war side by side with a prophetic vision that, while awaiting the fulfillment of human history, involved perpetual war. It did not even have the virtue of compensating for actual war by predictions of future peace. A reading of Pareto would have revealed its inferiority. War regimes must lay claim to peace, oppressive regimes to freedom.

☆   ☆   ☆

I call progressive politics those that refuse to proclaim exclusively either a final goal to history or its complete regularity and that allow for irregular and undefined transformations toward a goal situated on the horizon, this goal being justified by abstract principles.

As we have seen, millenarianism collides with a fundamental difficulty: either the end of history is defined concretely with a prosaic event becoming a final goal or it is defined abstractly and becomes a principle, a rational law. It is then necessary to determine, in a concrete situation, what is required by the principle one appeals to. These alternatives become inevitable once the rational dialectic and the dialectic of reality fail to merge.

On the other hand, conservatism succeeds in specifying the traits, so far constant, of human nature and society. But even if we should accept these constant features, there remains the task of determining at what level of generalization they should be considered. For instance, there will always be rulers and ruled: to what extent can the former be controlled by the latter? To what extent can the privileges of the rulers be reduced?

Now, it is precisely this margin for historical change that it is important to define, as soon as one contemplates the uncertainties not of theory but of action. The recognition of a plurality of regimes, each with its virtues and defects, leaves freedom of choice intact. If one admits that certain virtues (freedom of individuals, greatness of the community) are incompatible, each is left to make his choice alone, in any case an unsatisfactory one.

Progressivism does not deny the idea of regularity or even of a final goal for history, but it consciously formalizes the end and generalizes the regularities. The goal of history is not a concrete event, near at hand, defined by the socialization of the means of production or the seizure of power by the communists: it is an idea of Reason—with a capital R, in the Kantian sense—and can well serve as a criterion. This idea is formal and no more allows for specific political or historical policies than Kantian maxims give an individual specific advice on what he must do. The Kantian idea of a kingdom of ends helps only to judge different regimes and measure their imperfections. It has meaning only in relation to a conception—religious and perhaps philosophical—of the unity of mankind and consequently the possible unity of human history.

On the plane of reality, this idea does not deny in any way the experience of plurality: plurality of social regimes or of civilizations. Certainly man thinks and acts politically in relation to this multiple and contradictory reality.

We will leave aside the difficulty, classical for philosophy, of progression toward an inaccessible end. We will restrict ourselves to concrete difficulties. It is easy to trace the growth of knowledge, the accumulation of technical virtuosity. It is legitimate to note the expanding sphere within which men become aware of each other. Though they are still far from putting this recognition into practice, they no longer limit their notions of human solidarity to the frontiers, the community feeling, of a tribe, a people, or a race. Likewise, within a civilization one can clearly observe improvements in this or that area—the standard of living of the many, the freedom of individuals. But if progressivism, understood as a concern for improving certain institutions within a community, is a reasonable attitude, it does not expand into a total conception of history. For, once again, the virtues of political regimes are not all compatible. A certain degree of individual freedom implies a certain degree of economic inequality. The transition from one regime to another does not always result in the betterment of the existing order but rather the substitution of one order for another. Any kind of progressive politics implies the acceptance of certain institutions, prejudices, and traditions not because they conform to the idea of human society in general but because they are inseparable from an existing society in its present structure. Progressivism is a self-sufficient political idea so long as it functions in a stable society, one not aware of its uniqueness or prone to challenge its roots. At a time of total confrontation between wills and doctrines, each with its freight of good and evil, progressivism is condemned to deplore human folly.

In calm and happy eras, each of these three attitudes has positive value and serves the common cause. Millenarianism teaches us never to be satisfied with what has been achieved; conservatism reminds us that through all the upheavals there are needs common to all societies and traditions that must be safeguarded; progressivism gives rise to statesmen who, between the dream of the ideal and the understanding of evil, seek the way of action, adapted at each moment to circumstances. In times of crisis, each of these attitudes takes on an extreme form, so that instead of combining they paralyze each other. Millenarians, instead of stimulating progressives, fight them without mercy, fearing that their reforms will delay the revolution. Conservatives, convinced that total subversion can be resisted only by refusing all concessions, denounce the progressives. Then deadly struggles ensue whose outcome demonstrates neither the worth of the victors nor the errors of the vanquished.

At the theoretical level, there is no further possibility of overcoming these conflicts. No philosophy of history can dogmatically dictate a political doctrine except by mystification (such as confusing a specific event with the goal of history). There is a need for the idea of a goal in history, but it should not be defined concretely in terms of institutions. Thus, when man must make temporal choices, he cannot escape from the conflict of values, the incompatibility between systems. Relativism is the authentic experience of political man. Without eliminating uncertainties, inseparable from this relativity, the religious man has the double advantage of never being completely committed to secular quarrels and of judging these in terms of absolute standards. Man without God risks his life for impure causes and cannot avoid doing so. He knows that humanity can create itself only through doubt and error. He acts not out of a will to be God but out of a wisdom that willingly falls short of the absolute. Atheist humanism can define itself only by accepting the limits of human existence.

13. The Social Responsibility of the Philosopher

THE PROBLEM OF THE social responsibility of the philosopher can be approached in two ways: either by considering philosophers or professors of philosophy as private individuals or by regarding them in their capacity as philosophers.

The first approach would, I fear, be sterile. It would mean indulging in solemn platitudes or pious exhortations. Professors of philosophy are good fathers, good husbands, good citizens. They work for peace, for the dignity of man, for mutual understanding. Agreement would be forthcoming all the more easily since each speaker would give the same words different meanings.

The second approach is the productive one, but difficult. One would have to determine wherein philosophy consists and from that infer the responsibility it assumes toward society.

I will examine here a few aspects of the social responsibility of the philosopher. What attitude does the philosopher as such take toward the polity, political parties, and historical conflicts?

The Technician, the Ideologue, and the Philosopher

The problem facing the philosopher in twentieth-century Europe was stated, with unsurpassable clarity, by the Greek thinkers of the fifth century before our era.

In Greece the city-states, which formed the framework of political

"The Social Responsibility of the Philosopher." Reprinted by permission of the publisher from *Dimensions de la Conscience Historique* by Raymond Aron, pp. 296–313, published by Librairie Plon.

life, had a vague awareness of belonging to a common civilization, but they were organized into different regimes, just as the groups opposing each other within Athens were held together by different ideologies. These groups—and we dare not call them classes since we exclude slaves and foreign residents and refer only to citizens—were unequal in wealth. They looked outward and sought a model conforming to their aspirations in the practices of a city-state that was often the enemy of their own. Internal quarrels were inextricably linked with the struggles between cities, and conflicts of interest were exaggerated and transformed by ideological discords.

In these historical circumstances where did the philosopher stand? He was, first of all, one of the speakers in the dialogue that in itself constitutes the life of the city and the life of the mind. Must not a ship's pilot know the laws of navigation? The carpenter must know how to cut wood, the doctor how to care for the body. Would one entrust a patient or a ship to an ignorant man, to unskilled hands? The pilot of the city-state must be as expert as the pilot of the ship. But what science should the head of state possess?

That science, answers the philosopher, is the science of good and evil. Technicians teach us to reach immediate goals. There is a military science, but what will be the purpose of victory? There is an economic science, but of what use are riches? The philosopher probes beyond the knowledge that establishes techniques not because he has no use for science but because his science is final, unconditional. It is the science of sciences; it reveals the meaning of the instrumental sciences; it points the way to the final goal of existence.

Is there such a science of sciences? If philosophy is not the science of sciences, it falls, in one fell swoop, below the instrumental sciences and becomes the occupation of sophists who indiscriminately defend any thesis. The philosopher thinks of himself as the exact reverse of the sophist (or, as we would say today, the ideologue) but the public has a hard time telling them apart. Furthermore, a man who thinks of himself as a philosopher may be taken for a sophist by one of his colleagues. Who is to decide? Who is to judge between rival claims? If we are all engaged in dialogue, there is no detached speaker, and only a detached speaker can arbitrate.

Sophists and philosophers alike note that "vérité en deçà des Pyrénées, erreur au-delà." They both draw attention to the diversity of customs and constitutions. They both become involved in what we call sociology, the objective study and explanation of institutions. Aristotle's *Politics* is, in part, a comparative study of city-states, of their strong and weak points, of their birth and death. But the sociologist abandons philosophy if he sees nothing beyond observation and scientific explanation.

How is one to discern the advantages and disadvantages of a regime if one ignores what is good? And who, if not the philosopher, will say what is good in itself? Consequently, far from justifying any side and hallowing the relativity of values, he alone is capable of grasping the true and the good, quite apart from historical relativism. If he is mistaken for the sophist, it is because their first steps are similar: he, too, does not accept the laws of the city as absolute. Since it is only one among others, he sees the laws of his own city as relative; yet his ambition is to discover the laws of the city that would be the best one for all.

However, the philosopher runs a double risk: can he find a good universally valid for all men, can he discover the best regime? Even granting that he succeeds, can he move from the conception of a life good in itself, or of the best regime, to a judgment on what is preferable here and now? When the philosopher participates in the quarrels of the city, is he not condemned to betray his calling and behave like a sophist?

The polemics that swirl around the persons and actions of Socrates and Plato—polemics of both the fifth century B.C. and the twentieth century A.D.—illustrates this double peril. What are these "Ideas" within the reach of the philosopher, the "Ideas" that give him a criterion for discerning the truth? Is not that best regime, the regime imagined in the *Republic,* in the final analysis but the transfiguration of reactionary nostalgia, the dreams of old patrician families? A twentieth-century critic will go further and call it a totalitarian regime. The claim of the philosopher to hold, along with absolute truth, the key to the best regime, the dream of entrusting "experts" with unconditional authority, lies at the very root of totalitarian tyranny.

Whatever may have been the direction of Plato's attempts to put his ideas into practice, whether Aristotle did or did not subtly plead the cause of the Macedonian monarchy, the fact is that once he is involved in his century, the Greek philosopher cannot always be distinguished from the sophist. Having chosen *one* side in order to achieve *one* program of reforms, he has lost the serene certitude of ideas and has plunged into the belligerent uncertainty of action.

The *social* responsibility of the philosopher? Let us first ponder the responsibility of the philosopher toward philosophy. Should he defend the laws of the city, whatever they may be, because he wishes to be a good citizen? Should he belittle the laws of *his* city because they are no better than those of another? Should he judge and reform the laws with reference to the best regime, to eternal ideas, to an intrinsically good life? The temptation is to answer all three questions affirmatively. The philosopher gives the example of obedience to the laws (Socrates accepts death). The philosopher teaches detachment from the imperatives of a particular time or place. The philosopher seeks eternal truth, beyond the disorder and diversity of this mundane world. But can he be at the same time respectful of the laws, conscious of historical relativity, and a lover of the Platonic "Ideas"? If he returns among his fellow citizens after having perceived the "Ideas," will he not be either revolutionary, since he will have measured the distance between the real and the ideal city, or else skeptical or conservative, since he will have measured the distance between *all* cities and the ideal one?

An Additional Dimension

The dialogue of the technician, the sophist, and the philosopher extends to our own time although it would seem that the technician and the sophist have henceforth an irresistible advantage and that the philosopher appears eclipsed by his rivals.

How is it possible to intervene in public affairs if one is ignorant of the probable consequences of the different policies pondered by both leaders and citizens? Should one prefer private or public ownership of the means of production? What is the meaning of a preference in this instance? Morality would imply, at the most, that henceforth the ownership of factories be looked upon as a social function. Is this social function best fulfilled if ownership, in the juridical sense of the term, is diffused among hundreds of thousands of shareholders or concentrated in the state? The question is not philosophical, it is sociological or political: science gives a probable answer from which the statesman must draw conclusions. We deliberately took a "marginal" example, for the issue is charged with ideological overtones. The illustration of our problem would have been that much easier if we had chosen one of the numerous questions daily put to leaders concerning interest rates, the expansion or reduction of total demand, the percentage of investments, etc. Can one say that the philosopher is alien to such concerns? But if he is indifferent to economic growth, he is indifferent by the same token to the means essential to fulfilling the tasks whose urgency he proclaims. How can society overcome class differences if the forces of production are not sufficiently developed? Either the philosopher is ignorant of economics, in which case he limits himself to setting goals without even knowing if they can be realized; or, imitating Marx, he studies economics—but then does he himself know when he is talking as a technician and when as a philosopher?

The sophist also receives powerful reinforcement from ethnographic or historical science and from present experience. Is it possible to find a common denominator between the ways of life of archaic and developed societies? In a sense, the former are no more imperfect than the latter: the individual is integrated within a meaningful whole, and no one would be able to state with certainty that the Yankee is happier the the Bororo. The superiority of modern societies is immediately evident if the criteria chosen are those on which industrial society lays stress: knowledge, the exploitation of natural resources, and the development of productive forces. Twentieth-century man—the man who in our time is responsible for Buchenwald, the atomic bomb on Hiroshima, the negative aspects of the cult of personality—that man is neither wiser nor more virtuous than the military commanders of Athens and Sparta, whose madness prolonged the Peloponnesian War to the exhaustion of all the combatants, or the emperors of Rome, Byzantium, or Moscow.

Let us set aside this diversity offered by the centuries. Let each of us remember his own life. Most European nations in the course of the century have known different regimes. The Kaiser's Germany, Weimar Germany, Hitler's Germany, the Germany of Pankow, the Germany of Bonn: to which will the German of good will turn? In 1932 Communists and Hitlerites denounced the Weimar Republic with the same violence. From 1941 to 1945 Communists and groups of democrats denounced the Third Reich with equal violence. Communists rail against the Federal Republic of Bonn with a violence reciprocated by democrats in their denunciation of the Pankow People's Republic. Each time men were found to support the status quo or revolt against it, and among these men were professors of philosophy. Where was the authentic philosopher in the course of these tragic episodes? Indifferent to the tumult of the forum, did he keep his eyes fixed on the Platonic "Ideas"? Did he condemn all regimes with equal or with wavering vigor? Had he, once and for all, chosen sides? The side of Western democracy because it tolerates heresy or the side of communism with its claim to be the wave of the future?

In what manner does our dialogue differ from that of the Greeks? It seems to me the greatest difference is that it has acquired with the notion of history an additional dimension. We are not reduced to hesitating between historical relativism and eternal ideas. Another solution is offered: historical diversity could be overcome not in the timeless world of "Ideas" but in the society of the future. Conflicts, however cruel, become instruments of reconciliation, stages on the way to a classless society.

Philosopher and ideologue would resume the Platonic dialogue, but the former would appeal not to "Ideas" but to the whole of history or the future, and the latter, prisoner of a particular society or resigned to the anarchy of values, would disregard the laws of change or the truth of the future.

The ideologue, like the sophist in the past, denies the claims of the philosopher. In the eyes of the ideologue the philosopher is doubly an ideologue because he is an unwitting ideologue who wrongly imagines himself immune to the limitations of the human condition.

It is even more difficult in the twentieth century of our era than in the fifth century B.C. to choose among the three obligations that tradition, whether by turns or simultaneously, imposes on the philosopher. How to teach respect for the laws, such as they are in times like those of the Third Reich or other terrorist regimes? How can the philosopher remain above the fray of wars and revolutions when politics control the destiny of our very souls? What regime can sustain a confrontation with the "Ideas"? How to ascertain among competing regimes the one that paves the way to the future?

Once again the issue is not so much the social responsibility of the philosopher as the responsibility of philosophy itself. With what does philosophy supply us—faith or skepticism, relativism or eternal truth?

The Search for Truth

If there were no middle ground or compromise between these two antithetical terms the position of the philosopher would be a desperate one. He would have either to support fanaticism or to destroy faith: in both cases damaging the welfare of the city or community of cities. The citizen who no longer believes in the values of his city is as deadly as the one who clings to them with an exclusive passion.

The conflicting option between historical relativism and eternal "Ideas" cannot be overcome once and for all, but only day by day through the exertions of philosophic thought. Customs are diverse and disrespect for the customs of others is proof of philosophical as well as historical provincialism. The persecution of racial, religious, or political minorities cannot be condoned as expressions of institutional diversity. Such persecution violates a formal rule—respect for others—that can be held to be eternally valid though the methods of its application may differ. This analysis, crude in view of the difficulty of the problem, aims only at suggesting propositions or variables whose elaboration is the task of philosophy. There are customs whose diversity is legitimate, and it would be wrong to judge them as being true or false or even to rank them in hierarchic order. They express a creative and inventive genius that cannot be frozen into a single model.

Social behavior usually involves moral imperatives. However, these are universally valid only if they are formalized. It is a truth both eternal and scarcely instructive that there is among human beings a universal principle of reciprocity and equality. The meaning that time and civilizations give this principle varies. Rigorously applied, the principle would condemn all hierarchic and inegalitarian societies. Applied too loosely, it would condemn nothing and no one. In every period the principle has been interpreted in a particular way, without entailing total approval or disapproval of social reality.

Philosophers agree neither on the meaning that formal principles have in any given period nor on the eternal meaning with which they can be endowed. But the discussion among philosophers on the historical and universal aspects of these principles is nevertheless far from fruitless. It is a good precaution against simplistic dogmatisms; it is the proper approach to political and ethical inquiry. The natural sciences represent the the history of discovery, the accumulation of propositions in ever more precise terms, whose truth, within certain bounds, is definitely acquired. The discovery of values or of morality differs from that of scientific truth. What is lacking is verification, confirmation by experiment. But the history of thought, the history of political reality itself, does permit, through the discernment of formal rules and institutional diversities, the elaboration of shared values.

The critical approach to history has the same function: it reveals the illusory nature of opposing the particular to the universal. Historicism runs the risk of driving the philosopher back toward the camp of the sophists: if philosophy as such is inseparable from a particular period, class, or polity, the conscious awareness of this position can only destroy naive beliefs. Why should the philosopher remain faithful to the values of parliamentary democracy if the latter is but the instrument of bourgeois domination? The same fate would await the values of socialism if it in turn were to be merely the camouflage for domination by another class. Historicist thought avoids complete relativism only by postulating a final goal to history and the truth of the evolution toward it. There is the leap from proclaiming the illigitimacy of bourgeois democracy to the absolute legitimacy of socialist democracy because it appears at the end of the struggle, because it is the goal of humanity itself. In the framework of this historicist philosophy, one is caught in the following dilemma: either to belittle the regime that had been proclaimed as final, whereby one comes back to the generalizations of relativism; or to affirm the absolute worth of a regime and become wedded to fanaticism. The proper critical approach to history reveals the error behind this spurious dilemma.

Most regimes in our century (the Hitlerian regime, of course, excluded) lay claim to the same values: development of productive forces in order to guarantee all men the conditions of an honorable existence, rejection of hereditary inequalities, and dedication to the legal and moral equality of citizens. Economic growth and universal citizenship equally characterize regimes going by the name of people's democracies and regimes said to be Western democracies.

Neither of these two regimes is wholly faithful to its own principles. Neither has eliminated inequality of income; neither has done away with the hierarchy of offices and reputations; neither has overcome distinctions between social groups. On the other hand, neither seems incapable of growth, and neither seems paralyzed by internal contradictions. The bourgeois democracies have reached the stage of the welfare state; whereas the people's democracies are wrestling with what is left of the cult of personality. The colonial empires, built by the nations of Europe in the last century, are in the final process of disintegration or of transformation into confederations. The people's democracies have yet to put into practice the principles of national independence and equality between states.

Why should either one of these regimes boast of being final or absolute? The prophecies of the last century assumed that economies founded on private property were incapable of growth, beyond a certain point, or incapable of distributing to all the benefits of technological progress. Things have turned out quite differently. The economies of the bourgeois democracies guarantee a relatively high standard of living, perhaps a less rapid growth insofar as the percentage of investments in relation to the gross national product is lower. But Marx considered rapid accumulation characteristic of capitalism.

If the Eastern and Western systems are ruled by the same necessities, the philosopher has no reason to give absolute worth to one and none to the other: no determinism ordains in advance an implacable struggle between them and the total victory of one over the other; no moral consideration sanctions our attributing all the merits to one, all the demerits to the other.

It may well be that the struggle between these two regimes will be waged to the end (as it was between Athens and Sparta). It would be neither the first nor the last time that violence settled a dispute. All that the philosopher can and must assert is that history in a global context is not part of a dialectic that guarantees in advance the victory of one side and allows us to predict the outcome.

The whole of history has not been completed. We do not know the outcome of the adventure, the destined result. We have no right to invoke an inevitable future to justify a contemporary regime, as imperfect as any other (whether more or less imperfect matters little). At a time when humanity possesses the means to blow itself up, to render life impossible on the planet, it would require singular confidence or a singular blindness to put oneself in God's place (without believing in him) and contemplate the "happy ending" beyond the dark centuries. Even if we set aside the risks and perils that despite the reasonable nature of man remain tied to human irrationality, to appeal to a historical destiny (in the sense of a predetermined future) would still be uncalled for: those features of the future system that one can legitimately take to be inevitable do not describe one of the contenders only; they can be fulfilled by the victory of either. Economic growth, universal citizenship, collective well-being, and individual equality are credible in the distant future of both Western democracies and people's democracies.

Similarly, none of the regimes that profess as their objective the reconciliation of mankind should be completely supported or condemned by philosophy. All industrial social orders in our time are characterized by varied social groupings, but whether the instruments of production are in private or public hands, none completely realizes the idea of a classless society or of mutual human respect. Yet all aspire in different terms to this goal. One must have recourse to sociological analysis to be able to assert that it is possible or impossible, probable or improbable, to achieve the intrinsic aims set by these regimes.

The historical dimension gives new meaning to the debate between the sophist and the philosopher, the ideologue and the dialectician. But it does not essentially change their dialogue. There would be a basic change if the dialectician could legitimately identify one camp, one party, one regime with the purpose of history. But the dialectician would be untrue to dialectics in perpetrating such a confusion, as the philosopher would be untrue to philosophy if he endowed any one regime with the dignity of the "Idea." The contribution of the historical dimension is the projection in time of the dialogue between the particular and the universal. It is through time, through struggles and violence, and not only in the immobility of an eternal dialogue that the search for the "Idea" takes place, that the polity is fashioned, in which citizens can live according to morality and positive laws.

These analyses do not belittle the stakes of historical conflicts or hold that the philosopher can or should be indifferent to them. Quite the contrary. It is of vital importance to the philosopher that the establishment allow him the freedom to think and criticize and not force him to glorify the status quo. All we mean to say is that history, no more than the "Idea," gives the philosopher the right to idealize one regime and execrate all others, and also that the condemnation brought to bear on an institution by a philosopher refers to an abstract norm but yet implies a judgment based on facts and causal relations that pertain more to sociology than philosophy. Awarding all power to one party is not and cannot be the last word in politics since it eliminates from the polity and robs of freedom all those not belonging to the privileged minority. However, a historical (therefore relative) judgment might be that this single party is acceptable or deplorable according to the results one expects of it, according, as one sees it, to the possibility or impossibility, probability or improbability, of a breakup of the single party and the restoration of full citizenship to all. Opinions on one-party or multiple-party regimes are based on a comparative and objective study of institutions. The philosopher, as such, can only point out what is lacking in one or the other for the full realization of their proclaimed goals.

Civic Duty

The philosopher is first of all responsible to philosophy. To the extent that he serves philosophy and truth he serves society. Circumstances nevertheless tend to create contradictions between the various duties that the philosopher as such takes upon himself.

The philosopher, captivated by ideas or gazing toward the remote totality of the future, cannot endow the particular laws of his community with the unconditional worth that would be bestowed on them naively by the unthinking or insisted upon by fanatics. Even when the philosopher calls for obedience to positive laws, he tends to base this obedience on arguments that easily pass for irreverence. Socrates' enemies confuse him with the sophists; he is accused of weakening tradition, the authority of customs.

One can readily imagine situations wherein obedience without respect is not even a solution. Must obedience to laws be taught when the arbitrary prevails and where laws (which imply at least formal universality) have in a certain sense disappeared? The decision to submit or to revolt cannot, as such, be dictated by philosophy alone. It was a heroic philosopher who wrote on the door of the executioners: *ultimi barbarorum*. If he had simply continued his meditations, alone, deaf to the tumult of events, his act would have been no betrayal.

The philosopher feels a greater responsibility toward society in our time than in any other because events seem to influence the spiritual destiny of humanity and because the just organization of the community becomes the final goal once faith in the transcendent is lost. Thus, he aspires to be a technician as well as a philosopher, often prone to state as universal truth prudent suggestions that may be timely but are certainly debatable, sometimes also confusing ends and means, the particular and the whole, and unable to maintain the fine distinctions and proper relationships between the historical and the universal, between institutions of the moment and the ultimate society, conceivable but not concretely predictable.

Philosophy is, so to speak, the dialogue between means and ends, relativism and truth. Philosophy is untrue to itself if it cuts short the dialogue to the advantage of one term or the other. It remains faithful to itself and its social responsibilities to the extent that it refuses to sacrifice any of the terms whose contradictory solidarity distinguishes the condition of the thinking man.

It remains to be seen whether society itself will tolerate the philosopher who never completely submits to authority. Also, once the responsibilities that the philosopher can and should assume toward the community have been determined, how can one not ask oneself what responsibilities the community would like to impose on the philosopher?

Indeed, one of the most disquieting features of our time is the existence of regimes that are not content with the passive or indifferent obedience of the masses. These regimes want to be loved, admired, adored by all, by the very people who have solid reason to detest them. In the previous century, when Alsace and Lorraine were annexed by the German empire, representatives of the two provinces solemnly protested the violence done to them. In our century victims of annexations sing the praises of this violence and 99.9 percent of the voters ratify it. The more the tyrant is abhorred deep in people's hearts, the more he is deified by the very ones who plot his death. What the government asks of the philosopher is no longer simply to obey but to justify obedience.

Certain partisans of reflexology maintain that an efficient manipulation of reflexes delivers results equivalent to conversion. Ideologues will supply the mental scheme that is to be instilled into heretics and unbelievers. The philosopher is threatened in the sacred part of his being: he would become the instrument of a technique, while aspiring to mastery over all techniques, since it is he who determines their values and goals.

As in the era of religious persecutions, the philosopher seeks refuge in silence or guile. He does not always have the recourse of saying nothing and despising the powers that be. Condemned to speak out, he will reserve somewhere in his conscience the secret of his freedom. Does he risk losing his own integrity through verbal concessions to the government? I believe that in the last analysis the spirit breaks free from the tyrant, even a tyrant armed with the instruments of science. If the philosopher is in essence one who seeks truth and resists coercion, we can say that in our century he has been often threatened but never definitely vanquished.

Whether he meditates on the world or engages in action, whether he teaches obedience to laws or respect for authentic values, whether he urges revolt or encourages persistent efforts toward reform, the philosopher fulfills his calling inside and outside the polity, sharing the risks but not the illusions of his chosen party. He would cease to deserve the name of philosopher only on the day that he came to share the fanaticism or skepticism of ideologues, the day that he subscribed to inquisition by theologian-judges. No one can blame him for using the language of those in power if it is the price of his survival. Adviser to the *Prince*, sincerely convinced that a certain regime corresponds to the logic of history, he participates in the struggle and accepts its conditions. But if he turns away from the search for truth or encourages the mindless to believe they hold the ultimate truth, then he abjures his calling. The philosopher no longer exists—only the technician or the ideologue. Rich in means and not knowing the ends, men will oscillate between historical relativism and the frenetic, unreasoning attachment to a cause.

The philosopher is one who holds a dialogue with himself and others in order actively to overcome this oscillation. Such is his civic duty; such is his duty to society.

Chronology of Raymond Aron's Academic Career

1924–28	Student at the Ecole normale supérieure, Paris
1928	Agrégé de philosophie
1938	Docteur ès Lettres
1930–31	Reader at the University of Cologne
1931–33	Boarder at the Maison académique of Berlin
1933–34	Professor at the Lycée of LeHâvre
1935–39	Secretary of the Centre de documentation sociale of the Ecole normale supérieure; professor at the Ecole normale supérieure of Saint-Cloud
1939	Maitre de conférence at the Faculté des Lettres of the University of Toulouse
1945–55	Courses at the Institut d'études politiques and at the Ecole nationale d'administration
1954	Gastprofessor at the University of Tübingen
1955–68	Professor at the Faculté des Lettres et sciences humaines of the University of Paris
1960	Director of studies at the Ecole pratique des hautes études, VI section
1960–61	Research professor at Harvard University
1970	Professor at the Collège de France

Professor-at-large at Cornell University (1965);
Doctor *honoris causa* from Harvard (1958);
Yale (1960); Brussels (1962); Columbia (1966);
Southampton (1968); Jerusalem (1972); Oxford
(1972); Louvain (1973); Seoul (1976); Brandeis (1978)
Foreign honorary member of the American Academy
of Arts and Sciences
Member of the American Philosophic Society
Foreign Member of the British Academy
Foreign Member of the Royal Academy of Belgium

Member of the Académie des sciences morales et
politiques
Member of the executive committee of the *Revue
de métaphysique et de morale; Revue française de
science politique; Archives europeènnes de sociologie;*
and *History* and *Theory*
Officer of the Legion of Honor
Commandeur of the Ordre national du mérite

List of Raymond Aron's Principal Works in French and English

La Sociologie allemande contemporaine. Paris: Alcan, 1935 (2d ed. 1950).

German Sociology, translated by Mary Bottomore and Thomas Bottomore. London: Heinemann, 1957. New York: Free Press, 1957.

Essai sur la théorie de l'histoire dans l'Allemagne contemporaine: La Philosophie critique de l'histoire. Paris: Vrin, 1938 (2nd ed. 1950).

Introduction à la philosophie de l'histoire: Essai sur les limites de l'objectivité historique. Paris: Gallimard, 1938.

Introduction to the Philosophy of History: An Essay on the Limits of Historical Objectivity, translated by George J. Irwin. Boston: Beacon, 1961.

Le Grand Schisme. Paris: Gallimard, 1948.

Les Guerres en chaine. Paris: Gallimard, 1951.

The Century of Total War. Garden City, N.Y.: Doubleday, 1954. Boston: Beacon, 1955.

Polemiques. Paris: Gallimard, 1955.

L'Opium des intellectuels. Paris: Calmann-Lévy, 1955.

The Opium of the Intellectuals, translated by Terence Kilmartin. London: Secker & Warburg, 1957; Garden City, N.Y.: Doubleday, 1957. New York: Norton, 1962.

Espoir et peur du siècle. Paris: Calmann-Lévy, 1957.

La Tragédie algérienne. Paris: Plon, 1957.

L'Algérie et la République. Paris: Plon, 1958.

Immuable et changeante: De la IVe à la Ve République. Paris: Calmann-Lévy, 1959.

France, Steadfast and Changing: From the Fourth to the Fifth Republic, translated by George J. Irwin and Luigi Einaudi. Cambridge, Mass.: Harvard University Press, 1960.

La Société industrielle et la guerre, suivi d'un tableau de la diplomatie mondiale en 1958. Paris: Plon, 1959.

Dimensions de la conscience historique. Paris: Plon, 1960.

Paix et guerre entre les nations. Paris: Calmann-Lévy, 1961.

Peace and War: A Theory of International Relations, translated by Richard Howard and Annette Baker Fox. Garden City, N.Y.: Doubleday, 1966. An abridged edition prepared by Remy Inglis Hall, translated by Richard Howard and Annette Baker Fox. Garden City, N.Y.: Doubleday, Anchor, 1973.

Le Grand Débat. Paris: Calmann-Lévy, 1963.

The Great Debate: Theories of Nuclear Strategy, translated by Ernst Pawel. Garden City, N.Y.: Doubleday, 1965.

Dix-huit leçons sur la société industrielle (Cours de Sorbonne). Paris: Gallimard, 1963.

Eighteen Lectures on Industrial Society, translated by M. K. Bottomore. London: Weidenfeld & Nicolson, 1967.

La Lutte de classes (Cours de Sorbonne). Paris: Gallimard, 1964.

Démocratie et totalitarisme (Cours de Sorbonne). Paris: Gallimard, 1965.

Democracy and Totalitarianism, translated by Valence Ionescu. New York: Praeger, 1969.

Essai sur les libertés. Paris: Calmann-Lévy, 1965.

An Essay on Freedom, translated by Helen Weaver. New York: World, 1970.

Trois Essais sur l'age industriel. Paris: Plon, 1966.

The Industrial Society: Three Essays on Ideology and Development. New York: Simon and Schuster, 1966. New York: Praeger, 1967.

Les Etapes de la pensée sociologique. Paris: Gallimard, 1967.

Main Currents in Sociological Thought, translated by Richard Howard and Helen Weaver. Two volumes. New York: Basic Books, 1965, 1967. London: Weidenfeld & Nicolson, 1965. Garden City, N.Y.: Doubleday, Anchor, 1970.

De Gaulle, Israël, et les juifs. Paris: Plon, 1968.

De Gaulle, Israel, and the Jews, translated by John Sturrock. New York: Praeger, 1969.

La Révolution introuvable. Paris: Fayard, 1968.

The Elusive Revolution: Anatomy of a Student Revolt, translated by Gordon Clough. New York: Praeger, 1969.

D'une sainte famille à l'autre: Essai sur les marxismes imaginaires. Paris: Gallimard, 1969.

Les Désillusions du progrès: Essai sur la dialectique de la modernité. Paris: Calmann-Lévy, 1969.

Progress and Disillusion: The Dialectics of Modern Society. New York: Praeger, 1970.

Etudes politiques. Paris: Gallimard, 1972.

Histoire et dialectique de la violence. Paris: Gallimard, 1973.

History and the Dialectic of Violence: An Analysis of Sartre's Critique de la raison dialectique, translated by Barry Cooper. Oxford: Blackwell, 1975.

République impériale: Les Etats-Unis dans le monde, 1945–1972. Paris: Calmann-Lévy, 1973.

The Imperial Republic: The United States and the World, 1945–1973, translated by Frank Jellinek. Englewood Cliffs, N.J.: Prentice-Hall, 1974.

264

Penser la guerre, Clausewitz. Volume 1: *L'Age européen.* Volume 2: *L'Age planétaire.* Paris: Gallimard, 1976.

Plaidoyer pour l'Europe décadente. Paris: Laffont, 1977.

Les Eléctions de Mars et la Vè République. Paris: Julliard, 1978.

INDEX

Index